READING SITES
Social Difference and
Reader Response

READING SITES
Social Difference and Reader Response

Edited by
Patrocinio P. Schweickart
and Elizabeth A. Flynn

The Modern Language Association of America
New York 2004

© 2004 by The Modern Language Association of America
All rights reserved. Printed in the United States of America

For information about obtaining permission to reprint material from
MLA book publications, send your request by mail (see address below),
e-mail (permissions@mla.org), or fax (646 458-0030).

Library of Congress Cataloging-in-Publication Data

Reading sites: social difference and reader response / edited by
Patrocinio P. Schweickart and Elizabeth A. Flynn.
    p. cm.
Includes bibliographical references and index.
    ISBN 0-87352-984-7 (alk. paper) — ISBN 0-87352-985-5 (pbk. : alk. paper)
1.   Reader-response criticism. 2.   Literature and society. 3.   Books and
reading. I. Schweickart, Patrocinio P. II. Flynn, Elizabeth A., 1944-
    PN98.R38R427 2004
    801' .95—dc22   2003022482

Cover illustration of the paperback edition: Girl Reading at a Table (1934),
by Pablo Picasso. Metropolitan Museum of Art, bequest of Florene M.
Schoenborn, in honor of William Lieberman, 1995. (1996.403.1).
Photograph © 1996 The Metropolitan Museum of Art. © 2004 Estate
of Pablo Picasso / Artists Rights Society (ARS), New York.

Published by The Modern Language Association of America
26 Broadway, New York, New York 10004-1789
www.mla.org

Contents

Preface

Reading Sites addresses a concern that was latent if not evident in our earlier volume, *Gender and Reading*, namely, the way that the interacting social categories of gender, race, ethnicity, and class both condition and shape reader response. Despite the passing of more than fifteen years, the dynamics of reading within and across social difference remains underdeveloped within both literary studies and rhetoric and composition.

Special thanks go to our contributors, who have remained committed to the project despite what has turned out to be a rather long haul. Sonia Kane, acquisitions editor at the MLA, has been with us from the beginning and has handled the reviewing process efficiently and with considerable tact and diplomacy. At crucial stages of the reviewing process, Martha Evans, former director of MLA Book Publications, was also very helpful. Our reviewers, one of whom, Peter Rabinowitz, chose to reveal his identity, provided cogent readings of the manuscript and offered excellent suggestions for revision. We also received very helpful suggestions for revision from members of the MLA Publications Committee.

Patrocinio Schweickart thanks Thomas Adler, head of the English department, and Berenice Carroll, director of women's studies, for the research leave that enabled a significant portion of the work for the volume to be performed.

Elizabeth Flynn is grateful for the support of Bob Johnson, chair of the Department of Humanities at Michigan Technological University, and for the assistance of Sue Niemi, of the Department of Humanities. A sabbatical leave in spring 2001 was helpful in the final stages of the project as were two Faculty Scholarship Grants from Michigan Tech.

Introduction

Patrocinio P. Schweickart and Elizabeth A. Flynn

R eader-response criticism emerged in the 1970s and quickly gained widespread support—a session on reading at the 1976 MLA convention attracted an audience of over one thousand (Bleich, "Changing Reader" 31). Also notable during the 1970s and early 1980s was the publication of important books on reading by critics with diverse orientations, among them Roland Barthes, David Bleich, Jonathan Culler, Umberto Eco, Judith Fetterley, Stanley Fish, Norman Holland, Wolfgang Iser, Hans Robert Jauss, Gerald Prince, Louise Rosenblatt, and two important edited collections, *Reader-Response Criticism*, by Jane Tompkins, and *The Reader in the Text*, by Susan R. Suleiman and Inge Crosman.

It is safe to say that today reader-response criticism is not just something some critics do but something all critics necessarily do: all critics are readers, and all criticism is someone's response to a text. Moreover, a broad consensus has developed on three main tenets of reader-response criticism. First, the text is not a container of stable objective meaning, so interpretive disputes cannot be decided simply by reference to the objective properties of the text. Second, the reader is a producer of meaning; what one reads out of a text is always a function of the prior experiences; ideological

1

commitments; interpretive strategies; and cognitive, moral, psychological and political interests that one brings to the reading. And third, readings are necessarily various; there is no single noncontroversial set of standards for adjudicating interpretive disputes.

Despite strong support, however, reader-response criticism is still challenged by critics who hold positivistic views. For example, in *Literature Lost: Social Agendas and the Corruption of the Humanities*, John Ellis criticizes what he calls the "gender-race-class orthodoxy" and laments the abandonment in the humanities of the disinterested search for objective truth (7). A prime target are feminist critics, who in his view are unable to make intelligent contributions to the understanding of literature because of their emphasis on the theme of patriarchy and their "unrealistic and anachronistic victim-centered framework" (74).

Reader-response criticism has not adequately addressed charges such as those posed by Ellis and others.[1] Early work in reader response tended to focus on a universalized and unaffiliated reader and was itself often influenced by positivistic attitudes toward reading. The movement only turned its attention to gender and race in the 1980s and early 1990s, with the publication of books such as our *Gender and Reading* and James Machor's *Readers in History*. Moreover, little work has been done to relate the more recent branch of reader-response criticism that attends to gender, race, class, and other categories of social difference to the growing literature on the ethics of reading. Lawrence Buell in his introduction to the recent *PMLA* special topic Ethics and Literary Study, for instance, says, "Perhaps the touchiest single issue for both exemplars and critics of the ethical turn is the issue of whether it boils down, whatever the nominal agenda, to a privatization of human relations that makes the social and the political secondary" (14). One reason for this scant attention is that the social and the political connect the conversation to a traumatic history and to current social and cultural arrangements that involve high personal and collective stakes. But apart from the perhaps understandable desire to avoid difficult and volatile topics, one can also point out that the "privatization" of ethics is a function of the situation of ethics within a philosophical tradition that is defined by a strong commitment to the method of universalizing abstraction. The bracketing out of the social and the political is a consequence of the framing of ethical or moral reflection in terms of concepts—autonomy, freedom, norm, self, other—that have been stripped of all particularity.

Reading Sites explores diverse sites of reading and makes clear the importance of attending to the situation of readers as they interact with other readers and with authors in particular contexts that involve social hierarchy and difference. Thus it enters into and extends two conversations: reader-response theory as it attempts to explore relations between reading and factors such as gender, race, and class and discussions of the ethics of reading as these attempt to understand how readers interact with textual and authorial others in social contexts.

Reader-Response Theory

The major accomplishment of the reader-response theory that emerged in the 1970s and 1980s is the demonstration of the various roles the subjectivity of the reader play in the production of the meaning of the text. This development, not surprisingly, raised the perennial problems regarding subject-object relations. Is meaning objectively in the text to be read out by readers, or does it come from the subjectivity of the reader? Is the reader's role to discern the meaning of the text, or do readers truly produce the poems they read? It may be true that readers can read in various ways, but are all these ways equally valid, valuable, or acceptable? If the reader is a producer of meaning, what is the role of the text?

The pressure of these questions induced the division of reader-response theory into two camps: a text-dominant camp, represented most prominently by Prince and Iser, privileging the way the text and the reader in the text set the agenda for the reading; and a reader-dominant camp represented by Holland and Bleich, privileging the motivations, interests, and experiences of the reader. However, because the problematics of reading were posed in terms of the question of control over meaning, what was given at one end was taken away from the other. Emphasis on reader response tended to efface the significance of the text and the creative agency of the author; conversely, emphasis on the guiding role of the text tended to efface the agency of the reader. The development of reader-response theory depended on avoiding the two theoretical dead ends identified by Culler—the "monism of the text" and the "monism of the reader"—but the idea of reading as an interaction between two different entities proved difficult to maintain (74–78). Of particular significance in this regard is Rosenblatt, an early proponent of the study of reading (whose work was unfortunately excluded from the collections by both Tompkins and Suleiman and Crosman). Drawing on the work of the American pragmatists John Dewey and Charles Sanders Peirce, Rosenblatt argues that reading is best understood as a give-and-take process between reader and text. "Readers bringing to the text different personalities, different syntactical and semantic habits, different values and knowledge, different cultures, will under its guidance and control fashion different syntheses, live through different 'works'" (122). By bringing their unique backgrounds and values to the words on the page, readers actualize the text into a meaningful work that in turn stimulates response. Meaning, therefore, should be attributed not to the text or the reader but to the dynamic transaction between the two.

Admitting the role of the reader as producer of meaning brings forth two other problems related to but distinct from the risk of the nullification of the text, namely, the twin problems of error and interpretive chaos. In accordance with the positivism dominant in his intellectual milieu, I. A. Richards saw the subjectivity of the reader mainly as a source of error. If genuine knowledge of literature is to be distinguished from prejudice, taste, sentiment, and mere opinion, reading must be kept as free as possible of the "misleading effects of the reader's being reminded of some personal scene or adventure, erratic associations, the interference of emotional reverberations from a past which may have nothing to do with the poem" (13). The second problem—the danger of interpretive chaos (or relativism)—was the main motivation for the New Critical injunction against the affective fallacy. If the reader is a legitimate producer of meaning, then potentially we could have as many meanings as there are readers. As E. D. Hirsch has argued, the study of literature as a coherent academic discipline depends on finding efficient ways of regulating the proliferation of interpretations, of distinguishing interpretations that are competent, valid, and appropriate to the study of literature from those that are incompetent, invalid, or irrelevant. For Richards, the New Critics, and Hirsch, establishing the text as the ruling principle is the only effective way of safeguarding the study of literature from the dangers of error and disorder stemming from the subjectivity of readers.

Reader-response criticism has shown that the positivist presuppositions of this approach are untenable. Meaning is not objectively latent in the text, and the subjectivity of the reader cannot simply be ruled out as a source of error. All readings, including those that claim to be objective, are shaped—biased—by the reader's experiences, interests, and personality. Two ways of addressing the problem of interpretive chaos have emerged. The first, exemplified by Iser, gives the text a structuring rather than a ruling function. Written into every text, according to Iser, is an implied reader who sets the stage for actual readers. Readers fill in the gaps and connect the dots presented by the text. The substance of their response— the material that fills the gaps and connects the dots—comes from the reader's experience, knowledge, concerns, and interests. But the structure of the response—the gaps and the dots—are in the text. Different readers will read the text differently, but the implied reader that takes us through the process of apprehending the textual structure serves as a reference point for all interpretations.

Another proposal along this line is Peter Rabinowitz's idea of an "authorial audience." Rabinowitz observes that authors necessarily must make assumptions about "readers' beliefs, knowledge, and familiarity with conventions. . . . they design their books

rhetorically for some more or less specific *hypothetical* audience"
(21). Rabinowitz argues that by "treating [authorial intention] as
a matter of social convention rather than of individual psychology," his idea of an authorial audience "allows us to treat the
reader's attempt to read as the author intended, not as a search for
the author's private psyche, but rather as the joining of a particular social/interpretive community" (22). Like the implied reader,
the authorial audience functions as a "necessary fiction" for criticism, "guaranteeing the consistency of a specific reading without
guaranteeing its validity in any absolute sense" (Suleiman 11; qtd.
in Rabinowitz 23). The point is not to eliminate interpretive differences (there are many audiences, and not everyone will agree
to join the authorial audience) but rather to devise a way of orga-
nizing critical disagreements (I am doing an authorial reading,
you are not), to generate a class of interpretations that acknowledge the same point of departure, and to identify differences that
are not amenable to reasonable discussion.

A second way to address the problem of chaos arises from the
recognition that we read with the anticipation of discussing our
responses with others and that the meaning of a text is not the product of isolated readers but the collaborative product of a community
of readers. The development from subjectivity to intersubjectivity is
clearest in Fish's notion of the authority of interpretive communities and in Bleich's pedagogical practice of asking the members of
a class (students and teacher alike) to write responses that they subsequently share with one another ("Intersubjective Reading").
Whereas Bleich's main concern is to encourage the formation of
collaborative, mutually supportive, democratic communities of
readers, Fish's emphasis is on arguing that the regulatory and disciplinary power of interpretive communities mitigates the risk of interpretive chaos. Fish's interpretive communities refer not simply to
groups of readers but rather to readers operating within institutions
devoted to the study of literature. At any given point, these communities are governed by norms that determine the acceptability of
interpretations and critical strategies. Because there are different

interpretive communities, the interpretive field will remain heterogeneous. Nevertheless, what we will have is not chaos but an organized, structured, methodical, regulated, civilized pluralism.

Although Fish's approach to the authority of interpretive communities has connotations that become particularly ominous in light of Foucault's theory of the close connection between knowledge projects and regimes of power (*Power/Knowledge*), it has the advantage of underlining that as an academic discipline, the study of literature is governed by canons of acceptability, and the institutions where it is practiced are well equipped with mechanisms for cultivating certain readings—and readers—and impeding others. Fish's theory affirms the view that reading always takes place in a context where ideological and political interests intersect and connects reader-response criticism to the field of reception studies that was given its initial impetus by the German theorist Hans Jauss. According to Jauss, literary history should be concerned not only with authors and the cultural and historical contexts of their lives and works but also with the history of "the participation of the reader in the historically progressive actualization of meaning." Jauss proposes the idea of a "horizon of expectations" ("Identity" 23) to account for the changing contexts of beliefs, paradigms, and values that condition readers' responses to texts. Other notable examples of reception study are Steven Mailloux's method of "rhetorical hermeneutics" for exploring the cultural and political divisions that shape the reception of American literature ("Interpretation"); Tony Bennett's study of "reading formations," which connects reception study to Marxist theory and cultural studies; and Janice Radway's study of the women readers of popular romances, which connects reception study to feminist criticism and studies of popular culture.

Postmodernism and Feminist Criticism

Two other movements, postmodernism and feminist criticism, converged with reader-response criticism to propel the problematics of reading to the forefront of critical discussion. Influenced by the work of Jacques Derrida, Mikhail Bakhtin, Michel Foucault, Julia Kristeva, and others, postmodern perspectives on reading question both the presupposition of a unified reading subject and that of a text with a determinate meaning. The risk of misreading in this view comes not from the intrusion of subjective elements but rather from totalizing tendencies (effects of the reading subject's desire to maintain the illusion of a unified consciousness) that obscure the fluidity and multiplicity of textual meaning. The Derridean reading explored by Jeffrey Nealon in *Double Reading*, for instance, consists of a double move: the first, a critical reading from within the confines of a system or institution; the second, a self-reflexive reading that questions its own motives and attends to what was excluded in the first reading (18). The influence of Bakhtin is apparent in approaches that portray reading as taking place in a contact zone where voices contend with one another and marginalized perspectives struggle against the authoritative cultural discourses.[2] The work of Foucault is especially influential in new historicist reception studies that examine the ways in which historically specific audiences read particular texts, though the attempt to identify such reception is itself recognized as an interpretive activity that is neither neutral nor objective. History is seen as a constructed representation of events rather than as an exact account of them, and simple linear and foundational explanations of historical development are replaced by nonfoundational ones that recognize the multiplicity of factors that lead to historical change. This approach has been particularly fruitful in studies of nineteenth-century American literature that foreground the social, cultural, and material construction of gender and race.[3]

Feminist criticism introduced gender as an issue in critical discourse. The earliest approaches were critiques of the images of women in literature that have marginalized and devalued women and reinforced the social and cultural norms of male dominance, but in the late 1970s and 1980s, attention turned from the criticism of specific works to the critique of the literary canon. Feminists observed the overwhelming androcentricity of the works included in the literary curriculum and sought to remedy the situation by conducting research on women writers and by developing critical strategies appropriate to their works. *A Literature of Their Own*, by Elaine Showalter, and *The Madwoman in the Attic*, by Sandra Gilbert and Susan Gubar, inspired numerous studies that have led to the rediscovery of "lost" women writers and to the revision of the critical reception that has relegated most women writers to the margins of the canon.

At the same time, feminist critics began to attend to the situation of women readers. Fetterley's *The Resisting Reader*, published in 1978, argues that women readers need to resist canonical texts by male writers such as Ernest Hemingway, F. Scott Fitzgerald, and Henry James. These writers "immasculate" women readers, forcing them to identify against themselves and submit to the androcentric "designs" of works that marginalize women and define them as other (ix). An important concern of essays in our volume *Gender and Reading* was the development of a feminist theory of reading. Schweickart argues that reader-response criticism and feminist criticism need to encounter each other in a serious and sustained way. She observes that a feminist reading of some (though not all) male texts merits a dual hermeneutic: a negative one that discloses their complicity with patriarchal ideology and a positive one that recuperates the utopian moment that gave rise to it (43–44). Moreover, using the example of Adrienne Rich reading Emily Dickinson, she proposes a model for feminist readings of texts by women authors that involves construing the text not as an object but as the voice of another woman (47). Although feminist readings of male texts involve ideological unmasking, feminist readings of female texts are oriented toward "recovering, articulating, and elaborating positive expressions of women's point of view" and toward "celebrating the survival of this point of view in spite of the formidable forces that have been ranged against it" (51). Jean Kennard in "Ourself behind Ourself: A Theory for Lesbian Readers" formulates a theory of reading from the standpoint of the lesbian reader. Other essays in the volume explore the different ways in which male and female readers respond to literature, although the differences identified are not always pronounced or clear-cut. Holland and Leona Sherman suggest that male readers sometimes dismiss certain genres of literature, such as Gothic romances, because they find them threatening, while female readers some-times identify with the same texts, seeing them as invoking themes of woman's quest for self-knowledge and authenticity. Bleich finds that men tend to objectify the texts they read, while women have a less urgent need to do so. Flynn finds that men sometimes domi-nate texts by imposing meaning on them, while women more often interact with texts.

In most critical approaches the paradigm of reading is taken to be that done by professional critics and scholars in the course of their work—teaching and research—in academic institutions. The read-ing subject of these approaches, Foucault might say, is the effect of the discipline of literary study. By contrast, reader-response criti-cism has actively sought to pluralize readers, to explore reading as a cultural practice in a variety of contexts, including the practices of ordinary people in the course of their personal, social, and cultural lives, no less than those of professors and students within the acad-emy. Under the influence of feminist criticism and postmodernism, this interest in actual readers set the stage for the examination of how the activity of the reader is implicated in the prevailing social and cultural differences—first the category of gender and eventu-ally the categories of race, ethnicity, class, and sexual orientation. *Reading Sites* participates in this latter development by looking at reading from the point of view of actual readers in concrete situa-tions and by emphasizing theoretical and practical explorations of reading across categories of social difference—in particular, those of gender, race, ethnicity, and class.

The essays in this volume differ in their specific focus, but all begin with the recognition that an objectivist paradigm based on the fiction of the view from nowhere is untenable. As we have seen, acknowledging that interpretations are a function of the perspectives and interests of readers raises challenging questions regarding the validity of interpretations. Are all readings equally valid? How does one distinguish valid, competent, careful readings from incompetent, idiosyncratic, careless misreadings? How do we articulate the reader's responsibility with regard to the text he or she is reading? In addressing these questions, *Reading Sites* takes advantage of the insight in reader-response criticism that the intersubjectivity of interpretation allows us to think of validity as a product of a discursive process, to dispense with the notion of objective textual meanings, and to reframe the question of validity in terms of an ethics of reading.

The Ethics of Reading

"Ethics" may be understood in several ways. First, it has to do with the distinction between right and wrong. Being ethical in this sense means acting not on impulse but according to the appropriate norms. Second, ethics may refer to one's relationship with an other, to considerations of one's duty with regard to someone or something outside oneself. Today, under the influence of feminist criticism, postmodernism, and the work of Emmanuel Levinas, the second view of ethics is perhaps the most prominent (see Champagne). However, ethics has a third meaning that emphasizes one's relationship with oneself. To be ethical is to strive to cultivate the good in oneself and to live a good life. This notion of ethics is implicit in the work of Alasdair MacIntyre and other virtue ethicists, as well as in Foucault's idea of the "care of the self." The ethical framework of *Reading Sites* stretches across these three meanings of ethics.

Two books from sharply divergent points of view—*The Ethics of Reading*, by J. Hillis Miller, and *The Company We Keep*, by Wayne Booth—sparked the current "pursuit of ethics," to use Buell's term, in literary studies. Miller's motivation is to defend "the rhetorical study of literature," by which he means "deconstruction," against "opponents . . . from both sides of the political spectrum who continue to misrepresent it as ahistorical and apolitical" ("Is There an Ethics" 84; see also *Ethics* 1–11).

According to Miller, the ethical moment of reading faces in two directions. First, "it is a response to something, responsible to it, responsive to it, respectful of it," "something" that presents an imperative, "some 'I must' or *Ich kann nicht anders*. I must do this. I cannot do otherwise. If the response is not one of necessity, . . . if it is a freedom to do what one likes, for example to make a literary text mean what one likes, then it is not ethical" (*Ethics* 4). Second, reading is ethical to the extent that it is "a doing that does other things in turn" (85), an act that "enters into the social, political, and institutional realms, for example in what the teacher says to the class or in what the critic says" (4). Within this Kantian framework, the ethical as "duty" is the opposite of personal or social "inclinations." Ethical conduct is governed only by "the highest and unconditional good," an absolute universal that is abstracted of all particular values and goods and can only be found in the "pure will of a rational being" to respect the "law in itself" or "the law as such" (*Ethics* 16).

To explain what this means, Miller takes us through a close reading of a footnote in *Foundations of the Metaphysics of Morals*, in which Kant endeavors to distinguish the ethical feeling of respect from other feelings, specifically those of inclination and fear. The difference, according to Kant, is that inclination and fear are responses to outside influences, while respect is "self-wrought by a rational concept" and depends only on "the consciousness of the submission of the will to the law." Kant further writes, "All respect for a person is only respect for the law . . . of which the person provides an example" (qtd. in Miller, *Ethics* 17–18). Miller's ethics of reading stems from an extension of this Kantian analogy: "our respect for a text is like our respect for a person, that is, it is a respect not for the text in itself but respect for a law which the text exemplifies" (*Ethics* 18). The German word Kant uses for "respect," *Achtung*, joins the senses of "attention, heed" and "esteem, respect, regard" to the suggestion of "a coerced or alarmed taking notice of something possibly dangerous," as in its current use as a warning:

"look out! take care! beware!" (*Ethics* 16). The ethical, then, is associated with the sensation of something difficult and dangerous (if it is easy or pleasant, it is probably not ethical). The ethical reader "is like a man walking a knife-edge on a mountain-top, with an abyss on either side, the abyss of productive spontaneity on one side, the abyss of passive receptivity on the other" (19). And true to the expectations raised by deconstruction, Miller eventually shows that the "knife-edge itself turns into an abyss" (19). "What the good reader [of Kant, and in general of any text] confronts in the end is not moral law brought into the open at last by a clear example, but the unreadability of the text" (33).

In "Is There an Ethics of Reading?" Miller clearly spells out the implications and consequences of his point of view. The ethics of reading, "if there is such a thing," must be a response to the "law of language whereby a work fails to disclose itself fully or coincide unambiguously with itself or round itself off in a single coherent design with a single determinable meaning. Literature gives the reader literature, language gives him or her language" (97). For the sake of the "good" of this "insight into the real relations of language to society, history, and politics, which the rhetorical study of literature [i.e., deconstruction] alone can give," and for the sake of avoiding the "disaster of a misuse of literature for didactic ends for which it offers no sound basis," we must "give up, sacrifice, renounce . . . the desire to draw ethical conclusions from thematic readings" of literary texts. We "must give up the warm attractive project of looking at literature as the transmitter and creator, through language, of [our] culture's highest values." Thus starting from very different premises and by taking a stringently ethical stance, Miller arrives at recommendations that confirm the strictures of New Criticism: In our reading, teaching, and writing, "we should give up the attempt to transfer ethical themes directly from literature to life. . . . English departments of literature should reduce their function to a kind of linguistic hygiene, that is, to a study of the rhetoric of literature, what might be called 'literariness.' The rest should be left to departments of history, philosophy, religion, American Studies, Victorian studies, programs in 'modern thought,' and so on, where the rest belongs" (99).

Where Miller's conception of the ethics of reading is parsimonious, Booth's is capacious and includes all the "rest" that Miller renounces, namely, the appraisal of the "ethical value" of the "stories we tell each other," the discussion of the moral and political implications and effects of thematic and formal narrative choices, and the evaluation of the various "ethical powers" of literary works, "their power to add 'life' upon 'life'—for good or ill" (Booth 14). His view of ethics is Aristotelian rather than Kantian and advocates an ethical criticism that considers literature from the point of view of its contributions to the formation of "ethos"—the character of persons, of their interactions, and of the social and cultural world they inhabit.

The moral, intellectual, and political pressure brought on by the increased attention to gender, race, ethnicity, sexual orientation, and other categories of social difference is evident in both Miller and Booth. However, while Miller offers only a vague prophecy that a "millennium of good readers," as he has defined them, will usher in "the end of wars and of class conflict, an eternal reign of justice, peace, and happiness" ("Is There an Ethics" 100), Booth addresses the specific critical challenges posed by the categories of race and gender. *The Company We Keep* is a belated response to Paul Moses, an African American colleague of Booth's at the University of Chicago, who twenty-five years ago caused a "minor scandal" by refusing to continue teaching *Huckleberry Finn* because he did not think "it is right to subject students, black or white, to the many distorted views of race on which the book is based." In Moses's view, Twain's novel "is just bad education, and the fact that it's so cleverly written makes it even more troublesome to me" (qtd. in Booth 3). Rereading Twain in the light of the criticism of Moses and other African American critics, Booth found alongside "the marvelously warm and funny novel I had always loved," one that is distressingly similar to the one Moses read: "Twain, the great liberator, keeps Jim enslaved as long as possible . . . milking every possible laugh out of a situation which now seems less frequently and less wholeheartedly funny than it once did" (466–67). The novel "feeds stereotypes . . . that insult all black readers, and it redeems itself only by inciting some few sophisticated critics, many decades later, to think hard about how the book implicates white readers in unpleasant truths" (471). Booth considers various ways of redeeming Twain, but, he says,

> always, at my back I hear the voices of those readers—including myself now—who see that the infatuation is not after all innocent. They remind me that the hours I spend in that world *are* after all fantasy hours; whether or not I see them as that, they have the power to deflect my imagination in dangerous ways. . . . [Twain's] story . . . offers every invitation to miseducate ourselves, and therein lies the task of ethical criticism: to help us avoid that miseducation. (477)

Booth's rereading of Twain in the light of Moses's critique of the racism of Twain's book has its precedent in his rereading, five years earlier, of Rabelais's *Gargantua and Pantagruel* in response to feminist objections to the sexist attitudes it represents and promotes. On what basis do we decide the soundness of the specific ethical assertions we make upon reading about a literary work? The indeterminacy of the text, argues Miller, implies that there can be no indisputably sound basis for such assertions; this is precisely why we must abstain from making them. Booth, for his part, is compelled to tackle head-on the question of the validity of ethical assertions about literary texts. The logic of making defensible appraisals of literary works, he argues, is not the logic of deduction from clear premises or that of induction from specific instances but rather that of a method he calls *coduction*.

Coduction has three features. First, it attends to the subjectivity of the reader; to the reader's intellectual, emotional, and moral response to a text; and to the knowledge and experiences, literary and nonliterary, that the reader brings to the reading. Second, it relies on comparisons of works and reading experiences that generate a sense of similarities and differences that enable judgments of relative value. Third, coduction avoids the ever-present danger of subjectivism by requiring intersubjective verification. Coductions "can never be performed with confidence by one person alone." One must present to others one's views and one's reasons for holding them. "The validity of our coductions must always be corrected in conversations about the coductions of others whom we trust. They will always be subject to the corrections of time: time alone can yield the further comparisons that can teach us, again by coduction, whether our original appraisals can confirm themselves in further experience" (Booth 73).

One might argue against Booth that the requirement of intersubjective validation only trades one problem—that of individual bias—for another, more difficult one, that of the problem of power as a formative factor in the ideological commitments and collective authority of any community. Booth recognizes the problems of individual and collective bias, but, finally, rests his claims on his faith in the possibility that one can have rational discourse with others, a faith that is confirmed by his own "conversion" experiences— the correction, in time, of his personal and cultural biases as a result of conversations with critics who initially represented radically different perspectives.

The Other

The ethics of reading, as the examples of Miller and Booth show, concerns the reader's conduct with regard to an other and thus depends on the meaning one gives to this term. In Miller, the other refers to an abstract notion, an impersonal imperative—analogous to Kant's idea of the law and of "the highest and unconditioned good"—that stems from the linguistic nature of literature. It signifies the difference (*différance*) that both compels and defeats reading. In Booth, the other signifies other people—authors, fictional characters, friends, acquaintances, colleagues, other readers— particular others to whom he is answerable for his interpretations and value claims. These two conceptions of the other, polarized in

Miller and Booth, often coexist and commute with (that is, pass into and for) each other.

The pressure of these two notions of the other is especially evident in feminist theories of reading. Schweickart's representation of reading as communication is set in dialectical tension with the deconstructive conception of language as a barrier to communication: Rich's drive to communicate with Dickinson is undermined and ultimately defeated by texts that never fully disclose themselves. A similar tension is evident, from the opposite direction, in the work of postmodern feminist critics who have been especially concerned to develop strategies to guard against the ever-present danger of readings that enclose the text in a totalizing frame of reference. Kristeva recommends a form of analytical reading that recognizes and displays the incompleteness of any interpretation. Similarly, Gayatri Spivak advocates strategies that specify the particularities of the reading situation, emphasize the provisionality and fluidity of whatever labels are used to signify gender identity, and make evident that reading is always contingent on biographical and historical contexts. In Kristeva's and Spivak's view, reading, when properly done, is faithful to the ultimate unreadable otherness of the text, to the way texts disperse themselves and resist efforts to grasp their "essence." The responsible reader must follow the text's meandering movements, attend to its heterogeneous meanings, restrain the impulse to assimilate these into one point of view, acknowledge the partiality and contingency of all interpretations and their rootedness in the reader's social and cultural location. Feminist critics do not, however, conclude, with Miller, that to be ethical, literary critics must resolutely forego explicit discussion of the ways literature addresses and is implicated in social and cultural categories of differential privilege and power.

While on the surface postmodern feminist critics appear to emphasize the idea of the other as the ungraspable, irreducible *différance* of language, the stress on the multiplicity and mobility of the text in feminist works suggests not so much an abstract unreadable "something else," as in Miller, but rather many other things, differences, that one cannot, ought not, force into the "logic of the same." Thus the problem of the reader's conduct in the face of the otherness of language shades into the problem of reading others, across concrete differences of points of view, political interests, gender, race, ethnicity, and other categories of social and cultural difference. This is evident in Tina Chanter, who defends Derrida by offering a deconstructive analysis of Toni Morrison's *Beloved* that attends to the racial differences that are often muted or overlooked in the work of feminist opponents of Derrida. For postmodern feminists, deconstruction functions as a strategy for guarding against the impulse (well documented by Holland) to interpret all texts in terms of one's own identity theme, as well as against the essentialist tendency of some white feminists to homogenize all differences into the master category of gender. Such homogenizing excludes other categories of difference. The concern to develop reading strategies that attend to the otherness of the text is of a piece with the concern to attend to other people with different experiences and perspectives, to resist totalizing interpretive frameworks, and to recognize multiple systems of social and cultural domination.

Although the tension between a personal and an impersonal other is discernible in the essays in *Reading Sites*, the emphasis is on a personal other, and considerations of ethical responsibility revolve around the person-to-person obligations of recognition, nonviolence, assistance, care, and compassion (see Schweickart, "Reading, Teaching"). While other approaches tend to focus on a generalized other, *Reading Sites* affirms the feminist commitment to attend to the specificities of persons and situations, to think not of one general other but of particular others, differentiated, among other things, by race, ethnicity, and class.[4]

Reading and Social Difference

The method of coduction represents Booth's attempt to base value judgments on rational discussions with other "more or less qualified" readers. Aside from the politics of deciding which readers are more and which are less qualified to participate in critical discussions, it is important to note that for Booth, as for Fish and Bleich, the emphasis on intersubjectivity of interpretation has the effect of transforming readers into writers of readings. Coduction "collapses the distinction between how we arrive at a value judgment and how we defend it" (73) and in doing so covers up the difference between the experience and process of reading and the composed presentation of readings to others. In the first essay in *Reading Sites*, James Phelan shows that the problem of reading across social difference necessitates a closer look at what readers are doing when they are (silently) reading, apart from the (spoken or written) readings they present to others. In "Reading across Identity Borders: A Rhetorical Analysis of John Edgar Wideman's 'Doc's Story,'" Phelan proposes a "rhetorical reader-response criticism" that "views literature as the sending by an author and the receiving by a reader of a multileveled communication through the medium of the text." Underlying Phelan's model of reading is a dual conception of authors and readers. The flesh-and-blood author is a particular person, situated in a particular historical context, possessing certain personality traits and bearing identity markers, such as gender and race. The implied author is a hypothetical construct drawn from the narrative choices realized in the text. Phelan conceives of reading as involving a real reader, the flesh-and-blood person whose response to the text is conditioned by the reader's particular personality and situatedness, and a hypothetical reader representing the "authorial audience, the implied author's ideal addressee." Phelan's account of reading involves a significant revision of the idea of an "authorial audience" originally proposed by Peter Rabinowitz. Using "Doc's Story," Phelan demonstrates how he bridges the gap between the particularities of his own subjectivity and situatedness as a white man and the authorial audience addressed by Wideman's story of an African American male, who consoles himself for the loss of a white female lover by recalling the story of Doc, a blind African American man who can play basketball.

Phelan's account of his effort to join the authorial audience and to render himself in a position to receive the communication offered by the author through the narrative gives us what Booth does not, an extended reflection on his own identity and situation as a middle-class white male professor and on the way these particulars condition his response to Wideman's story. He gives us an account of the twists and turns of the play of similarity against difference, and he sets his capacity to understand and be moved against the necessary limitations of his sympathy and understanding. Phelan stretches his interpretive resources beyond the limits of his own flesh-and-blood experience and puts these efforts in the service of another's (Wideman's) communicative project. He shows that to discharge his readerly obligation, he must maintain the tension between deploying his subjective capacities and restraining them, between trusting his reactions and questioning them. His method is meditative where Booth's coduction is assertive and argumentative. He tests and corrects his responses not against what other readers might say but against the response that is called for by the hypothetical author he draws from the text. He reads the text before he responds. And then he reads again to test and correct his response. Phelan thus portrays reader and author as discourse partners.

Phelan's idea of a rhetorical reader-response criticism goes against the strong aversion in dominant twentieth-century Euro-American critical theory to the view that literature is a form of communication. The binary opposition between the communicative and the aesthetic is a fundamental element of the formalist poetics of New Criticism. A poem is an art object to the degree that it does not convey a message or to the degree that whatever message it can be said to convey is peripheral to its intrinsic poetic properties. In contemporary theory, the marginalization of the communicative function of language is reinforced by Derrida's critique of logocentricity and by the post-structuralist thesis that the meaning of the text is unreadable. However, like ethical criticism, the view that literature is a form of communication continues to be widely affirmed in practice even though it is theoretically proscribed. "Whenever a human practice refuses to die in spite of centuries of assault from theory, there must be something wrong with the theory" (Booth 6). Part of what is wrong is that theoretical concepts are often generalizations of the reading practices of their authors, in this case, the largely Euro-American male academic elite.

In "Colored *Readings*; or, Interpretation and the Raciogendered Body," Angeletta KM Gourdine elaborates a notion of *reading* drawn from African American oral culture and premised on the integration of communicative and literary values. *Reading* capitalizes on two oral practices: the black-church practice of "taking a text" in which a preacher uses a scriptural passage as a vehicle for commenting on the current concerns of the congregation and the practice, usually associated with black women, of "reading" an offensive or belligerent person by telling them the "biting truth" about themselves. The conjunction of these two practices results in a *reading* that is a response to previous statements (a scriptural text or a verbal affront) and at the same time is an occasion for saying something new beyond the terms set by the previous utterance. In her essay, Gourdine, a black woman, *reads* the works of black women writers—Zora Neale Hurston, Toni Morrison, Terry McMillan, Ama Ata Aidoo—as *readings* of the dominant cultural representations of raciogendered bodies of white and black women.

Gourdine's approach complicates Phelan's idea of an authorial audience. On the most obvious level, Gourdine is a black woman responding to the writings of other black women. She starts out as a member of the authorial audience for the texts she has selected—she does not have to work to join it. But is it true that black women writers writing about race from the perspective of black female protagonists are writing for an audience consisting entirely of black women? This is evidently not true with Hurston. "How It Feels to Be Colored Me" is a clever retort to white people whose ideas about being colored are at best patronizing if benevolent and at worst malicious and insulting. Hurston is *reading* white people— she is telling them off and doing them one better. Moreover, although she is speaking directly to white people, she is doing so with the expectation that black people are in the audience. Like Hurston, Morrison, McMillan, Aidoo, and other black writers presuppose a racially mixed audience.

Phelan's recursive rhetorical reading gives an account of his effort to join Wideman's African American authorial audience, from which, he assumes, he is excluded by virtue of his racial identity. However, while it is true that people of color do not figure among the ideal addressees of white writers (e.g., Jane Austen, Henry James, Mark Twain, and even, we would argue, William Faulkner),[5] Gourdine's essay suggests that the authorial audience of African American texts is often racially mixed: reading across racial difference is exactly what the hypothetical author expects from white readers. Moreover, black people do read the canonical texts that discount them as readers, and the model of reading across racial difference proposed by Phelan is problematic—indeed, hazardous—for them. For a black reader, reading a white text poses a threat similar to the risk of immasculation that, according to Fetterley, women readers face when they read male texts. As Morrison put it more precisely, black women reading white texts imbued with the white ideology of female beauty are at the receiving end of discourse designed to produce the conviction that they are ugly (*The Bluest Eye*). Because white racial ideology is culturally ubiquitous, black women cannot simply refuse to read white texts. They need to *read* them in Gourdine's sense.

"In Another Place: Postcolonial Perspectives on Reading," by Louise Yelin, focuses on three late twentieth-century reinterpretations of Victorian masterpieces: *Jack Maggs,* by Peter Carey; *Cambridge,* by Caryl Phillips; and *Windward Heights,* by Maryse Condé, recall and respond to *Great Expectations,* by Charles Dickens; *Mansfield Park,* by Jane Austen; and *Wuthering Heights,* by Emily Brontë. Carey, Phillips, and Condé illustrate what it means to read and write at a moment when the national literary traditions that were formed within the context of European colonial projects were being revised and rearticulated in the context of postcolonial economic, political, and cultural globalization. Like Gourdine, Yelin is concerned to elaborate protocols of reading from unexpected locations and perspectives. Carey, Phillips, and Condé capitalize on diverse vantage points (in Australia, the Carribean, francophone West Africa, France, England, and the United States) that supplement the insular geographic and historical perspective of Dickens, Austen, and Brontë and allow for the explicit disclosure of the history of colonialism, slavery, and racism that is latent but largely invisible from canonical European texts and traditions. In the process, Yelin argues, these authors illuminate the problem of bridging the divisions of gender, race, ethnicity, and class that connect us in our present moment to that history, and they prompt us "to listen for what remains to be said by those—nonreaders and nonwriters—whose perspectives have not yet been voiced, or heard, in contemporary literature."

Reading and the Self

The essays above explore the cognitive and moral implications of reading as a response to an other—language, a text, the discourse of another person, perspectives on the margins of the dominant culture. The next three essays explore another consequence of the critical turn toward the reader, namely the validation of the involvement of reading in various processes of self-realization and development.

The strong self-involvement encouraged by reader-response criticism adds a new twist to the problem of subjectivist reading: what is at issue is not only the risk of cognitive error but also the moral risk of self-absorption and of being unable to see anything except in terms of one's own perspective. But as much as this objection is well-taken, it is important not to overcompensate in the opposite direction: reading is involvement with the self no less than involvement with an other, and for many actual readers, reading is explicitly part of the process of becoming, maintaining, and cultivating one's self.

In "When a 'Speck' Begins to Read: Literacy and the Politics of Self-Improvement in Nineteenth-Century British Working-Class Autobiography," Kelly J. Mays examines the role played by reading in working-class narratives of self-development. In these stories, learning to read transforms an "ignorant brute" into "a worthy member of society." Moreover, the crucial event is not, as one might expect, the acquisition of literacy itself but rather the "great change" when an avid reader no longer reads just for the pleasure of stories but for ideas that contribute to the realization of a "higher self." Mays focuses particularly on *Memoirs of a Social Atom*, by William Edwin Adams, and *Memoirs of a Militant*, by Annie Kenney. Both Adams and Kenney were working-class activists.

Adams and Kenney speak of themselves as readers devoted to the fantastic, sentimental, and sensational stories published in "penny dreadfuls" and weekly girls' papers. However, literacy and a passion for reading did not distinguish them from the "great masses" of "poor lads" and factory girls. Both associate the development of autonomous individuality and the recognition of personal agency with a change in reading habits: a preference for texts that offered serious ideas and useful knowledge and a reflective attitude toward rather than absorption in the text. The change, predictably, is presented as the transition from childhood to adulthood, but Mays notes that it coincides for both Adams and Kenney with entering the labor force. Reading is, in a sense, a form of resistance against the conditions of labor. Becoming a worker is a destiny, not a choice; as a worker, one takes one's place as a "social atom" among other social atoms. However, becoming a "great reader" is a choice, to give one's "hands" for "wages" during working hours but to devote leisure hours away from the factory to putting one's "brain" and "higher self" to "nobler uses."

It might be argued that in spite of initial appearances, the pattern of reading Adams and Kenney describe is not necessarily emancipatory. One can appreciate the emancipatory aspirations that motivate their efforts to partake of the "culture of literacy," but ironically the result is their estrangement from their class and the adoption of forms of reason and notions of self-development that are governed by the ideals of bourgeois individualism. By tracing the specific linkings of the story of reading with the other elements of the lives and political careers of Adams and Kenney, Mays shows that while the bourgeois values encoded in texts are indeed a hazard for the working-class reader, the idea of "embourgeoisement" oversimplifies the complex and multifaceted relation of self-development and reading. Adams and Kenney associate reading not only with the realization of themselves as individuals with talents and ability and with the right to question prevailing conditions but also with the recognition of themselves as politically responsible members of their class. These autobiographies, Mays concludes, do not exemplify the role of reading in the adoption of bourgeois individualism but rather in mediating and facilitating the development of a distinctly politicized form of working-class consciousness.

Mays's essay suggests that careful studies of working-class autobiographies complicate the postmodern thesis that whenever one thinks of oneself as a subject, whenever one frames one's moral and political claims in terms of subjectivity, one necessarily becomes implicated in the reproduction of the normative white male bourgeois subject. Following Mays, we could argue that subject formation results not in a single hegemonic form but in various forms of subjectivity. Adams and Kenney become subjects, but not bourgeois subjects. Using Foucault's terms, we can regard working-class autobiographies as repositories of subjugated knowledge—specifically of knowledge bearing on the formation of working-class subjects—knowledge refined out of the notion of the subject adopted by the dominant academic disciplines.

"Some of Their Stories Are like My Life, I Guess: Working-Class Women Readers and Confessional Magazines," by Jane Greer, focuses on a much maligned group of readers—working-class women consumers of confessional magazines in the 1950s whose lamentable taste for "true trash" and alarming penchant for mistaking fiction for reality have been decried by moralists, educators, social reformers, and cultural critics. Greer's study seeks to amplify the voices of this group of readers and to bring out the varied and energetic forms of readerly agency they employed in appropriating the narratives they found in confessional magazines.

True Story, founded in 1919, was the first of the confessional magazines offering first-person real-life stories of "sin, suffering, and sorrow" written by "common people" rather than by professional writers. *True Story* was an instant success and was soon followed by imitators. By the 1960s, the aggregate circulation of confessional magazines was estimated at over 8,500,000. Greer bases her account of the responses of actual readers on a 1955 sociopsychological study conducted by Lee Rainwater, Richard P. Coleman, and Gerald Handel of 150 working-class women who were longtime readers of *True Story*. She argues that the readers Coleman interviewed adopted a specific reading strategy, which she calls "flexible moral realism." They accepted the narratives as realistic depictions of the challenges of everyday life, and they judged these stories according to flexible moral standards that were based on the understanding that because the complex circumstances of life made moral lapses likely, such lapses need not bar anyone from achieving a reasonably happy life. The stories in confessional magazines mitigated the sense of loneliness of troubled readers and provided an important source of information on how to deal with problems like illicit love affairs and unplanned pregnancies. Greer concludes that contrary to the stereotype of passive, manipulated mass consumers, the working-class women who read confessional magazines during the first half of the century were productive and active, energetically insisting through the strategies they adopted that they were not leading vulnerable or ruined lives and that their experiences were worthy of circulation in the wider print culture.

Anne G. Berggren and Erin A. Smith, the next two contributors, continue the feminist tradition of ethnographic participant-observer studies focusing on women readers. In "Reading like a Woman," Berggren makes her experience the point of departure for her study of women who, like herself, are lifelong passionate readers. Her subjects are white, middle-class, highly educated readers with professional careers, but her study shares two of the features of Greer's study of working-class readers. First, Berggren, like Greer, conducts her research against the background of the general disparagement of women readers, their tastes in reading material, and their reading practices that has persisted for at least four centuries. The similarity in the patterns of criticism noted by Greer and Berggren offers an opportunity to observe the interaction between class and gender. At first glance, we are struck by the saliency of gender. Both working-class women and middle-class women are castigated for stereotypical feminine deficiencies — trivial tastes, sentimentality, and the tendency to be taken in by stories. However, on closer inspection, we see how gender works as a proxy for class and how class works as an intensifier of gender. The disparagement of the working-class readers of Greer's study is accomplished by attributing to them a concentrated form of the female qualities that have been the perennial targets of the critics of femininity.

Second, the practice of reading "like a woman" that Berggren and her subjects favor and explicitly assert against their academic training is consonant with the "flexible moral realism" Greer found in working-class readers. Reading like a woman rather than reading like a "scholar" involves allowing for, indeed capitalizing on, the permeability between fiction and the real world, responding to characters and their predicaments as if they were real people and as if their worlds were extensions of one's own. According to Berggren, critics have accurately observed that women who love to read fiction become passionately absorbed in their reading. However, she argues that these critics have been unable to appreciate that for many women, reading fiction has functioned effectively as an occasion for developing self-knowledge, for enlarging one's experience of other people and of the world, and for critical reflection about specific life circumstances as well as about fundamental issues.

In "Both a Woman and a Complete Professional: Women Readers and Women's Hard-Boiled Detective Fiction," Smith takes issue with the generally formalist or structuralist approaches that characterize scholarship on detective fiction, which emphasize the denouement where the mystery is solved and the social order is reestablished. According to Smith, Fredric Jameson's contention that mystery fans "read for the ending" (132) degrades the rest of the novel as a means to an end. In fact, Smith found fans of women's hard-boiled detective fiction do not give much importance to the plot—they seldom remember the ending. Instead, they focus on the middle of the novels—on the female detective and her personality and on the typical situation in which she finds herself. Smith found a strong element of rehearsal in the way the (professional, highly educated, middle-class white) women she interviewed read the detective fiction. The readers identify with the woman detective, and through this identification they imaginatively live out certain character traits (e.g., physical courage, iron will) and certain situations (of danger, confusion, adventure) that are akin to real-life situations they have faced or may face.

Reading as Social Enterprise: The Community and the Classroom

The intersubjectivity of reading faces in two directions—toward the authorial subject and toward other readers. The last essays in the volume focus on the social production of meaning in various communities of readers. In "That, My Dear, Is Called Reading: Oprah's Book Club and the Construction of a Readership," Rona Kaufman shows that Oprah's very successful book club orchestrates a variety of locations (the television studio, the book-club meeting place, the private location of the individual reader or viewer) and a multitude of relationships (reader with text, reader with writer, readers and viewers with each other, and Oprah with everyone else). The club, Kaufman stresses, was not about the passage from illiteracy to literacy (all the club members can read) but about the passage from aliteracy to literacy—club members are converted from people who know how to read but do not to people who read regularly and passionately.

Significantly, Oprah's Book Club also represents concrete experiments in reading and conversing across racial line. In the episodes Kaufman discusses, Oprah, an African American woman, hosted and orchestrated conversations between Toni Morrison, an African American writer, and her mostly white audience. Kaufmann stresses Oprah's leading role. Oprah's admiration, respect, and love for Morrison and her works were vividly displayed when Morrison was a guest on the show and served as a catalyst for similar responses from book-club members, the studio audience, and the larger viewing audience. One might question the sincerity of this response—after all, Oprah and her staff staged and managed the show. However, using an idea from Smith, we can also say that the show offered the mostly white book-club members and audience an opportunity to rehearse responsible ways of reading works of African American writers writing about African American concerns.

For most of us, the classroom provides the most immediate practical examples of reading as a collaborative hermeneutic project where different readers formulate and refine their responses to texts in discussions with others. Mary Louise Pratt conceives of the classroom as a contact zone, a social space "where cultures meet, clash, and grapple with each other, often in contexts of highly asymmetrical relations of power" (34). In "Rhetorizing the Contact Zone: Multicultural Texts in Writing Classrooms," Laurie Grobman points out that while teaching and learning in a multicultural contact zone can be an exhilarating experience, most of us who have attempted such an educational project know that issues of racial and ethnic difference can be explosive and that despite our best intentions, communicating across or on the edge of the color line can be difficult, frustrating, painful, and frightening to teachers and students alike. It is important to invite students to reexamine their deeply held views about race and ethnicity, but it is also important to make the classroom into a space where students can engage the conflict-ridden issues implicit in multiculturalism without the fear, hostility, and defensiveness that are inimical to learning. To this end, Grobman devised a method she calls "rhetorizing the contact zone" of multicultural texts[6] and applied it to the composition courses she taught in spring 1999.

Taking her cue from Pratt and Bakhtin, Grobman argues that a multicultural text can be read as a contact zone where heterogeneous value systems, ideologies, and cultural structures meet, interact with, interanimate, and contest one another. In Grobman's usage, "rhetoric" refers to the art of composing publicly persuasive discourse, and "rhetorizing" the textual contact zone means analyzing it in terms of the competing rhetorical systems it contains. In her composition courses, instead of using a multicultural reader (the typical choice), Grobman used a single text, *The House on Mango Street*, by Sandra Cisneros. She structured the reading of this novel around four discourses: the American dream, American individualism, the bildungsroman tradition, and the feminist counterdiscourse to the discourse of fairy tales. In the writing assignments, the students were asked to comment on how Cisneros's text engages each of these four discourses. As each essay underwent a series of revisions, Grobman shows how the students progressed from vague and predictable statements about these familiar themes to a greater appreciation of the complex ways that Cisneros's novel engaged them. In this way, Cisneros's text works as a multicultural contact zone enabling thinking and writing about language and meaning, literacy and power, national identity and cultural diversity.

Rhetorizing the contact zone of the text has two important pedagogical advantages. First, it offers a model for the interaction of diverse points of view. The students see that the differences and disagreements that arise in class discussion have been anticipated by the text. Phrasing their own reactions within the rhetorical framework of the text produces just enough detachment to allow for a critical examination of these reactions. Second, the focus on rhetoric fits in with the mission of a composition course to teach students about the complex relation of language and meaning and about the effective use of reading and writing skills for formulating and testing ideas, persuading others, and influencing social and institutional decisions.

Bleich in "What Literature Is 'Ours'?" observes that, ironically, the call for the reform of the literary curriculum to reflect the reality of cultural diversity comes at a time when literature itself has been relegated to the cultural margins. Bleich suggests that literature no longer matters because we have ceased to attend to its fundamental materiality as language. Readers familiar with his work may be surprised by this statement. Has Bleich, who is perhaps the best-known champion of the subjective prerogatives of the reader and a proponent of a pedagogy that encourages the collaborative examination of responses, converted to the deconstructionist study of literature recommended by J. Hillis Miller?

Bleich's concern stems from his observation that students, even those who are most engaged and moved by the texts they read, tend to formulate their responses in terms of predictable themes (such as being "truly independent" and "believing in yourself") that tend to homogenize their responses to literature. Students who resort to stock responses, according to Bleich, are not reading the text but reading past it.

Bleich cites the responses of Brenda Daly and her student collaborators to *A Thousand Acres*, by Jane Smiley, as examples of what needs to happen if literature is to matter. Daly and the students take issue with Smiley's choice of the word "seduced" to signify the occurrence of incest. They argue that the father did not "seduce" his daughters—he "raped" them. In this example, taking the language of the text seriously means appreciating the weight of the writer's linguistic choices and, if necessary, disputing them. Here again we see tension between the conception of the other as impersonal matter (language) outside oneself and the conception of the other as another person. For Bleich, the matter of the language of a literary text is our access to the voice and the point of view of the writer. If reading is to be a conversation, we need to take in the language of the text and incorporate it into our responses. Bleich decries the loss of the facility to quote texts from memory and to incorporate such quotes into everyday conversations. To make literature matter, he argues, we need to make the language in which it is written partake of the living language by which we conduct our social interactions with others. His concern with language is of a piece not with Miller's poststructuralist recommendations for the study of literature but with his own enduring commitment to cultivation of socially responsible conceptions of reading and writing.

"Reading 'Whiteness,' Unreading 'Race': (De)Racialized Reading Tactics in the Classroom" by AnaLouise Keating points out some of the dangers of the recent trends in exposing and analyzing "whiteness" as a racial category. Although scholarship "denormalizing" whiteness is a welcome development, Keating is troubled by the lack of attention to the possible deleterious impact in the classroom of reading strategies that racialize whiteness. It is not enough to teach students to read whiteness in previously unmarked texts. Unless one does so carefully, one is likely to trigger white backlash and to reinforce the belief in permanent racial categories. What is called for, Keating argues, are "(de)racialized tactics" (along the lines Octavia Butler uses in her novels) that on the one hand teach students to recognize that all characters and texts are racialized and on the other enact these racialized readings in unexpected, temporarily deracialized ways that underscore the contingent, fluid, and relational nature of all racialized identities.

Keating's strategy for teaching students how to read "whiteness" as a racial category involves four steps. First, one must select texts that thematize whiteness as a racial category without reinforcing the widespread belief that race is a natural category. Keating applies her method to the teaching of *White Noise*, by Don DeLillo, and *Ceremony*, by Leslie Marmon Silko. Second, one must delay racialization. Keating recommends that discussions begin with topics that do not foreground race. For example, the protagonists of *White Noise* and *Ceremony* are both men in the throes of an identity crisis related to World War II. Because the initial omission of race fits in with the students' training in ignoring the "whiteness" of white people and white culture, it sets the stage for the explicit discussion of whiteness as the unmarked, normalized, racial category. The third step is the discussion of race as a "denaturalized" category. Keating historicizes terms like "white" and "black." She points out that the Puritans identified themselves as "Christian" or "English" or "free" but not "white" and that the term is an artifact of the racialization of slavery; that racial terms like "black" and "white" imply unwarranted homogeneity where in reality we have a diversity of ethnicities, languages, and cultures; that racial categories are politically motivated and unstable—the category "white" includes groups (such as the Irish, Jews, and Italians) that are relatively recent additions; and that racial purity is an untenable fiction. The fourth step is the deconstruction of whiteness. Keating takes the class through close readings of particular passages in DeLillo and Silko that illustrate the selective racialization of characters, the direct or subtle allusions to whiteness, and the way whiteness functions symbolically in each novel.

Charles Mills argues that "the world we are living in" has been constituted by a "racial contract," which he defines as a set of formal and informal agreements among "whites," the general purpose of which is "the differential privileging of whites as a group with respect to nonwhites as a group." By means of the contract, whites give themselves the status of full persons and give "nonwhites" the "different and inferior moral status [of] subpersons" (11). Mills stresses that while nonwhites may acquiesce or cooperate with the contract, they are not genuinely consenting parties. The contract "is between those categorized as white *over* nonwhites, who are thus objects rather than subjects of the agreement" (12).[7] Mills's theory of a racial contract is modeled on Carole Pateman's theory of patriarchy as a sexual contract—a set of agreements by means of which men secure their political, social, and cultural dominance over women. Following Pateman and Mills, we can easily conceive of the idea of a class contract that secures the socioeconomic domination of one class over another. These three contracts "[underwrite] the modern social contract and [are] continually being rewritten" (Mills 62).

The above references to the work of Mills and Pateman underscore the stark political realities that form the context for *Reading Sites*. The connection between reading and the politics of social difference is suggested by Mills's argument that the racial contract *prescribes* an "epistemology of ignorance" on racial matters:

> [O]ne could say, . . . as a general rule, that *white misunderstanding, misrepresentation, evasion, and self-deception on matters related to race* are among the most pervasive mental phenomena of the past few hundred years. . . . And these phenomena are in no way *accidental*, but [are] *prescribed* by the terms of the Racial Contract, which requires a certain schedule of structured blindnesses and opacities in order to establish and maintain the white polity. (19)

Following and extending Mills, we can see that along with instruction in reading skills and cultural literacy, literacy education trains us to misrecognize and misunderstand race, gender, class, and the other categories of difference that structure our world. The activity of reading is one of the ways of securing our consent, if we belong to the privileged group, and our acquiescence, if we belong to the inferiorized group, to the terms of the social contracts that maintain these unequal relations. But if literacy education and the study of literature have been deeply implicated in the concerted production of ignorance on categories of difference, the essays in *Reading Sites* suggest how they can become a means for overcoming such ignorance, and how reading practices can contribute to the project of repealing inequitable social and cultural arrangements.

NOTES

1. For example, Balbert finds that feminists do not understand D. H. Lawrence's fundamental vision, hence their reductive and misleading treatments of his work (3); Levin accuses feminists of misreading Shakespeare's tragedies and asserts that the most productive approach to the plays is "a scientific study of

the complex factors in human development, which would investigate the similarities as well as the differences between women and men based on evidence that compelled the assent of all rational people regardless of their gender or ideology" (136). Flynn discusses the attacks on feminism by Ellis, Balbert, and Levin more fully in "Misreading"; see also *Feminism*.

2. For an example of a Bakhtinian perspective on reading narrative, see Beaty.
3. Essays in Machor's edited collection *Readers in History*, for example, deal with Margaret Fuller's review of Frederick Douglass's autobiography (Mailloux, "Interpretation"), black responses to Harriet Beecher Stowe's *Uncle Tom's Cabin* (Banks), and the cultural authority of nineteenth-century women (Harris). Also, see Flint, *The Woman Reader 1837–1914*.
4. In critical theory, as Chow has observed, the other is an idealistic concept, purified of all the "vulgarities" of actual specific social, racial, and cultural differences, whose main function is to do the "work of the negative," to accomplish "the othering, the making-heterogeneous of Western thought from within" (xvi–xxii).
5. Morrison makes a stronger claim: "until very recently, and regardless of the race of the author, the readers of virtually all American fiction have been positioned as white" (*Playing* xii).
6. A "multicultural text" is shorthand for literature written from the perspective of the nonwhite ethnic minority populations of the United States. See Grobman's explanation for using this awkward term.
7. "All whites are *beneficiaries* of the Contract, though some whites are not *signatories* to it" (Mills 11). Mills explains in a long footnote that although he is focusing on race, he is aware that racial domination coexists and interacts with gender and class domination (137–38n3).

WORKS CITED

Balbert, Peter. *D. H. Lawrence and the Phallic Imagination: Essays on Sexual Identity and Feminist Misreading*. New York: St. Martin's, 1989.

Banks, Marva. "*Uncle Tom's Cabin* and Antebellum Black Response." Machor 209–27.

Beaty, Jerome. *Misreading Jane Eyre: A Postformalist Paradigm*. Columbus: Ohio State UP, 1996.

Bennett, Tony. "Texts in History: The Determinations of Readings and Their Texts." Machor 61–74.

Bleich, David. "The Changing Reader." *Reader* 43 (2000): 31–32.

———. "Gender Interests in Reading and Language." Flynn and Schweickart 234–66.

————."Intersubjective Reading." *New Literary History* 17 (1986): 401–22.

Booth, Wayne C. *The Company We Keep: An Ethics of Fiction*. Berkeley: U of California P, 1988.

Buell, Lawrence. "Introduction: In Pursuit of Ethics." *PMLA* 114 (1999): 7–19.

Champagne, Roland. *The Ethics of Reading according to Emmanuel Levinas*. Amsterdam: Rodopi, 1998.

Chanter, Tina. "On Not Reading Derrida's Texts: Mistaking Hermeneutics, Misreading Sexual Difference, and Neutralizing Narration." *Derrida and Feminism: Recasting the Question of Woman*. Ed. Ellen K. Feder, Mary C. Rawlinson, and Emily Zakin. New York: Routledge, 1997. 87–113.

Chow, Rey. *Ethics after Idealism: Theory-Culture-Ethnicity-Reading*. Bloomington: Indiana UP, 1998.

Culler, Jonathan. *On Deconstruction: Theory and Criticism after Structuralism*. Ithaca: Cornell UP, 1982.

Ellis, John M. *Literature Lost: Social Agendas and the Corruption of the Humanities*. New Haven: Yale UP, 1997.

Fetterley, Judith. *The Resisting Reader: A Feminist Approach to American Fiction*. Bloomington: Indiana UP, 1978.

Flint, Kate. *The Woman Reader 1837–1914*. Oxford: Oxford UP, 1993.

Flynn, Elizabeth A. *Feminism beyond Modernism*. Carbondale: Southern Illinois UP, 2002.

————. "Gender and Reading." Flynn and Schweickart 267–88.

————."Misreading (and) Feminism." *Reader* 49 (2003): 65–90.

Flynn, Elizabeth A., and Patrocinio P. Schweickart, eds. *Gender and Reading: Essays on Readers, Texts, and Contexts*. Baltimore: Johns Hopkins UP, 1986.

Foucault, Michel. *The Care of the Self*. Trans. Robert Hurley. New York: Random, 1986.

————. *Power/Knowledge: Selected Interviews and Other Writings, 1972–1977*. Ed. and trans. Colin Gordon. New York: Pantheon, 1980.

Gilbert, Sandra, and Susan Gubar. *The Madwoman in the Attic: The Woman Writer and the Nineteenth-Century Literary Imagination*. New Haven: Yale UP, 1979.

Harris, Susan K. "Responding to the Text(s): Women Readers and the Quest for Higher Education." Machor 259–82.

Hirsch, E. D. *Validity in Interpretation*. New Haven: Yale UP, 1967.

Holland, Norman, and Leona Sherman. "Gothic Possibilities." Flynn and Schweickart 215–33.

Jameson, Fredric. "Reification and Utopia in Mass Culture." *Social Text* 1 (1979): 130–48.

Jauss, Hans Robert. "The Identity of the Poetic Text in the Changing Horizon of Understanding." Machor and Goldstein 7–28.

Kant, Immanuel. *Foundations of the Metaphysics of Morals*. Trans. Lewis W. Beck. Indianapolis: Bobbs-Merrill, 1978.

Kennard, Jean E. "Ourself behind Ourself: A Theory for Lesbian Readers." Flynn and Schweickart 63–80.

Kristeva, Julia. "Psychoanalysis and the Polis." *The Kristeva Reader.* Ed. Toril Moi. New York: Columbia UP, 1986. 301–20.

Levin, Richard. "Feminist Thematics and Shakespearean Tragedy." *PMLA* 103 (1988): 125–38.

Machor, James L., ed. *Readers in History: Nineteenth-Century American Literature and the Contexts of Response.* Baltimore: Johns Hopkins UP, 1993.

Machor, James L., and Philip Goldstein, eds. *Reception Study: From Literary Theory to Cultural Studies.* New York: Routledge, 2001.

MacIntyre, Alasdair. *After Virtue: A Study in Moral Theory.* Notre Dame: U of Notre Dame P, 1984.

Mailloux, Steven. "Interpretation and Rhetorical Hermeneutics." Machor 39–60.

———. *Rhetorical Power.* Ithaca: Cornell UP, 1989.

Miller, J. Hillis. *The Ethics of Reading: Kant, de Man, Eliot, Trollope, James, and Benjamin.* New York: Columbia UP, 1987.

———. "Is There an Ethics of Reading?" Ed. James Phelan. *Reading Narrative: Form, Ethics, Ideology.* Columbus: Ohio State UP, 1989. 79–101.

Mills, Charles W. *The Racial Contract.* Ithaca: Cornell UP, 1997.

Morrison, Toni. *Playing in the Dark: Whiteness and the Literary Imagination.* Cambridge: Harvard UP, 1992.

Nealon, Jeffrey T. *Double Reading: Postmodernism after Deconstruction.* Ithaca: Cornell UP, 1993.

Pateman, Carole. *The Sexual Contract.* Stanford: Stanford UP, 1988.

Pratt, Mary Louise. "Arts of the Contact Zone." *Profession 91.* New York: MLA, 1991. 33–40.

Rabinowitz, Peter J. *Before Reading: Narrative Conventions and the Politics of Interpretation.* Ithaca: Cornell UP, 1987.

Radway, Janice. *Reading the Romance: Women, Patriarchy, and Popular Literature.* Chapel Hill: U of North Carolina P, 1984.

Richards, I. A. *Practical Criticism: A Study of Literary Judgment.* New York: Harcourt, 1929.

Rosenblatt, Louise. *The Reader, the Text, the Poem: The Transactional Theory of the Literary Work.* Carbondale: Southern Illinois UP, 1978.

Schweickart, Patrocinio P. "Reading Ourselves: Toward a Feminist Theory of Reading." Flynn and Schweickart 31–62.

———. "Reading, Teaching and the Ethic of Care." *Gender in the Classroom: Power and Pedagogy.* Ed. Susan Gabriel and Isaiah Smithson. Urbana: U of Illinois P, 1990. 78–95.

Showalter, Elaine. *A Literature of Their Own: British Women Novelists from Brontë to Lessing*. Princeton: Princeton UP, 1977.

Spivak, Gayatri Chakravorty. "Finding Feminist Readings: Dante—Yeats." *In Other Worlds: Essays in Cultural Politics*. New York: Routledge, 1988. 15–29.

Suleiman, Susan R. "Introduction: Varieties of Reader-Oriented Criticism." Suleiman and Crosman 3–45.

Suleiman, Susan R., and Inge Crosman, eds. *The Reader in the Text: Essays on Audience and Interpretation*. Princeton: Princeton UP, 1980.

Tompkins, Jane, ed. *Reader-Response Criticism: From Formalism to Post-structuralism*. Baltimore: Johns Hopkins UP, 1980.

Reading across Identity Borders:
A Rhetorical Analysis of
John Edgar Wideman's "Doc's Story"

James Phelan

> *I try to invite the reader into the process of writing, into the mysteries, into the intricacies of how things are made and so, therefore, I fore-ground the self-consciousness of the act of writing. And try to get the reader to experience that, so that the reader is participating in the creation of the fiction. . . .*

> *There's often a confusion between the person I am and what I do in my work. If the work is serious it should stand on its own. It shouldn't need the prop of personality behind it. Another side of this cult of personality is that it perpetuates our confusion about race. The author's race or sex determines the kind of critical commentary that appears about his or her work. This stupidity is institutionalized in traditional literary studies.*

> —JOHN EDGAR WIDEMAN

Rhetorical Reader Response and the Question of Difference

One commonplace of our poststructuralist, postmodern critical age is that all knowledge is relative to analytical frameworks, episte-mological perspectives, and subject positions. Unfortunately, atten-tion to this commonplace often obscures an important question that follows from it: to what extent can knowledge and understanding be shared across frameworks, perspectives, and positions? With the rise of multiculturalism and developments in feminist and queer theory, one version of this question has become especially pressing for reader-response criticism: to what extent, if any, can readers of literary texts cross the identity borders of gender, race, class, sexual orientation, and nationality?[1] As John Edgar Wideman cautions in the second epigraph above, however, we need to avoid the assumption that writers or readers will treat or respond to certain subject matters in predictable, identity-specific ways. With this caution in mind, I here pursue an answer to the question of whether we can read across difference, and I do so in connection with what I call rhetorical reader-response criticism in *Narrative as Rhetoric* and with a narrative text that is itself concerned with how people can relate across racial and gender borders. Wideman's "Doc's Story" was first published in his 1989 collection *Fever*, and it is one of several stories in the collection concerned with relating across difference.[2] How do I, a white male reader, come to understand and evaluate this story by an African American male writer about an African American man's relationship with a white woman? I also use "Doc's Story" because it exemplifies the point Wideman makes in the first epigraph: the narrative requires the reader's active participation for its completion.

Rhetorical reader-response criticism is best understood as part of a broader rhetorical approach to literature. This approach views literature as the sending by an author and the receiving by a reader of a multileveled communication through the medium of the text. The communication engages readers intellectually, emotionally, psychologically, and ethically, and its dynamics involve recursive relations among authorial agency, textual phenomena (including structures, techniques, literary conventions, and intertextual relations), and reader response. Because the relations are recursive, no one of these three main components of the communicational dynamics dominates the other two; because the communication is recursive, an initial focus on any one of the components necessarily leads to attention to the other two (for more on the approach, see my *Reading People* and *Narrative as Rhetoric*).

Pairing this rhetorical approach with the question of reading across differences is especially intriguing because the approach takes a dual view of authors and readers, recognizing them as both flesh-and-blood individuals and hypothetical constructs. The flesh-

and-blood author is a particular person, situated in a particular historical context, possessing particular skills, beliefs, politics, values, attitudes, opinions, and biases. The hypothetical or implied author is the streamlined version of the flesh-and-blood author that he or she inscribes in the text; or to put it another way, the implied author is the consciousness responsible for the text being this way rather than that way and therefore responsible for inviting the audience to respond in these ways rather than those.[3] Since the implied author is a version of the real author, identity markers such as race and gender are likely to be relevant to, though not determinative of, the construction of the implied author. The real reader is the flesh-and-blood person whose individuality and situatedness affect the way in which he or she attends to, understands, and responds to the text. The hypothetical reader is the authorial audience, the implied author's ideal addressee who is fully attentive to, fully comprehending of, and thus fully responsive to the authorial communication. As these descriptions indicate, there is likely to be a gap between any individual flesh-and-blood reader and the authorial audience (for more on audiences in narrative, see Rabinowitz, "Truth in Fiction" and *Before Reading*).

The rhetorical approach posits that it is both possible and desirable for real readers to join the authorial audience: joining that audience means that readers are getting beyond their own subjectivities and encountering another's. At the same time, the approach recognizes that, because of the gap between flesh-and-blood readers and the author's ideal audience, such joining is not automatic and, indeed, is often less than completely successful. The question of reading across differences highlights the two key bridges leading to successful rhetorical interchange: the authorial bridge, which runs between flesh-and-blood author and implied author and which is formed by the specific construction of the text (in these ways rather than those); and the audience bridge, which runs between the flesh-and-blood reader's subjectivity and the knowledge, beliefs, and values of the authorial audience and which is formed out of the flesh-and-blood reader's engagement with the otherness of the constructed text. Thus different readers might form different bridges, but those bridges will lead to the same destination. Furthermore, once over the bridge, the flesh-and-blood reader does not simply fade away but instead seeks to evaluate the destination: what does it mean, cognitively, emotively, and especially ethically, to accept or reject the invitations of the implied author? I turn now to construct one audience bridge for "Doc's Story," beginning with a brief summary of it and an account of my initial response as flesh-and-blood reader.

Toward a Rhetorical Reading: Text and Response

In "Doc's Story," the narrative present is some unspecified winter in the post–civil rights era of American history; the protagonist, an unnamed adult African American male living in Philadelphia, has broken up with his white lover (also unnamed) the previous spring and finds himself in need of the right story "to get him through [the] long winter because she's gone and won't leave him alone" (146). That story, which he first heard on the basketball court in Regent Park the previous summer, is about Doc, a Regent Park regular who was successful in the white world and who, after going blind, played a legendary game of basketball in the park in which he "held his own" (152). Wideman presents the protagonist's remembering of the story as a rehearing of it; because the voice shifts from that of the heterodiegetic narrator to that of one of the park regulars, Doc's story becomes a narrative embedded within Wideman's "Doc's Story." After the vivid remembrance, the story returns to the narrative present, when the protagonist thinks of his departed lover, including the final moments she spent with him in Regent Park. During that meeting, something got in his eyes, temporarily blurring his vision, and "before he could blink her back into focus, before he could speak, she was gone" (153). The story concludes with the protagonist wondering whether telling his lover Doc's story would have persuaded her that the two of them could make it as a couple: *"If a blind man could play basketball, surely we . . . If he* had known Doc's story, would it have saved them? He hears himself saying the words. The ball arches from Doc's fingertips, the miracle of it sinking. Would she have believed any of it?" (153).

I find the story's ending exceptionally moving: the protagonist's sense of loss and especially his longing are painfully acute, and my empathy with him is deep. As I participate in completing the fiction by trying to answer the protagonist's final questions, I infer that his vision of both himself and his lover is still occluded, that he doesn't see that Doc's story would not have saved them. But I also feel that this inference increases the emotional power of the story, because it emphasizes the gap between desire and its effects, on the one hand, and the actual state of affairs between the lovers, on the other. At the same time, this relation between my cognitive understanding (the protagonist does not understand his situation) and my emotional response (I find his situation even more poignant than I would if his vision were clear) raises questions about the role of readerly judgment in this story. Is there a connection between the protagonist's failure to see and his ethical relationship to the lover—or even to himself? Furthermore, even as I stand in the position of claiming to see more than the protagonist in this story about occluded vision, I can't help wondering, especially given the identity borders between me and Wideman, about my vision of his story: What am I not seeing? is a question that inevitably hangs over my responses and inferences. Consequently, as I move to consider the sources of those responses and inferences in the textual phenomena, I seek not simply to confirm but also to test them.

Sources of Response;
or, Design and Inference

"Doc's Story" is built on the interrelations between the embedded narrative of Doc and the frame narrative of the protagonist. A flesh-and-blood reader can enter the authorial audience—and, in Wideman's words, participate in the making of the fiction—by inferring the comparisons and contrasts Wideman builds into his construction of the two narratives. To track the comparisons, contrasts, and corresponding inferences, I distinguish among three nested narratives: the innermost story about Doc, which I will call "Doc Plays Ball"; the middle-level story about the unnamed protagonist, which I will call "The Protagonist Longs"; and "Doc's Story" itself, the synthesis of the first two stories.

The most salient feature of "Doc's Story" is "Doc Plays Ball." Not only is this embedded story given the most space in the text, it is also the main textual source for the inference that the racial identity of the author is shared by the implied author. For in "Doc Plays Ball," the implied Wideman draws on the rich tradition of African American oral narrative. The tale, whose exact "orbit was unpredictable" (147), clearly circulates among the basketball players and is clearly marked as community property. Wideman identifies the teller of the version the protagonist remembers only as "one of the fellows" (148). Furthermore, this version is a kind of tour de force of oral narrative in Black English Vernacular, full of metaphor, hyperbole, and innovative syntax. The style is in marked contrast to the more standard diction and syntax of "The Protagonist Longs," though here too Wideman proves to be a master stylist. There is no doubt that "Doc Plays Ball" resonates differently for someone who uses Black English Vernacular and is intimately familiar with African American oral narrative traditions than it does for me. There is also no doubt that "Doc Plays Ball" resonates differently for someone like me who has played serious playground basketball than for readers who have not. Nevertheless, the functions of "Doc Plays Ball" within "Doc's Story" are equally available to these different kinds of readers: all of us can still enter the authorial audience, even if we do not all sit in the same row.

Although lacking the surface brilliance of "Doc Plays Ball," "The Protagonist Longs" is a rich and innovative story in its own right. This story departs from the standard structure of narrative, which consists of a beginning, middle, and end identified by the introduction, complication, and resolution of unstable relations between characters or within a single character.[4] Although the story makes a gesture toward such a structure through the narrator's comment that the protagonist is in need of a story and through his turning to Doc's, this gesture is contained within a wider narrative situation in which virtually nothing happens. That is, the central instability of the lover's situation—his sense of loss and longing in the absence of his beloved—is both present and essentially unchanged throughout the beginning, middle, and end of the story. What changes, instead, is the audience's understanding of that situation. To put the point another way, the progression governing "The Protagonist Longs" is not what we associate with narrative but what we associate with lyric: instead of an unfolding of events that track a character's movement from one situation to another, the story gives us a gradual revelation of character and situation that allows us to understand—and empathize with—the character in that fixed situation. This dimension of the story is reinforced by the use of the present tense and by the relatively short passage of narrative time between the beginning of the story and the end. "The Protagonist Longs," however, is not in itself sufficient for a full revelation of character and situation.

A striking feature of "The Protagonist Longs" is how little of Wideman's text is explicitly devoted to it. The story begins in the present tense as the narrator slides into the protagonist's perspective and his memories of his lover: "He thinks of her small, white hands, blue veined, gaunt, awkwardly knuckled. He'd teased her about the smallness of her hands" (145). Soon the fundamental instability of the protagonist's situation is introduced: she left the previous May, he misses her acutely, and while waiting for summer and a return to the solace offered by the companionship of the basketball games and the shared stories in Regent Park, he needs a story to tide him over.

That story of course turns out to be "Doc Plays Ball," but before we hear it we learn not more about the protagonist but more about Doc: he was a pioneer, integrating his block on Regent Square, playing ball as a student at "the University" (of Pennsylvania, the Ivy League) and then teaching there. Once the text returns to "The Protagonist Longs," the final paragraphs reveal a little more about the lovers' shared past, review their final meeting, and return to the present with the concluding questions about whether Doc's story would have mattered.

By itself, then, "The Protagonist Longs" is a slight narrative: it does not give us a detailed portrait of the main character, and it offers few specifics about the lovers' relationship, though they had been together for years. One consequence of this relative slightness is that the few specifics offered take on considerable importance. We learn that the lovers were "opposites attracting" (152), that they'd picketed a Woolworth's "for two years" (145), that she was hardheaded and practical and so regarded as "superstition" the supernatural stories about slavery he would sometimes tell (152). We also learn that at the end "it was clear to both of them that things weren't going to work out" but also that "more and more as the years went by, he wanted her with him, wanted them to be together" (152). These details and the scene in which she leaves while he is not looking lead to the inference that she acted on her hardheaded practicality. If it were up to him, they'd still be trying to work things out, however clear it was that they wouldn't succeed.

But it is not until we examine the interaction between "Doc Plays Ball" and "The Protagonist Longs" and particularly until we try to understand why the protagonist turns to "Doc Plays Ball" for solace that we can get at the emotional power of the ending. While the protagonist provides the obvious connection between Doc's story and his own situation in his imagined appeal to his lover, "*If a blind man could play basketball, surely we,*" Wideman invites the authorial audience to recognize other comparisons and contrasts that the protagonist himself recognizes either dimly or not at all. Some of these connections depend as much on the background information about Doc as on "Doc Plays Ball." The major connection is that Doc himself is a role model for the protagonist, someone able to achieve what the protagonist desires. First, Doc has succeeded in the white world, not just as an athlete but also as a man: he taught at the university, integrated a white neighborhood, and was neither deterred by the racism that accompanied these efforts nor forgetful of his roots. When he was teaching,

"Doc used to laugh when white people asked him if he was in the Athletic Department"— "until the joke got old" (147). Doc's white neighbors didn't like his bringing his friends from the playground to his house to cool off with water from his hose, "didn't like a whole bunch of loud, sweaty, half-naked niggers backed up in their nice street," but "Doc didn't care. He was just out there like everybody else having a good time" (147).

For the protagonist, succeeding in the white world would mean being able to maintain his relationship with his lover without forgetting his own roots. The limited details of their relationship indicate that they are ultimately driven apart by disagreements and other conflicts stemming from their racial difference. Though the picketing of Woolworth's suggests their shared concern with civil rights, her regarding as superstition the stories of slavery days—"when Africans could fly, change themselves to cats and hummingbirds, when black hoodoo priests and conjure queens were feared by powerful whites" (152)—indicates the cultural divide between them. For her the stories were interesting because of what they suggested about "the psychology, the pathology of the oppressed" (152). Since her hardheaded practicality is one sign that they were "opposites attracting," his recollection that she never listened expecting to "hear truth" implies that he did find such truth in the stories (152). The protagonist recognizes their differences but desperately wants to believe that those differences could have been overcome. In Doc himself and in "Doc Plays Ball," he recognizes, at some level of his consciousness, not just a story about overcoming seemingly insurmountable obstacles but also the possibility of successfully negotiating the cultural divide between white and black.

Moreover, the protagonist is attracted to "Doc Plays Ball" because it shows that Doc is able to take command of any situation, as exemplified in the sequence of actions that leads him to play despite his blindness. This sequence forms a traditional narrative, one with initial instabilities, complications of those instabilities, and a final clear resolution of them. The main instability is introduced when Doc, usually an unerring free-throw shooter, misses badly on one summer Sunday, and a younger player, aptly nicknamed Sky, snatches the ball out of the air and dunks it for him. The instabilities are complicated by what happens next: the assembled players loudly applaud Sky's dunk, but Doc quiets everybody by saying, "Didn't ask for no help, Sky. Why'd you fuck with my shot, Sky? . . . You must think I'm some kind of chump" (150–51). After keeping Sky standing uncomfortably before him long enough to make his point that Sky's action was an insult, however unintentional, Doc tells Sky to forget it and asks to play winners. Doc's position in the group is such that no one, especially not Leroy, the player picking the next team, will deny Doc's request. Once Leroy picks Doc for his team, resolution quickly follows: the game "was a helluva run. . . . Overtime and shit. . . . And Doc? Doc ain't been out on the court for a while but Doc is Doc, you know. Held his own" (152). In short, "Doc Plays Ball" is a narrative whose initial instability puts Doc on the verge of losing status in his community but whose resolution shows Doc substantially enhancing that status. Indeed, the teller of "Doc Plays Ball" briefly suggests that Doc is so in command that he has orchestrated the whole sequence: ". . . that Sunday something went wrong. Couldna been wind cause wasn't no wind. I was there. I know. Maybe Doc had playing on his mind. Couldn't help have playing on his mind cause it was one those days wasn't nothing better to do in the world than play. Whatever it was, soon as the ball left his hands, you could see Doc was missing, missing real bad" (150).

The protagonist desires a similar kind of command in his life, a command that he clearly lacked in the final meeting with his lover.

> They were walking in Regent Park and dusk had turned the tree trunks black. . . . Perhaps he had listened too intently for his own voice to fill the emptiness. When he turned back to her, his eyes were glazed, stinging. Grit, chemicals, whatever it was coloring, poisoning the sky, blurred his vision. Before he could blink her into focus, before he could speak, she was gone. (152)

The implicit contrast with Doc is hard to miss. Doc's blindness is something that he overcomes or even uses to his advantage. The protagonist's blindness, though momentary, puts him at such a disadvantage that his lover leaves even before he realizes it.

Thus the protagonist turns to "Doc Plays Ball" because it gives him hope not only for the relationship but also for himself—not to be Doc, exactly, but to have Doc's abilities. But Doc's story also "bothered him most" (147) because he worries that he lacks those abilities. In testing my initial inference that the protagonist's worries are well founded and his hopes unrealistic, I find considerable confirming evidence. First, the protagonist reacts to losing his lover not by seeking ways to bridge the cultural divide between them but by moving further into a subculture distinct from hers: the Regent Park playground is not just an African American space, it is an African American male space. The basketball games and the stories emphasize the point. The protagonist remembers that, on the occasion when he first heard "Doc Plays Ball," it was immediately preceded by "the one about gang warring in North Philly" in which one gang "lynched this dude they caught on their turf. Hung him up on the goddamn poles behind the backboard," where the next morning "little kids" found him "with his tongue hanging out and shit down his legs" (148). Furthermore, "Doc Plays Ball" is very much a story of the African American male urban subculture: it is about a male hero, whose heroism consists of individual achievements, especially, though not exclusively, athletic ones.

Second, the protagonist seems unable to understand something that Wideman invites his audience to see: the difference between the protagonist's response to "Doc Plays Ball" and the likely response of his lover. For him, it is literal truth, verified by an eyewitness ("I was there. I know" [150]). For her, we infer, it would be an urban legend, no more truthful than the stories about Africans who could fly. Furthermore, the protagonist's denial, the occluded vision that prevents him from seeing how the woman would respond to the story, also suggests ways in which he is not like Doc. "Doc Plays Ball," indeed Doc's whole life, is about a man overcoming obstacles, not about a man denying them.

Emotion, Judgment, and the Ending of "Doc's Story"

At this point, we are ready to return to the question of how readerly judgment works in "Doc's Story," especially in relation to Doc and to the protagonist. Like the protagonist, we judge Doc positively, admire his abilities, want him to succeed, and take some satisfaction in his success. But we also always see him from the outside, filtered through the perspective of the protagonist and of the vernacular teller of "Doc Plays Ball." Indeed, because we see his story through these filters, we subordinate our responses to Doc to our responses to the protagonist. And those responses are more complicated, since the protagonist is less fully characterized than Doc, since the protagonist does not act in ways that alter his initial situation, and since we nevertheless see his vision of his situation as inadequate. Perhaps the most significant element of our complicated reaction is that we do not see any ethical consequence to his limited vision: that is, the protagonist's failure to see his situation clearly is not a sign of an ethical deficiency but instead a sign of the depth of his heartache and desire. Furthermore, Wideman's limited characterization of the protagonist in combination with the lyric structure of the narrative and the technique of focalizing the story through the protagonist's consciousness allows us to see him not from the outside but from the inside. Rather than judge him, we participate in his feelings of loss and longing much as we participate in the feelings of a speaker in a dramatic lyric such as Wordsworth's "I Wandered Lonely as a Cloud" or Frost's "Stopping by Woods on a Snowy Evening." The power of the ending, then, arises through the synthesis of our clearer vision of the protagonist's situation and our capacity to feel with him. In sum, Wideman has invited his audience to participate in completing the fiction by recognizing his innovative narrative structure, one that harnesses the powerful vernacular narrative of "Doc Plays Ball" to the lyric revelation of "The Protagonist Longs" and that also uses our understanding of the protagonist's limited vision to deepen the poignancy of his heartache and longing.

Reexamining the Design, Complicating the Inferences

What, then, about the possible limits of my vision as I try to move from my responses as flesh-and-blood reader to an understanding of Wideman's invitations to his audience? Although of course one cannot finally see what one is unable to see, I find that some elements of the story lead me to reconsider some of my claims. "Doc's Story" is, in part, a narrative about ways of reading: the lover has one way of reading the protagonist's stories of the supernatural and the protagonist himself has another; the protagonist has one way of reading "Doc Plays Ball," and Wideman's audience, I claim, has another. It makes sense to compare Wideman's representations of different ways of reading with the kind of reading I have offered to this point. So far, that reading is close to the lover's mode: with hardheaded practicality, I have concluded that the answers to the protagonist's final questions are negative. This realization gives me pause, because I infer that Wideman wants us to question the lover's mode of reading. She is an exemplar of the nonrhetorical reader, one who does not bother to enter the authorial audience, preferring instead (however unreflectively) to impose her own cultural assumptions on another culture's narratives. By reading Wideman's story with hardheaded practicality—and attributing that reading to the authorial audience—am I doing the same thing? One way to answer this question is to consider how Wideman wants his audience to answer the question, Is "Doc Plays Ball" a true story? Should we regard its tour de force quality as evidence that Wideman wants us to regard it as an urban legend—it's wonderful but of course it's not true? In other words, does Wideman invite us to adopt the protagonist's view of the story, his lover's likely view, or some third view—and if the last, what is it?

The flesh-and-blood Wideman, who himself was an all–Ivy League basketball player at the University of Pennsylvania and has written about his experiences playing basketball in *Hoop Roots*, knows that playing the game with any skill without being able to see is impossible, very much the stuff of urban legend. Passing, catching, shooting, cutting, rebounding: a blind man, no matter how gifted and capable of compensating for loss of sight with his other senses, simply couldn't do these things well enough to "hold his own" in a serious playground game. Yet the implied Wideman constructs many elements of the text to make "Doc Plays Ball" a plausible story up until the resolution, including having the protagonist remember what he knows about Doc beyond "Doc Plays Ball." The information about Doc's success in the white world is authoritative. "Doc Plays Ball" itself has a plausible starting point because a formerly skilled player who loses his vision could become an accurate free-throw shooter. And the story is itself so loaded with specific, concrete details—not just the names of players such as Sky and Leroy but also the ways in which Doc uses his knowledge of the players to take command of the situation—that it sounds at least as much like history as legend. Yet some important elements suggest it is legend. As noted above, it is not a story that is owned by—or closely associated with—an individual teller but rather one that belongs to and circulates in the whole community. In addition, the details of the game itself are very sketchy: Leroy is the only other player identified, there is no testimony about any particular moves Doc makes, and no definitive report on which team won. It's as if Wideman wants us to focus on everything until the resolution as the literal truth and to recognize the resolution as entering the realm of legend.

More generally, we can infer that Wideman wants his audience to understand the story not as literally true but as capturing some truth about both Doc and the community that is so invested in his story. Doc is an extraordinary person whose achievements in his subculture and in the white world are not just tellable but significant, because they offer those who share his story hope and even inspiration. Furthermore, members of the community are invested in the story because they need it to counter the truths in stories such as the one about gang wars.

Significantly, this answer moves the authorial audience away from simple hardheaded practicality without fully deviating from the reading strategy of the white woman: it interprets "Doc Plays Ball" as revealing something about the psychology—though not the pathology—of the community in which the story circulates. And this movement, along with the inference that the story is a legend with some basis in literal truth, opens up another set of answers to the protagonist's final question, would she have believed any of it? The difference between "Doc Plays Ball" and the supernatural tales of Africans flying may be sufficient for the woman to believe some of "Doc Plays Ball"—and also to hear behind Doc's story the truth of the protagonist's love and of his desire for them to be together. Given that she stayed in the relationship for so many years, we can readily infer that she too has a certain desire for it to work and that she might find some hope in the protagonist's telling of Doc's story. In other words, these inferences shake the confidence with which I have answered no to the protagonist's questions without moving me toward a confident yes. Instead, these inferences render the story's final questions open not just for the protagonist but also for the authorial audience.

Understanding the final questions as genuinely open has several significant consequences. First and most evidently, this understanding injects an element of hope into the ending, even as the depth of the protagonist's longing—and our empathy with it—remains unchanged. Second, this understanding alters our sense of the protagonist's flawed vision: although he is too invested in the possibility that "Doc Plays Ball" would have made a difference to recognize why it might not have, that investment itself now seems less rooted in denial. Third, this understanding alters our inferences about Wideman's treatment of reading across differences. The first conclusion makes the content of the story run somewhat counter to Wideman's own invitation to his readers: in that account, Wideman closes but does not fully bridge the gap across the racial and gender differences of the protagonist and his lover, even as Wideman asks those readers who are not male and African American to bridge whatever gaps there may be between him and them. I do not mean to suggest that this initial reading uncovers a flawed logic in Wideman's construction or that it shows that the story is at cross-purposes with itself: certainly one could imagine a successful story written along these lines. But the revised view invites us to thematize questions of reading across differences both on the level of the protagonist's relationship with his lover and on that of Wideman's relation to his audience. In each case, the story suggests, we need to remain conscious of the gaps, but in each case, there is hope, though not certainty, that the gaps can be bridged.

In this connection, it is worth emphasizing that even if the lover were to have her faith in their future restored by "Doc Plays Ball," her reading of that story would still be different from the protagonist's. He would believe "It happened" (152), and she would believe that it ultimately conveys a figurative rather than literal truth. The differences between the lovers would remain, and those differences would continue to be a source of both attraction and contention. Similarly, this revised understanding of Wideman's communication does not erase all difference between him and his audience, and it does not stop me from continuing to wonder, what am I not seeing? At the same time, however, it does make me more optimistic that both Wideman and I are right to believe that communication across differences is possible.

Finally, this new understanding sheds further light on the relation between the narrative form of "Doc Plays Ball" and the lyric mode of "The Protagonist Longs" and indeed of "Doc's Story" itself. As noted above, one of the innovative features of "Doc's Story" is the way it subordinates the embedded narrative to the larger lyric structure. Understanding that subordination as one that leads to the conclusion that the protagonist's final questions are genuinely open helps us recognize the effectiveness of Wideman's technique. The clear narrative resolution of "Doc Plays Ball" sets up the openness of the lyric structure of "Doc's Story." And that openness makes the lyric itself more effective than if there were a clear answer, positive or negative, to the protagonist's questions. Because the authorial audience sees both possibilities, we move closer to the protagonist as we appreciate and participate in his sense of loss and longing.

Ethical Response

To assess the ethical dimensions of rhetorical reading, we need to consider the experience of taking on the values underlying an author's communication to the authorial audience. Adopting the values goes hand in hand with entering the authorial audience. Indeed, it is the recognition of this phenomenon that fuels debates about whether some books should be removed from school reading lists. Those who argue that, say, *Huckleberry Finn* should be removed from such lists often put their case this way: since there are racist elements to Twain's communication in *Huckleberry Finn*, readers of the book are encouraged to adopt racist attitudes while they read—and, given the book's reputation as a masterwork of American literature, after they are finished reading.[5]

Wideman's communication in "Doc's Story" endorses at least two sets of values and beliefs, the first having to do with the story's characters and events and Wideman's treatment of them, and the second having to do with the story's self-reflexiveness—its thematizing of its own form—and the reader's awareness of that element of the story. The first set includes the following ideas: difficult obstacles can be overcome; those who are able to overcome such obstacles not only deserve respect but rightfully inspire others to overcome the obstacles they face; communication, even love, across racial barriers is one such obstacle. The second set includes a belief in the power of narrative, a similar faith in the power of lyric empathy, and an overriding commitment to communication across racial borders. At the same time, Wideman's endorsement of the values concerned with communication across borders is tempered by a realization of the difficulty of such communication. In taking on Wideman's values while we read, we are of course being persuaded, however subtly, to adopt them more generally, and as individual flesh-and-blood readers we need to come to terms with this persuasion. For my part, I am not only willingly persuaded but also greatly encouraged by Wideman's vision of possibility—and I suspect that many other readers, regardless of their own particular racial identities, will respond in similar ways.

But I do not expect that all readers will respond this way: some are likely to find Wideman's vision naive, and some are likely to find it self-indulgent for a fiction writer to proclaim the power of narrative; others may object to what they see as the myth of heroic individualism in "Doc Plays Ball," and still others to the treatment of the white woman, who is never given her own voice and is always seen through the perspective of the protagonist.

At the stage of ethical evaluation, the rhetorical framework is much less concerned with bridging differences among readers than with trying to move from initial response to entering the authorial audience. If the effort to read as a member of the authorial audience is an effort to get beyond oneself and encounter another, the effort to do ethical evaluation is an effort to return to the self and assess that encounter. That assessment will inevitably lead to different results for different readers. What is important for the rhetorical theorist, however, is that flesh-and-blood readers continue to remain other-directed in the sense of wanting to know—and to discuss—how other readers assess the encounter.[6]

Generalizing from "Doc's Story"

From the rhetorical perspective, "Doc's Story" is both a typical and a special case of reading across differences. The story is a typical case because all rhetorical reading involves entering the authorial audience and virtually all such entrances involve moving beyond one's individual identity. Sometimes the move is a simple one—to the backyard or across the street; and sometimes it requires considerable effort both in preparation and in execution—a move across an ocean, into a new layer of the atmosphere, or back through several centuries. If we were to ask whether the obstacles to entering the authorial audience are greater in "Doc's Story" or in, say, *Sir Gawain and the Green Knight*, most readers, certainly most of our current undergraduate students, would choose *Sir Gawain*. But "Doc's Story" is a special case because the issues of racial difference are more charged in our contemporary cultural and literary climate than issues of historical difference. More than that, "Doc's Story" is a special case because the effort to enter its authorial audience is one that involves overturning some still entrenched hierarchies of our institution. The effort not only acknowledges the aesthetic and political value of the story but also implicitly says that the issue of racial difference ought to be neither erased nor regarded as an insuperable obstacle. In other words, "Doc's Story," finally, is a special case because its take on difference is much like that of rhetorical reader-response criticism.

"The ball arches from Doc's fingertips, the miracle of it sinking"(153). The meanings flow from author to audience, writer to reader, and then back again, the miracle of literary communication. Can you share our belief in it?

NOTES

The quotations in the epigraphs are in Wideman, Interview 77, 79.

1. Practitioners of reader-response criticism, unlike those of some other critical movements, have never subscribed to a single set of critical principles and a single way to do interpretation. But certainly one important stream of work has been on the role of difference; Flynn and Schweickart's *Gender and Reading* is an exemplar. For that reason, I find it all the more significant that Schweickart has recently called for more attention to the question of reading across differences. ("Reading")

   One useful model that arises from work on difference is the adaptation of Anzaldúa's notion of "mestiza consciousness" to the act of reading: all readers have multiple parts of their identities, some of them in paradoxical relation to each other, but to read well, each of us must be able to draw on those different parts of our identities at different times. I find such an adaptation useful for talking about flesh-and-blood readers. In this essay, however, I focus not on differences among individual readers but on possible common ground in the authorial audience.

2. Especially noteworthy are "The Statue of Liberty" and "Hostages," though these stories are formally very different from "Doc's Story" and from each other. It's not possible to do justice to the complexities of these stories in this essay, but it's fair to say that, like "Doc's Story," they both acknowledge the importance of racial difference and imagine ways of overcoming that difference.

3. In recent years, the concept of the implied author, introduced by Booth in 1961 in *The Rhetoric of Fiction*, has come under attack by some narratologists on the grounds that it is unnecessary or too vague (see Genette; Nunning). I find some of the debate about the concept to be a disagreement over terminology—those who find the term *implied author* unnecessary do not disagree with the point that some authorial consciousness constructs the text for a hypothetical audience; at the same time, I continue to find the distinction between the flesh-and-blood author and the version of himself or herself that an author creates in the writing of a text to be useful, because it underlines the rhetorical strategies involved in the construction of a text. Thus the version of himself that Wideman creates here includes his race because there are textual signals that underline it; however, the implied Wideman is different from the flesh-and-blood Wideman in that the latter is married to a white woman and the former's marital status is not a salient part of his identity. This point helps explain the difference between a rhetorical and biographical approach, though both are concerned with authors. The rhetorical focuses on the implied author, the biographical on the flesh-and-blood author. In this essay I use "Wideman" as shorthand for "the implied Wideman"; when I refer to the historical author, I use the term "the flesh-and-blood Wideman."

4. For more on this way of analyzing narrative structure, see my *Reading People, Reading Plots*.

5. I hasten to add that this case against *Huckleberry Finn* is not one I agree with. Although, in my view, the book does have racist elements, its underlying values are strongly antiracist—and students are better served by reading the book and debating its value structure than by having it removed from reading lists. For more on the debates about *Huckleberry Finn*, see Arac; Graff and Phelan.

6. The ideas in this paragraph are indebted to but not the same as Booth's ideas about coduction. See Booth's *The Company We Keep*.

Works Cited

Anzaldúa, Gloria. *Borderlands / La Frontera: The New Mestiza*. San Francisco: Spinsters / Aunt Lute, 1987.

Arac, Jonathan. *Huckleberry Finn as Idol and Target: The Functions of Criticism in Our Time*. Madison: U of Wisconsin P, 1997.

Booth, Wayne C. *The Company We Keep: An Ethics of Fiction*. Berkeley: U of California P, 1989.

———. *The Rhetoric of Fiction*. 2nd ed. Chicago: U of Chicago P, 1983.

Flynn, Elizabeth A., and Patrocinio P. Schweickart, eds. *Gender and Reading: Essays on Readers, Texts, and Contexts*. Baltimore: Johns Hopkins UP, 1986.

Genette, Gérard. *Narrative Discourse Revisited*. Trans. Jane E. Lewin. Ithaca: Cornell UP, 1988.

Graff, Gerald, and James Phelan, eds. Adventures of Huckleberry Finn: *A Case Study in Critical Controversy*. Boston: Bedford, 1995.

Nünning, Ansgar. "Deconstructing and Reconceptualizing the Implied Author." *Grenzueberschreitungen: Narratologie im Kontext / Transcending Boundaries: Narratology in Context*. Ed. Andreas Solbach and Walter Gruenzweig. Tuebingen: Narr, 1999. 95–116.

Phelan, James. *Narrative as Rhetoric: Technique, Audiences, Ethics, Ideology*. Columbus: Ohio State UP, 1996.

———. *Reading People, Reading Plots. Character, Progression, and the Interpretation of Narrative*. Chicago: U of Chicago P, 1989.

Rabinowitz, Peter J. *Before Reading: Narrative Conventions and the Politics of Interpretation*. Columbus: Ohio State UP, 1998.

———. "Truth in Fiction: A Reexamination of Audiences." *Critical Inquiry* 4 (1977): 121–41.

Schweickart, Patrocinio P. "Reading as Communicative Action." *Reader* 43 (2000): 70–75.

TuSmith, Bonnie, ed. *Conversations with John Edgar Wideman*. Jackson: U of Mississippi P, 1998.

Wideman, John Edgar. "Doc's Story." 1989. *The Stories of John Edgar Wideman*. New York: Pantheon, 1992. 145–53.

———. *Hoop Roots: Basketball, Race, and Love*. Boston: Houghton, 2001.

———. Interview with James W. Coleman. TuSmith 62–80.

Colored *Readings*; or, Interpretation and the Raciogendered Body

Angeletta KM Gourdine

I recall that as a child I was frequently warned away from a tendency to behave as though certain games or activities favored by my peers were beneath me. As I sneered at a unanimous decision to play dodgeball rather than play school or have a spelling bee, I was brought back to the moment with a stern cautioning: "don't let me *read*, write, and erase you." This sense of *reading*, common in the black community, is interpretation of the highest order, and as such it both encompasses and excludes literary connotations.[1] Moreover, as my childhood recollection demonstrates, *reading* can be accompanied by writing and erasing. These two acts indicate the *reader's* desire not only to tell you about yourself but also to craft an other self that amends the self your previous behavior encodes. The *reading*, then, renders an interpretation that supersedes previous interpretations.

Reading, first of all, involves taking a text, translating a text into immediately relevant terms. In *Black Talk*, Geneva Smitherman tells us that "to take a text" is synonymous with *reading* (320). Though this definition primarily refers to the tradition in the black church whereby the "Scriptural reference and message of the sermon" are announced (320), the parallel between this sacred practice and the secular task of textual analysis is nonetheless striking. In both cases, the objective is a clear and corrective message. The preacher uses biblical scripture to comment on the behavior of his or her congregation, and *readers* interpret behavior while also providing a critique of the beliefs that license such behavior.

Specifically, to *read* is to take ideology as text and to render an interpretation that both lays bare and critiques behaviors and the attitudes that account for them. An interpretation rendered through *reading* stands for something beyond the text's uncovered meaning; it always carries an underlying, implicit commentary. To be *read* is both to be exposed and to be told about yourself. Blackwomen[2] have for ages had dominion over this form of social criticism, and the power of our ability to *read* and the biting truth that comes from our *readings* have given us the reputation for "a bluntness. A going to the heart of the matter even if it [gives] everyone concerned a heart attack" (Walker 119).

Because *reading* traditionally occurs in conversations, it has been understood only as a form of signifyin'.[3] However, while signifyin' is generally characterized by indirection, *reading* is most effective and potent when the *reader* is forced to "turn it out." In *Black Ice*, Lorene Cary recalls the moments her mother was compelled to *read* someone most acutely:

> I always saw it coming. Some white department-store manager would look at my mother and see no more than a modestly dressed young black woman making a tiresome complaint. He'd use that tone of voice they used when they had *important work elsewhere.* Uh-oh. Then he'd dismiss her with his eyes. I'd feel her body stiffen next to me, and I'd know that he'd set her off. . . .
>
> And then it began in earnest, the turning out. She never moved back. . . . Sometimes she'd talk through her teeth, her lips moving double time to bite out the consonants. Then she'd get personal. . . . (58–59)

Here Cary indicates what occasions *reading*, why blackwomen *read*, and how we prepare to take a text of experience and interpret it "not [as] a matter of style" but as an act of "black power and duty" (59). In such instances *reading* is responsive action, directing its "cold indignation as well as hot fury" at any text that renders blackwomen's bodies into muted spectacles. On these occasions, *reading* is a way to talk back, to gain an ear and confound the listener.

Manifesting the twoness of W. E. B. Du Bois's double consciousness, *reading* is simultaneously a response to previous statements and a significant assertion in its own right. For example, Toni Morrison's *Beloved* responds to certain muted facets of blackwomen's experiences in slavery, but it also comments on the future of a nation that seeks security in such silenced histories (see my "Hearing"). This simultaneous enactment of assertion and response clarifies the ways in which, in their texts, blackwomen have abandoned any attempt to "respond to a situation as though both we (blackwomen) and they (white people and/or men) are operating within the same codes of conduct" (Holloway 31).

In this essay, *reading* is both a response to and a statement about the ways in which histories of race and gender have encoded narratives that manifest stereotypes of blackwomen's bodies and experiences. I discuss *reading* as a verbal style, a narrative strategy, and an interpretive approach. This essay develops a theory of interpretation based on this verbal art and as such *reads* as it reads, relating critical commentary closely to the position of blackwomen's bodies as texts seen and interpreted but not often heard. My first text is Zora Neale Hurston's "How It Feels to Be Colored Me." Hurston shows how the ideology of race organizes social responses to blackwomen generally, and to herself particularly. Her *reading* of how both colored and white people read race-color and its relation to class establishes a foundation for my analysis of Toni Morrison's *The Bluest Eye*, a novel that questions the narratives of human value that underwrite myths of physical beauty. Similarly, I analyze how Terry McMillan's *Waiting to Exhale* challenges notions of how black women can have it all. From these texts, I move to Ama Ata Aidoo's *Changes* to advance the second part of my argument, that *reading* functions not only as a narrative strategy but also as an interpretive lens for critical analysis.

I/Eye Must Read, Write, and Erase; or, Color Me Black and Beautiful

Hurston begins "How It Feels to Be Colored Me" by exclaiming, "I am colored and I offer nothing in the way of extenuating circumstances except the fact that I am the only Negro in the United States whose great grandfather on the mother's side was *not* an Indian chief" (1008). Thus Hurston satirically responds to that desire within some black people to erase the curse of their blackness by alluding to their mixed genealogy. In *Codes of Conduct* Karla Holloway points out the ways in which a "racialized discourse" depends on our "reifying the lie of a biological referent" (5). It is this reification that Hurston resists, and *reads*. Hurston continues, "I am not tragically colored. There is no great sorrow dammed up in my soul or lurking behind my eyes" (1009). Rejecting the stereotype of the lowly Negro cursed by the misfortune of race and placing intellect center stage, Hurston reasons that the curse is not the fact of her blackness but the interpretation of her race as a license for social and political retaliation. In this vein, Hurston *reads* what she appropriately identifies as textual misreadings of her biological, historical, and social body.

On the surface, Hurston's words speak to her particular experience as a colored woman. She declares:

> Someone is always at my elbow reminding me that I am the granddaughter of slaves. It fails to register depression with me. . . . The terrible struggle that made an American out of a potential slave said "On the line!" The reconstruction said "Get set!" and the generation before said "Go!" I am off to a flying start and I must not halt in the stretch to look behind and weep. . . . It is thrilling to think—to know that for any act of mine, I shall get twice as much praise or twice as much blame. It is quite exciting to hold the center of the national stage, with spectators not knowing whether to laugh or to weep.
>
> The position of my white neighbor is much more difficult. No brown specter pulls up a chair beside me when I sit down to eat. No dark ghost thrusts its legs against mine in bed. (1009)

If we examine the construction of her text with an eye alert to the art of *reading*, we see that Hurston is turning it out. In taking racial animus as her text, she subtly reminds us that the "ghost" of race creates a site where all Americans reside and a mark that all Americans bear. By invoking historical moments of supposed racial progress, Hurston invites us to reconsider who is really a victim here: the person who is taunted for being a racially marked body or the person who is haunted by the memory of participating in racial marking.

Hurston cleverly cloaks her biting social commentary within an experiential narrative, all the while exposing the tyranny of racial codes and racialized conduct. Delivered with verbal élan, Hurston's *reading* draws our attention to the title of the piece itself. She says she will explore "how it feels to be colored me," but *colored* is ambiguous: is it the obvious reference to racial semantics, namely, *colored* as an identity marker, or is it *colored* as a past tense verb, as in "I have been colored"? Each reading of the term offers a different level on which the text can be interpreted. In the first sense, the subject is strictly Zora; the "me" becomes the focus of interpretation. Yet, in the second sense, though the presence of "me" is maintained, the emphasis is on the one who has, could, or would color "me."

Hurston is fully aware that her body is a sign provoking "a certain stereotype" and initiating "a particular response" (Holloway 34). Recognizing the stereotype as part of her reality, Hurston takes control of her image. By refusing to offer "extenuating circumstances," she responds to the act of her coloring and not the fact of her coloredness. This response is then coupled with an assertion. Though blackwomen have characteristically been mules of the world, Hurston makes it clear that she no longer will carry the load. Though aware that there are some things "nice girls who are dark" dare not do, Hurston brashly claims her own body, acts with and through a pride in her color (Holloway 16).[4] In doing so, though, she reminds us that because black people are not haunted by brown specters or dark ghosts, her white neighbors have become mules of a different order.

While Hurston reinterprets a narrative of human value founded on premises of white superiority, Morrison's *Bluest Eye* highlights the impossibility of separating such narratives from myths of physical beauty. The ability to get one's mind around such separation is a privilege that dark-skinned black girls are not readily afforded. Indeed, blackwomen are absent from the majority of general studies of beauty. With the exception of *Beauty Secrets*, by Wendy Chapkis, and *Face Value*, by Robin Lakoff and Raquel Scherr, studies of beauty in American culture have focused on white women. Though it promised to be not only a comprehensive study of beauty in our culture but also a feminist one, Naomi Wolf's *The Beauty Myth* avoids engaging the intimately related, though historically distinct and separated, experiences of black and white women with respect to beauty standards.

Left out of academic conversations, black women have addressed beauty standards in two primary ways: through novels and through sociological and psychological studies of black children's fondness for white dolls. *The Bluest Eye* merges these two traditions. Through the little girl Pecola Breedlove's fascination with Shirley Temple and with the blue eyes of white dolls, the novel shows how black people's lives are contained by and subjected to dominant cultural values. Pecola's idolization of representations of little white girls clarifies the ideology of beauty—"the descriptive vocabulary of day to day existence, through which people make sense of the social reality that they live and create from day to day"—that has victimized black women (Fields 109).

Lisa Jones describes the pre-1968 doll industry, before the creation of Christy, "Barbie's black friend," and asks why, post-Christy, little black girls still "grow up slaughtering or idolizing pink fleshed, blue-eyed doll babies? Even after two black cultural nationalist movements, four black Miss Americas and integrated shelves at Kiddie City and Toys R Us?" (150). In her view, the black girl has two options—either deify or crucify these images of pure womanness. We surely see these options confronted by the character of Claudia McTeer, one of the narrators in *The Bluest Eye*. Like the "Dick and

Jane" excerpts that frame *The Bluest Eye*'s central narrative, the doll industry's racialized practices highlight blackwomen's invisibility and the ugliness attributed to their being. Though Mattel designed Shani as "tomorrow's *African American* woman" (emphasis added), she operates within the European construct of "long combable hair" as a "key seller" (151). Shirley Temple, the white dolls Pecola covets, and Shani confirm that European physical features translate into physical as well as economic beauty. In a society driven by capitalist impulses the valuable human is the one who can be translated into a profitable commodity. For our world as for the doll industry and the world in which the Breedloves live, economic value determines the degree to which one is able to be beautiful and to be loved. By offering Pecola Breedlove as one consequence of equating a European beauty aesthetic with human value and virtue, Morrison's novel claims that the ideals of romantic love and physical beauty are "[p]robably the most destructive ideas in the history of human thought. Both originated in envy, thrived in insecurity, and ended in disillusion" (97).

The Bluest Eye was written during the heyday of "black is beautiful," the maxim demanding respect in the face of social and political neglect. Like Hurston's refusal to be "tragically colored," "black is beautiful" called for pride and attempted to erase previous narratives that connect ideas of European physical beauty to human virtue. The potential of this movement to usher in a revision of beauty standards was limited by several factors. First, men also had a stake in "black is beautiful."[5] In other words, pride in blackness (or racial pride) overshadowed any focus on pride in the physicality indicated by the second half of the maxim. Second, women's concerns were muted and made secondary to the larger concerns of race that were embodied and championed by men. Championing a revision of beauty standards (a concern that seemed specific to women) did not appear to be a significant contribution to the goal of dismantling institutional racism.

The Bluest Eye works around these restrictions by *reading* the ideology of ugliness. Ugliness, like any ideology, is performative and must be constantly created or verified or it dies (Fields 112). The sense of ugliness that wreaks havoc for Pecola Breedlove persists not only because she has inherited it but also because people in her world, the readers included, interpretively re-create it and read her through it. To put it succinctly, ugliness in the text is wedded to race and poverty:

> The Breedloves did not live in a storefront because they were having a temporary difficulty adjusting to the cutbacks. . . . They lived there because they were poor and black, and they stayed there because they were ugly. . . . You looked at them and wondered why they were so ugly; you looked closely and could not find the source. Then you realized that it came from conviction, their conviction. (34)

Morrison's *reading*, like Hurston's, hinges on the interpretation of one term: *conviction*. If we read *conviction* as a spirited determination, we would read this passage as Morrison's informing us of the ways in which the Breedloves participate in their own oppression. However, if we read *conviction* within the context of judicial action, we are forced to ask for what crime the Breedloves received "their conviction." Their conviction results from being poor and black and so locates them on the wrong side of the law that constitutes whiteness as the only right beauty. This visible violation of the basic code for human value and beauty is their crime. They are convicted for the crime of social, ethnic, and economic ugliness. The *reading* in the novel explains Pecola's desire for blue eyes as a response to her family's conviction; she must extricate herself from a punishable position. Blue eyes erase her blackness, allowing her no longer to be ugly, thus no longer to be poor. Pecola's decision to acquire blue eyes signifies her attempt to sever the prevailing equation of race and class with human value. In this light, the ending of the novel is a critique of the reader's acquiescence to this equation and the form of insanity it sanctions.

Moreover, Morrison skillfully literalizes W. E. B. Du Bois's concept of double consciousness—Pecola literally splits into two selves. While Du Bois's double consciousness situates the black body in a "world which yields [her] no true self-consciousness, but only lets [her] see [her]self through the revelation of the other world," in Morrison *reading* the doubling of consciousness enables the attainment of "second-sight" (Du Bois 5). In the final chapter, Pecola, now endowed with magical blue eyes, finds a friend to talk to and play with. Realizing that she is her own best friend, Pecola is no longer a black body tortured by the white gaze. She transforms herself into a black body invested with a power that escapes the logic of white supremacy.

Beauty Is the Mane Thing

In addition to color, kinky hair is a feature that marks black-women as ugly, economically and physically.[6] While Hurston and Morrison *read* racial codes of color, McMillan *reads* codes of hair. *Waiting to Exhale* revolves around four women—Bernadine Harris, Savannah Jackson, Gloria Matthews, and Robin Stokes—all of whom are struggling emotionally, though not financially, as single women who find their lives frustratingly lonely and incomplete. Hillary Radner observes that the novel "does not exclude heterosexual exchange as a moment of feminine pleasure. . . . The hero is no longer all powerful, but in his place; he generates only one relationship among many in a community in which the feminine dominates" (116–17). However, through Bernadine Harris, McMillan resists following Radner's counterscript exactly, for that script too is written within mainstream American discourse, which imposes the cultural ideals of white patriarchal domesticity across the borders of race and class. McMillan instead ushers in yet another counternarrative that challenges the persistence of any single relationship. She establishes a continuum of relationships, all of which aid the women in negotiating a new sense of heterosexual togetherness and a clear understanding of the role of female friendships in their struggle to establish their sense of themselves.

After a marriage of eleven years, which epitomized the black conquest of the material American dream—"a dream house in a picture perfect neighborhood . . . filled with picture perfect furnishings"—Bernadine's husband, John, informs her that he is leaving her for a white woman (26). As she reflects on the past few years of their life together as husband and wife, she realizes that "John was doing nothing more than imitating the white folks he had seen on TV or read about in *Money* magazine" (26). Their beautiful life was a material asset, and she too had bought into the dream. She has sacrificed herself to the myth of beauty, stability, and happiness with the handsome prince.

Bernadine's faith in whiteness, wealth, and beauty—her buying in—becomes evident as she contemplates a chemical treatment for her daughter's hair. Depressed over the separation, Bernadine has confined herself to bed, ignoring household duties, including the combing of her daughter's hair, which she now identifies as "a mess." She remembers once wanting to let Gloria, a hair stylist and owner of the Oasis Hair Salon, "give the girl a perm, but John refused to let her put any chemicals in his daughter's hair" (83). It is ironic that this man, so obsessed with whiteness, would refuse to allow his daughter one of its defining features–straight, silken, and easily combable hair. This moment not only takes us back to Jones's discussion of the doll industry's practices and Pecola's obsession with the long blond hair of the dolls she covets; it also brings us to Noliwe Rooks's *Hair Raising*.

Rooks explains how blackwomen are lured by advertisements such as one from Lustrasilk, which makes clear that "if African American women want a 'different' life, complete with 'beauty comfort and lasting peace of mind' as well as a 'smile of confidence,'" they should surely use hair-altering products (130). Blackwomen are enticed by the suggestion that straight hair means not only ease of life but also beauty and social acceptance. With straight hair, blackwomen too can have it all.

Gloria Wade-Gayles suggests that a black woman's hairstyle choice is directly linked to the degree to which she has felt oppressed: "Straightened hair became a weight pulling my head down when I wanted to hold it up" (157). Similarly, Bernadine realizes her complicity in John's white dream and immediately sets out to divest herself of the associated signs of beauty, the first of which is her hair: "Within an hour, Bernadine went from what felt like pounds of hair on her head to a very short two- or three-ounce style" (134). McMillan makes clear that shedding her long, relaxed hair ushers in self-assurance and freedom. A new sense of beauty, in fact, emerges. Bernadine's new do startles one of the hair stylists into exclaiming, "I didn't know you were that pretty" (134).

Hair is a significant aspect of blackwomen's fantastical obsession with whiteness, and this obsession leads us to torturous means. The anguish with which the stylist cuts Bernadine's hair raises the issue of male desire as well as the cultural encoding of the hair as an index of woman's glory, her crown of virtue. In the background, though, Desiree—the only other female stylist at Oasis—sarcastically referred to later as "Miss Black America," stands gazing upon the spectacle with her long flowing hair weave intact. The reference to Desiree as "Miss Black America" surely intends us to recall the first black Miss America, Vanessa Williams, pale skinned, green eyed, and she had long blond-like hair. Within this frame, in the shadow of Desiree—and the conjured iconography of beauty—Bernadine sheds her hair. Long flowing hair symbolizes both strength and contrition. While Bernadine's long hair signified her belief in the relation among color, class, and physical beauty, she recognizes that, unlike Samson, long hair makes her weak.[7] Although we as readers want to support Bernadine's desire to rid herself of the weight of her hair, we are simultaneously forced into a moment of self-reflection about what our hair means for us.

For blackwomen, especially those born with dark skin, the most easily manipulated beauty feature is hair. As Bertram Ashe notes, "black women sometimes opt for cosmetic surgery or colored contact lenses," but "hair alteration (i.e., hair-straightening 'permanents,' hair weaves, braid extensions, Jheri curls, etc.) remains the most popular way to approximate a white female standard of beauty" (582). McMillan uses this most popular approximation of a mainstream beauty ideal to *read* not only the beauty myth but also our complicity, knowing or innocent, in the continuing re-production of the ideology behind that myth.[8]

The novel's focus on hair is also encoded by Savannah's adoration of hats. Like the hair they hide, hats are metonymic of the various ways that women adorn themselves for acceptance. When Robin comments that Savannah wears many hats and looks good in all of them, she is acknowledging not only Savannah's astute fashion sense but also the multiple demands placed on her as a single, professional black woman. Savannah's hats hide her hair but reveal the weight she carries.

> I'm tired of these have-their-cake-and-eat-it-too motherfuckers. I'm through. Finished. From here on out, my pussy will be much harder to get, my heart no longer on display. It's going to take a whole lot more than a juicy dick, a sparkling swimming pool, some iced tea, a thick moustache, a pretty body, a handsome face, a Bible class, smooth conversation, and a serenade to get me to drop my guard. (373)

In the final chapter, the women come "back to life." Robin is content to raise her child with the help of her friends, Gloria has survived a near fatal heart attack and is now involved with her neighbor, Savannah has sworn off her married lover and is embracing her life alone, and Bernadine has risen out of the depths of her despair to live and love again. When Bernadine gets almost a million dollars in her divorce settlement, her first thought is to go on vacation, "for it is time" (405). London is a perfect location, since not only does "the queen of fucking England" live there but "they've got the best hats in the world in London" (405). Bernadine plans a celebration party for herself and her three friends, at which they must all wear hats. At this point, McMillan's *reading* again shows itself, for the hats symbolize the process of hair alteration and the desire for blue eyes; they emphasize the lengths to which blackwomen must go, the exhaustive number of roles that we must perform—hats we must wear—to survive within existing ideologies.

However, when Robin confesses that she does not own a hat, Bernadine responds, "[W]ell, buy one" (402). This requirement of wearing a hat, it seems, invokes the image of their burden, a burden Savannah and Bernadine herself have previously disclaimed. Perhaps readers can see McMillan's ending as a simple closure to a narrative of individual weaknesses overcome by the strength of collective female struggle, and the settlement as their reward. But, as a *reading*, the code of hats also suggests an alternative interpretation.

These women have existed within a paradigm that negates them for so long that even their moments of resistance are inscribed by it and replicate it. The chapter title reminds me of the song "Back to Life" by Soul II Soul. One verse beckons "Back to Life, Back to reality, Back to the here and now," while the chorus exclaims, "however do you want me, however do you need me, however do you want me." The song's lyrics help me hear the women *reading* at the end of *Waiting to Exhale*. True, they have again surrendered themselves to the demands of material beauty; however, the hats they will inevitably wear are of their own choosing. They are willing to love and be loved; the celebration makes clear that the settlement is freedom for Bernadine and all the women. There is a pregnant pause—a *however* that lingers. The space of the *however* indicates the reality that they must come back to.

From Narrative Strategy to Interpretive Lens; or, Polygamous Allegiances in Aidoo's Changes

In the previous sections, I have examined the ways in which African American women writers *read*. I argued that Hurston, Morrison, and McMillan indeed use *reading* as a narrative form. However, here, I *read*; that is, I use my understanding of the art of *reading* to analyze an African woman's text. As a result of the increased political visibility of Alice Walker's *Possessing the Secret of Joy*, the world of African women is often mistaken as one organized around the politics of sexual mutilation. However, for Ama Ata Aidoo, such categorizing is not always appropriate, and she revises

Walker's idea in her casting of the female characters in *Changes*.

Changes is the story of Esi Sekyi and her quest for love on acceptable terms. Though married, she feels stifled by the demands on her as wife and mother. Esi's story is framed by two other narratives. The first focuses on Esi's relationship with her best friend, Opokuya Dakwa. A nurse by profession, Opokuya, like Esi, is struggling to negotiate her way among the roles of wife, mother, and professional. Opokuya's constant arguments with her husband, Kubi, over who should drive their car highlight Esi's effort to situate the changing parameters of male and female relationships. The second framing narrative, focusing on Fusena Kondey, offers another version of an African woman, wife, mother, daughter, and professional. Fusena manages her home and a kiosk. Through these three women, I see Aidoo examining the relation between financial autonomy and the erotics of patriarchy.

Until about twenty years ago, African texts were generally written by men and therefore presented monolithic characterizations of African women's experiences. Furthermore, these stereotypes licensed Western, mostly white middle-class, feminists to apply sexual liberationist politics to African women.[9] Aidoo tells us that some feminists have gone so far as to declare that women like her are "bourgeois African women [who] are in no position to speak for ordinary African women in the village" ("Capacious Topic" 153). Beyond the obvious arrogance of such claims, the gender universalism of Western feminism allowed Western feminists to ignore their own colonial influences. Esi, Opokuya, and Fusena, each in her own way, undercut ideological assumptions that African women live under a patriarchy more extreme than that in the West. These strong female characters show that "to be constituted by a discourse" is not necessarily "to be *determined* by discourse where determination forecloses the possibility of agency" (Butler 143).

As the novel opens, we meet Esi, a professional woman "from the Department of Urban Statistics," who we later learn is also a wife and mother (4). A Eurocentric feminist reader would be inclined to see Esi as confronting that "paramount question": "how can the contemporary African woman negotiate her way between the claims of tradition and modernization?" (Frank 18). This commanding issue has been termed by Katherine Frank and others as the African woman's "bind"; by Aidoo in her play *Dilemma of a Ghost*, a "dilemma"; and even, borrowing from Buchi Emecheta's novel, "the double yoke" (Umeh 178). Oko, Esi's husband, worries that "she definitely puts her career well above any duties she has as a wife" (8) and argues in a "loud male voice" that Esi does not fit the mold of "an African woman" (8–9). However, Aidoo's characters work to refute the presumption that African women must make an unavoidable choice between social and financial independence on the one hand and motherhood, even Africanness, on the other. Interestingly, even Oko must concede not only that Esi is an African woman but also that there are "plenty of them [women like Esi] around these days" (8). Aidoo's female characters labor to survive as gendered subjects and as contributing members of a society struggling to revolutionize itself. This dual task is not a "bind," nor are the often conflicting requirements of this existence a "dilemma" the women must resolve.[10]

Esi's story is told on several levels. There are dialogues, clearly indicated by the use of quotation marks, and there is omniscient narration. However, the novel presents another voice—graphically represented by single-spaced type and double indentions—that offers an interpretive perspective on the narrated events and that is at once text to be read and a text that *reads*. This voice signifies on, talks back to, Western feminist readers and erases the images of African women they have constructed.

Early in the novel, Esi is trying to come to terms with her feelings about what she describes as a "marital rape" and is attempting to decide her course of action. Esi imagines herself presenting a paper entitled "The Prevalence of Marital Rape in the Urban African Environment" (10). Her presentation, she imagines, receives "boos from the men, and uncomfortable titters from the women" (11).

The question and answer period consists of only one, quite elaborate question:

> Yes, we told you, didn't we? What is burying us now are all these imported feminist ideas . . . And dear lady colleague, how would you describe "marital rape" in Akan?
> Igbo? . . . Yoruba?
> Wolof? . . . or Temne? (11)

The questioner intimates, as most Western feminists also imply, that all feminism in Africa has been brought to it from the outside and that such imported ideas are of no consequence in explaining behaviors in Africa.[11] The objection is recast and uttered by what I term the *reading* voice:

> She was caught in her own trap. Hadn't she some time ago said in an argument that you cannot go around claiming an idea or an item was imported into a given society unless you could also conclude that to the best of your knowledge, there is not, and never was any word or phrase in that society's indigenous language which describes that idea or item?
>
> By which and other proof, the claim that "plantain" "cassava" and other African staples came from Asia or the Americas could only be sustained by racist historians and lazy African academics? . . . African staples coming from America? Ha, ha, ha! . . . And incidentally, what did the slaves take there with them in the way of something to grow and eat? . . . What a magnificent way to turn history on its head! (12)

In this excerpt, the *reading* narrator takes as text the assertion of imported ideologies. Like Hurston's, Morrison's, and McMillan's texts, Aidoo's text suggests that through the corporeal, the ideological is deftly *read*. The tone here casts a clear visual image of this narrator's posturing to turn it out; there is not indirection but outright assertion of "black power and duty" (Cary 59).

Most effectively, this moment manages to capture the duality of *reading* as a linguistic form, merging its sacred and secular facets. By leaving Oko and later divorcing him, Esi endorses her secular commitment to be free of oppressive male influence. However, she begins a relationship with Ali Kondey, the "managing director of Linga Hide Aways," a tour and travel agency (22). In the representation of their relationship, I detect a *reading* of feminist interrogations of African sexual politics.[12] A primary facet of that politics for feminist critics is the practice of polygamy—one of the most "glaringly sexist feature[s] of traditional African society" (Frank 18).

Ali and Esi, after agreeing that they would marry, try to decide on a wedding date and the day Ali will travel to meet with Esi's fathers, the male elders of her village. Eagerly, Ali decides that he should go the next day, Saturday. Esi's response shows her determination to reconcile sacred and newly emergent secular traditions. She explains to Ali that "her people didn't consider Saturdays as good days for betrothal and such" because it is a masculine day (89).

The appeal to tradition is the root of the novel's *reading*. As a femcentric writer,[13] Aidoo, in a seeming contradiction, allows Esi to support the very tradition feminists claim oppresses women like her. Interestingly, Esi splits cultural hairs and raises an issue of terminology. When Ali asks Esi to wear his ring, she bluntly asks him if what they are doing, what he is doing by having two women wear his rings, is not bigamy. Ali angrily responds:

> When put like that, yes, we are committing a crime. Polygamy, bigamy. To the people who created the concepts, these are all crimes. Like homicide, rape and arson. Why have we got so used to describing our cultural dynamics with the condemnatory tone of our masters' voices? We have got marriage in Africa, Esi. In Muslim Africa. In non-Muslim Africa. And in our marriages a man has a choice—to have one or more wives. . . . As long as he can look after them properly. (90)

Esi wrestles with the Western definition of bigamy versus what Islam understands as polygamy. In doing so, Esi effectively forces an anthropologizing of the West, which forces us to examine the intersections and divergences of these two concepts. The implications, though, are not that having two wives is bigamy or that polygamy is unlawful and equal to bigamy. The *reading* is two-pronged.

First, Ali's objections are outright rejections of Western critiques of polygamy. His *reading* is response. Second, Esi's *reading* is a statement that comes from an analysis of their situation within their own cultural tenets. She reasons that some traditions are worth preserving and others are not. By divorcing Oko, for example, Esi deviated from traditional marriage practice. Yet, although Esi is not a Muslim, she recognizes that there are customs, Islamic and non-Islamic alike, that must be followed if her marriage to Ali is to be legitimate and honest. Clearly, she tells Ali, the idea of two women wearing one man's rings is a departure from the traditional "way of doing the two or more wives business" (90). Esi recognizes that in the polygamous marriage the second wife is never to undermine the power and status of the first wife and that wearing Ali's ring would do just that to the status of Ali's other wife, Fusena, as "Mrs. Ali Kondey" (90).

Western readers think nothing of Esi's divorce from Oko—Esi confesses she never loved him, and, beyond this, he is guilty of marital rape. In Western secular traditions divorce—certainly under such circumstances—is not controversial. However, this is precisely where and how I see Aidoo *reading* most effectively. Though Western women are outspoken about the effects of polygamy on women, they do not raise similar concerns about the effects of serial polygamy, divorce, in their own world. The controversial nature of this interpretation, and my suggestion that this is Aidoo's critique, begs a somewhat digressive explanation.

As a citizen of a dominant Western nation, I am aware of the presumed separation of church and state, a division between the sacred and the secular. Such division supports our notions of individual freedom. However, an anthropologizing of our social and political behaviors would reveal the secular state and the sacred church—embodied most notably by the Judeo-Christian tradition—are not as separate as we would like to think. The "pledge of allegiance" acknowledges that the United States is "one nation under God." Capitalism, as our economic ideology, is grounded in religious faith, for as our currency reminds us "in God we trust." Insiders, whether individuals or collectives, may choose to ignore or elide the influence of the Judeo-Christian tradition, but to an outsider the legitimacy of such elision is not so clear. Aidoo's novel, in effect, *reads* divorce in the same way that some Western feminists have read polygamy. If we frame marriage as Esi does, as a religious institution, then according to Christian doctrine—excepting adultery—divorce is unlawful. Significantly, while in the United States bigamy is a crime against civil law, adultery is a crime against Christian moral and religious law.[14]

Esi's return to Qur'anic instruction on polygamy, which allows her to distinguish this religious practice from the secular notion of bigamy, *reads* Western feminists who ignore how Western divorce practices highlight the ambiguity of the ideological relationship between the secular and sacred. That Esi can both divorce Oko and, without betraying her principles, become second wife to Ali is a nuance that *reading* yields. With this, *Changes reads* Western secular laws that write divorce yet do not manage to comprehend Ali's and Esi's conflicting approaches to polygamy. The novel therefore points to the evolution of divorce in Western society as evidence that traditions, sacred or secular, are not necessarily fixed but are "socially created" and re-created (Spillers 253; see also 251–52).[15]

I started this essay claiming that *reading* is both statement and response, and I conclude it likewise. Each of the texts I discuss presents blackwomen who, not willing to just sit and wait for things to happen, make things happen. Hurston and the fictional characters Pecola, Bernadine, and Esi change, go through changes and are put through changes; and each struggles to change the world and the discourses that they are compelled to inhabit. These blackwomen—the characters and the writers themselves—take notions of beauty, romantic love, having it all, and togetherness as a text, and then they proceed to *read*, (re)write, and erase the aspects of those notions that would frustrate their aspirations to claim, reform, and inform the traditions they have inherited and to shape a future that values their individual and collective power and integrity.

NOTES

1. I use italics to designate this particular practice.

2. In my work, I make a distinction between the references "black women" and "blackwomen." I use "black women" to refer to women of African descent in the United States and "blackwomen" to women of African descent throughout the world, including but not limited to the United States. In this essay, the latter, more inclusive reference seems more appropriate.

3. This verbal art of insult is generally nonmalicious. The point is to be quick-witted and to be the most clever in one's critique. I offer "signifyin'" here as the discipline of insult and critique, and *reading* is one genre of that art (another being the dozens, for example). Though most forms of signifyin' are ritualized ways of poking fun and demonstrating humor, *reading* is always used to make a point of principle.

4. Additionally, I paraphrase Holloway's discussion of the instructive lesson black mothers give their children when they misbehave, "Act your age, not your color" (3). Such a reprimand, Holloway argues, and I concur, demonstrates the relation between "color and character," a relation that Hurston reads and disrupts (Holloway 4).

5. One cannot escape the commentary on men's participation in the myths that confound Pecola and the ideologies that the narrative engages. The family name, Breedlove, recalls the instance of Trueblood incest in Ralph Ellison's *Invisible Man*. For a discussion of this intertextuality see Awkward.

6. See Ashe; see also Neal and Wilson, who explain that "compared to Black males, Black females have been more profoundly affected by the prejudicial fallout surrounding issues of skin color, facial features, and hair [. . . due] in large part to the importance of physical attractiveness for all women" (328).

7. Here I refer to the biblical association of hair, particularly women's hair, with penance, as indicated by Mary Magdalene, the epitome of the penitent sinner who washed the feet of Christ and wiped them with her hair (Luke 7.37–38, King James version). Long flowing hair became associated with virgins, those women who possessed a strong spiritual commitment to Christ (such as Saint Agnes, who, when she was cast into a brothel for refusing to marry, let her hair grow long to cover her body, wanting her body to remain pure for Christ) and with men who possessed physical strength (such as Samson).

8. Forrest Whittaker's film adaptation of the novel casts three slenderesque, light-skinned women and a heavy dark-skinned woman in the major roles, and all of them have altered hair—relaxers in all four cases and a weave in the case of Bernadine, who is played by Angela Bassett. Although

adherence to the European body aesthetic is a related issue, it is beyond my particular focus here. Nonetheless, the color dynamics are inescapable in the visual medium of the film, revealing the ways in which the color ideology is an interpretive lens for understanding the story in *Waiting to Exhale.* Specifically, the ambiguity I note here in terms of Bernadine's hair style is presented in the film as a move from one relaxed hair style to another. My observation in no way means to suggest that it is impossible for a black woman to have naturally straight hair, but it is made to draw readers' attention to the particular casting choices and to invite an evaluation of the ideological message spoken by those choices.

9. Fishburn's *Reading Buchi Emecheta* provides an extensive discussion of Western feminist politics as it relates to the reading of and critical response to African women's literature. Fishburn's discussion is specific to Emecheta's novels but Fishburn's critiques of certain Western feminist readings of Emecheta's gender politics offer a larger scope and inform quite appropriately the issue I raise here.

10. "Bind" and "dilemma" refer to ideas discussed by the feminist critics Frank and Umeh and refer to Aidoo's play *Dilemma of a Ghost.* I discuss these in more detail below.

11. In an essay about two of the primary positions under debate in feminist sexual politics, Ferguson clarifies the grounding of Frank's ideas about "the feminist novel in Africa." Ferguson suggests that while radical feminists argue that "sexual freedom requires sexual equality of partners and their equal respect for one another as both subjects and body," libertarian feminists consider that "sexual freedom requires oppositional practices, that is, transgressing socially respectable categories of sexuality and refusing to draw the line on what counts as politically correct sexuality" (108-09). The African woman's bind, then, reflects repressive social categories of sexuality, which preclude "equal respect" for women as subjects and bodies. In fact, Frank tells us that the African woman writer is involved in a "repudiation of prevailing patriarchal roles and norms" in order to "delineate fully the new life of the African New Woman" (32).

12. I borrow the term "femcentric" from Haynes, who uses it to avoid the equating of woman-centered approaches, ideologies, and practices with feminism. While the two perspectives exist on a continuum of woman-focused cultural and social practice, feminism carries a particularly political tone that I am trying to unravel. I make the distinction in deference to Aidoo's claim that she is not a feminist because she writes about women and centers her stories on their lives and based on my own polygamous allegiances to womanism and anti-antifeminism.

13. I especially find this blurring of the lines between the sacred and the secular interesting with respect to the recent instances where the military has

punished (even with discharge) men and women who engage in adulterous behavior. Having pledged allegiance to God, nation, and military unit, adulterers who break codes associated with any of these institutions signal their dishonor to all of them. I recognize, however, that the military raises a host of other issues, but as a secular institution and a branch of the state, its claim that adultery as a moral grievance affects civil order warrants mention. While Catholicism more stringently enforces the scriptural rules on marriage and divorce, these ideas are part of the Christian faith generally. See Matt. 5.31–21, 19.3–9; Mark 10.9, 11–12; Luke 16.18; and 1 Cor. 7.10–11 (King James version).

14. Particularly, Ali and Esi come from different regions, and each brings a different conception of relationships, especially male and female relationships, to bear on their relationship together. Hence, Ali's and Esi's constructions of their relationship are built on a tradition that they remake and reshape as they negotiate their partnership.

Works Cited

Aidoo, Ama Ata. *Changes: A Love Story*. London: Women's, 1991.

———. *Dilemma of a Ghost*. London: Longman, 1970.

———. "'That Capacious Topic': Gender Politics." *Critical Fictions: The Politics of Imaginative Writing*. Ed. Philomena Maraani. Seattle: Bay, 1991. 151–54.

Ashe, Bertram. "'Why Don't He Like My Hair?': Constructing African-American Standards of Beauty in Toni Morrison's *Song of Solomon* and Zora Neale Hurston's *Their Eyes Were Watching God*." *African American Review* 29.4 (1995): 579–91.

Awkward, Michael. "The Evil of Fulfillment: Scapegoating and Narration in *The Bluest Eye*." Gates and Appiah 175–209.

Butler, Judith. *Gender Trouble: Feminism and the Subversion of Identity*. New York: Routledge, 1990.

Cary, Lorene. *Black Ice*. New York: Vintage, 1991.

Chapkis, Wendy. *Beauty Secrets: Women and the Politics of Appearance*. Boston: South End, 1986.

Du Bois, W. E. B. *The Souls of Black Folk*. 1903. New York: Viking, 1989.

Ferguson, Ann. "Sex Wars: The Debate between Radical and Libertarian Feminists." *Signs* 10 (1984): 106–12.

Fields, Barbara J. "Slavery, Race and Ideology in the United States." *New Left Review* 181 (1990): 95–118.

Fishburn, Katherine. *Reading Buchi Emecheta*. New York: Greenwood, 1994.

Frank, Katherine. "Women without Men: The Feminist Novel in Africa." *Women in African Literature Today*. Ed. E. D. Jones, E. Palmer, and M. Jones. Spec. issue of *African Literature Today* 15 (1987): 14–34.

Gates, Henry Louis, Jr., and Anthony Appiah. *Toni Morrison: Critical Perspectives Past and Present*. New York: Amistad, 1993.

Gourdine, Angeletta KM. "Hearing, *Reading,* and Being Read by Beloved." *NWSA Journal* 10.2 (1998): 13–31.

Haynes, Laura Sams. "Christio-Conjure in Twentieth-Century Black Women's Writing." Diss. Louisiana State Univ, 2002.

Holloway, Karla FC. *Codes of Conduct*. New Brunswick: Rutgers UP, 1995.

Hurston, Zora Neale. "How It Feels to Be Colored Me." *Norton Anthology of African American Literature*. Ed. Henry Louis Gates, Jr., and Nellie McKay. New York: Norton, 1997. 1008–11.

Jones, Lisa. *Bulletproof Diva*. New York: Doubleday, 1994.

Lakoff, Robin, and Raquel Scherr. *Face Value: The Politics of Beauty*. Boston: Routledge, 1984.

McMillan, Terry. *Waiting to Exhale*. New York: Viking, 1992.

Morrison, Toni. *The Bluest Eye*. New York: Pocket, 1972.

Neal, Angela M., and Midge L. Wilson. "The Role of Skin Color and Features in the Black Community: Implications for Black Women and Therapy." *Clinical Psychology Review* 9 (1989): 323–33.

Radner, Hillary. *Shopping Around: Feminine Culture and the Pursuit of Pleasure*. New York : Routledge, 1995.

Rooks, Noliwe. *Hair Raising: Beauty, Culture, and African American Women*. New Brunswick: Rutgers UP, 1996.

Smitherman, Geneva. *Black Talk: Words and Phrases from the 'Hood to the Amen Corner*. Boston: Houghton, 1994.

Soul II Soul. "Back to Life." Audiocassette. Virgin, 1989. CD. Virgin, 1992.

Spillers, Hortense. "Afterword: Cross-Currents, Discontinuities." *Conjuring: Black Women's Fiction and Literary Tradition*. Ed. Marjorie Pryse and Spillers. Bloomington: Indiana UP, 1985. 249–61.

Umeh, Marie. "Reintegration with the Lost Self: A Study of Buchi Emecheta's *Double Yoke.*" *Ngambika: Studies of Women in African Literature*. Ed. Carole Boyce Davies and Anne Adams Graves. Trenton: Africa World, 1986. 173–80.

Wade-Gayles, Gloria. *Pushed Back to Strength: A Black Woman's Journey Home*. Boston: Beacon, 1993.

Walker, Alice. *Possessing the Secret of Joy*. New York: Pocket, 1992.

Wolf, Naomi. *The Beauty Myth: How Images of Beauty Are Used against Women*. New York: Morrow, 1991.

In Another Place:
Postcolonial Perspectives on Reading

Louise Yelin

Opening Maryse Condé's *Windward Heights* (1995), a reader encounters the novel's exuberant dedication: "To Emily Brontë / Who I hope will approve of this interpretation of her masterpiece. / Honour and respect!" In this epigraph, Condé announces that for her, at least, rereading and rewriting are part of the same project, the celebration and explication of a "masterpiece" so compelling that she need not name it. (The original French title, *La migration des cœurs*, evokes Brontë's theme but does not echo Brontë's title as the English version does.) Condé's "interpretation" transposes the characters and events in *Wuthering Heights* from Britain at the turn of the nineteenth century to Guadeloupe and its environs at the turn of the twentieth century. In different ways, Caryl Phillips's *Cambridge* and Peter Carey's *Jack Maggs* also reread nineteenth-century British literature by rewriting it. Reimagining the articulation of class and colonialism in *Great Expectations,* Carey foregrounds the Australian histories suppressed or assigned an instrumental role in Dickens's novel. While Phillips does not explicitly refer to particular texts, he alludes to and borrows from a variety of sources, including novels, slave narratives, poetry, and travel writing; the unmarked quotations

inserted into the distinct narratives that make up *Cambridge* comment on one another and on Phillips's narrators.

In this essay, I explore what Carey's, Phillips's, and Condé's late-
twentieth-century interpretations of nineteenth-century British
narratives tell us about reading at a moment when traditional,
national literatures are being transformed by economic, political,
and cultural globalization. *Jack Maggs, Cambridge,* and *Windward
Heights* all bridge distances of time and place, gender and generation, race and nationality. These novels represent nineteenth-century
Britain and its colonial empire from the disparate vantage points of
Australia, where Carey was born; the Caribbean, birthplace of
Phillips and Condé; England, where Phillips grew up and was educated; France and francophone West Africa, where Condé lived
before returning to her native Guadeloupe; and New York, where
all three writers now live. All three novels offer versions of what
Edward W. Said terms "contrapuntal reading": they make explicit
what is latent, invisible, or otherwise suppressed in canonical texts
and traditions, revealing the ways these texts and traditions are
formed or deformed by the exigencies of European imperialism
(32). Products of their authors' reading and of the various locations
in which their authors lived, read, and wrote, these novels
expose lacunae in particular nineteenth-century British texts, in
the nineteenth-century British novel as a historically specific
national genre, and in the written documents and official histories
recorded and preserved in archives. Elucidating or imagining what
is dimly glimpsed or not seen, what is barely heard or not said in
Victorian classics such as *Great Expectations* and *Wuthering Heights*,
Carey, Phillips, and Condé not only rewrite and reread Charles
Dickens and Emily Brontë but also thematize the act of reading
itself. Nomadic, cosmopolitan, contemporary, postcolonial, these
works broaden the temporal and spatial contexts in which the
nineteenthcentury British novel is embedded; thus, I suggest, they
give us protocols of reading and writing "in another place."

In what follows, I take as a point of departure the conception of
reading outlined by Patrocinio Schweickart in "Reading Ourselves:

Toward a Feminist Theory of Reading." Exposing the ellipses and elisions of women's perspectives in the work of canonical male writers and in traditional notions of critical reading, she offers what her subtitle calls a feminist theory of reading. Schweickart delineates two moments of feminist reading practice: a negative hermeneutic of "ideological unmasking" or critique and an affirmative project of recuperation whose aim is the "recovery and cultivation of women's culture" (51; see also 43–45). Writing in the 1980s, Schweickart notes a shift in the emphasis of feminist criticism from critique to recuperation, yet she also treats the two moments as complementary aspects of a larger project. Like Condé, that is, she suggests that reading and writing are reciprocal practices, each shaped and modified by the other.[1] Schweickart represents reading as revision, a way of seeing again or seeing anew that enables women to find themselves in the texts they read. Carey, Phillips, and Condé expand Schweickart's notion of revision: reading and writing "in another place," they elaborate ways of seeing afresh that perforce encompass exigencies of distance and difference.

Jack Maggs: *Reading Upside Down*

Peter Carey describes *Jack Maggs* as a "rereading" of *Great Expectations* (Conversation); it recalls other Victorian novels as well. His explanation of the novel's genesis points to the reciprocal, if not necessarily symmetrical, relation of reading and writing, the ways that each is implicated in and in turn influences the other. In Carey's account, both reading and writing are inflected by and reproduce the colonial political and cultural economies that link Australia— and Australians—to Britain. In deciphering, then decentering the colonial inscription of Australian literature, Carey articulates an antipodean politics of reading.

Carey was prompted to read *Great Expectations*, a novel he had previously avoided, and to write *Jack Maggs* when he read Said's *Culture and Imperialism* (Conversation). In this book, Said lays bare the ensemble of affiliations between culture and empire. Relating apparently "discrepant" experiences, he interprets "the archive of modern . . . European and American culture with an effort to extend, give emphasis and voice to what is silent or marginally present or ideologically represented" (66). Carey also cites as an influence Miriam Dixson's *The Real Matilda*, a feminist history of Australia that gives women a prominent role in a narrative from which they had largely been effaced (Conversation). In *Jack Maggs*, Carey emphasizes what Dickens suppresses or relegates to the background, the Australian story that underwrites Dickens's narrative and especially the role of Australian women in this story. That is, Carey highlights the colonial underpinnings of British culture. At the same time, in *Jack Maggs* he develops both the critical genealogy of Australian identity that preoccupies *Oscar and Lucinda* (and is further explored in *The True History of the Kelly Gang*) and the anatomy of colonial mentalities in *The Unusual Life of Tristan Smith*.[2] In the process, he points to a mode of reading that embraces the multiple sites and discrepant experiences that literature simultaneously discloses and occludes.

The title character of *Jack Maggs* is a convicted felon transported to Australia for life. The novel begins with Maggs's return to England in search of one Henry Phipps, who, as a young boy, befriended him. At the home of Phipps's neighbor, Percy Buckle, Maggs meets a young writer named Tobias Oates. A self-styled "cartographer" of "the criminal mind" (85), Oates, who is reminiscent of Dickens but lacks Dickens's genius, "steals" Maggs's story, transforming it by entangling in it his own needs, desires, and conflicts. Throughout, the novel sets Oates's account of Maggs's life against Maggs's own version, as rendered in his memories and journal.

Carey's revisions of Dickens are telling. Exploring the nexus of class and colonialism, Carey shows us how class relations in Britain are reproduced—and transformed—in Australia; thus, he sharpens both the class and colonial plots that animate *Great Expectations*. Jack Maggs's poverty, like that of Dickens's Abel Magwitch, virtually dooms him to a life of crime. Abandoned at birth, Maggs is sold by scavengers to a man who, in turn, pays a midwife and abortionist known as Ma Britten to put him to use. Maggs is trained as a thief and sent out with a young girl named Sophina, with whom he falls in love. When Sophina becomes pregnant, Ma Britten forcibly aborts the child. In Carey's schematic reading of the nineteenth century, Ma Britten (read: Mother Britain [see Hassall 130]), who symbolizes the quintessential rejecting mother (mother country) and the nation that values the sovereign (property and monarch alike), violently prevents the birth of the nascent, working-class British subject and forestalls the emergence of the British working-class family. Sophina is condemned to death by hanging; Maggs is transported to Australia.

The oppression and brutality that Maggs suffers in England are intensified in the penal colony in Australia. The shame of the convict past, embodied in the scars Maggs conceals under gentleman's clothing, is a repressed history that Australians still carry with them and that even now haunts Australia. Yet, seeking Phipps, Maggs returns to the class and culture that rejected, criminalized, and tortured him—or, more precisely, to the bogus representative of that class that he himself has invented (Carey, Conversation). Like Dickens's Magwitch, Maggs makes a fortune in Australia. He uses his vast wealth to make a gentleman out of Phipps, who, like Dickens's Pip, refuses to acknowledge his connection to the convict. In *Great Expectations* and *Jack Maggs* alike, the bourgeois culture of Britain, exemplified by the pretensions of Pip and Phipps, is dependent on a colonial economy based on the forced labor of convicts and the violent appropriation of aboriginal lands. But where Dickens focuses on the British ramifications of this scenario, Carey is particularly concerned with Australia. In the trajectory of Maggs, exemplary Australian, Carey suggests that Australia and Australians must free themselves from the metropolitan culture that holds them in thrall.

Great Expectations dramatizes Pip's process of enlightenment, an enlightenment associated with his overcoming his futile hankering after gentility and his acknowledgment of his ties with the convict Magwitch and the blacksmith Joe Gargery. In *Jack Maggs*, however, enlightenment is the province not of Phipps but of Maggs, who comes to accept himself by more or less acknowledging what it means to be Australian. Yet Carey is true to Dickens's belief in the redemptive power of love. The agent of Maggs's transformation is Mercy Larkin, a young girl whose mother sold her to one Percy Buckle. In his quest for Phipps, Maggs leaves two sons in Australia. When Mercy taxes Maggs with his abandonment of his "real children," he initially demurs that he is "not of that race . . . the race of Australians" (291–92). Eventually, though, Mercy and Maggs create a new family by reclaiming Maggs's sons and raising them with their own children, "five further members of 'That Race'" (305).

Throughout the novel, Carey punctures the illusions that deform Australian ways of seeing. He urges readers to decipher the colonial myths inscribed in cultural artifacts of all kinds. Maggs carries with him a portrait of Phipps that is actually a "likeness" of "George IV dressed as a commoner" (244). That is, the miniature that Maggs cherishes depicts the sovereign during whose Regency he was transported. Through much of the novel, Oates acquires Maggs's story by mesmerizing him. He claims to be cataloging the demons that plague Maggs, yet he sees Maggs mainly as "a mirror held up to his own turbulent and fearful soul" (85–86).

Maggs is, in fact, tormented by a "phantom." He has recurring visions of the soldier, a captain in the 57th Regiment, who tortured him at Moreton Bay. At the end of the novel, Phipps, who has thus far avoided meeting Maggs, appears in the uniform of the 57th Regiment: that is, as an incarnation of Maggs's "nightmare" (301). Maggs concedes, at last, that this apparition is not his son; thus, he exorcises a phantom that symbolizes a British culture as corrupt as George IV, as rapacious as Ma Britten, and as artificial as Mr. Turveydrop, the "Master of Deportment" in *Bleak House*. Many years afterward, Oates publishes *The Death of Maggs*, a novel in which Mercy Larkin is not mentioned (305). Oates uncritically parrots the worldview of Ma Britten and her minions, consigning Maggs to defeat or death and erasing Mercy altogether. But the real Maggs returns to Australia and reclaims his place as husband, father, citizen: that is, as progenitor of a family that prefigures the Australian nation. Like Maggs, Carey suggests, Australia must confront the specter of its past and, in allaying the ghost of Ma Britten, emancipate itself from its pernicious infatuation with the colonizing mother country.

No doubt, *Jack Maggs* can be read as a manifesto for (white) Australian writers and others similarly situated, whether in Australia or, like Carey, elsewhere.[3] I wish to focus, however, on what the novel implies about reading. Maggs's shortcomings as a reader are the result of systematic exploitation, deprivation, and abuse. In London, his only education is instruction in identifying—"reading"— the different hallmarks of the silver he finds in the grand houses he robs (97–99). Maggs is drawn to Ma Britten (Britain) even though she brutally beats him. Later, at Moreton Bay, he tries to stave off the pain of flogging by building "London in his mind" and recalling his vision, on entering the first house he robbed, of "what he later knew was meant by authors when they wrote of England, and of Englishmen" (300). Carey suggests that as long as Maggs—or the Australians he stands for—sustains the illusion of England that he acquires under the aegis of Ma Britten and fetishizes in his image of Phipps, he will neither understand his world nor take his proper place in it.

As an antidote to Maggs's blindness, subjection to illusion, and inability to decode the world he inhabits, Carey sketches antipodean reading practices that limn the "ensemble of affiliations," to borrow Said's phrase, in which literature is embedded and which, in turn, it reimagines. When Maggs arrives in England, he records his story in mirror writing, using an ink that quickly fades into invisibility (70). The intended recipient of this narrative is Phipps. The novel's readers encounter Maggs's story before Phipps's repudiation of its author causes it to disappear. By showing readers what is initially written backwards and soon becomes invisible, Carey urges us to decipher elisions and ellipses in the historical record. In other words, he asks us to restore what has been erased or otherwise omitted and to tease out meanings hitherto obscured. At the same time, he cautions us about the limits of interpretation. At the very end of the novel, we discover that Maggs has not read Oates's book but that Mercy "compensate[s]" for this lack. In fact, she donates several copies of *The Death of Maggs* to the Mitchell Library in Sydney. But, in the novel's last words, "The Mitchell's librarian has noted on each index card the 'v. rough excision' of that page which reads: *Affectionately Inscribed to* PERCIVAL CLARENCE BUCKLE, *A Man of Letters, a Patron of the Arts*" (306). *Jack Maggs*'s readers, once again, are privy to information unknown to the novel's characters. Mercy, Carey's version of the "real Matilda," plays a crucial part in the unmasking of Ma Britten; the excision of her tormentor, like her own absence from Oates's text, symptomatizes what cannot be known even as it demonstrates that reading must make visible the widely discrepant experiences that culture inscribes.

Cambridge: *Reading Broken History*

If Carey chiefly addresses Australian culture, Phillips is primarily interested in Britain. *Cambridge* is part of a larger project in which Phillips traces the genealogy of the black European and especially the black Briton. The novel dramatizes the role of black slaves whose labor in the Caribbean made possible the industrial revolution and the emergence of modern Britain. At the same time, it counters the racist, exclusionary notions of Britishness advanced by Enoch Powell and Margaret Thatcher by asserting the claim of blacks—those long settled in Britain as well as newly arrived immigrants from the Caribbean and their children—to British identity.[4]

Like *Jack Maggs*, *Cambridge* draws on British texts that it rereads, to use Carey's term, and in the process rewrites.[5] Once again, reading and writing are implicitly presented as reciprocal practices. But Phillips's use of source material differs somewhat from Carey's. Unlike *Jack Maggs*, which directly engages *Great Expectations*, *Cambridge* refers obliquely to such nineteenth-century British novels as *Mansfield Park* and *Wuthering Heights* and to the nineteenth-century British novel in general. The setting of *Cambridge*—a plantation in the Caribbean at a moment of crisis in the political economy of plantation slavery—recalls *Mansfield Park*, which describes the reverberations in Britain of events that occur in Antigua. In naming the protagonist Emily and the man that she is supposed to marry (but does not), Thomas Lockwood, Phillips evokes the author and narrator of *Wuthering Heights*. (Hawthorn cottage, where Emily takes refuge at the end of Phillips's novel, is almost an anagram for the Brontës' Haworth.) Phillips also draws on such genres as travel writing, slave narrative, abolitionist poetry, and colonial records and on his wide reading in histories that document the lives of black people in Britain and its empire from the sixteenth century to the twentieth century.[6]

Cambridge, set in the Caribbean in the early nineteenth century, juxtaposes several narratives that present different versions of the same events. The two protagonists and principal narrators are Emily Cartwright, a white Englishwoman who travels to her father's plantation on the eve of the marriage he has arranged for her with an unappealing, elderly widower, and Cambridge, a black slave on the plantation, who kills a brutal overseer and is lynched. The first-person narratives of Emily and Cambridge are followed by a third account of the killing and its aftermath as they might be represented in plantation records, court documents, the local press, and island lore. Commenting on and contradicting as well as reinforcing each other, these narratives model for us the ways that writing is always already a species of reading.

Vulnerable to the power of white middle- and upper-class men in England and the Caribbean alike, Emily oscillates between one set of beliefs and another. She attempts to resist but sometimes acquiesces to the patriarchal gender constraints represented most prominently by her father and the colonial establishment. Similarly, she alternately expresses opposition to slavery and echoes its apologists. Emily's journey across the Atlantic is a paradigmatic instance of the voyage that turns Europeans into Americans. Her experience at once resembles and differs from that of Cambridge, who—in Phillips's sly underscoring of the importance of the journey during which Africans are transformed into Americans—undergoes the Middle

Passage twice. Once on the island, Emily relates her observations in the conventional manner of (European) travel writing. On the one hand, she assimilates the island landscape to an English scene, likening the "infamous sugar canes" with "young shoots that billowed in the cooling breeze" to "fields of green barley." On the other hand, she relies on the commonplace of the "tropical paradise" (18). In describing the slaves, she lurches from one set of clichés to another: "that the black is addicted to theft and deceit"; that the "negro village is a picturesque scene" (39, 42). Emily's observations are influenced by the doctor, managers, clergymen—and the planto-crats to whom they are subservient and on whom their livelihood depends—who guide her around the plantation and the island's principal city. Like Carey, Phillips challenges readers to correct for the distortions in his character's point of view.

Cambridge supplies much of what Emily leaves unsaid—and, by extension, what is excluded from and makes possible such nineteenth-century British novels as *Wuthering Heights*, *Jane Eyre*, and *Mansfield Park*. Like *The History of Mary Prince* (1831), a slave narrative published in England, Cambridge's narrative is a confession retrospectively shaped by the subject's conversion and by the Christian notion of the fortunate Fall. It also recalls Olaudah Equiano's and Ukawsaw Gronniosaw's accounts of black London-ers in the late eighteenth century.[7] Cambridge, who adopts the homiletic style of evangelical Christianity, is stodgy, even plodding, in his recital of a "history truly broken" (137). Cambridge has little knowledge of his early life. The story proper begins with the Middle Passage: that is, at a point when his original identity, if not his name, Olumide, is already lost to memory. Cambridge notes that the "English talk" of his captors "resembled . . . the manic chatter of baboons" and says that he "wondered . . . if [the white men] were not truly intent upon cooking and eating us" (135). In Cambridge's inversion of racist commonplaces, Phillips winks at such foundational instances of European colonial discourse as Montaigne's essay "Of Cannibals" and Shakespeare's appropriation of Montaigne in *The Tempest*.[8] Cambridge is taken to England immediately after he arrives in Carolina; on the way, he is given a new name, Thomas. In London, he marries a fellow servant; under her influence, he becomes a Christian, an itinerant preacher, and an abolitionist orator. Renamed again—he is now called David Henderson—he rejoices: "Truly I was now an Englishman, albeit a little smudgy of complexion! Africa spoke to me only of a history I had cast aside" (147). If Cambridge seems too quick to dismiss his African history, he also evokes the black British culture of the 1980s in asserting an identity forged in diaspora.[9]

Cambridge's assumption of Englishness is premature, however. As the excess of names suggests, his national identity—like that of the black Britons he figures and prefigures—is repeatedly put into question. Sent by a missionary society to convert the African heathen, he is once again enslaved, this time by the ship's captain. Taken to the Caribbean and renamed Cambridge, this "virtual Englishman" becomes "manifestly a West Indian slave" (157, 159). On the plantation, he befriends a young girl who becomes his wife; although she practices obeah, he attempts to convert her and, imitating his masters, gives her a new name, Christiania. He is sent to protect Emily, but, he says, "the Englishwoman didn't concern me" (164). His lack of interest in her deflates the myth—a staple of British colonial discourse beginning with *The Tempest*—of white women as the object of black men's desire. He tries to talk "as one man to another" (166) to the brutal overseer Brown; when Brown strikes him, he resists, killing Brown then praying for forgiveness.

The third section of the novel, which omits the motives and feelings that Emily and Cambridge detail, offers a truncated version of the events they describe. Christiania and Stella, a slave who instructs Emily in the customs of plantation life and tends to her when she goes mad at the end of the novel, are muted in the narratives of Emily and Cambridge; they are utterly invisible in this third account. In the conspicuous absence of these black women from a story in which they play significant parts, Phillips asks readers to notice and critically mark what is missing—what is unmarked and unremarked—from the official record of plantation slavery.

Cambridge represents Caribbean colonial—and, by extension, postcolonial—culture as the result of a process of "creolization" that transforms black and white alike. Emily herself refers to both blacks and whites as "creoles"; she describes the emergence, after the slave trade is made illegal, of "creole" slaves "deemed to have safely entered this new tropical life or . . . born in this zone" (38). In Emily's use of the word "creole"—that is, in the use of the term by a white Englishwoman—Phillips engages in conversation with a contemporary French (francophone) exploration of the term in *Eloge de la Créolité* ("In Praise of Creoleness") by Jean Bernabé, Patrick Chamoiseau, and Raphaël Confiant.[10] This influential text begins, "Neither Europeans, nor Africans, nor Asians, we proclaim ourselves Creoles" (886). Bernabé, Chamoiseau, and Confiant elaborate a conception of creoleness that transcends geography and encompasses other locales (Mauritius, for example) as well as the Carribbean. They eschew clear-cut definitions of *créole* or *créolité* ("creoleness") and reject both the "claim of a universality ruled by Western values" and "traditional raciological distinctions." Rather, they adopt a rhetoric of enunciation that treats creolenesss as an *"interactional or transactional aggregate* of Caribbean, European, African, Asian, and Levantine cultural elements, united on the same soil by the yoke of history": that is, as a hybrid formation, a process of negotiation, a "question to be lived" (890–93).

Emily describes two variants of colonial—creole—culture and distinguishes their different "transactions," to borrow from Bernabé, Chamoiseau, and Confiant, with the metropolitan culture transported to or imposed on the island where most of the novel's events take place. On the one hand, the colonial, particularly the culture of the colonizers, is a parodic imitation, a pastiche of the excesses in the metropolitan original. Thus, Emily remarks the "ostentation," "vulgar extravagance," and "addiction to ornament" she finds among the planters and in Baytown, the island's principal city (102, 117). On the other hand, colonial culture, particularly the culture of the colonized, in mimicking both British and colonial (white creole) models, inscribes covert expressions of resistance. In Emily's misprision of what she encounters, a misprision fostered by the colonial functionaries and plantation managers who shape her perceptions, Phillips highlights the interpretive challenges posed by creole cultures, in the Caribbean and elsewhere, that have chiefly been represented by adherents of the western universalism with which Bernabé, Chamoiseau, and Confiant take issue. At the same time, Phillips urges readers to seek traces of agency in actions whose meanings are distorted or hidden altogether in the historical record.

Traveling the island with Emily, we discern in her observations aspects of the local scene of which she seems unaware. Emily is baffled, for example, by the song of a free black cobbler, yet her confused account offers us a glimpse of the cobbler's self-fashioning creativity:

> He sang a tune in a minor key which Mr. Brown identified as negro music, but which to my ear seemed a corrupt version of an old Welsh air. . . . On observing us the black rolled up his eyes until only the whites were visible, and then . . . he prostrated himself before us in a gesture of base supplication. . . . I was unsure, in the case of this *sambo*, whether he was making sport of us, for I detected about his free person touches of wit which he appeared to be only partly concealing, but to what purpose I could not fathom. (105)

Emily does comprehend some of what she notices. She hears the cobbler's song as a corruption of a Welsh air—that is, as a faulty copy of a provincial original. But she senses that his wit is somehow a sign of his freedom. Her discomfort is intensified a few moments later when she observes the "proceedings of a slave court." She remarks with unwitting irony that "[a] formal system of law whereby any offender, irrespective of colour or quality, is meted out just punishment seems not to have taken hold on this island" (105). In the double voicing—by Emily in Baytown, by the author in England—of the words "this island," Phillips discloses connections of which Emily is unaware. Indeed, the novel insists that readers recognize—that an adequate reading make manifest—connections latent or implicit in the world the characters inhabit.

Neither Emily nor Cambridge, however, can acknowledge what they might have in common. (Nor, for that matter, can either see what Emily might have in common with Christiania or Cambridge with Brown.) Emily never recognizes Cambridge as an equal—as he puts it, "one man to another" (166). In her susceptibility to patriarchal imperatives and his tenuous assumption of English identity, Phillips not only represents the early nineteenth-century Caribbean but also addresses contemporary Britain, in which Cambridge's predicament is echoed in that of blacks—descendants of those Emily describes as Creole slaves—born in Britain but excluded by restrictive, racist notions of Britishness. *Cambridge* begins with the word "England" and ends with the name "Stella": Phillips invites readers to connect the two terms, to construct a sentence that, like the novel's plot, relates the one to the other. Reading and rewriting nineteenth-century narratives from the perspective of a black British culture that refuses restrictive, racist constructions of English, or British, identity, restoring to view the lives of Stella, Christiania, Cambridge, and their descendants, Phillips seeks to repair the broken history of Britain.

La migration des cœurs / Windward Heights: *Reading across Language and Culture*

In *La migration des cœurs* (translated into English as *Windward Heights*), Maryse Condé rereads and rewrites *Wuthering Heights*. Condé's "interpretation" of "Brontë's masterpiece" expands Brontë's dissection of the relation between property—selfhood, material possessions—and desire. By setting *Windward Heights* in the context of plantation slavery and its aftermath in the Caribbean, Condé gives prominence to a race plot that is not emphasized in *Wuthering Heights*.[11] Like Carey and Phillips, that is, she emphasizes narratives suppressed or obscured in nineteenth-century British novels. But Condé amplifies the notion of reading elaborated in *Jack Maggs* and *Cambridge*, for *Windward Heights* situates Brontë in a frame of reference not limited to British, or anglophone, literature. Indeed, Condé observed that she was unaware, when as a young girl she read a French translation of *Wuthering Heights*, that the novel had originally been written in English (Conversation). What Françoise Lionnet identifies as the "cross-cultural poetics" of *Windward Heights* performs a "comparatist" reading of Brontë's text and proposes protocols of reading comparatively: that is, as a translation across national and linguistic boundaries.[12]

Condé's plot recalls Brontë's in its broad outlines. Like *Wuthering Heights*, *Windward Heights* traces through several generations the intertwined fortunes of two families, here, the Gagneurs, who struggle to survive on the harsh terrain of L'Engoulvent, and the wealthy Linsseuils, who own a plantation named Belles-Feuilles. Generational differences within the same family register the pressure of historical events on everyday life. As in *Wuthering Heights*, both families and the relationship between them are transformed when an outsider, here, a foundling named Razyé, enters the seemingly closed environment they inhabit. Like his prototype Heathcliff, Razyé evokes strong feelings in those he encounters—generally, sympathy in women and antipathy in men. Brought by Hubert Gagneur to L'Engoulvent, Razyé becomes the childhood companion of Hubert's daughter Cathy, Condé's version of Catherine Earnshaw. After Cathy's marriage to the sickly, feminine, "civilized" Aymeric Linsseuil, Razyé marries Aymeric's sister Irmine, whom he treats cruelly and later abandons. Eventually, Razyé commandeers, or more precisely, appropriates by legal and extralegal means, much of the wealth of the neighborhood. His hungry accumulation, like that of Heathcliff, is an attempt to seek compensation for the humiliation he suffers at the hands of the Gagneurs and Linsseuils alike, to satisfy his thwarted desires by acquiring worldly goods, and to establish his claim to respectability.

If, as this brief summary suggests, Condé retains the basic structure of Brontë's novel, she also complicates it in important ways. Her modifications challenge readers to extend what Hans Robert Jauss calls the "horizon of expectations" beyond the confines outlined by one national culture, one language, one set of literary traditions.[13] Condé shifts the action of Brontë's novel forward about one hundred years, from the turn of the eighteenth century to the turn of the nineteenth century. *Wuthering Heights* begins in 1801, when Lockwood arrives at Thrushcross Grange, which he has rented from Heathcliff. It moves back into the last third of the eighteenth century, as Nelly Dean, once a servant at Wuthering Heights and now the housekeeper at Thrushcross Grange, recounts for Lockwood the tale of the Earnshaws and the Lintons. And it concludes in 1802, when Lockwood returns to the neighborhood and learns that Heathcliff has died and that the second Catherine, Catherine Linton, is soon to be married to Hareton Earnshaw.[14] *Windward Heights* begins in 1898, moves back to the mid-nineteenth century, as several narrators recount the entangled histories of the Gagneurs and the Linsseuils, and concludes in the early twentieth century with the birth of a child who looks toward a future unrealized in the text: that is, toward the present moment in which the novel was written.

Condé also expands Brontë's geographical range, transferring the action from a remote corner of England to the Caribbean: Condé herself said recently that she has always thought of *Wuthering Heights* as a Caribbean text (Conversation). Most of *Windward Heights* is set in the French colony of Guadeloupe. (In 1946, Guadeloupe, along with Martinique, became part of France as one of its "overseas departments.") Some of the action occurs in Cuba, a Spanish colony, and in the British colony of Dominica. The multilingual territory traversed by the characters in *Windward Heights* is an arena for the competing colonial ambitions of England, France, and Spain. A place where, as Caryl Phillips puts it, "Africa met Europe on somebody else's soil" (Interview with Graham Swift 102), Condé's Caribbean is a polyglot, transnational, geographic (geopolitical) entity, a site of a history still in process.[15]

Condé's temporal and spatial relocation of Brontë's plot emphasizes a narrative that is muted in or displaced from the surface of *Wuthering Heights*, the story of the "triangular trade" and of plantation slavery in the Americas. Heathcliff is picked up by Mr. Earnshaw in Liverpool, which was, in the late eighteenth century, the most active port in the British slave trade. By the 1840s, when Brontë wrote the novel, slavery had been abolished in Britain and its colonial empire. (In 1807, the slave trade was abolished; an 1833 act of parliament freed the slaves throughout the British empire [see Fryer, *Staying Power* 203, 207]). The gap between the events the novel describes and the moment in which it was written may be one reason that slavery is not explicitly mentioned, but rather tacitly acknowledged in its figurative language (see Von Sneidern). This gap also makes possible the untenable and implausible assumption that the author did not know what her novel does not say: that is, that Emily Brontë was unaware of the slave trade and the abolitionist activity of Britain's blacks in Leeds and Liverpool, cities not far from the Brontës' native Haworth, and elsewhere.[16]

At once sharpening Brontë's focus and extending her purview, Condé specifies the historical context in which the plot of *Windward Heights* unfolds. The actual events to which the novel alludes and that punctuate the lives of its characters are events in the history of slavery and its sequelae, including anticolonial political movements involving former slaves and their descendants in both Cuba and Guadeloupe. Like Brontë, Condé rarely dates the events she mentions; as in Brontë, the omission of dates gives us history as it is experienced in or as a backdrop to everyday life. At the same time, Condé compels readers unfamiliar with the Caribbean—readers, perhaps, of Brontë or other nineteenth-century British novelists—to fill in the outlines of the narrative by consulting histories of the area.

The first scene of *Windward Heights* places Razyé in Havana as the battleship *Maine* is being blown up in the harbor: in other words, after the death of José Martí (1895) and at a pivotal moment in which an emergent American imperialism, not Martí's anticolonial nationalism, displaces European—here, Spanish—colonial domination of the Western Hemisphere. *Windward Heights* also alludes to the end of slavery in the French empire (1848) but suggests that in Guadeloupe, at least, the maintenance of a political economy based on sugar vitiated formal abolition. Condé details, on the one hand, the luxury supported by the Linsseuils' ownership of a plantation and, later, a factory where sugar is refined and, on the other, the harsh conditions of labor and the deprivations suffered by the slaves and their descendants alike. As one of the novel's narrators remarks, "The abolition of slavery hadn't changed anything at all. . . . It was still the rich white planters who laid down the law and the blacks who lived from hand to mouth" (19).[17]

Toward the end of the novel, Cathy Linsseuil, the daughter of Cathy Gagneur and Aymeric Linsseuil, goes to teach school in the town of Roseau, in Dominica. As a British colony that had previously been the possession of France, Dominica completes the picture the novel gives of the Caribbean at the turn of the nineteenth century. Perhaps more important, Dominica was the birthplace of Jean Rhys. Condé was inspired to write *Windward Heights* at least in part by the example of Rhys's revision of *Jane Eyre* in *Wide Sargasso Sea* (Conversation). Dominica here not only signifies Condé's homage to Rhys but also affirms Caribbean affiliations across race, language, and nationality. Indeed, the range of Condé's intertextual allusions—to *David Copperfield*, Aimé Césaire's *Notebook of a Return to the Native Land*, Simone de Beauvoir's *The Second Sex*, and Tayeb Salih's *Season of Migration to the North*, among others—sketches the global context in which she situates her own work and points to the need for transnational, translational, multilingual, that is, comparatist, reading practices and interpretive frameworks.

Condé opens up Brontë's text narratively as well as chronologically and spatially. Like Brontë, Condé presents her novel as a written version of stories passed down orally. But Condé makes a different use of this structure than Brontë does. In *Wuthering Heights*, Lockwood recounts for the novel's readers what he is told by Nelly Dean, who, in turn, incorporates the accounts she is given by some of the characters she describes. Heathcliff and Cathy, however, appear only at several removes, as they are observed and represented by others. Condé gives the role of Nelly to a series of narrators. Almost all are women; most are servants; several are illiterate, speakers of Creole, not French; some occupy ambiguous positions in the social hierarchy as offspring of extralegal liaisons and, in some cases, of rape. Some are the children of slaves; some are the daughters and granddaughters of Indians and others brought to Guadeloupe as laborers after abolition. Taken together, Condé's narrators embody the history of Guadeloupe as it is experienced and remembered by those absent from the official record—poor women, mainly.[18] Their stories are not contained, as is that of Brontë's Nelly Dean, by a frame narrator like the quintessentially unreliable Lockwood. Rather, an unidentified, omniscient third-person narrator, the voice of the novel, presents their tales without comment, thereby authorizing their memories as the stuff of history and in particular of a history missing from the archive. Finally, unlike Heathcliff, whose motives must be inferred from his speech and action, Razyé is represented—in free indirect discourse—as the subject of consciousness (thoughts and feelings). Eschewing the representation of her male protagonist as a mysterious object of attention and speculation, Condé demystifies both Razyé and the plot that he sets in motion.

If *Wuthering Heights* traces the beginnings of modernity in Heathcliff's disruption of relationships between parents and children, sisters and brothers, husbands and wives, masters and servants, Wuthering Heights, Thrushcross Grange, and the nearby village of Gimmerton, *Windward Heights* shows us in Razyé's destructive influence the beginnings of the contemporary world we inhabit. In both novels, parents love other parents' children more than their own; in both novels, status is in flux. Condé, however, explicitly represents what Brontë hints at: the ways that race, as it is constructed in the system of plantation slavery and its aftermath, and slippages between race and class intensify the instability of class identities. The Linsseuils are a family of "rich white creoles," while the paterfamilias of the Gagneurs is a "tawny-colored mulatto" (18) and his children reflect a range of racial characteristics.

Like the racially indeterminate Heathcliff, Razyé is, as Françoise Lionnet points out, a collection of discrete, indeed conflicting, racial signifiers ("Narrating the Americas" 8). In this respect, Razyé might be seen as a gloss on a remark made by Nelly Dean in *Wuthering*

Heights. To console Heathcliff for Cathy's apparent preference for Edgar Linton, Nelly says:

> A good heart will help you to a bonny face, my lad, . . . if you were a regular black; and a bad one will turn the bonniest into something worse than ugly. . . . You're fit for a prince in disguise. Who knows, but your father was Emperor of China, and your mother an Indian queen, each of them able to buy up, with one week's income, Wuthering Heights and Thrushcross Grange together? And you were kidnapped by wicked sailors and brought to England. (57)

When Condé's Nelly, surnamed Raboteur, consoles Razyé, she makes explicit the racial subtext of Nelly Dean's remark, but unlike Nelly Dean, she does not conflate racial, aesthetic, and moral categories. In using the first-person plural, she also identifies herself with Razyé: "You know you're handsome in your own way, with that Ashanti black skin, that fine curly hair and all those marks on your cheeks. Perhaps your ancestors were princes and princesses? Who knows what *our* parents were before we were brought here as slaves!" (30; emphasis added). In Condé's Caribbean, a world defined by racial miscegenation and racial and cultural *métissage*,[19] the association of racial and moral characteristics is shown to be arbitrary, contingent on material conditions.

Yet material conditions—abstracted in such conceptual categories as race, class, and gender—are not the whole story, in either Brontë's text or Condé's. Indeed, Condé's title, *La migration des cœurs*, evokes both the global circulation of populations that inaugurates modernity and the vagaries of desire. At the beginning of *Windward Heights*, Razyé is in Havana, having fought as a mercenary on the side of the Spanish colonizers. Later, he aligns himself with the socialist and anticolonial political parties working against the French. In Cuba, he seeks the assistance of a "*babalawo*, a high priest of *santeria*" (5) in contacting the spirit of his beloved Cathy. Throughout, he attempts to regain her through the effort of *kimbwaze*, or priests. Yet, Condé suggests, even the quest for the other is mediated by an economy in which race cannot be discounted or the devastating effects of racial hierarchies wished away. Indeed, she presents the abjection of Cathy's daughter and the bravado of Razyé's son as legacies of slavery, colonial psychosexual constellations that persist long after abolition; thus, she asks us to read contemporary articulations of race and gender as signs of histories buried, suppressed, forgotten.

At the end of *Windward Heights*, Condé's second Cathy dies bearing a daughter. Jack Maggs's posterity is similarly assured, Oates's distortions notwithstanding, by the Australian family he leaves behind. These children look toward futures unrealized in the novels and still in the process of unfolding. The ending of *Cambridge* is somewhat more ambiguous. Emily gives birth to a stillborn child, yet her narrative transmits to readers the memory of her Caribbean journey and thus of the system of slavery. All three novels call on readers to recover what Cambridge calls "broken history." They supplement the histories of European modernity imagined by Dickens, Brontë, and Austen, among others, by setting these histories in a global context. Thus they suggest that understanding these histories is accomplished, paradoxically, by reading them in another place.

Writing in the postcolonial present, Carey, Phillips, and Condé give us new versions of familiar narratives. Augmenting and amending once-standard accounts of slavery and its aftermath, of European and especially British imperialism, of colonial constructions of class and culture, these writers reiterate for us the ineluctably partial character of all reading—and, for that matter, of all writing. They show us, that is, how the meaning of any text is crucially influenced by the situation of the reader, the time and place in which the reader is located, the histories the reader incarnates. Taking up Brontë and Dickens, Equiano and Austen, Carey, Phillips, and Condé also illustrate the persistent authority of the literary traditions and cultural formations in which they themselves were schooled. Yet their own histories of migration and that they read and write from multiple locations—Australia and New York; London, Saint Kitts, and New York; Guadeloupe, Paris, and New

York—caution us to see meaning too as nomadic, migrating, and in flux. Making palpable what is buried in or absent from their sources, these writers also urge us to listen for what remains to be said by those—nonreaders and nonwriters—whose perspectives have not yet been voiced, or heard, in contemporary literature. Indeed, in revisiting the past, Carey, Phillips, and Condé also address the present and point to the future. Imaginatively excavating the painful legacies of the plantation and the penal colony, these writers hear—and ask readers to heed—their echoes in the racial inequality, oppression, and violence that continue to haunt contemporary discussions of identity. Reading the past in another place, they prompt dreams of a different kind of future.

NOTES

Parts of this essay were first presented at an MLA panel entitled "Rethinking Victorian Realism" (San Francisco, December 1998); thanks to Hilary Schor and the session participants for stimulating my thinking about the topic. Peter Carey, Maryse Condé, and Caryl Phillips generously shared with me their ideas about reading. Special thanks go to Caryl Phillips, who set this essay in motion when he told me how Carey came to write *Jack Maggs* and introduced me to *Windward Heights*, published in England in the Faber Caribbean Literature series he edits. I thank Elizabeth Flynn, Patrocinio Schweickart, Peter Rabinowitz, and an anonymous reader for the MLA for helpful comments on an earlier version of this essay and Robert Friedman, top editor *extraordinaire*. Through many conversations over the years, Bella Brodzki, Françoise Lionnet, and Ronnie Scharfman made this essay possible by broadening the context of my own reading; I hope I do them justice.

1. I thank Patrocinio Schweickart and Peter Rabinowitz for pointing out the importance of this reciprocity.
2. Ashcroft, Griffin, and Tiffin (133, 135) regard the establishment of "indigeneity"—that is, an authentic identity—as a crucial issue for the literature of white settler colonies.
3. Hassall connects Carey with David Malouf and Alex Miller as "mythmakers" who "(re)mythologise Australia in its own terms" (135).
4. In a 1968 address, Enoch Powell warned that the growth of Britain's black population would flood the nation. In the run-up to the 1979 elections,

Margaret Thatcher asserted that Britain was in danger of being "swamped" by its enemies. On the history of blacks in Britain, see Fryer, *Staying Power* and *Black People*; on identity, see Hall; Bhabha; and Phillips and Phillips, especially chs. 24 and 29.

5. Sharrad notes that Phillips's "post-colonial textuality is partly constructed out of a *reading . . .* of other texts" (216).

6. See O'Callahan on Phillips's use of words, phrases, and passages taken from Monk Lewis's *Journal of a West India Proprietor*, Lady Nugent's *Journal*, Mrs. Carmichael's *Domestic Manners and Social Condition of the White, Coloured, and Negro Population of the West Indies*, and *The Interesting Narrative of the Life of Olaudah Equiano, or Gustavus Vassa the African. Written by Himself*. Sharrad links Cambridge's story to that of the protagonist of "The Dying Slave," a "well-known abolitionist poem" (211–12). Phillips cites especially the work of James Walvin and Peter Fryer as influences (Conversation).

7. Gronniosaw was the author of *A Narrative of the Most Remarkable Particulars in the Life of James Albert Ukawsaw Gronniosaw, an African Prince, As Related by Himself* (1770). On Gronniosaw, see Fryer, *Staying Power* 89–91, and Phillips, *Extravagant Strangers* 1–5.

8. The slaves' belief that their captors were cannibals also figures in Fred d'Aguiar's novel about the Middle Passage, *Feeding the Ghosts*. See also De Andrade's "Cannibal Manifesto." I thank Maryse Condé for introducing me to this remarkable text.

9. See Hall and Phillips and Phillips, chs. 28 and 29, on the diasporic character of black British identities.

10. I thank Ronnie Scharfman for introducing me to the *Eloge* and helping me to understand it in the context of debates in the francophone world.

11. On race in *Wuthering Heights*, see Meyer, ch. 3, and Von Sneidern.

12. Lionnet, "Transnationalism" 33; on feminist comparatist reading practices, see Lionnet, "Transnationalism" 34, and the essays collected in Higonnet.

13. "The coherence of literature as an event is primarily mediated in the horizon of expectations of the literary experience of contemporary and later readers, critics, and authors" (Jauss 22).

14. The best summary of *Wuthering Heights* is that of Sanger, who meticulously maps virtually every incident of the novel. Sanger's chronology places the events of the novel in a crucial moment in the history of slavery in the British West Indies, the last third of the eighteenth century.

15. On the "transcolonial" history of the Caribbean, see Lionnet, "Transnationalism."

16. Fryer, *Staying Power* 207–27. Phillips, "Interview with Louise Yelin" 54.

17. Condé herself made the same point when she asserted that the legacy of slavery, its "persistence in our minds," calls into question the very notion of "abolition" ("Symposium").

18. As Condé told Wolf: "In a society like the Caribbean, who knows more than the servants about the construction of society, the details of society? Nobody ever asks them their opinion, but they are there, they are witnesses; they are the ones who see, they are the ones who arrange everything" (Interview 77).

19. *Métissage* means, literally, mixing; Lionnet uses the term in ways that move beyond discourses of race. She defines *métissage* as a "dynamic model of relationality" that creates "complex identities and interrelated, if not overlapping, spaces" (*Postcolonial Representations* 4, 7).

WORKS CITED

Ashcroft, Bill, Gareth Griffin, and Helen Tiffin. *The Empire Writes Back: Theory and Practice in Post-colonial Literatures*. New York: Routledge, 1989.

Bernabé, Jean, Patrick Chamoiseau, and Raphaël Confiant. "In Praise of Creoleness." Trans. Mohamed B. Teleb Khyar. *Callaloo* 13 (1990): 886–909

Bhabha, Homi K. "DissemiNation: Time, Narrative, and the Margins of the Modern Nation." *The Location of Culture*. New York: Routledge, 1994. 139–70.

Brontë, Emily. *Wuthering Heights*. 1847. New York: Penguin, 1995.

Carey, Peter. Conversation with author, New York City, July 1999.

———. *Jack Maggs*. New York: Knopf, 1998.

Condé, Maryse. Conversation with author, New York City, June 1999.

———. Interview with Rebecca Wolf. *Bomb* Summer 1999: 74–80.

———. "Symposium." Slave Routes: The Long Memory. Conference at Columbia University, 7 Oct. 1999.

———. *Windward Heights*. Trans. Richard Philcox. London: Faber, 1998; New York: Soho, 1999.

D'Aguiar, Fred. *Feeding the Ghosts*. Hopewell: Ecco, 1999.

De Andrade, Oswaldo. "Cannibal Manifesto." Trans. Mary Ann Caws and Claudia Caliman. *Exquisite Corpse: A Journal of Letters and Life* 11 (2002). 27 Oct. 2002 <http://www.corpse.org/issue_11/manifestos/deandrade.html>.

Dixson, Miriam. *The Real Matilda: Woman and Identity in Australia from 1788 to the Present*. 1976. Rev. ed. Ringwood, Austral.: Penguin, 1984.

Fryer, Peter. *Black People in the British Empire: An Introduction*. 1988. London: Pluto, 1993.

———. *Staying Power: The History of Black People in Britain*. London: Pluto, 1984.

Hall, Stuart. "Cultural Identity and Diaspora." *Identity: Community, Culture, Difference*. Ed. J. Rutherford. London: Lawrence, 1990. 222–37.

Hassall, Anthony J. "A Tale of Two Countries: *Jack Maggs* and Peter Carey's Fiction." *Australian Literary Studies* 18 (1997): 128–35.

Higonnet, Margaret R., ed. *Borderwork: Feminist Engagements with Comparative Literature*. Ithaca: Cornell UP, 1994.

Jauss, Hans Robert. *Toward an Aesthetic of Reception*. Trans. Timothy Bahti. Minneapolis: U of Minnesota P, 1982.

Lionnet, Françoise. "Narrating the Americas: Trans-colonial Métissage and Maryse Condé's *La migration des cœurs*." Changing the Map: The Worlds of Comparative Literature. Whitney Humanities Center, Yale University. 6 Feb. 1999.

———. *Postcolonial Representations: Women, Literature, Identity*. Ithaca: Cornell UP, 1995.

———. "Transnationalism, Post-colonialism or Transcolonialism? Reflections on Los Angeles, Geography, and the Uses of Theory." *Emergences* 10.1 (2000): 25–34.

Meyer, Susan. *Imperialism at Home: Race and Victorian Women's Fiction*. Ithaca: Cornell UP, 1996.

O'Callahan, Evelyn. "Historical Fiction and Fictional History: Caryl Phillips's *Cambridge*." *Journal of Commonwealth Literature* 29.2 (1993): 34–47.

Phillips, Caryl. *Cambridge*. 1991. New York: Vintage, 1993.

———. Conversation with author, New York City, Jan. 1998.

———, ed. *Extravagant Strangers: A Literature of Belonging*. New York: Vintage, 1999.

———. Interview with Graham Swift. *Kunapipi* 13.3 (1991): 96–103.

———. Interview with Louise Yelin. *Culturefront* 7.2 (1998): 52–54, 80.

Phillips, Mike, and Trevor Phillips. *Windrush: The Irresistible Rise of Multiracial Britain*. London: Harper, 1999.

Said, Edward W. *Culture and Imperialism*. New York: Knopf, 1993.

Sanger, C. P. "The Structure of *Wuthering Heights*." Wuthering Heights: *A Norton Critical Edition*. Ed. Willliam M. Sale, Jr. 2nd ed. New York: Norton, 1962. 286–98.

Schweickart, Patrocinio P. "Reading Ourselves: Toward a Feminist Theory of Reading." *Gender and Reading: Essays on Readers, Texts, and Contexts*. Ed. Elizabeth A. Flynn and Schweickart. Baltimore: Johns Hopkins UP, 1986. 31–62.

Sharrad, Paul. "Speaking the Unspeakable: London, Cambridge, and the Caribbean." *De-scribing Empire: Post-colonialism and Textuality*. Ed. Chris Tiffin and Alan Lawson. New York: Routledge, 1994.

Von Sneidern, Maja-Lisa. "*Wuthering Heights* and the Slave Trade." *ELH* 62 (1995): 171–97.

When a "Speck" Begins to Read: Literacy and the Politics of Self-Improvement in Nineteenth-Century British Working-Class Autobiography

Kelly J. Mays

> *Another ignorant brute of a spinner whom I pieced for, had a great incli-*
> *nation to use his hand as an instrument of punishment. . . . I am glad,*
> *however, to hear that he has since learned to read, and has become a*
> *worthy member of society.*
> WILLIAM DODD, 1841

In 1824, Thomas Cooper made a vow. Giving up the Lincolnshire dialect he had grown up speaking, the nineteen-year-old shoe-maker promised himself that he would henceforth "speak grammat-ically, and pronounce with propriety" (56). It was a difficult promise to make and keep mainly because it changed his relationships with others. As he explains in his autobiography:

> Now, to hear a youth in mean clothing, sitting at the shoemaker's stall, pursuing one of the lowliest callings, speak in what seemed to some of [the neighbors] almost a foreign dialect, raised positive anger and scorn in some, and amazement in others. Who was I, that I should sit on the cobbler's stall, and "talk fine"! They could not understand it. With Whillock and my intellectual friends I had con-versed in the best and most refined English I could command; but I had used our plain old Lincolnshire dialect in talking to the neigh-bours. This was all to be laid aside now, and it took some courage to do it. Yet I persevered until the Doric was conquered. . . . (56–57)

Conquering "the Doric" demanded perseverance. But Cooper's "courage" was tested only because changing his speech meant both violating others' expectations about the behavior appropriate to a man of his station and endangering the sense of community with others secured by that behavior. Cleansing his speech of the dialect that he had grown up speaking and that his mother and neighbors continued to speak, Cooper publicly differentiated himself from them. Adopting the "fine" language he had learned through books and "intellectual converse" (53), he announced his allegiance not only to his "intellectual friends" but also to what we might, following Benedict Anderson, call the imagined community of Standard English speakers. Yet Cooper continues to identify with all these communities and never presents the choice to speak grammatically as an attempt to claim middle-class status. In fact, he expresses uncertainty about whether he can fully communicate the cost of such behavior to readers who "can scarcely understand" (56). Cooper thus displays at least as much self-consciousness about the difference between himself and his non-working-class readers as about the difference between himself and his working-class neighbors. This moment of Cooper's narrative enacts the very thing it also describes—an acute sense of living across and trying to reconcile two cultures, two communities, and two identities.

Cooper's vow to speak grammatically was the most public of a series of vows through which he sought to reshape his life, community, and self in terms of an ideal learned from, and embodied in his commitment to, print and reading. Rocked by the death of one friend, encouraged by another, and inspired by reading Dr. Samuel Lee's biography and Kirke White's *Remains*, Cooper determined to be, like these men, "a scholar" (53). If his goal was straightforward, the route to it definitely was not. In addition to giving up his native dialect, Cooper vowed to have "no friend in addition to my new friend John Hough"; "to spend a couple of hours or more, every Saturday night, in intellectual converse" with Hough (53); to "combine the study of languages with that of mathematics; complete a full course [of reading] in ancient and modern history, and get an accurate and ample acquaintance with the literature of the day" (55); to memorize "the entire 'Paradise Lost' and seven of the best plays of Shakspeare" (57; spelling original); to pursue "a course of reading on the Evidences of Christianity" (56); and to "lead a strictly moral life," retiring "to pray at least once in the day-time" (57).

Both the nature of Cooper's vow and that he wrote them down underscore the role of print and reading in defining the new life, self, and community he sought to forge. Cooper's scheme centered on a commitment to studious reading, to the language of print, and to the friendship of those who shared this devotion and language. Print was the medium for, and reading his primary means of access to, all the courses of study he pursued. Thus if the changes in Cooper's speech most palpably and publicly marked the transformation of shoe-maker into scholar, reading was the means and measure of that transformation.

Cooper's *Life* is justifiably regarded as the prototypical story of the nineteenth-century working man dedicated to reading and self-improvement. Certainly it brings to the fore the vision of read-ing implicit in other working-class autobiographies. Some of the assumptions integral to this vision are succinctly expressed in my epigraph. Here, with almost breathtaking assurance, a self-described "factory cripple," William Dodd, informs his readers that the spinner who so often beat him during his early days in the cotton mill has "since learned to read" and thus "become a worthy member of society" (279). For Dodd, literacy measures and bridges the distance between ignorance and enlightenment and between animal violence and humanity, the mere ability to read producing profound and seemingly permanent changes in individual character and behavior. Dodd's vision of the change wrought by literacy is ultimately very like that expressed by Cooper and a host of other working-class readers who became autobiographers. Yet there is a key difference between Dodd and Cooper: Whereas Dodd implies that literacy is sufficient to trans-form brute into citizen, Cooper argues that this transformation results from using literacy the right way.

Cooper's view predominates in nineteenth-century working-class autobiographies. Few of them represent learning to read as the turning point it is for Dodd's spinner. But many do, like Cooper's, hinge on a dramatic moment in which the autobiographer's relation to books and the act of reading suddenly changes in a way that profoundly and irrevocably changes him or her. Autobiographers typically describe themselves as becoming—in and through this moment—"a student or an earnest reader," "a scholar," or "a great reader" (J. Wood 9; Cooper 53; Burt 46). They thus tend to describe what Annie Kenney labels the "great change" as unique because it is self-directed and as crucial because it transforms the reader into the worthy citizen described by Dodd. Though reading is often not the only activity associated with this change—as Cooper's almost dizzying list of vows illustrates—it does play a major role in what the historian David Vincent aptly labels a "secularized conversion experience," whose effects radiate outward, leaving "no part of the readers' lives untouched" (136). Key to that experience is a new sense of selfhood and agency predicated on a reconceptualization of the relation between reading and other activities, between leisure and work, and between the great reader and others.

To investigate further these elements of the great change and the role it plays in nineteenth-century working-class life narratives, the rest of this essay focuses primarily on two texts—William Edwin Adams's *Memoirs of a Social Atom*, first published serially from 1901 to 1902, and Annie Kenney's *Memories of a Militant*, first published in 1924. Both Adams and Kenney were political activists, or "politicians" in the nineteenth-century sense. A factory worker in her youth, Kenney left the factory to become a trade-unionist before helping to found and run the Women's Social and Political Union, turning herself into one of the most influential of the early suffragettes. Adams, born nearly a half century before Kenney, played an equally prominent role in a different cause. Trained as a printer, Adams wrote for and edited a series of radical newspapers and participated actively in the Chartist and Republican movements.

This essay argues that Adams, Kenney, and other working-class scholar-activists adopt the assumptions and values endemic to what the historian Thomas Laqueur calls the "culture of literacy."

Yet Laqueur's conclusions about the social and political ramifications of that adoption need to be complicated. Especially problematic are his assertions both that working-class men and women thereby demonstrated a "powerfu[l] attach[ment]" to "bourgeois definitions of improvement" and that this embourgeoisement hampered the development of working-class consciousness and solidarity (270). To complicate that conclusion, I build on Regenia Gagnier's arguments about the vision of subjectivity and community embodied in the texture and rhythm of working-class autobiographies. Accepting Gagnier's provocative claim that "there would have been no subjects of the modern labor movement without the creation of socio-political agency that actually occurs in" these narratives (164), I argue that reading plays a key role in this creation. In fact, at least some nineteenth-century working-class autobiographers thought literacy led not to embourgeoisement but to politicized forms of working-class and feminist consciousness.

"The Story Was the Great Thing": Early Reading Experiences and the Question of Agency

As Gagnier shows, a characteristic feature of nineteenth-century working-class autobiographies is their authors' tendency not to accept as a "given" the sense of individuality that middle-class autobiographers usually take for granted. Typically, the working-class writer registers an inability or unwillingness to see himself or herself as either "a significant agent worthy of the regard of others" or "an individuated 'ego.'" Instead, these writers begin their narratives by identifying themselves as indistinguishable parts of "the undifferentiated 'masses'" (141). Playing on his surname, for example, Adams opens his *Memoirs* by declaring, "I call myself a Social Atom—a small speck on the surface of society. The term indicates my insignificance. . . . In a word, I am just an ordinary person" (xiii).

Such "rhetorical modesty" arguably had everything to do with the autobiographers' status as "hands" whose working conditions "often mitigated against self-perception as an integrated, autonomous agent" (Gagnier 142). Demonstrating this connection in a peculiarly forthright way, Kenney describes becoming a full-time factory worker at thirteen as a matter of "join[ing] the great masses whose lives were spent spinning and weaving cotton" (18). To her—as to other writers—this event confirms her own lack of individuality and agency, as well as her family's powerlessness. In her words, "It was not my parents' fault that I was sent to the factory at such an early age. It was force of circumstances" (20). Continuing to stress the "force of circumstances," Kenney recounts her first years as a full timer: "A few years passed, all very much the same, work all day, play at night; on Saturday afternoons, play; on Sundays, Sunday School, Church, walks; and on Monday work again" (20). Reducing four years of her life to a single sentence without a subject, Kenney highlights the way in which her life—like that of those around her—followed an unchanging pattern defined by the factory and the church. And, indeed, Kenney implies that finally becoming a full-timer merely affirmed the power the factory had always exercised over the texture and rhythm of her family's life: each night during her early years, she remembers, "all the children, including myself and the others younger than I" would sit "on the window-sill watching the lights in the cotton factory, a few miles away, gradually going out. Those lights were our signal to retire" (3).

At least initially, then, Kenney and Adams derive their identity and writerly authority from their very insignificance. Their lack of individuality and agency enables them to speak as and for all "specks" and "social atoms."

And Adams and Kenney continue to speak from the position of the ordinary worker as they sketch the history of their early lives as readers. Though they explain how they learned to read, they don't envision reading as distinguishing them from other members of society. As Adams writes of his experience at a private academy,

"I learned to read and write—that was all" (76). Adams refers in the third person to "the nervous and excited reader" he was as a child, encouraging us to believe that his reading habits made him like all the "poor lads of sixty years ago" who "had to be satisfied with literary matter of a parlous character" (107). Similarly, Kenney turns to the first-person plural when she remembers the "one redeeming feature" of her life as a half-timer: "We used to go shares in a weekly girls' paper" (16).

For Kenney, such readerly acts weren't distinctive largely because the experience of reading the stories offered in the weekly girls' paper seemed very like the experience of listening to the stories adults told or read to her. Like Kenney, most of the autobiographers began their lives in a world filled with storytelling and reading—a world in which there seemed little distinction between the two.

The stories themselves link these various acts and experiences. For the autobiographers, the awareness of these stories drives and defines early efforts as reader. During her first stint away from home, the domestic servant Janet Bathgate taught herself to read only because she wanted to "read for herself the stories" in the Bible (84). According to Adams, the "story was the great thing" (101).

The desire for this "great thing" determined what and how young readers chose to read (when given any choice). The rather infamous Chartist and Nonconformist minister Joseph Barker, for example, sought any "fairy tales [he] could get hold of, and any kind of wild and foolish romances" (117), and he approached every text with the aim of extracting from it just such a tale: "My chief reason for wishing to see [Richard Burdsall's *Memoirs*] was, that I had heard there were some ghost stories in it. . . . I cared little about the rest of the book. I was impatient till I came to that story, and then I was satisfied. The other parts of the book I either did not understand or did not relish. But that story I did relish . . ." (116–17).

Likewise, the tailor Thomas Carter navigated around "the merely perceptive and . . . doctrinal parts of the Scriptures" to get to the exciting stories or "wonderful events" related there (29–30), and the weaver-poet Samuel Bamford regarded the New Testament as a "storybook," "read[ing] it all through and through," "more for the interest the marvelous passages excited, than from any religious impression which they created" (89).

Through such aggressively selective reading, young readers could and did make the most of their limited reading matter. The London-born George Acorn became adept at turning texts designed for others' purposes into ones that suited his own:

> I used to skip the parts that moralized, or painted verbal scenery, a practice at which I became very dexterous. Such mental gymnastics were forced upon me by the flood of goody-goody literature which was poured in upon us. Kindly institutions sought to lead us into the right path by giving us endless tracts, or books in which the comparative pill of religious teaching was clumsily coated by a mild story. It was necessary in self-defence to pick out the interesting parts, which to me at that time were certainly not those that led to the hero's conversion, or the heroine's first prayer. (50)

Converting any and every text into the storybook for which he longed, Acorn rejected the ideological "pill" in order to relish its delicious "coat."

Yet in describing their childhood reading, most autobiographers in fact tend to highlight not the mental dexterity and independence entailed in such "mental gymnastics," but rather the lack of judgment, discernment, or even agency displayed in the process. Above all, they lament the youthful inability to discriminate between life and literature, fact and fiction, or history and romance. After Adams borrowed a copy of *Villeroy, or the Horrors of Zindorf Castle* (105), he felt so certain that the "robbers and murderers" of the story were about to come through the front door that he read the chapbook with "the carving knife on the table beside him" (106). The bookbinder and labor unionist Frederick Rogers says he ran "with a beating heart" through the "dark street[s]" of East London "lest I should meet any of the evil things Bunyan so vividly described" (6). In the words of Thomas Burt, a miner turned Labour member of Parliament, the greatest "gusto" was felt for "highly-spiced" "adventures" and "wild, romantic stories" (114). But the autobiographers repeatedly avow that in their youth they read such stories as "book[s] of history," "real matter of fact" (Barker 116).

In these terms the most common and revealing scenes are those, like Rogers's, that focus on first encounters with John Bunyan's *Pilgrim's Progress*. Barker, for example, reports that he "regarded" the book "as a history. I had no idea that it was a parable or an allegory. My impression was, that the whole was literal and true,— that there was, somewhere in the world, a real city of destruction and a new Jerusalem, and that from the one to the other there was a path through some part of the country . . ." (116). Burt viewed Pilgrim's story not "as a dream or allegory, but as solid literal history," noting that he "believed every word of it" (115). So convinced of the book's veracity was the weaver-poet John Leatherland that he "often wished [his] mother to set out, with [him] and [his] sister, upon the journey." Though his mother "endeavoured to explain that it set forth the pilgrimage through this world to a better," Leatherland "could not understand how it could be, and longed to visit the House Beautiful . . ." (4–5). Such confusions of fact and fancy could and did occur with many works besides Bunyan's, as Adams's remarks about his failure to comprehend either the "religious meaning" of *Pilgrim's Progress* or the "satirical meaning" of *Gulliver's Travels* indicate (101). However, the wide availability and popularity of *Pilgrim's Progress* combined with its obviously allegorical form to ensure that encounters with it were memorable and meaningful, especially in terms of demonstrating the guileless literal-mindedness of young readers.

These accounts of early reading represent the inability to tell fact from fiction as a kind of failure—the hallmark of a reading process that involves a great deal of sensual or bodily engagement, activity, and pleasure, on the one hand, and, on the other, the reader's utter mental subjection. Depicting himself as following "the development of the drama" of *Villeroy* "with absorbing interest and terror," Adams portrays himself as one possessed. The fact that he armed himself with a knife proves, he says, how

"entirely . . . this idea" (that he was about to be robbed or mur-
dered by *Villeroy*'s characters) "obtain[ed] possession of his morbid and juvenile mind" (106). Adams encourages us to dwell on
the young reader's helplessness and intellectual passivity, letting
"this idea" dominate his sentence just as it once dominated his
mind and stressing his fear of what others might do to him.

In this way the child's inability or unwillingness to distinguish
fact from fiction, his or her mental subjection to the text, and the
emphatically bodily character of a reading process driven by the
desire for story seem to feed the autobiographers' inability to experience or represent themselves as "integrated autonomous agent[s]"
(Gagnier 142). And it seems no accident that the stories that Adams
and Kenney read in their youth are either tales that focus wholly on
aristocratic life or tales in which (active) aristocratic characters vic-
timize or rescue (passive) working-class characters. Kenney explicitly draws attention to this characteristic in the weekly girls' paper
when she explains that they featured "titles, wealth, Mayfair, dukes,
and factory girls" (16).

The Great Change: Forging the Autonomous Self through "Earnest Reading"

De-emphasizing the extraordinariness of the ability to read and
their early reading experiences, most autobiographers organize their
narratives around the later and more-definitive change in their reading that occurs when they become "a student or an earnest reader,"
"a scholar," or "a great reader." According to such narratives a great
reader is defined by a conscientious dedication to reading and a tendency to read to gain the permanent possession of ideas and useful
knowledge rather than to experience temporary pleasure. Through
their approach to reading the autobiographers ironically become new
persons by becoming more thoroughly themselves—experiencing
themselves as individuals, self-determining agents in ways they had
not previously. The great change thus fosters a new sense of self
predicated on an understanding of the relations between reading

and other activities; between the great reader and other people; and between past, present, and future. Reading is thus not play or bodily pleasure but a uniquely educative act crucial to the lifelong process of mental and moral improvement.

To convey a vivid sense of the particular shape this literary conversion experience takes, I quote from the relevant passages in Adams's and Kenney's autobiographies. The following passage from Adams's *Memoirs* comes directly after his account of reading *Villeroy*:

> It may be that stories of the "Villeroy" stamp . . . encouraged and developed the taste for reading; and the taste for reading, once acquired, came in due course to need higher pabulum to satisfy it. Before it could be satisfied, a complete revolution in companions became necessary. Frequent occasions had arisen for feeling dissatisfied with the chums of my boyhood—once particularly when some of them, having taken a bird's nest, tore the little fledglings to pieces. . . . Other incidents occurred to produce estrangement. Some of the lads had already begun to contract bad habits. Was there not a danger that bad habits would be contracted by all the rest? I resolved to sever the connection. One Sunday afternoon the usual call was made for a ramble in the fields. Word was sent to the callers that their old companion was not going to join them. I heard from an upper room, not without a certain amount of tremor, their exclamations of surprise. They wandered off into the fields in one direction; I, with a new companion, wandered off into the fields of another. My new companion was Young's "Night Thoughts." The old companions were never joined again. A new life had begun. (107–08)

The dramatic turn in Kenney's narrative follows her one-sentence description of factory life. Here she recounts the moment when, at age seventeen, she went alone to the Oldham Library and there read "with the greatest fervour" a special issue of the *Rational Review* dedicated to Voltaire:

> In the same *Review* it said: "Voltaire did more than any other Frenchman to make the people think." I can only say that he started a train of thought within me which has never ceased to vibrate.

> One thought leads to another, one discovery leads to other unex-
> plored regions. This year came the great change in my life. Out-
> wardly I was the same happy-go-lucky-devil-may-care-come-and-go
> person as before. Inwardly it was a year of self-contemplation, deep
> meditation and secret communion with my higher self. . . .
> When I was twenty life wore a still more serious aspect. I became
> interested in Labour, or I should say in Robert Blatchford's articles
> appearing in the *Clarion*. . . . Thousands of men and women in the
> Lancashire factories owe their education to Robert Blatchford. (22–23)

Kenney's reference to Blatchford as her "literary father and mother," like Adams's reference to his "new life," casts the great change as a kind of rebirth into selfhood that is associated with a bourgeoning desire for solitude. Thus whether venturing alone into the Oldham Library to hold converse with Voltaire, forsaking "boyhood" "chums" to wander alone in the fields with a book of poems, or vowing not to speak in dialect, Adams, Kenney, and Cooper literally and symbolically begin to distance themselves from other ordinary "lads" and factory girls. The new sense of individuality secured through spatial as well as social segregation is communicated in a variety of ways. Adams, for example, uses the first-person singular rather than the first-person plural. Kenney calls attention to the split between the outward "happy-go-lucky" person she still appeared to be to others and the "higher self" others never saw, while Cooper does much the same thing by dividing this portion of his life into two chapters entitled "Shoe-maker Life: Early Friendships" and "Student Life: Its Enjoyments."

Cooper's organizational strategy, like Kenney's choice to move straight from her sentence about factory life to the story of her morning in the Oldham Library, foregrounds a pattern many auto-biographies follow. Most describe the great change as occurring just after the autobiographers become full-time workers or appren-tices, regardless of the chronological relation between these events. On the one hand, such narrative timing ensures that the great change becomes materially and symbolically linked to the movement into the world beyond the family and immediate neighborhood and

toward socioeconomic independence and the adult status this con-
fers. Adams describes his apprenticeship to a printer at fourteen as
the beginning of "the real business of life": "The regret felt at leaving school just then . . . was speedily submerged by the new delight
of mixing with men in a workshop. I was a boy still, but I thought
myself a man" (80). Likewise, Mary Smith asserts that her "woman's
life in reality commenced" the day she began to work alongside her
brother managing a grocery and provision shop (50). Again, the
great change immediately follows the commencement of working
life, and becoming a scholar thus seems like a natural extension
of maturation.

On the other hand, however, this sequence differentiates, even as
it aligns, the two experiences. Although Adams "thought himself a
man" when he went to work, he also felt "regret" at leaving school;
and although he was among the lucky few whose parents were able
to apprentice him and allow him some choice about which trade he
would enter, he had little say about whether and when those
choices would be made: "the time had arrived when I must choose"
(80). Smith claims she had no choice at all. Though entrance into
the world of work signified socioeconomic independence and adulthood, it was seldom seen as a matter of individual, or even familial,
choice. The move thus often signals both the interdependence of
the family's various members and the family's limited power in the
world. As the Dundee factory boy puts it, his mother was "forced to
make her child a slave," "depending for bread on the use of its bones
and sinews" (*Chapters* 11). The autobiographers repeatedly draw
attention to the mandatory nature of work for them and their families, as well as their lack of control over the poor conditions of the
workplace.

Acorn remembers his initiation into full-time work in a chapter
called "I Am Launched," a title that communicates much about the
ambiguities of being "launched" by others into economic selfhood.
So too does Carter's statement, "When the time of my going to
school was ended, the question arose *how I should be disposed
of . . .*" (67; emphasis mine). Though Bathgate uses the third

person to refer to herself throughout her autobiography, this narrative strategy takes on a new resonance and a new poignancy when she recalls being sent into service for the first time: "Jenny's consent was never asked," she writes (88).

Even as descriptions of the great change clearly draw on and enhance correlations among independence, adulthood, and work, they also suggest that earnest reading enables a kind of independence, selfhood, and agency that isn't fostered by being a worker. The autobiographers insist that they had little or no choice about whether, when, and how to be workers. But they clearly and unanimously affirm that they chose to be great readers, that this choice had everything to do with taking control of their characters and their lives, and that the great reader was, by definition, a person who could and did exercise the power to choose in a way unlike social atoms and factory girls.

Not surprisingly, the workplace often temporarily disappears from the autobiographies in the wake of the great change as leisure time and activities become more significant than the hours spent in factory, workshop, or mine. Recognizing a split between the outwardly carefree person she had always been in the factory and the serious, inward meditator she became in the Oldham Library, Kenney discovers and cultivates her new self during her leisure hours and through her far from leisurely reading.

The reading practices of Kenney and the other autobiographers emphasize mind rather than body and depend on the oppositions encoded in Adams's assertion that "[t]he hands were for wages; but the brain was for nobler uses" and on the assumption that serious reading was preeminent among the nobler uses of self and leisure (397). As Bamford writes, "When I first plunged, as it were, into the blessed habit of reading, faculties which had hitherto given but small intimation of existence, suddenly sprung into vigorous action" (91). "[M]y mind seemed to be awakened to a new mental existence," reports the Chartist William Lovett (36). Through its very redundancy the phrase "mental" awakening of "mind," like Bamford's reference to the springing into "action" of once-dormant "faculties," eloquently and economically articulates the Enlightenment-tinged parameters of the great change. Though mind is, Lovett and Bamford imply, an innate faculty, its awakening proves to be a transformative experience for someone who had previously seen himself or herself only as a working body. Making this point in similar terms, Sam Neil, coal hewer and secretary of the Northumberland Miners' Association, urged his fellow miners to support university extension in 1884: "You, on whose shoulders the drudgery of the world falls—you, whose physical energies are taxed to the utmost—you are asked to make possible the cultivation of those moral and intellectual faculties which you in common with all men possess. . . . these are the faculties which raise men above the brute creation, and . . . it is only by their cultivation that he can enjoy his life thoroughly" (qtd. in Rogers 100–01). Taxing only "physical energies," the drudgery of work dehumanizes by reducing the individual to the "brute" body or even its component parts, hands and shoulders.

Neil's remarks remind us of Dodd's "ignorant brute of a spinner" transformed through literacy and the Dundee factory boy's vision of himself as a collection of marketable body parts. Tellingly, the factory boy was rescued by an accidental encounter with a book that first "awakened" and "stirred" his "mind" and "set [him] on a career of reading and thinking" (*Chapters* 35). For the factory boy, as for Hannah Mitchell and so many others, the result is a new sense of the self as an integrated, autonomous being "with [one's] own individuality [and] soul" and, above all, one's own active and developing mind (Mitchell 242). In the words of the shoemaker John Younger, "I began . . . to regard my own mind as the only wealth of property I should ever possess in this world, and therefore determined to take care of its health, whatever might be the servitude to which the attached body might be subjected" (qtd. in Vincent 164). To Younger, as to Cooper and Kenney, the mind-centered self cultivated through reading is not only independent but also authentic in a way the laboring, body-centered self is not. When the London-born Kathleen Woodward first secured a room in which she could pore alone over the books that were her only private property, she saw it as her "citadel," the "reward of [her] imposture at the factory" (134). In its "solitude," she was "recreated . . . girded, armored for the day . . . and [for] the people whose very presence laughed at [her] secret thoughts" (135).

Only in her room and through her reading can Woodward begin both to see herself as more than a serviceable body and to resist the subjection of mind to body that she sees as simultaneously the product, sign, and cause of workers' economic, social, and political subjection and abjection. In this way, reading facilitates the mental liberation that alone makes more worldly kinds of liberation thinkable. Describing his neighbors in the slums of East London, Acorn laments, "These people lead mechanical lives. . . . The mind is never used at all; it is simply animal against animal, via conventional routes" (65). Key here is the equation between animality and conventionality on the one hand and intellection and active resistance on the other. For what most disturbs Acorn is his fellow slum dwellers' fatalism, their tendency to see their condition as inevitable and natural. Acorn conceives his difference from them— a difference vouchsafed by and demonstrated through his reading—as inhering in his ability and desire to question the adverse circumstances and low social position that he shares with them:

> I had too much self-esteem quietly to accept the social status in which I found myself, whereas, so far as I could see, my companions were not only contented, but had never thought of questioning their lives. I had always questioned my environment, although to be sure at first it caused me to wonder whether my discontent was not due to some moral obliquity or mental kink which prevented me from falling peacefully into my allotted place and position in life.
>
> As I grew older . . . I came to see . . . that I was not like a section of a jigsaw puzzle, formed simply for the purpose of fitting into one particular corner of the social picture. . . . (81–82)

Unlike Acorn, who avows that he "had always questioned [his] environment," most of the autobiographers see themselves as having to be awakened to this capacity to question. Only through reading did Lovett "for the first time" realize "how deficient" he was in "being able to give a reason for the opinions and the hopes [he] entertained" (35–36). Reading alone, it seems, produces the desire and ability to question one's environment, to analyze the beliefs that one had accepted before, and to articulate one's own views.

Earnest reading differs from work in part simply because one freely chooses to do it and is valued because it enables one to recognize and embrace the very power to choose, if only—at first—what to think and believe. As Robert Lowery writes of his time in a Canadian hospital:

> At this time commenced the more complete exercise of my thinking and reflective faculties. Up to this time I had read but few books, . . . and had therefore no ideas, so to speak, of my own. Those I had, had been given me by others, and had not been analyzed by me, or made my own. As I sat in bed day and night, . . . the mind as it were rose and came forth, to ask of, and examine, this and that of life and its future, which I had scarcely thought of before. (54–55)

For Lowery and others, this ability to master and own ideas distinguishes human beings from animals and adults from children (as well as, perhaps, men from women) in a way working never could: "Men of strong minds rest not till they have a reason to give for the faith that is in them, and in passing from boyhood into the full manhood of their existence . . . they begin to question the opinions which they have received. . . . They desire to be *masters* of the opinions which hitherto they have only *submitted* to" (71; emphasis mine).

Lowery's diction suggests the social, class-inflected framework within which he and others understand the nature and significance of mental independence. Here, mastery of ideas through reading translates into criticism and at least potential mastery of material, social, and economic conditions or what Kenney calls "the force of circumstances." Although Dodd "pursu[ed]" his "studies" because they afforded escape from "thoughts of [his] unhappy condition," their most significant effect was to make him aware just how unjust, unnatural, and changeable that condition was:

[I]n proportion as the truths of science were unfolded to my wondering sight, and the mists of ignorance chased from my mind, so the horrors of my situation became daily more and more apparent, and made me, if possible, still more fretful and unhappy! It was evident to me, that I was intended for a nobler purpose than to be a factory slave! and I longed for an opportunity to burst the trammels by which I was kept in bondage! (288)

For Dodd, as for Lowery, reading's significance resides in its emancipatory effects, the way it enables one to recognize injustices and to feel capable of effecting change.

Of course, the autobiographers do not believe all reading has such emancipatory effects. Instead, and as the retrospective accounts of childhood reading demonstrate, these effects both depend on and encourage specific reading strategies and specific textual choices. For example, I have quoted Lowery as saying simply that "Up to th[e] time" of his intellectual awakening he "had read but few books. . . ." Yet the full sentence in fact reads, "Up to this time I had read but few books, *merely feeling interest in the poetry, imagination, or incidents*, and had therefore no ideas, so to speak, of my own" (54–55; emphasis mine). Lowery implies that adult, emancipatory reading entails valuing texts not for their "poetry" and "incidents" but for the "ideas" texts contain and the critical thinking they inspire. Whereas reading for incident is a thing of the moment, reading for ideas is a means of preparing for the future, both by increasing one's "deposit of knowledge" and by learning to "form [one's] own judgment" (T. Wood 9; Smith 203).

To some extent, this sense of forward-looking purpose renders reading serious and scholarly regardless of what is read. Thomas Carter argues that because his "prevailing desire was to obtain some useful knowledge," his reading of light literature did him more good than "harm" (28). Yet Carter and others typically portray intellectual awakening as also beginning with and inspiring profound changes in what, as well as how, they read. After all, the pivotal moment in Kenney's life occurs when she substitutes the

Rational Review for the weekly girls' paper, in Adams's when he chooses Young's poetry over *Villeroy*. Most of the autobiographers recount similar changes as they begin to seek out texts very different from those they had most enjoyed as children.

Fact is now distinguished from and often valued over fiction, the newly serious self finding its most appropriate food in serious reading matter. In the wake of his own intellectual and religious conversion, Barker gave up "novels" and vowed instead—in a fashion reminiscent of Cooper—to read "the scriptures daily," to commit "some portions" of them "to memory" "every day," and to learn "nearly all the hymns" in his hymnal (111–12). As he explains, "After I began to be religious I began to read a new order of books altogether. I thought it my duty to read chiefly religious books, and I acted accordingly" (122). Though Barker's emphasis on religion distinguishes his intellectual conversion from some others, his narrative makes clear that Barker was guided primarily by a rationalist preference for fact over fiction. Formerly Barker had sought out the most "wild and foolish romances" and taken them for "history"(116–17). Now he not only eschews fiction but also expresses distaste for nonfictional works that seem full of "confusion, inconsistency, and folly." Above all, Barker "wanted something plain and true; something rational and practical" (123). This desire soon led him to widen the scope of his reading dramatically, as he turned from "reading books on religion" to teaching himself Latin, Greek, and "a system of shorthand writing"; to "study[ing] Arithmetic," "Grammar, Mensuration, Algebra, and the like"; and to reading "History, especially the History of England, and Rollins's Ancient History" (138–39). In its variety and ambition and in its rationalist leanings, this course of scholarly reading closely parallels that which Cooper and many other autobiographers undertook in the years of intensive study that followed the great change.

The commitment to logic and reason that was so crucial a part of the great change determined both the preference for nonfiction and the standards by which all reading matter was judged. That preference obviously grows out of the association of fiction with animality, childishness, and subjection. Thus Adams opposes "bad habits," mindless violence, and "exciting" "stories of the 'Villeroy' stamp" to good habits and the "higher pabulum" of Young's poetry. Kenney juxtaposes factory life, "happy-go-lucky" mindlessness, and "wild romances" with solitude, intellection, and the *Rational Review*. And both narrators depict themselves as reborn through the act of foregoing what Barker calls "wild" and "fitful" "ecstasies" and seeking out the "stable pleasures" of "the healthy and rational man [sic]" (102).

Though each of the autobiographies has its unique elements, the basic outline of the great change and the terms that give it shape and meaning are remarkably consistent—the association of reading with seriousness and rationality; with the pursuit of useful knowledge; with an assertion of the author's difference and independence from neighbors, family members, and workmates; with a realignment of the relations between work and leisure; with the discovery of a private, higher self capable and worthy of cultivation. The great change thus had everything to do with recognizing and affirming that, in Acorn's words, "it was a man's duty to perfect himself during this life" (288); that the mind was the primary site of one's perfectible individuality; that reason was the single most important mental faculty; and that reading was the best way to cultivate self, mind, and reason.

The "Interest in Labour," the "Passion for Politics": The Communities of Working-Class Scholar-Activists

Adams and Kenney launch themselves on the path of self-improvement through their reading habits, and their choosing the companionship of a text over that of their friends is significant. For in all of these narratives, the sense of individuality fostered by reading entails a "long[ing] for solitude" (Mitchell 240), a determination to "become solitary" (Cooper 53). And this desire for spatial separation from others sometimes has profound social consequences, which is clear in Adams's autobiography. The oppositions—between body and mind, bad habits and good ones, brutality

and enlightenment—differentiate the new adult Adams from the
old childish one by separating him from the nameless "poor lads"
who had once been his constant companions. In "Coddling and Culture," the chapter that follows the story of that fateful Sunday, these
social distinctions are rendered explicit and general. For here Adams
argues that the "few facilities" available to the poor in his youth distinguished all "those who had the perseverance and the capacity to
penetrate" "culture" from all those who lacked these qualities, all
those who "kept our tools bright and keen with constant friction"
from all those who "neglected" those tools and "left" them "to rust
and decay" (111). The agency Adams sees himself as achieving and
demonstrating through earnest reading turns into a general standard for discriminating between "the fit and the unfit," those who
used the tools of literacy and print to emancipate themselves and
those who remained the tools of others.

At least to this point, Adams's narrative exemplifies the more
individualist elements and divisive effects of the paradigm of literacy
and improvement sketched in these autobiographies. For, like
Cooper, Kenney, and Woodward, Adams here embraces a model of
autonomous selfhood and agency that we might describe as bourgeois and that secures distinctions among workers. Labeling as
bourgeois these narratives and the assumptions and values that
drive them would mean interpreting them in the same way that
Cooper feared his neighbors would interpret his choice to speak
grammatically—as demonstrating that he repudiated the community from which he sprang. This interpretation accords with
Laqueur's argument that working-class scholar-activists demonstrate their bourgeois allegiance by embracing the culture of literacy. By this logic, Dodd's condemnation of the base and illiterate
spinner, Acorn's desire to distance himself from his animalistic peers,
Woodward's retreat into her private room, and Adams's decision
not to play with old friends illustrate how the "new cultural meaning of literacy" "drove a wedge through the working class" by
sharply dividing "the respectable from the non-respectable poor"
(Laqueur 270).

On the one hand, Laqueur is right: these great readers do see their reading as enlightening and emancipating them, giving them a sense of individual autonomy and agency that differentiates them from other unenlightened, nonrespectable, or even unfit workers. In some ways, that achievement, as well as the mature, critical reading process so central to it, was the very condition of possibility for the autobiographies themselves, enabling these writers to analyze their experiences and inspiring them to share it. They emphasize the great change precisely because, as they look back over their lives, they are moved both by a desire to understand and explain how they learned to master the forces that once threatened to overmaster them and by a sense of pride in the achievements that mastery made possible.

On the other hand, however, Laqueur's argument needs to be complicated (as Cooper's fear that his behavior will be misinterpreted by others begins to suggest). For Cooper and his fellow autobiographers want to explain how they liberated themselves through reading precisely because they identify with other workers, even or especially those unenlightened workers who, in their eyes, continue to be controlled by circumstances and by others' words and ideas—just as they once had been. As we've seen in Cooper's example, the imagined and real audience for these autobiographies clearly crossed class divides. But Cooper, like his fellow writers, pays special attention to young working-class readers, his goal being to serve as an inspiration and role model for them just as the weaver-poet Kirke White did for him. Burt, who greatly admired *The Narrative of Frederick Douglass*, hopes that by recounting his own efforts "to acquire knowledge and self-discipline under extreme difficulties," he "may encourage youths of the working class, with better opportunities than [his], to put forth their utmost efforts in the same direction" (19–20). John Wilson highlights the sense of mission and of class solidarity, tradition, and pride that the autobiographies seek to foster when he concludes his *Memories of a Labour Leader* by warning his young readers that they are "debtors" to the past. Owing their manifold "opportunities" to "the great hearts who laboured" on their behalf, young readers should feel equally indebted to the present and future, being "in duty bound to hand that legacy on in increased value to [their] successors" (317). Through his Bunyanesque language, Wilson exhorts young working-class readers to become pilgrims in an ongoing, collective march toward the figurative celestial city (317).

As Wilson's words amply demonstrate, the great change does not turn these autobiographers into aloof individualists bent solely on bettering either their own personal condition or that of a respectable elite. Instead, the great change leads to a political awakening grounded in a critical stance toward the class system; a palpable sense of belonging to the imagined community of workers and, sometimes, women; and a commitment to actualizing that community. Reading leads not to embourgeoisement but to politicized forms of group consciousness and to forms of collective activism designed to foster group solidarity and emancipation. In these narratives, the moment of individuation, differentiation, and retreat to the private realm is just that—a moment—and one that is important precisely because it facilitates a subsequent movement outward as these scholars become public activists.

Tellingly, Adams begins to describe the new life by asserting his likeness to other workers: "I was only a very ordinary lad," "a very youthful atom" (112). At the same time, he returns to a plural narrative voice: "We were fond of controversy in those days, some of us because we wanted to propagate what we thought were new ideas" (116). "[O]ff with the old companions and . . . on with the new" (112), Adams writes, once again defining himself as an indistinguishable part of a collectivity. Far from recounting the wholesale retreat into solitary, private study that one might expect, Adams reports that he began to study French "with another youth" and phonography with a "disciple" of Pitman, attending "classes or meetings every night in the week" (112–13). Adams and his fellow students brought this rhetoric to life and created organizations devoted to educational, social, and political activities and goals. These organizations included the Cheltenham General Literary Union, the People's Institute, the

National Charter Association, and eventually the Cheltenham Republican Association. Adams henceforth consistently represents reading and improvement as simultaneously communal and individual enterprises.

Similarly, Kenney ends her narrative of the great change by avowing that reading led to her decision to join a socialist choir and eventually the trade union and the Women's Social and Political Union. "The reading of books made me more serious," she explains, "and at last I decided to join the Oldham Clarion Vocal Union. I could not sing, but I . . . felt I should meet others whose ideas were very much like my own, which really meant that they were *Clarion* readers" (24). By joining the Clarion choir, Kenney, like Adams, began to seek out those who were equally dedicated to cultivating their own minds to change the world around them. "Secret communion with [her] higher self" through private reading turns into communion with others and into relationships based on ideas and ideals rather than circumstances.

These relationships are grounded in ideas in the sense that they actualize the idea of community produced, in Kenney's eyes, by her reading. As she "became interested in Labour," she began to see herself and those around her as laborers, appreciating in a new way their connection to the "[t]housands of men and women in the Lancashire factories" and, eventually, what it meant to be a woman (23). Because of these overlapping interests and commitments, Kenney would eventually leave the factory and the companions of her youth. She mourned that separation, depicting her first visit to the Pankhurst home as the second major turning point in her story: "For the first time in my life I experienced great loneliness. I instinctively felt that a[nother] great change had come. I was losing my old girlfriends of the factory" (28). Yet Kenney suggests that losing contact with her old girlfriends was a necessary step on the road to devoting her life to changing theirs. Her subsequent activism expressed her commitment to "the simple, big-hearted, book-loving, wisdom-seeking people whose lives were spent in the dark mines and the over-heated cotton factories of the North" (24). In fact, leaving the factory ensured that Kenney would always be—for herself and others—a factory girl. She fully appreciated the truth and the irony of that label. Of her first public speech (in support of Keir Hardie's Parliamentary campaign), she declares, "It could not have been my eloquence that was the draw, for my speeches were too often incoherent. But I had worked in a factory!" (56).

The later histories of Adams and other working-class autobiographers obviously differ a great deal from Kenney's. Few achieved Kenney's renown or left manual labor permanently behind them. But underlying all these histories is the same connection between culture and politics, self and mutual improvement, intellectual awakening and activism. To take just one more example, Frederick Rogers—the little boy who once ran through London's dark streets to escape the "evil things . . . so vividly described" in *Pilgrim's Progress*—eventually assumed leadership roles in—to name just a few—the East London University Extension movement, the Toynbee Hall education committee and its Elizabethan Literary Society (which he helped to found), the Vellum Binders' Trade Society, the London Trades Council, the National Committee of Organised Labour, and the committee's successful campaign to make old-age pensions "the law of the land" (266–67). In other words, Adams speaks for Rogers and many others when he declares, "With the desire for culture there had come a passion for politics" (112), when he insists that the activism spawned by this passion was undertaken on behalf of the whole working population (237), and when he figures this struggle as one that links individual (mental and moral) and mutual (social, economic, and political) improvement.

For these autobiographers, scholarship and activism were one. Earnest reading and the achievement of mind over matter that reading enabled were crucial to efforts to ensure that no worker was simply a hand destined to do others' work but was instead a human being with the same faculties, desires, and rights as those who "had the leisure to do as [they] pleased" (Shaw 21). Mature readers' ability to separate fact from fiction translates into a refusal either to remain sociopolitical children or to accept the fictions that justified social distinctions and injustice. However much the culture of literacy may have divided the respectable from the nonrespectable or the working woman from the working man, it also did much to create both the idea of a community that transcended those divisions and the agency and passion necessary to make that ideal real.

WORKS CITED

Acorn, George [pseud.]. *One of the Multitude.* London: Heinemann, 1911.

Adams, William Edwin. *Memoirs of a Social Atom.* 2 vols. London, 1903. 2 vols. in 1. New York: Kelley, 1968.

Anderson, Benedict. *Imagined Communities: Reflections on the Origin and Spread of Nationalism.* London: Verso, 1983.

Bamford, Samuel. *Early Days.* London: Simpkin, 1849. Rpt. in *The Autobiography of Samuel Bamford.* Volume 1. Ed. W. H. Chaloner. New York: Kelley, 1967.

[Barker, Joseph]. *The History and Confessions of a Man . . . Showing How He Became a Methodist and Methodist Preacher. . . .* London: Chapman, 1846.

Bathgate, Janet. *Aunt Janet's Legacy to Her Nieces: Recollections of Humble Life in Yarrow in the Beginning of the Nineteenth Century.* 3rd ed. [?] Selkirk: Lewis, 1901.

Burt, Thomas. *An Autobiography.* Supp. chs. by Aaron Watson. London: Unwin, 1924.

[Carter, Thomas]. *Memoirs of a Working Man.* London: Knight, 1845. Rpt. from *Penny Magazine* 11 May 1844.

Chapters in the Life of a Dundee Factory Boy. An Autobiography. Dundee: Myles, 1850.

Cooper, Thomas. *The Life of Thomas Cooper: Written by Himself.* 4th ed. London: Hodder, 1873.

Dodd, William. *A Narrative of the Experiences and Sufferings of William Dodd, a Factory Cripple, Written by Himself.* London, 1841. Cass Lib. of Industrial Classics 10. London: Cass, 1968.

Gagnier, Regenia. *Subjectivities: A History of Self-Representation in Britain, 1832–1920.* New York: Oxford UP, 1991.

Kenney, Annie. *Memories of a Militant.* London: Arnold, 1924.

Laqueur, Thomas. "The Cultural Origins of Popular Literacy in England, 1500–1850." *Oxford Review of Education* 2.3 (1976): 255–75.

Leatherland, J. A. *Essays and Poems, with a Brief Autobiographical Memoir.* London: Tweedie, 1862.

Lovett, William. *The Life and Struggles of William Lovett, in His Pursuit of Bread, Knowledge, and Freedom.* . . . London, 1876. The World of Labour, English Workers, 1850–1890. New York: Garland, 1984.

[Lowery, Robert]. "Passages in the Life of a Temperance Lecturer, Connected with the Public Movements of the Working Classes for the Last Twenty Years. By One of Their Order." *Weekly Record of the Temperance Movement* 15 Apr.; 30 May 1857. Rpt. in *Robert Lowery, Radical and Chartist.* Ed. Brian Harrison and Patricia Hollis. London: Europa, 1979. 37–194.

Mitchell, Hannah. *The Hard Way Up: The Autobiography of Hannah Mitchell, Suffragette and Rebel.* Ed. Geoffrey Mitchell. London: Faber, 1968.

Rogers, Frederick. *Labour, Life and Literature: Some Memories of Sixty Years.* London, 1913. Soc. and the Victorians Ser. 7. Brighton: Harvester, 1973.

[Shaw, Charles]. *When I Was a Child.* London, 1903. Firle, Eng.: Caliban, 1977.

Smith, Mary. *The Autobiography of Mary Smith, Schoolmistress and Nonconformist.* . . . London: Bemrose, 1892.

Vincent, David. *Bread, Knowledge, and Freedom: A Study of Nineteenth-Century Working Class Autobiography.* London: Europa, 1981.

Wilson, John. *Memories of a Labour Leader.* 1910. Firle, Eng.: Caliban, 1980.

Wood, John. *Autobiography of John Wood, an Old and Well Known Bradfordian, Written in the Seventy-Fifth Year of His Age.* Bradford: Chronicle and Mail, 1877.

Wood, Thomas. "Autobiography, 1822–1880." *Keighley News* 3, 10, 17, 24 Mar. 1956; 7, 14 Apr. 1956. Offprint in booklet form.

Woodward, Kathleen. *Jipping Street: Childhood in a London Slum.* New York: Harper, 1928.

"Some of Their Stories Are like My Life, I Guess": Working-Class Women Readers and Confessional Magazines

Jane Greer

Margaret Atwood opens her short story "True Trash" by describing a fictional reading site out of the 1950s. As the young waitresses at Camp Adanaqui sunbathe on their afternoon break, they read out loud from a *True Romance* magazine. On this particular afternoon, it is Joanne who is seemingly in control at this site as she reads "in a serious, histrionic voice" (5) with "a fake English accent" thrown in for "extra hilarity" (6). Joanne has selected the story of Marleen, a high school girl who works part-time in a shoe store to help her divorced mother meet their household expenses. Marleen is being pursued by two of the store's clerks. One is dependable and has matrimonial intentions; the other, named Dirk, "rides a motorcycle and has a knowing, audacious grin that turns Marleen's knees to jelly" (6). As Joanne moves through Marleen's story, most of the other waitresses (Hilary, Pat, Liz, Stephanie, Alex, Tricia, and Sandy) chime in with editorial comments and snickering asides. When Marleen's mother nags her about her falling grades, Hilary pipes up, "Oh God. . . . Someone please give her a double Scotch" (6). Liz brazenly suggests, "Maybe she [Marleen] should try out both of them [the store clerks], to see which one's the best" (6). And when Marleen finally submits to Dirk's advances and Joanne reads, "*And then—dot dot*

dot—*we were One*, Capital O, exclamation mark" (8), the waitresses are silent for a moment before erupting into laughter. Atwood writes, "Their laughter is outraged, disbelieving. *One*. Just like that. There has to be more to it" (8). Before Joanne can continue the story and describe the aftermath of Marleen and Dirk's moment of passion, Hilary announces that the storytelling must come to an end—only ten minutes remain of the waitresses' afternoon break. As Hilary and several other waitresses plunge into the lake to rinse off their tanning oil, Ronette, a waitress who has been silent throughout the reading, leans over to Joanne. "'Yeah, but,' she says to Joanne, 'why is it funny?'" (9).

That Ronette is a different kind of reader and a different kind of young woman from the other waitresses at Camp Adanaqui becomes apparent as Atwood's story unfolds. Unlike Hilary, Joanne, and the other waitresses who will eventually go to university, Ronette is one of the "town girls, . . . the ones who stand in line at the . . . movie theater, chewing gum and wearing their boyfriends' leather jackets, their ruminating mouths glistening and deep red like mushed-up raspberries" (4). Outwardly marked as a member of the working class, Ronette is an enigma to both the young male campers and her fellow waitresses, and they all project their own desires and fears onto her.[1] The campers

> make bets over whether they will get her at their table. When she
> leans over to clear the plates, they try to look down the front of her
> sedate but V-necked uniform. They angle towards her, breathing her
> in: she smells of hair spray, nail polish, something artificial and too
> sweet. Cheap. . . . It's an enticing word. . . . Most of the things
> in [their lives] are expensive, and not very interesting. (4)

For the other waitresses (especially Joanne, "who has a bad habit of novelizing"), Ronette seems to have a knowledge that their college-preparatory educations have not given them. She "knows other things, hidden things. Secrets. And these other things are older, and on some level more important. More fundamental. Closer to the bone" (13).

The inadequacy, though, of these interpretations of Ronette becomes obvious as Atwood's story concludes eleven years after the summer of reading tales and waiting tables at camp. Joanne, now a struggling copywriter living in Toronto, runs into Donny, who had been a sensitive, if confused, fourteen-year-old camper. Over coffee with Donny, Joanne realizes that he—not the rakish counselor Darce—is responsible for the pregnancy that Ronette had announced at the end of the summer. As Atwood's story ends, Joanne muses:

> Donny, sitting sweetly across the table from her, is in all probability the father of a ten-year-old child, and he knows nothing about it at all.
>
> Should she tell him? The melodrama tempts her, the idea of a revelation, a sensation, a neat ending.
>
> But it would not be an ending, it would only be the beginning of something else. (30)

While Joanne contemplates her narrative options, Ronette is "left behind in the past, dappled by its chiaroscuro, stained and haloed by it, stuck with other people's adjectives" (30).

In offering "True Trash" as a multilayered fiction of reading, Atwood calls attention to the range of responses possible among variously positioned readers. For Hilary, Joanne, and the other waitresses who share ties to the middle class, the "Moan-o-drama" magazines provide an opportunity for them to demonstrate their savvy skepticism (5). They pride themselves on not being vulnerable to the fantasy worlds proffered by the confessional magazines. But even more interesting, Atwood deftly dramatizes the silence of Ronette and other readers like her who have been "left behind in the past" and whose responses to texts do not often have a place in critical histories and ethnographies of reading. In "True Trash," Ronette stands as an example of what Joseph Harris has termed "the other reader," that is, a seemingly naive reader who is duped by the mass media, a reader for whom "true trash" is serious. For Harris, this other reader stands as a problematic foil to the typical cultural critic, whose self-proclaimed textual acumen allows him or her to resist the messages of the hegemonic culture that are encoded in print ads, music videos, and television commercials. Harris goes on to urge those of us in English studies to begin considering seriously how the voices of other readers like Ronette might cause us to revise our current textual strategies:

> Can we imagine a kind of criticism in which the comments of ordinary readers (or students) function not only as material for the writer to work with and explain—as examples of what she herself has to say, perhaps, or as illustrations of the problem she wants to address—but also as checks against the bias of her own reading, as statements of views she must in some way respond to? (31)

Like Harris, I believe that reconstructing the lives of real readers and acknowledging the diversity and creativity of their textual activities can help us better understand our own responses to texts and the range of possible reading lives available today. My project in this essay, then, is to amplify the voices of the real readers on whom the fictional Ronette seems based and to reconstruct the reading lives of working-class women who enjoyed confessional magazines (*True Story*, *True Confessions*, *Modern Romances*, etc.) in the middle decades of the twentieth century.

More specifically, I describe how working-class women resisted the calls for the reformation of working-class reading tastes that were issued by social activists with various political agendas. Instead, many working-class women remained avid readers of the confessional magazines and used a reading strategy that can be termed *flexible moral realism*.[2] Such a reading strategy privileges the correspondences between events in a narrative and events a working-class woman reader recognizes as likely to take place in her own life or in the lives of people she knows. Additionally, flexible moral realism necessitates that such a reader apply an elastic code of ethics in judging the behavior of characters found in the magazines' pages. While such a reading strategy was practiced privately by individual readers of the confessional magazines, I also suggest that choosing to value the mimetic dimensions of the confessional magazines and making generous ethical judgments helped lay the groundwork for some working-class women to resist their isolation and develop a nascent sense of community among themselves. Through common texts and shared reading strategies, working-class women could begin to feel connected to other similarly circumstanced women. Ultimately, I hope that my descriptions of the individual and collective reading lives of working-class women might help initiate a re-valuation of ways of reading that acknowledges the power of identifying with characters and narrative situations that seem real. While the predominance of poststructuralism in today's academic circles necessitates an always-already awareness of the artifice of the text, the possibility that more realistic ways of understanding and identifying with texts might productively bring together groups of readers merits further consideration, especially if a woman like Ronette could find a place to do more than whisper in such a group. Before I take up these issues, though, it may be useful to review the history of the confessional magazines.

"Sin, Suffering, and Sorrow": The Origins of the Confessional Magazines

True Story was the first of the confessional magazines. Founded in 1919 by Bernarr Macfadden, *True Story* originated from the reader mail of Macfadden's first magazine venture, *Physical Culture*—a vehicle for his ideas on health and fitness. *Physical Culture* featured advice columns and first-person narratives dealing with physical and psychological problems. Many readers sent in letters about their own experiences. The editors received letters from girls who "confessed their sexual mistakes and thought they were fallen women" and "broken-hearted women . . . [who] had done two hundred knee bends, twice a day, and had thrown away their corsets" yet still found themselves unlucky in love (Macfadden and Gauvreau 218–19). In her autobiography, Mary Macfadden, Bernarr's wife, describes how she encouraged her husband to create a new

magazine out of these letters, a magazine that would surely succeed because its stories would be written by its own readers. Early
issues featured narratives with titles like "How I Learned to Hate
My Parents," "I Said It Could Never Happen to Me," "Why I Will
Never Marry," and "My Wild Ride."

From the beginning, Bernarr Macfadden was clear about the criteria used to judge such first-person narratives as they were submitted for publication by *True Story*'s readers. He described his
magazine's editorial principles: "We want stories only from the
common people. . . . We've got to keep out 'writing writers' who
want to make a business of it" (Peterson 299). In a promotion for
one submission contest, he wrote, "Remember . . . the story is the
thing that counts—not literary skill. . . . Tell it naturally, simply,
in your own words. . . . If it contains the human quality we seek,
it will receive preference over tales of less merit no matter how
cleverly, beautifully, or skillfully written they may be" (Fabian 59).
According to Mary Macfadden, "if a narrative sounded too 'highbrow,' my husband asked the office elevator operator to read it. If it
was over his head it went back to the author. A wag on the editorial
staff had written a piece for barroom reading entitled: 'How I Was
Demoted to Editor of *True Story* and Worked My Way Up to Elevator Man Again'" (223–24).

With its unique fusion of the roles of reader and writer and its
promise of real-life tales of "sin, suffering, and sorrow," *True Story*
was an immediate success. The first issue sold 60,000 copies out of
an initial printing of 100,000 (Nourie and Nourie 511). Harland
Manchester reports that by the mid-1930s yearly circulation of
True Story topped 2,200,000 and advertising space sold for nearly
$4,000,000 (26).

Hoping to duplicate Macfadden's success, a number of other
publishers brought out imitations of *True Story*. Fawcett Publications introduced *True Confessions* in 1922, and Dell Publishing Company debuted *Modern Romances* in 1930. Seeking to maintain his
dominance in the confessional magazine market, Macfadden even
launched his own imitations of *True Story*: he began publishing

True Experiences in 1922 and quickly followed it with *Love and Romance* (Peterson 300). Acknowledging the difficulty of precisely determining the total audience for confessional magazines, Theodore Peterson estimates that the aggregate circulation of these magazines had grown to over 8,500,000 by the early 1960s (302).

Sociologically oriented research conducted by librarians during the middle decades of the twentieth century indicates that most of the millions of readers who helped make the confessional magazines a success and who ensured their steady growth were indeed working-class women.[3] In a study of how the Great Depression affected the number and types of texts read in a neighborhood in South Chicago and in a more affluent suburb of Saint Louis, Douglas Waples (one of the guiding forces behind the University of Chicago's Graduate Library School) found that while the confessional magazines accounted for 13.2% of the total magazines read in the industrial neighborhoods of South Chicago, only 1.4% of the readers in an affluent suburb of Saint Louis read them (151). Robert Miller's detailed comparison of the reading lives of the residents of two census tracts in South Chicago builds on Waples's research. Miller found that in the tract characterized as "a middle-class residential area," whose population had higher levels of education, more income, and greater access to a range of printed materials (books, magazines, and newspapers), residents read widely from the diverse materials available to them (753). For Miller, the most striking difference between this middle-class community and the second tract, which had a much higher concentration of unskilled laborers, many "foreign born or of foreign parentage," was in the "comparative circulation of detective, adventure, and confessional and love periodicals" (738). Although the residents of the prosperous tract read a greater number of texts, the working-class residents of the second tract read nearly twice as many of the pulp periodicals, including confessional magazines (751).

The findings of other librarians and sociologists bear out the claims made by Waples and Miller. In a longitudinal study of the

reading habits of students who attended the Milwaukee Vocational
School from 1924 to 1936, William Rasche found that in 1924 *True
Story* held first place on the list of magazines most popular with
the working-class student body. In 1932, *True Story* was still the
most popular magazine among young women at the school, while
Popular Mechanics claimed the top spot on the list of magazines
read by the male students (76–77). In a study of African American
families in Chicago, E. Franklin Frazier, a professor of sociology at
Fisk University, also commented on the pervasiveness of the confessional magazines, which were helping to define the meaning of
sex for many young women.[4] Frazier notes that "the remark of one
girl that she read '*Love Stories, True Stories, Love Affairs, True Confession,* and *Fairy Tales*' was common" and that even in narrating
their life histories, young women would often shift into retellings of
narratives they had read in confessional magazines (199). The
local findings of Waples, Miller, Rasche, and Frazier are consistent
with the national research of the sociologists Paul F. Lazarsfeld
and Rowena Wyant, who reported in their study of ninety American cities that the higher the population of industrial workers
(both African American and white), the higher the circulation of
confessional magazines (37).

Waples and other reading researchers centered in graduate
schools of library science hoped their work would ultimately become
a "sociology of reading" (200) that could explain the power of print
as a socializing force, not just serve as a compilation of statistics on
the production and distribution of reading materials. Stephen
Karetzky has noted, though, that the reading research movement of
the 1920s and 1930s failed to achieve this ambitious goal because of
"deficiencies of the library profession at large, which lacked a critical mass of socially oriented intellectual energy, a belief in the value
and usefulness of scientific research, and an appropriate system of
rewards that would encourage and support such research activity
and the application of its results" (356). While the reading
researchers in graduate library schools lacked a professional

infrastructure that would have supported their research and enabled them to make more precise claims about the reading lives of individuals and larger social groups, social reformers of various political orientations were all too willing to step into the breach with their perspectives on the reading habits of working-class readers. The confessional magazines, with their quick success and steadily growing circulation figures among working-class women readers, quickly came to occupy a central position in the conversations of reform-minded activists from across the political spectrum.

The Concerns of Social Reformers

In lamenting the prominent role of the confessional magazines in the lives of working-class women, social reformers on both the left and the right were largely concerned that these magazines were shouldering aside more appropriate reading. Although the Communist Party's *Working Woman* published and promoted works by women worker-writers like Grace Lumpkin, Mary Heaton Vorse, Meridel Le Sueur, and Myra Page, Henry Hart reported at the 1935 American Writers' Conference that even the most popular proletarian novels sold fewer than 3,000 copies at full price (161). Following Hart's speech, Alexander Trachtenberg called for action: "We must admit that the value of imaginative literature has not been sufficiently stressed in the revolutionary movement. . . . It is up to us, in our workers schools, in our bookshops, in our forums, in our study groups, our reading circles, to overcome this gap in our work, to bring proletarian literature to the workers" (163).

But Trotskyites like Louis Adamic were raising serious questions about reaching the masses through proletarian literature. In the *Saturday Review of Literature*, Adamic took up the project of defining "what the proletariat reads." According to Adamic, "The sad answer is that the overwhelming majority of the American working class does not read books and serious, purposeful magazines. In fact, the American working class hardly reads anything apart from the local daily and Sunday newspaper and occasional copy of *Liberty*,

True Stories, Wild West Tales, or *Screen Romances*" (321). Adamic goes
on to remark:

> In Flint, Michigan, I met a number of factory girls who had read
> Catherine Brody's "Nobody Starves" because they had heard they
> were in the story, and all of them declared to me they did not like the
> novel. I asked them why. The replies were that the story was not
> true; at least parts of it were untrue. The conditions among the
> workers in Flint were not quite as bad, they said, as the author
> described them. . . . One girl remarked: "I got sore reading the
> book. We wear much nicer clothes than she says we do!" (322)

Though advocates of proletarian literature might dismiss the
attitude of the young woman from Flint as a reflection of a mis-
placed bourgeois mentality, respondents to Adamic's article
offered a number of reasons why workers rejected proletarian literature in favor of confessional and pulp magazines: that so-called
proletarian writers living in Greenwich Village studios were out of
touch with the broad mass of American workers (Calverton); that
outmoded pedagogical methods in public schools "smothered" students' interests in *any* serious literature (Clark); that American
proletarian writers had not sufficiently adapted Soviet models to
the American context and were themselves conflicted in their
desires to pursue art for art's sake as well as to produce socially relevant literature (Calmer).[5]

Just as the literary left lamented the questionable reading choices
of working-class readers, so too did more conservative forces fret
over workers' lack of interest in genteel literature. An unsigned *Literary Digest* article titled "The Drive against Dirt" was highly critical of "articles and stories professing to make 'realistic' disclosures
of the 'truth of life'" (16). The article concludes with a lengthy
quote from the Baltimore *Southern Methodist* that exhorted readers
to "[b]uy good magazines, surround your children with whole-
some books, and support that which is worthwhile, including the
church press, and this dangerous literature will not find lodgment
in our own families" (16). Similarly positioning "periodicals that

print what are called true confessions and true romances" as one of four types of pulp magazines (10), Aldous Huxley was concerned about the ways in which the publishing industry of the 1930s was being shaped by the low tastes of working-class readers. Huxley describes his attempt to purchase a book on American geography while on an automobile trip through Florida. Though he could find no bookstore in a seaside town, "[i]n the main street alone I found no less than six shops devoted to the sale of nothing else than periodical pulp. From the brilliantly lighted windows scores and hundreds of highly colored female faces, either floating in the void, or else attached to female figures in a state of partial undress, gazed out from the covers of magazines" (10). Huxley laments that "Ours is the first cultural dispensation, so far as I am aware, under which large numbers of men, women, and children have contracted the habit of taking regular doses of dilute literary sadism" (11).

Though widely divergent in their political agendas, critics from Huxley to Trachtenberg were united in their narrow focus on the reading choices—not the reading strategies—of the working class. Their concern for what working-class women were reading arises out of a common assumption that working-class readers were isolated individuals who passively consumed the texts they encountered. To reform themselves, the members of the working class only needed to begin partaking in a healthier print diet—either proletarian literature or more genteel classics. But Janice Radway cautions us that "reading is not eating." She challenges the metaphor of consumption—the process of uncritically ingesting a text or eating it up. Radway argues that such a metaphor distorts the complicated social processes involved in the distribution and selection of printed material by readers and the intense interactions that take place between readers and texts. According to Radway, the metaphor of textual consumption reduces readers "to purely physical entities that are either mechanically moved by the objects that come in contact with them or chemically transformed by those that they consume. They have absolutely no power themselves to act on their environment, to select some objects over others, to use them in

creative ways, or to construct their significance idiosyncratically" (11).
Like Radway, I believe it is imperative that we forego a metaphor of
consumption and instead investigate how readers appropriate and
interact with the texts available to them.

The Flexible Moral Realism of Working-Class Women Readers

Attempting to investigate how a historically remote population
of readers interacted with texts presents many problems of accessi-
bility and recovery. In media studies today, ethnographers can
interview actual readers and viewers and gauge their responses.
Radway's 1984 study of romance readers (*Reading the Romance*)
and her 1997 work on the reading practices of staff members at the
Book-of-the-Month Club (*A Feeling for Books*), Jackie Stacey's study
of female film spectatorship, Bridget Fowler's analysis of the reading lives of 115 women in the west of Scotland, and Linda K. Christian-Smith's research on teenage readers of young-adult romance
novels in three middle schools in a large city in the American Mid-
west are useful models of contemporary investigations that explore
how people make use of the cultural texts that are part of their
everyday lives. But historians interested in readers who are no
longer available for interviews must be more inventive. In general,
the emotional experience of reading is not well documented, nor
are records of reading often preserved in forms easily accessible to
researchers. In particular, working-class readers like Atwood's
Ronette left limited traces of their emotional and intellectual
engagement with texts as ephemeral as the confessional magazines.
Few readers who enjoyed tales of sin, suffering, and sorrow
recorded their responses to the printed texts in their lives.

In attempting to reconstruct the reading habits of working-class
women, I have thus had to draw on a variety of sources: the work
of the Chicago sociologists Lee Rainwater, Richard P. Coleman, and
Gerald Handel, who interviewed working-class women about their
reading lives in the 1950s; the work of more recent media scholars,

like David Sonenschein, who have studied the editorial practices of the confessional magazines; and the scholarship of historians such as Regina Kunzel, who have explored other issues of concern to working-class women, such as family planning, birth control, and options for dealing with unplanned pregnancies.

What I found was that working-class women seemed to use a strategy that can be called flexible moral realism. As I use the term, flexible moral realism denotes a reader's decision to accept the events portrayed in a narrative as a realistic depiction of the challenges of everyday lived experience and to resist the imposition of rigid moral standards when judging the actions of characters who move through such a mimetic narrative world. A brief summary of a 1941 narrative from *True Story* allows me to provide a general outline of this reading strategy. "Our Fourth Daughter" details the struggles of a man to make a place for his illegitimate granddaughter, Susan, in his own family while keeping her identity secret. The grandfather suffers great anxiety when Susan, on learning of her true parentage, runs away from home. Susan ultimately returns for an unexpected Christmas Eve reunion with her grandparents, but she does not succumb to pleas that she reside permanently on their farm. Instead, she returns to her job in a metropolitan department store, with promises to visit her grandparents often. Within the framework of flexible moral realism, a confessional magazine reader would see in this narrative a mimetic description of events that might unfold in her own life. Moreover, the grandfather's questionable decision not to reveal Susan's true parentage when she reaches adulthood must be weighed against his desire to fulfill the wishes of Susan's mother, his daughter Irene, who had died while giving birth to Susan. Irene had been a likeable young woman who, during the early months of the United States' involvement in World War I, had erred only in wanting to give an upstanding young man from the community "some little memory to take with him into the mud and slime" of the trench warfare in France (83). Both Irene's decision to "give herself" to a young man who would soon give his life for his country and the grandfather's decision to deceive the adult Susan about the identity of her biological parents occur within a context of competing moral imperatives. In justifying her decision to engage in premarital sex, Irene explains, "I'm not bad. It just—happened—because I cared, and because France is so far away" (83); in explaining his decision to lie about Susan's true parentage, the grandfather explains that he was motivated by his genuine desire to protect Susan and to "not mix her up" (79). When confronting such a complex ethical situation, the readers of confessional magazines would likely apply a flexible moral code that acknowledged the good intentions and bad decisions, the stoic suffering and partial victories of narrators and characters who find themselves inexperienced and vulnerable in trying situations. In short, flexible moral decisions are made that acknowledge the complicated circumstances that lead to sin, suffering, and sorrow. For readers who use this strategy in moving through a text, the most satisfying stories feature a character who is able to achieve a reasonably happy life despite understandable ethical lapses.

Flexible moral realism as a reading strategy allowed working-class women to make two simultaneous moves. First, they were privileging the realistic or mimetic dimensions of the narrative worlds they found in confessional magazines on the basis of their sense of the correspondence between the narrative world and their own life experiences. Second, they were applying a flexible ethical code as they responded to the dilemmas faced by the narrators and characters they encountered in the magazines. To illustrate how working-class women made these two moves in reading confessional magazines, let me take each one in turn.

As readers, working-class women chose to accept and value as realistic the events portrayed in magazines like *True Story*: unplanned pregnancies, unfaithful lovers, and petty criminal activity. As one of the women interviewed by Rainwater, Coleman, and Handel explained, "You can tell those stories are true, there are things like that just happen. Well, like wives getting abandoned or raising children" (129). Another reader commented, "*True Story* is, well, it's down to earth more. They [the stories] devote their time to facts you know, it's there and you deal with it, and sometimes it's love and sometimes it's sad—just like life generally" (129). In fact, when Rainwater, Coleman, and Handel asked women whether they could write a story based on their own experiences or the experiences of family and friends that would be appropriate for a confessional magazine, they answered affirmatively. As one woman mused, "some of their stories are like my life, I guess. Some of the problems. We always manage to work them out though; maybe not the same way they do in [*True Story*]. Well, in a certain way, they compare with my life, everybody has problems" (129). As Rainwater, Coleman, and Handel observe, these remarks show that readers appreciated as realistic the magazines' focus on the daily dramas of average people's lives. The narratives presented readers with characters and situations that seemed close to their own sense of identity.

A 1937 "human interest textbook" published by *True Story* confirms that the confessional magazines' realistic focus was crucial to readers. One monthly feature in *True Story* was the "Home Problems Forum"—an advice column that presented the real-life problem of a reader and then asked other readers to respond to the magazine by letter with possible solutions. Typical problems included whether parents should let a grown daughter return to their home when her marriage becomes difficult, whether strict discipline is appropriate with a recalcitrant stepchild, and whether a young newlywed should share the intimate details of her married life with her sister. According to *True Story* editors, "Some problems bring letters by the thousands—others by the thin hundreds" (*How to Get People Excited* 5). Most pertinent to my point is that the editors were clear about what types of problems drew the greatest responses:

First, and most fundamental, it has seemed true that common, everyday situations which are familiar to everyone, generally pull the full mail pouches. Ideally, the most exciting situation will be one that has happened or reasonably could happen to every person who reads it. The in-law theme, for example, almost always draws a top response. (6)

The reality of the narratives in the confessional magazines was further bolstered by the posed photographs that typically accompanied each story. Resembling movie stills, these photographs make the narrators and characters palpable.[6] The external physical details of the photographs (e.g., clothing, hairstyles, makes and models of automobiles) help solidify the confessional magazines' portrayal of everyday life.

The confessional magazines not only used photographs to heighten the mimetic qualities of the narratives, they also presented typically happy endings for most stories that included conflicting details that heightened the stories' realism. In one story that appeared in the 1930s, a car wreck ends an unplanned pregnancy, but the young woman genuinely mourns the loss of the child that had been fathered by an irresponsible college student. While the young woman is excited by a potential relationship with another young man, the hero who pulled her from the wrecked automobile, his career as a musician does not promise financial security. In the conclusion of another confession, a debutante who weds a shop clerk acknowledges that despite her nuptial bliss, she regrets that her relationship with her mother has been shattered. David Sonenschein's study of the contents of confessional magazines from the 1960s confirms that the narrative endings were usually far from rosy. Sonenschein reports that "forty-eight percent end on a note of the narrator having mixed feelings of guilt and hope, punishment and salvation. . . . Nineteen percent of the stories end on a completely sad tone, where punishment has come about with the tacit admittance by the narrator that she deserved what she got in the end" ("Love" 405). The realistically stubborn details that surface in the endings of confessional narratives and the narrators' own mixed feelings disrupt any fairy-tale quality the stories might have. The stories' *relatively* happy endings underscore the possibility of positive outcomes, even for people in desperate circumstances.

These relatively happy endings do more, though, than play into readers' decisions to accept the stories as realistic. The basically up-beat endings are also part of the readers' sense that a flexible moral code is required if one is to respond ethically and empathetically to the narrators and characters in the magazines' pages.[7]

The consistent pattern in nearly all the confessional narratives is the narrator's fall from innocence and security as a result of her or his inability to respond to competing ethical demands, a short period of privation and unhappiness, and repentance followed by restoration to more favorable circumstances. For example, a *True Story* narrative from the 1930s recounts a young working-class woman's despair over the injuries her little sister sustains when a badly constructed school collapses. However, the young woman is not condemned for failing to report her prior knowledge of the shoddy building contractor's illegal practices to the police. Instead, her silence occurs in the context of her loving devotion to the con-tractor's upstanding son and her unwillingness to hurt him by embar-rassing his family. Though the young woman is racked by guilt as her little sister recovers from her injuries and rejects any assistance from the contractor's son, the two lovers are ultimately reconciled and decide to marry. This protagonist and most others found in the pages of confessional magazines are basically moral women who must negotiate conflicting ethical imperatives.

Rainwater, Coleman, and Handel found that *True Story* readers were most satisfied by such narratives because they "allow . . . for the play of human emotions and some compromise" on the part of a woman "whose strivings are basically moral" (134). One reader re-membered a protagonist who makes bad decisions and gets into trouble as she deals with the emotional turmoil of being abandoned by her first lover. The interviewee was pleased, though, that the protagonist eventually met a new "fellow that fell head over heels in love with her and they were married and she was happier than ever before" (132–33). This interviewee stands as a representative of the many women in the Rainwater, Coleman, and Handel study who would "repetitively . . . recall and retell with evident satisfactions, stories of women who have [understandably] transgressed, and still manage to live a good life" (134).

By applying a flexible moral code as part of their reading strategy, working-class women were subtly insisting that a woman's moral status is never truly lost and that basically happy outcomes are possible in most real-life situations. In reading confessional magazines, working-class women acknowledged the likelihood of moral transgressions but insisted that guilt and shame need not be incapacitating (Rainwater, Coleman, and Handel 134).

Making the Private Public: Creating a Sense of Community among Readers

Reading can be an intensely private experience, but shared texts and common reading strategies may have also played a role in creating a sense of community among working-class women in the middle decades of the twentieth century. In choosing to value the mimetic dimensions of the confessional narratives and in applying a flexible code of ethics when judging the behavior of the lifelike characters, working-class women could begin to feel connected to other, similarly circumstanced readers. A number of studies do suggest that working-class women reduced their sense of loneliness by reading confessional magazines. The study by Rainwater, Coleman, and Handel reports that magazine readers often felt "isolated, friendless, intimidated in social contacts" (135). Similarly, Sonenschein cites the responses of the editors of confessional magazines who confirmed that "our readers are less educated and marry young. They don't have many people to talk to" ("Process" 404). Rainwater, Coleman, and Handel, though, found that by reading confessional magazines, working-class women felt "more . . . engaged with others" (135).

This nascent sense of community may arise in part from how confessional magazines make the private public in ways that seemed realistic to readers and did not violate their flexible moral code. Conversations about the supposedly shameful aspects of women's lives—illicit love affairs, unplanned pregnancies, minor criminal activities—are no longer taking place in hushed tones. Instead, the previously private dramas of women's lives take center stage. Irmengarde Eberle recognized the potential power in "the new confessional" just as the popularity of *True Story* and its sister magazines was soaring in the 1930s. In the *New Republic*, Eberle noted:

> Since the ugliness of sex has always been the result of shame and secrecy, this confessional literature . . . can in the long run, by virtue of its authenticity, do only good. It is bringing thoughts of sex out into the open, and, by acquainting its readers with the common experiences of men, it is gradually dissipating the morbid atmosphere that has gathered about certain natural functions. It is following a sound instinct in curing unhealthiness by exposing it to the sun. (70)

By emphasizing the authenticity of the portrayals of sexual experiences and by advocating the dissipation of the "morbid atmosphere" that typically surrounded conversations about sexuality, Eberle's analysis of the magazines suggests that they provided readers with an outlet to articulate important but unacknowledged aspects of their lives. In her important work on unmarried mothers, maternity homes, and the professionalization of social work, Kunzel extends Eberle's observations and develops a powerful portrait of the role confessional magazines played in the lives of young women dealing with unplanned pregnancies. Kunzel suggests that the confessional magazines recognized the power of female sexual desire in stories with titles like "The Story of a Repentant Woman," "The Price of Silence," "The Baby I Never Saw," and "I Said It Could Never Happen to Me." Departing from the Victorian norms expressed in the evangelical narratives of "villainous men and victimized" women that many social workers and reformers circulated, the confessional magazines acknowledged the pleasures of physical intimacy for women (Kunzel, *Fallen Women* 106). Female narrators unabashedly used language like "[my] blind terrific need of him . . . left me helpless and trembling in his arms"; "Then there were only two of us—just us two in all the world. Everything else, even the sound of the little wind over the water, was blotted out. . . . [There was just] the tenderness, the sweeping glory, the marching mood of madness." Such language lays the groundwork for new, feminine rhetorics of sexual desire. In fact, as Kunzel cogently argues, the dramatic language that many single pregnant women used to described their circumstances when they arrived at maternity homes was probably gleaned from confessional magazines (*Fallen Women* 105–06).

Kunzel also notes that women faced with unplanned pregnancies in the first half of the twentieth century may have learned more about options available to them from confessional magazines than from traditional sources such as family members or physicians. In her 1995 article on "pulp fictions and problem girls," Kunzel cites the report of a social worker in 1933 who described how women would arrive at maternity homes clutching copies of confessional magazines. They would explain to the disapproving matrons that "the stories are just like us" (1470).

Kunzel's *Fallen Women, Problem Girls* provides more details about the conflicts over reading habits that surfaced between working-class women and social workers in maternity homes and the tenacity with which working-class women clung to their preferred reading materials:

> The unmarried mothers' attachment to popular confessional magazines like *Real Love*, *Thrilling Love*, and *Sweetheart Stories* drove maternity home workers to distraction. Offended by the reading habits of one Door of Hope resident, the matron told her "about better reading being available" and advised her of "the damage such trashy reading could do her." She warned her that reading pulp magazines would "keep her emotions stirred up, that she would meet a problem in having had aroused in her all the feelings, emotions, and passions of an adult woman before she is mature enough

to know how to handle them." Giving her a copy of a respectable novel, she arranged to meet with the woman later to find out "if she liked it better than the cheap magazines." When they met to discuss it, however, the unmarried mother reported that she preferred her magazines to the book and continued to read them over the matron's protests. (*Fallen Women* 98)

By helping to generate a common discourse through which previously undiscussed female sexual pleasures and the often private experiences of single women dealing with unplanned pregnancies could begin to circulate in public realms, the confessional magazines held out to working-class women the possibility of membership in a broader community.

Although not entirely comfortable with the scandalous nature of the confessional magazines, some social service agencies necessarily recognized the power of these magazines in readers' lives. As Kunzel reports in "Pulp Fictions and Problem Girls," the National Florence Crittenton Mission, the largest chain of maternity homes for unwed mothers, decided to join forces with the pulp magazines in 1936.[8] It sponsored an article, "I Was an Unwed Mother," in *True Story*, and according to Kunzel, the response was overwhelming and immediate. The January 1937 *Florence Crittenton Bulletin* reported that the mission offices were "fairly swamped" with requests from thousands of single, pregnant women who had read the *True Story* article (Kunzel, "Pulp Fictions" 1467). Similarly, a 1949 *True Confessions* story, "The Terrifying Ordeal of an Unwed Mother," was accompanied by a column from the United States Children's Bureau, urging women to seek assistance through its offices. After studying the letters the bureau received in response to the story and column, Kunzel concludes the confessional magazines "provided readers with a lexicon of legitimacy and authority" (1479).

While such stories of loving not wisely, but too well, helped young women understand their own lives and offered them avenues for individually seeking assistance, by the 1940s many social workers began "to advocate placing single pregnant women in individual 'foster homes' with private families" since group maternity homes "would nurture a subversive group consciousness among single mothers" (Kunzel, "Pulp Fictions" 1479–80). As young women arrived at the maternity homes, they started to realize how many other women were dealing with similar issues in their lives. They began "losing their regret and conscience-stricken feeling" (1479) and came to see their pregnancies as part of broad "social problems" rather than as "private traumas" (1480).

Kunzel's research undermines the claims made by critics of the confessional magazines like George Gerbner, who argues that the confessional magazines are "loaded with editorial ammunition designed to . . . [make] social protest appear to be out of place, unrelated to the insecurities of working-class life" (32). For Gerbner, a narrative of sin, suffering, and sorrow was only a "spine-tingling object lesson in bearing up under relentless blows of half-understood events. . . . People, not society, must yield to what are assumed to be the inflexible hazards and demands of human life" (35–36). The women Kunzel describes and those interviewed by Rainwater, Coleman, and Handel have clearly learned lessons other than what Gerbner posits. By reading in ways that allowed them to find themselves and others like them in the pages of confessional magazines, as well as in group maternity homes, women readers created not just an abstract, interpretive community but also real, face-to-face communities with enough social power to resist the imposition of middle-class standards of taste that social workers in group homes sought to impose.

As Kunzel and Rainwater, Coleman, and Handel describe, reading confessional magazines allowed working-class women to see their lives in new ways.[9] By improvising with and appropriating narratives like those found in the pages of *True Story* and its sister magazines, women could insist that they were not leading vulnerable or ruined lives and that their experiences were worthy of circulation in a wider print culture. These working-class women were productive, active readers. In the confessional magazines, they found a mirror that they could tilt to reflect their own generous view that sinning is probably unavoidable but that redemption and a life of reasonable happiness are still attainable.

Like most readers, working-class women in the middle decades of the twentieth century were reading a variety of texts in imaginative and original ways. I offer my description of the reading lives of these women not as a definitive portrait of their textual activities; instead, my hope is that my work has opened a momentary aperture into how readers can appropriate, dismember, and contextualize the written texts available to them. Moreover, in holding out the tantalizing possibility that shared texts and common reading strategies can lay the groundwork for forging connections among otherwise isolated individuals, I hope that my work here might suggest the merit of further historical and ethnographic explorations of the ways in which printed texts and shared reading strategies can bring people together.

Such studies of real readers might also serve as a useful starting point for investigating and reevaluating the dismissal of ways of reading that value the mimetic dimensions of narrative situations and that acknowledge the power and pleasures of identifying with the seemingly real characters that can be created through words. One has only to recall Jane Austen's *Northanger Abbey*, Tabitha Gilman Tenney's *Female Quixotism*, or the many tirades against women's indiscriminate reading tastes that appeared in nineteenth-century periodicals (e.g., "Ladies and Romances," by L. L. Hamline; "Novel Reading," by John Edwards; "What Is the Harm of Novel-Reading?," by 'S' in the *Wesleyan-Methodist Magazine*) to realize that concern about the ways in which women identify too strongly with characters and confuse fiction and fact has a long and complex history. More recently, university scholars and graduate students have been thoroughly steeped in poststructuralism, and as Lynne Pearce has noted, "any consideration of there existing a 'relationship' between the reader and a textual character has been regarded as symptomatic of an outdated, and theoretically suspect, 'authentic realism' approach to textual analysis. Such involvement is seen as a sign of the reader losing sight of the 'textuality' of the reading experience" (17). I believe, though, that my study of readers of confessional magazines suggests that more realistic ways of understanding and identifying with texts has the potential to create a sense of collectivity among readers when they first encounter what they take to be a representation of their own lives in a printed text. Barbara Christian describes just such a moment when she first read Paule Marshall's *Brown Girl, Brownstones*. She writes that the novel

> was not just a text, it was an accurate and dynamic embodiment both of the possibilities and improbabilities of my own life. In it I encountered myself as object. In illuminating so clearly, so lovingly, the mesh of my own context, Marshall provided me with a guide, a way to contemplate my own situation and gave me back the memory, the embodied history of women like myself who had preceded me. . . . It was crucial to a deeper understanding of my own life. (197)

Like the working-class women who read confessional magazines, Christian found in a work of fiction a cultural resource that she could use to insist on the value of her own experiences. And as my own "true confession," I will admit to the near-compulsive need I have to read (and reread) the novels of Jane Austen, Charlotte Brontë, and George Eliot, primarily because such texts offer me fully realized, mimetic narrative worlds where I can, at least for a little while, identify with and admire other bookish women who are as witty as Elizabeth Bennet, as courageously independent as Jane Eyre, as large-hearted as Dorothea Brooke. Just as the working-class women readers found confessional magazines a useful way to frame their experiences, so too do I turn to texts to make sense of my hopes, my dreams, my life. I hope, though, that my exploration here of the productive nature of working-class women's reading strategies might prompt literary scholars to revisit questions about the powers and pitfalls of reading with realistic expectations and about the ways in which common texts and reading strategies can bring people together. I believe that it is by taking seriously the relations that diversely circumstanced readers have with the texts and with other readers that we can establish a more productive conversational space for pursuing vital questions about the role of print in our lives—a conversational space where Atwood's Ronette would not have to whisper, "Yeah, but . . . why is it funny?"

Notes

1. The interior lives of working-class men and women can be uniquely difficult to describe. As Zandy has noted in *Liberating Memory*, a working-class
   identity is generally "intended for disposal. In order to 'make it' into the
   dominant society, one 'overcomes' the class circumstances of birth, and
   moves into the middle and then the upper classes" (1). The challenges of
   describing working-class identities are particularly acute for scholars interested in the history of literacy and reading. Though working-class people in
   a variety of historical contexts have left written descriptions of their reading lives, such advanced literacy is too often inappropriately used as a
   marker that these men and women have made it and moved beyond their
   working-class origins. This erases much of the history of literate activity of
   the working class and is part of what makes it possible for dominant economic groups to conceive of a working-class identity as a tabula rasa onto
   which they can project their own desires and fears.

2. In their 1955 study of readers and nonreaders of *True Story*, Rainwater,
   Coleman, and Handel delimit a lengthier list of textual characteristics that
   made the magazine appealing to working-class women: its realistic nature,
   its concern with people, its youthfulness, its morality, and its positive focus.
   They briefly mention moral realism as a textual feature that distinguishes
   True Story from other magazines, not as a reading strategy. In addition to
   drawing on their work, I am also indebted to Mills's more recent discussion
   of "authentic realism" as a feminist reading strategy whereby women
   choose to emphasize relations between texts and their lives.

3. Social and academic pressures spurred a boom in sociologically oriented
   research by librarians in the 1930s, when the confessional magazines were
   hitting their stride. Such research typically sought to determine what people read and why, so that librarians could help Americans make wise reading decisions. In the early 1930s, libraries were called on to provide for the
   "greatly increased leisure" of the unemployed (Geller 151). But as the number of unemployed increased and their circumstances became more desperate, librarians and the library-using public began to ask whether the
   library should serve all members of the community, including the growing

number of tramps. Some librarians were strongly committed to welcoming people from all walks of life into their reading rooms; others, like Milton Ferguson of the Brooklyn Public Library, were equally adamant in asserting that libraries should primarily serve businessmen and college students. Ferguson even went so far as to quote John Cotton Dana, an early president of the American Library Association, who wanted to protect libraries from "those often so unfortunate as to be without a job . . . whose coats . . . give off an odor so unlike the perfumes of Araby" (Geller 151).

As the Great Depression deepened, though, large numbers of librarians began finding themselves among those "so unfortunate as to be without a job." Libraries had to compete for drastically reduced public and private funds, and they responded by laying off staff as well as drastically slashing acquisition budgets and undertaking other cost-cutting measures. In the midst of this crisis, Carleton Joeckel, an instructor at the University of Michigan's library school, expressed the growing concern that libraries were ineffectively responding to the Great Depression because they lacked a sense of overall purpose. He lamented that his field was locked in debates about "whether the library is for all the people or only for some of them, whether it shall supply books of ephemeral interest to its readers or leave such books to the tender mercies of the rental library, and so on. Am I going too far when I say that I doubt whether any other activity of government is as vague, as indefinite, and as generally inarticulate in defining its purpose and proper field of service?" (Geller 151).

The 1933 presidential report *Recent Social Trends in the United States* underscored Joeckel's concerns and added to the woes of librarians (Karet-zky 29). The fifteen-hundred-page report made only scattered references to the library's role in the life of the country. As William Haygood explained, the compilers of the report felt that libraries were important but omitted them because "unlike the public school or public health organizations or even recreational agencies, the public library is inarticulate when it tries to define its place among the institutions which index a nation's level of culture. In brief, it lacks the facility of measurement" (Karetzky 29). In response to these pressures, librarians began to undertake serious research projects about reading and library usage that would help them define their place in the edu-cational and cultural lives of the population of the United States.

4. Kunzel's *Fallen Women, Problem Girls* made me aware of the relevance of Frazier's research for scholars interested in historical studies of the reading habits of working-class women (105–06).

5. Though most of the respondents to Adamic's article excoriated either working-class readers for their low reading tastes or working-class writers for not appropriately addressing the interests of the majority of American workers, Cantwell offered a somewhat different response. He queries

whether it is fair for leftist critics not to develop a more well-rounded portrait of working-class readers, who might be rejecting proletarian literature in favor of other serious literature, rather than for confessional and pulp magazines. Cantwell cites the work of Charles Compton, a Saint Louis librarian who studied borrowing records from the early 1930s and found, among other things, that 317 unemployed men and women read books by Mark Twain (Compton 20); that two cooks, five African American maids, and three Pullman-car porters were readers of Thomas Hardy (Compton 39); and that an often unemployed bricklayer was a regular reader of George Bernard Shaw (Compton 72). Compton thus concludes that "lowbrows read good books" (34). Following Compton's lead, Cantwell holds out the possibility that "the working class perhaps makes up the majority of serious American readers, even though the majority of the working class may not read seriously" (270).

6. The use of such photographs in the confessional magazines was pioneered by Bernarr Macfadden. The models for the first photographs that appeared in *True Story* were members of the editor John Brennan's family; later aspiring young actors, including Frederic March, Jean Arthur, Norma Shearer, Anita Louise, Madge Evans, and Bebe Daniels were used as models (Peterson 209). Fabian has suggested that because of the cinematic qualities of the photographs, *True Story* needs to be read "through an interpretive grid provided by film" (62). Fabian continues: "Macfadden positioned *True Story* at this particular intersection of the cinematic and the literary, finding one means to profit from the extraordinary popularity of movies. . . . He offered his stories and their illustrations as occasions for readers to experiment with what they had seen on film, to debate, to discuss, to try out, and to cast themselves and their friends as players in tales of romance, adventure, and intrigue" (63).

7. Among the confessional magazines, *True Story* most particularly tried to position itself as a magazine that offered moral instruction. William Jordan Rapp, the editor of *True Story* from 1926 to 1942, organized a ministerial board of prominent clergymen to endorse the moral values of its stories. The board included the Reverend Ralph W. Keeler, Crawford Memorial Methodist Church; the Reverend Elliot E. Parry, Protestant Episcopal Church; Rabbi Ellsington P. Harris, Broadway Tabernacle; the Reverend James H. Munro, Presbyterian Church and Municipal Tombs Prison; and a Catholic priest who served anonymously on the ministerial board. Mary Macfadden described the function of the board as "blue-penciling broad expressions and sobering down tense scenes of passion often described at blood heat by our contributors" (234).

8. In the 1940s, the United States government also attempted to capitalize on the perceived power of the confessional magazines to shape public opinion.

Honey has documented the activities of the Office of War Information (OWI) and its Magazine Bureau, headed by the former journalist Dorothy Ducas. Under Ducas's leadership, the bureau published the *Magazine War Guide*, which gave editors information about particular patriotic themes the government wanted to stress. According to Honey, Ducas "boasted of having a 'great deal of success' in persuading confessions editors to support labor recruitment, mentioning the pleasant relationship she had with *True Story* in particular" (40). Honey further quotes from a Ducas memo in which the former journalist argues that the confessional magazines could and should "lead pulp readers into supporting home-front campaigns" and advocates the publication of stories that present "emotionally, the story of democracy's fight, the attitudes of good Americans, the stakes of all of us in the war" (45).

Through the efforts of Ducas and the Magazine Bureau, the confessional magazines did publish stories that featured war workers as exemplary patriots whose labor and cooperation with management would help ensure an American victory in the war. Furthermore, the magazines followed the OWI recommendations that writers establish unpatriotic behaviors as the source of romantic frustration for young women (43). Though Honey carefully documents the efforts of the United States government and the OWI to use *True Story* and its sister magazines to shape the attitudes and behaviors of working-class readers, I have found no sources detailing readers' responses to the government's efforts.

9. While I focus here on the reading lives of working-class women, it is important to note that many women also saw themselves as writers for the confessional magazines. During the 1930s, manuscripts arrived at the editorial offices at the rate of 70,000–100,000 a year. In Cantor and Jones's survey of *True Story* writers from the 1960s, one finds parallels between the motivations for reading confessional magazines and for writing one's own confessional narrative. Many writers who sought to publish their confessions expressed a serious commitment to helping others. Several of Cantor and Jones's respondents spoke of their hope that others would benefit from their mistakes. One woman explained that she wrote her story "for myself, not for *True Story*. Then I decided to submit it so other mothers might be encouraged if they had the same type of child" (124). And another writer included a note with a submission explaining the author's desire to "reach the heart of someone who had [similarly] suffered" and who might benefit from the story (Eberle 69).

Works Cited

Adamic, Louis. "What the Proletariat Reads: Conclusions Based on a Year's Study among Hundreds of Workers throughout the United States." *Saturday Review of Literature* 1 Dec. 1934: 321–22.

Atwood, Margaret. "True Trash." *Wilderness Tips*. New York: Doubleday, 1991. 1–30.

Calmer, Alan. "Portrait of the Artist as a Proletarian." *Saturday Review of Literature* 31 July 1937: 3+.

Calverton, V. F. "Proletarianitis." *Saturday Review of Literature* 9 Jan. 1937: 3+.

Cantor, Muriel G., and Elizabeth Jones. "Creating Fiction for Women." *Communication Research* 10 (1983): 111–37.

Cantwell, Robert. "What the Working Class Reads." *New Republic* 17 July 1935: 268–70.

Christian, Barbara. "Being the Subject and the Object: Reading African-American Women's Novels." *Changing Subjects: The Making of Feminist Literary Criticism*. Ed. Gayle Greene and Coppélia Kahn. New York: Routledge, 1993. 195–200.

Christian-Smith, Linda K. *Becoming a Woman through Romance*. New York: Routledge, 1990.

Clark, Earl. "Education for Reading." Letter. *Saturday Review of Literature* 22 Dec. 1934: 384.

Compton, Charles H. *Who Reads What? Essays on the Readers of Mark Twain, Hardy, Sandburg, Shaw, William James, and the Greek Classics*. New York: Wilson, 1935.

"The Drive against Dirt." *Literary Digest* 23 Jan. 1932: 16.

Eberle, Irmengarde. "The New Confessional." *New Republic* 4 June 1930: 68–70.

Edwards, John E. "Novel Reading." *Ladies' Repository* 3 (Apr. 1843): 115–17.

Fabian, Ann. "Making a Commodity of Truth: Speculations on the Career of Bernarr Macfadden." *American Literary History* 5 (1993): 51–76.

Fowler, Bridget. *The Alienated Reader: Women and Romantic Literature in the Twentieth Century*. New York: Harvester, 1991.

Frazier, E. Franklin. *The Negro Family in Chicago*. Chicago: U of Chicago P, 1932.

Geller, Evelyn. *Forbidden Books in American Public Libraries, 1876–1939: A Study in Cultural Change*. Westport: Greenwood, 1984.

Gerbner, George. "The Social Role of the Confession Magazine." *Social Problems* 6 (1958): 29–40.

Hamline, L. L. "Ladies and Romances." *Ladies Repository* 1 (Sept. 1841): 258–59.

Harris, Joseph. "The Other Reader." *Journal of Advanced Composition* 12 (1992): 27–37.

Hart, Henry. "Contemporary Publishing and the Revolutionary Writer." *American Writers' Congress*. Ed. Hart. New York: Intl., 1935. 159–62.

Honey, Maureen. "New Roles for Women and the Feminine Mystique: Popular Fiction of the 1940s." *American Studies* 24 (1983): 37–52.

How to Get People Excited: A Human Interest Text Book. New York: True Story, 1937.

Huxley, Aldous. "Pulp." *Saturday Review of Literature* 17 July 1937: 10–11.

Karetzky, Stephen. *Reading Research and Librarianship: A History and Analysis.* Westport: Greenwood, 1982.

Kunzel, Regina. *Fallen Women, Problem Girls: Unmarried Mothers and the Professionalization of Social Work, 1890–1945.* New Haven: Yale UP, 1993.

———."Pulp Fictions and Problem Girls: Reading and Rewriting Single Pregnancy in the Postwar United States." *American Historical Review* 100 (1995): 1465–87.

Lazarsfeld, Paul F., and Rowena Wyant. "Magazines in ninety Cities—Who Reads What?" *Public Opinion Quarterly* 1.4 (1937): 29–41.

Macfadden, Mary, and Emile Gauvreau. *Dumbbells and Carrot Strips: The Story of Bernarr Macfadden.* New York: Henry Holt, 1953.

Manchester, Harland. "True Stories." *Scribner's* Aug. 1938: 25+.

Miller, Robert A. "The Relation of Reading Characteristics to Social Indexes." *American Journal of Sociology* 41 (1936): 738–56.

Mills, Sara. "Authentic Realism." *Feminist Readings / Feminists Reading.* 2nd ed. Ed. Mills and Lynne Pearce. London: Prentice, 1996: 51–82.

Nourie, Alan, and Barbara Nourie, eds. *American Mass-Market Magazines.* New York: Greenwood, 1990.

"Our Fourth Daughter." *True Stories of 1941.* Ed Robert O. Ballou. New York: Bartholomew, 1941. 79–101.

Pearce, Lynne. *Feminism and the Politics of Reading.* London: Arnold, 1997.

Peterson, Theodore. *Magazines in the Twentieth Century.* Urbana: U of Illinois P, 1964.

Radway, Janice. *A Feeling for Books: The Book-of-the-Month Club, Literary Taste, and Middle Class Desire.* Chapel Hill: U of North Carolina P, 1997.

———. "Reading Is Not Eating: Mass-Produced Literature and the Theoretical, Methodological, and Political Consequences of a Metaphor." *Book Research Quarterly* 2 (1986): 7–29.

———. *Reading the Romance*: Women, Patriachy, and Popular Literature. Chapel Hill: U of North Carolina P, 1984.

Rainwater, Lee, Richard P. Coleman, and Gerald Handel. *Workingman's Wife: Her Personality, World, and Lifestyle.* New York: Oceana, 1959.

Rasche, William Frank. *The Reading Interests of Young Workers.* Chicago: U of Chicago Lib., 1937.

'S.' "What Is the Harm of Novel-Reading?" *Wesleyan-Methodist Magazine* 78 (1855): 933.

Sonenschein, David. "Love and Sex in the Romance Magazines." *Journal of Popular Culture* 4 (1970): 398–409.

———. "Process in the Production of Popular Culture: The Romance Magazine." *Journal of Popular Culture* 6 (1972): 399–406.

Stacey, Jackie. "The Lost Audience: Methodology, Cinema History, and Feminist Film Criticism." *Feminist Cultural Theory: Process and Production.* Ed. Beverley Skeggs. Manchester: Manchester UP, 1995. 97–118.

Trachtenberg, Alexander. "Publishing Revolutionary Literature." *American Writers' Congress.* Ed. Henry Hart. New York: International, 1935. 162–64.

Waples, Douglas. *People and Print: Social Aspects of Reading in the Depression.* Chicago: U of Chicago P, 1937.

Zandy, Janet. Introduction. *Liberating Memory: Our Work and Our Working-Class Consciousness.* Ed. Zandy. New Brunswick: Rutgers UP, 1995. 1–15.

Reading like a Woman

Anne G. Berggren

I begin with three images of myself as a reader of fiction:

It's about 1950. At age nine or ten, I am setting the table, novel in one hand, silverware in the other. Absorbed in my reading, I must have made my way several times from the kitchen to the dining room, carrying table mats, napkins, glasses; now I place the knives, forks, and spoons properly, using peripheral vision. Exasperated comments come from the kitchen or den: "She always has her nose in a book."

In 1985, I'm having a crisis triggered by watching the third episode of the Masterpiece Theatre television production of *Pride and Prejudice*. Although I have planned to put off rereading the book until all five episodes have aired, I find that, though I know perfectly well what will happen, I can't wait. So, I lie on my queen-sized bed, consumed by my already well-thumbed fake-leather volume. In my mid-forties, a wife, the mother of two small children, I have responsibilities; I need to clean the bathrooms, cook the meals. My unfinished projects litter the house. But I can't stop reading, starting the novel again every time I finish. After five or six readings, over a period of a week, the obsession runs its course, and I am again able to function.

In 1995, I'm in graduate school, in a class on the eighteenth-century novel, defending *Clarissa*. Someone has pointed out a contradiction, in that Richardson treats Clarissa as both free and unfree. "But that's an accurate depiction of girls' lives," I argue. "Clarissa believes in the democratic ideals she's been taught, and then it dawns on her that they don't apply to girls." It becomes clear to me that while others in the class are deconstructing the novel as artifact, I'm believing in it as historical and personal truth. To me, Clarissa is as real as a current neighbor or a friend from my past.

A passionate reader, a reader constantly immersed in novels, I've never been able to separate reading from life. I've identified with— and wept over—characters in fiction ranging from *Elsie Dinsmore* to *War and Peace* to romances from the back of *Redbook* magazine. I've whisked books out of sight to avoid being caught reading when I was neglecting duties, and I've turned to fiction for clues on dealing with sex, raising children, and other important aspects of life. I've reread novels obsessively and longed for sequels to tell me how the characters turned out and what happened next. When I entered a doctoral program in English and education at age fifty-two, I noticed immediately that my lifelong reading practices—personal, accepting, emotional, addictive—contrasted sharply with the critical, cognitive approaches to novels that my more recently trained fellow students employed.[1]

Thinking about how and why I had acquired these practices, I realized how much reading, for me, was entangled with gender: how, in my white, middle-class, small-town family, only women read and they seldom read anything but novels; how my favorite childhood stories, chosen by my mother from her own childhood favorites, called for an emotional response; how I graduated, in my early teens, to reading the same popular novels and magazine fiction my mother read; how Miss Whitelaw, my high school English teacher, encouraged me to read a huge number of historical novels—both literary and romantic—to get the flavor of the time periods we covered in American and English literature. Apparently, instead of reading like a scholar, I was reading like a woman.[2]

Then, as I began reading commentary about women readers, I was struck by how accurately the *negative* comments about women readers over the past four centuries described my own reading practices.[3] Since I had always regarded these reading habits as positive, indeed life-sustaining, I thought the critics of women readers must be overlooking or misinterpreting the positive values of a particular approach to reading that I, as a woman, had found useful. I set out to examine how these critics had constructed the woman reader. I also began to compare their observations with those of a small sample of contemporary white, middle-class women readers with reading practices similar to mine.

Constructing "the Woman Reader"

The practices of women readers have been belittled since at least the sixteenth century, by which time women readers were sufficiently numerous to influence the writing and publishing of books. In *Writing for Women: The Example of Woman as Reader in Elizabethan Romance*, Caroline Lucas points out that male authors often expressed embarrassment at having to earn their living by writing for women. Even in stories with strong and articulate women characters, Lucas shows, male writers included condescending remarks and editorial comments that portrayed women readers as weak, passive, and prone to misunderstanding. Flirting with readers, mocking women as silly or evil, and applying contorted interpretations to "neutralize" stories likely to empower women, they constructed "a role for the woman reader which is prescriptive and repressive [in that] the narrator constantly anticipates her reactions and arrogates her response" (4).

This dismissive concept of women readers had wide acceptance. Kate Flint, in *The Woman Reader, 1837–1914*, cites a number of rebukes of weak women readers. Edward Hakes, for instance, worried in 1574 that a woman reader could become "so nouseled in amorous bookes, vaine stories and fonde trifeling fancies, that shee smelleth of naughtiness even all hir lyfe after" (23). In 1800, the Reverend Vicesimus Knox claimed that women readers were likely to "pay the chief attention to the lively descriptions of love, and its effects" and then "eagerly wish to be actors in the scenes which they admire" (28). Thus, drawn to tawdry stories that would undermine their chastity, women were apt to adopt such stories as models for real life. Accepting fantasy as reality and consequently misconstruing reality, they might even expect their suitors or husbands to live up to the ideals of men in novels.

These deficiencies of women readers contributed to the popularity of the novel, according to early critics of that genre. Ian Watt points out that the novel contrasted with patrician male literary traditions that (its patrician adherents believed) required a formal education and specialized language skills to read. Anyone could read novels, which were based on ordinary domestic scenes and conversations and aimed, as Watt puts it, to "give the reader certain kinds of emotional experience" and to affect him or her personally and psychologically (Watt 215). Richard Steele, writing in the *Guardian* in 1713, warned that such an "unsettled way of reading. . . . naturally seduces us into a undetermined a manner of thinking. . . . [so that the] assemblage of words which is called a style becomes utterly annihilated. . . . The common defense of these people is, that they have no design in reading but for pleasure" (qtd. in Watt 48).

This "unsettled way of reading," which required no thinking and provided transient, useless pleasure without educating, was regarded as inherently appealing to women. Thus in an article entitled "Moral and Political Tendency of the Modern Novels," written in 1842, a critic declared, "The great bulk of novel readers are females; and to them such impressions (as are conveyed through fiction) are peculiarly mischievous: for, first, they are naturally more sensitive, more impressable, than the other sex; and secondly, their engagements are of a less engrossing character—they have more time as well as more inclination to indulge in reveries of fiction" (qtd. in Flint 12). The social critic W. R. Greg expressed a similar notion in 1859 when he described women as "always impressionable" readers "in whom at all times the emotional element is more awake and more powerful than the critical, whose

feelings are more easily aroused and whose estimates are more easily influenced than [men's]" (qtd. in Flint 12, 4). By the end of the
nineteenth century, medical textbooks were warning that novels
had insidious physical effects as well: the emotional reaction to
novels could cause the early onset of menstruation in girls and hys-
teria in women, dangers that could be avoided by reading about
practical subjects such as beekeeping (Flint 59).

One would assume that feminists would not share such distrust
of women readers. But in 1792 Mary Wollstonecraft railed in *A
Vindication of the Rights of Women* against "women who are
amused by the reveries of the stupid novelists, who, knowing little
of human nature, work up stale tales, and describe meretricious
scenes, all retailed in a sentimental jargon, which equally tend to
corrupt the taste, and draw the heart aside from its daily duties"
(qtd. in Flint 28). More recently, Janice Radway suggests in
Reading the Romance that getting away from "daily duties" was
in fact an important motive of the women romance readers she
interviewed. These readers, whom she calls the Smithton women,
claimed that romance novels met their needs perfectly, supplying
short, focused, literal "quick reads" (59) that bathed them in the
emotion of a one woman–one man romantic attachment, giving
them intense pleasure and an uplifting experience while affording
them a respite from the demands of husbands and children. Thus,
the Smithton women insisted, their chosen reading materials were
useful for both their content and the respite they provided.

While Radway's germinal work on women readers has been
invaluable, I see her as characterizing these women's reading as
naive in two ways.[4] First, she describes the Smithton readers as
"literal" readers who accept an author's assertions despite contrary
evidence in the text (190), regard "the romantic universe [as] identical to the universe inhabited by real women" (188), and believe in
language as "a system of names" for real-world objects and conditions that should be efficient and unambiguous (191). This view of
women readers is similar to the one Lucas ascribes to male writers
writing for women in the sixteenth century.

Second, Radway explores at length the ways in which the women's "practice and self-understanding have tacit, unintended effects and implications" (210). In explaining these effects, she cites the prevalent academic feminist view that romance novels are basically conservative, reinforcing for the Smithton readers the repressive trappings of the patriarchal system.[5] The Smithton readers, however, regarded feminism as disrespectful of their choice to make sacrifices as wives and mothers. Through repeated readings of romance novels, the women saw themselves as reinforcing their "womanness," allying themselves with their own sex.

Sara Mills uses the term "authentic realism" to denote the reading practice of women who, like Radway's romance readers and me, read primarily for pleasure, assess the events and female characters in novels against their own experience and their sense of "what women are *really* like," and feel an interest in and kinship with the author, especially if she too is female (Mills, "Authentic Realism" 58). Mills notes that this approach is "used by many ordinary women . . . as if it were mere common sense and self-evidently the proper method for analyzing women's texts . . . [and thus it] must be treated seriously, and not simply discounted as unacademic and theoretically naive" (53).

Despite the call for respectful treatment, however, Mills clearly thinks women who read for authentic realism need to advance to more complex forms of reading such as the rigorous critique of patriarchy used by Kate Millett in *Sexual Politics*, the "gynocriticism" proposed by Elaine Showalter in "Feminist Criticism in the Wilderness," French feminist practices, or Marxist feminism. These more systematic and critical methods involve setting oneself apart from the reading, regarding the novel as "text," and analyzing it from the outside rather than living in it as a participant. They involve, as the fourteenth-century scholar Christine de Pisan put it, "reading *as* a woman" rather than "reading *like* a woman" (qtd. in Schibanoff 95). While someone reading like a woman could immerse herself in the world of any novel that she believed to be authentic, someone reading as a woman would always be aware of herself as outside the text, looking on, ready to judge when the text departed from certain standards she held. On the basis of distinctions made by the earlier commentators previously cited, one might even say that then she would be reading like a man.[6]

One could argue that feminists promote critical reading to combat an organized effort by patriarchal society to keep women subservient and powerless by deliberately assigning to women (and to women readers) the characteristics men wish to disown and by using social, moral, intellectual, and cultural institutions to maintain a male-dominated power structure. But how does this explanation frame the way many women, including me, read? Are we indeed politically naive, if not passive and weak? Is there something wrong with our reading practices? Or are we simply engaging in processes and practices of reading that differ from those that critics of women's reading practices value?

Comparing Women's Stories of Reading

In an effort to see how typical or idiosyncratic my reading has been, as well as to understand how novel reading has functioned and continues to function in contemporary women's lives, I conducted a series of interviews with nine women about their experiences of reading from their earliest memories up to the present.[7] My aim in these interviews was not to generalize about women readers from such a small sample but to become more aware of how reading had been experienced by other women. I also hoped to find what phenomenologists call "transsituational similarities"—those that occur when an experience is "shared by different people at different times and places" under "similar circumstances" (Barritt, Beekman, et al. 26). For this reason, I chose to interview professional (but nonacademic) middle-class women between the ages of forty and sixty who, like me, described themselves as passionate readers since childhood. I hoped this choice might enable me to see some continuity between these readers (including me) and passionate, middle-class women readers in the past—readers most likely to mention their reading in diaries, letters, fiction, and other writings that might be used in historical studies. I further hoped to gauge how my respondents had been affected by previous constructions of the woman reader.

The stories of three of my respondents—Kim, Sylvia, and Nancy—illustrate three themes that emerged again and again in the interviews.

Kim and Resistance to Gender Roles

Kim, a civil rights lawyer now in her forties, recalls that at age ten or eleven, she would slip into her bedroom closet after she was supposed to be asleep, switch on the closet light, and read. It is probably not accidental that one of the books she would read over and over under these confined conditions was *The Diary of Anne Frank*. In the privacy and secrecy of her closet, Kim remembers being

> very envious of [Anne Frank's] ability to express herself and [I] remember reading that book a lot to try to understand what she was doing that was making so much sense to me. I liked the way that she talked; I felt she was talking to me. I think that was very special— that feeling of a personal connection. So often books are . . . told in the third person. But that was a book in which this girl who doesn't know me is being very intimate with me and letting me into her world. She was asking a lot of questions that I was asking.

This world that Anne Frank was describing, Kim believes, resembled in many respects the world Kim was trying to understand at the time. Kim recalls being "completely transfixed" in the late 1960s by the images on television of the marches on Washington, Martin Luther King's speeches, the assassinations of Bobby Kennedy and King, the Detroit riots, and the Vietnam War. These television images, she surmises, "shaped the way I was relating to the world, and I think I was looking for literature that also made that connection." Kim continues:

> I think I was also attracted very much to the situation [Anne Frank] was in, which was being in an environment that was secret and

protected, ostensibly, but not really all that safe because the world outside is very chaotic. And that was, I think, what I was experiencing at that time too, given all that was going on in the world.

Because Kim viewed their situations as similar and felt that this author was speaking directly to her in an intimate relationship, she was able to use Anne Frank as a model for her own behavior and character. As Kim puts it:

> Anne Frank gave me confidence that no matter how embattled you are, or how besieged your life is, you can still have integrity. You don't have to become a victim. . . . [S]he was a voice of reason that would survive, embodied in her diary, despite the chaos. That gave me confidence, because I felt embattled . . . [because of] what was going on outside, and [inside] my family. I was the only girl and I had two brothers who were pretty rough on me. I also was very shy and pretty isolated socially, so I didn't feel like I had a real comfortable social place to be. The Holocaust was very much a part of my family environment. And my grandparents were all immigrants and my mother's an immigrant from Canada, so I felt in some degree new to the country too.

Unlike most of the women I interviewed, Kim disliked Nancy Drew mysteries, feeling that Nancy was "cold" and inhabited an insider position that Kim did not recognize. She was searching instead for girl heroines "who were kind of on the outside, who saw themselves as outsiders, and whose being on the outside embodied a kind of truthfulness about their world." *The Secret Garden*, another story involving secrecy and enclosure, offered one such heroine. Mary Lennox, Kim explains, is "a young girl, an orphan, a guest in the house, on the outside, who, through her compassion and gentleness, built bridges between herself and other people and demonstrated a whole lot more common sense than the adults around her." Kim read this book "a million times." *Anne of Green Gables* also appealed to her. "Anne was the kind of girl I wished I could have been," Kim says. "[She was] very outspoken, very uninhibited, extremely imaginative and totally charming. . . . I didn't see myself that way." Although this book and its sequels were among those Kim reread many times, she recalls being very disappointed when Anne "[gave] up her writing for her husband the doctor, to be the wife and mother, [since] I thought she was also going to be a writer."

Jo March in *Little Women*, *Little Men*, and *Jo's Boys* provided a role model who did not abandon her dreams of being a writer even though she married and had children. While Kim's mother and all the women she knew were "very traditional," Kim notes that "Jo chose a nontraditional path, with the complete sanction of her mother. I found that very empowering, and I think I really internalized that, and it helped me as I grew up to make decisions that weren't necessarily the easiest as far as my family was concerned." Kim internalized the meaning of Jo's story through so many readings of *Little Women* that she wore out her copy of the book. When her mother bought her a new copy, she recalls rereading the novel, thinking, "Wow, I just hadn't realized this, I didn't see this before, I didn't see that before," and deriving from her new edition new meanings as she grew older.

For Kim, reading continued to be a space where she set her own standards. Just as she had never admired Nancy Drew, she also never took to popular novels such as *Gone with the Wind*. She based her rejection on political grounds:

> There was a real falsity, I thought, to my environment, and I was very bothered as a teenager by the lifestyles of the people around me. There was a real intolerance for people with different ethnicities, with different income levels, and I thought that people's politics . . . weren't reflected in their lifestyles. I felt a large sense of hypocrisy in the world around me and I felt that same [objectionable sense of values] in those books—those more popular books.

Instead of turning to adult novels in high school, then, Kim began to split her reading in two directions: first into classic historical nineteenth-century novels by Jane Austen, George Eliot, and others (which she still prefers today), and second into radical minority literature that critiqued the status quo. Somewhat later, she consciously turned to women authors: "I started reading

Eudora Welty, Kate Chopin, Maya Angelou, and Sylvia Plath. I loved Sylvia Plath: again this extremely alienated person. For a while—I'd say three or four years—I predominantly read books by women." In her reading today, she seeks "observations about human nature and about the characters" and notes, "I guess I'm looking for books that make sense to me, that tell me something about myself. So I probably read less for entertainment than I do for a search for some kind of enlightenment that I just can't find any other way."

Sylvia and the Quest for Knowledge

Sylvia, currently in her fifties, is a partner in a general-practice law firm. As a child, she was fascinated by knowledge, and she herself attributes this fascination to "a prurient interest in sex" prompted by the medical journals her father, a pediatrician, left lying around the house. Thus she found a "main source of reading delight" in her father's dictionary, which she often perused by flashlight under her covers at night. As she explains, the medical journals contained "all these pictures of people with weird lesions on their bodies, with their eyes blacked out, standing [naked]—particularly [those with] diseases of the genitals. And I would read these things, and there were all these words I would have to look up. Many of them were pieces of words in the dictionary, because there were all these lab words."

Like Kim, Sylvia considered herself socially isolated, a "misfit," an "outcast." The misfit feeling derived partly from Sylvia's skipping second grade and thus losing her same-age friends and being "teased about being a smart kid." She found another misfit in Superman and Superboy comics; she could identify with a character who had a powerful secret identity that contrasted with the drab and uninteresting persona he was required to display to the rest of the world. Sylvia says of Superman, "I loved the fantasy of it; I used to get lost in those comics, thinking about Krypton, Jor-El. . . . I could buy a comic and lock myself in my room and

read it. I would lift out over where I was and be in the book." She
continues:

> I remember, as a kid, walking around with books. I would bring
> books to the dinner table. I couldn't put them down. I would carry
> them everywhere with me; I'd get so distracted I couldn't put that
> aside and do what I was really supposed to be doing. It was great.

Because Sylvia viewed her home life as less than happy, she was
drawn to books in which the families were happy. Reading about
happy families in, say, *Cheaper by the Dozen* and *Belles on Their Toes*
would take Sylvia "out of the nuttiness that was going on around
me and would replace it with these happy mothers and fathers."
Also, the relative safety of small-town life in the 1950s afforded
Sylvia the freedom to court adventures in real life. So, on a steady
diet of classic girls' books, dog and horse stories, and Nancy Drew,
Hardy Boys, and Dana Girls mysteries, Sylvia recalls exploring the
city cemeteries and the dense woods along the river, "worrying
about who [she] might run into." She adds, "[There] was always
this thrill that something might happen. I remember the nervous-
ness, the agitation about testing myself: Is something bad going to
happen? What about ghosts?"

Through her constant reading, Sylvia feels she was "struggling
to find meaning, and somehow having a sense that there were
answers, that other people had the answers." She says, "I didn't
know the questions to ask to get to the answers, so [I had] this
difficult undertaking."

In her preadolescent search for answers, Sylvia turned from her
father's dictionary, kept on the bottom shelf of the bookcase just
inside her parents' bedroom door, to her mother's Leon Uris and
Henry Miller novels, housed on the out-of-reach shelves. Her
mother read these books sequestered in the bathroom, smoking
cigarettes, taking a break from her three children. Sylvia says:

> I remember rifling through [Henry Miller] looking for certain
> words. . . . I thought adults got to read stuff that was forbidden to
> me, and wouldn't it be great when I had access to that. Once I found

those books, I remember pulling them off the shelf and [trying to put them back exactly right], having the feeling that someone was always looking to see if books had been moved and I'd get caught.

In her early teens, Sylvia graduated to her mother's Readers' Digest Condensed Books and adult books such as *The Good Earth*, *Gone with the Wind*, *The Once and Future King*, and *Marjorie Morningstar*. Sylvia says of her reading experience, "When I read, I often have a sense of self and identity being like a permeable membrane, so that I spill over into the book and the book spills over into me. I get very lost in novels, and I insert myself into the character's circumstances and feelings." This permeability caused problems when Sylvia read Sylvia Plath's *The Bell Jar* shortly after she finished college. "I was emotionally ripped up and vulnerable," she recalls, "and I read that book and somehow I got enmeshed with Sylvia Plath and saw myself as her. . . . And then I started to think about her ending her life." In a recent reading of *Middlemarch*, Sylvia notes, "I was there. I could have been Dorothea on some level; I could look out of her eyes; I could feel her feelings. . . . It isn't so much a projection as really this permeability thing, because I feel sensations as I read." Reminded of her description of what it felt like as a child to "lift out" of her ordinary life and "be in the book," Sylvia says of *Middlemarch*, "I transposed myself [and was] like a bug on the wall, listening in on the conversations."

The tension between the permeability and "bug on the wall" experiences—the attempt to be both inside and outside a situation—may reflect Sylvia's ongoing quest for greater knowledge: knowledge of words and their derivations, knowledge that grown-ups had, knowledge that always seemed out of reach. She felt required to "find out whatever the message in the universe was for me." Sylvia says, "I always had the sense that there were really some answers to life. . . . I had to live the right kind of life; I had to live a moral life in the sense of doing right by the rest of the world and . . . being true to myself. But what did that mean, to be true to myself?" She struggled to fill in "gaps" in her knowledge, to make up for deficiencies she perceived in her upbringing and education. She describes a feeling of trying to "counter the entropy in the universe" and is still frustrated by the thought that knowledge is "growing by bounds and there's no way I can ever master it except if I start right now and read as much as I can." At one point, Sylvia began plotting how many books she could read a year and what her life expectancy was, in an effort to maximize her capacity for knowing.

Novels aid in this quest for knowledge because they provide a unique historical perspective. Thus with *Middlemarch* or with a Jane Austen novel or a war novel, Sylvia says:

> You have a picture of society that's different from what a historian writes, that's different from what you get from going to a museum or looking at paintings. . . . You're acquiring knowledge about how something was then, through someone else's eyes. . . . What I like about reading historical novels is the different flavor from the histories; it's nice to know the history of a time so that then you can take the historical novel and sort of fit the pieces in together.

For Sylvia, then, as for Kim, reading novels seems to offer "some kind of enlightenment" that can't be found elsewhere. A blurring of boundaries between herself and characters in a novel, a voyeuristic lifting out in which she is the observer of other people's lives, and an intellectual challenge in which she is fitting together pieces of historical information from fiction, histories, biographies, paintings, museums, and even maps (another of her interests) are necessary components of a holistic view of life.

Nancy and Life Trajectories

Nancy, a journalist and freelance writer now in her late fifties, notes that her reading and life have intertwined on several occasions, as she illustrates with the following story. Pregnant with her first child, Nancy read Sigrid Undset's novel *Kristin Lavransdatter.* In the novel Kristin gives birth kneeling on the floor and pulling with all her might on a rope hanging from the ceiling whenever she feels a contraction. When Nancy went into labor, she was given "twilight sleep," and in her periodic awakenings into semi-consciousness she began reenacting Kristin's birthing scene. "I was in this hospital bed with arms on it, and I kept struggling to find the rope," Nancy recalls. "I would pull myself up, and I would be grabbing the sides of the bed, trying to get upright, trying to use gravity to let the baby come out faster." At that point, she adds, "a nurse would come in and force me back down on the bed and I would clunk out again."

The story illustrates Nancy's search, in her adult reading, for ways to handle milestones in life. Nancy speaks, for instance, of the difficulty she had reconciling her expectation that she would fulfill a traditional woman's role with a decision to work outside the home. Nancy's father died when she was fifteen, and she observed firsthand the grief her mother experienced at having to return to work as a nurse after years of being "happy as a clam being a housewife." Then second-wave feminism, Nancy believes, changed conditions for her entire generation. "That was a struggle for me," she says, "because I was very reluctant to get a job. I wanted it both ways: I wanted to be free and independent and respected, but I didn't want to work." It was as though "you started out being taught how to play tennis and suddenly discovered that the game had changed into a game of football and you weren't prepared. You didn't have the padding; you didn't have the skills. But you were out there on the field anyway."

In this predicament, Nancy sought out authors who wrote "about people over the life course." She discovered Anne Tyler "purely by accident"—she was intrigued by one of Tyler's titles—and proceeded to read all her novels. She notes that Tyler deals

> with all those marriage and relationship issues and efforts to put meaning into your life as an individual woman [with]in the constraints of marriage. Her characters often walk away from marriage—but they always come back. She obviously believes that ultimately people have to be connected to be happy, but there's always a tremendous period of turmoil in making those decisions.

Tyler also explores another theme that Nancy believes she is drawn to in her reading: this author appreciates "the lack of planning and the accidental in life." Nancy views herself as "trying to decide whether things are accidental or whether there is some sort of design, either an unconscious design coming out of you, or some grand design." Describing herself as an atheist, Nancy says, "Rationally, I don't believe in a grand design; irrationally, I think I do."

In her forties, Nancy immersed herself in Robertson Davies's novels, especially the Salterten and Deptford trilogies, both of which she reread several times. She was drawn to these books partly because of their moral stance, "where good is rewarded and evil ultimately catches up with people." But also, she felt, Davies had "a very complex view of relationships" and the same appreciation of serendipity that she found in Tyler. "There's a great deal of happenstance, happy coincidence, a synchronicity in his books," she explains, so that "you begin to realize after a while that he believes in some sort of a pattern to relationships and the universe. I found that sort of structure comforting. . . . It was very helpful to me to have someone who could look at things from a distance and see things work out over time."

Recently Nancy retired—an agonizing decision for her because "it's a move away from structure and safety into taking advantage of a lot more freedom and dabbling" and because it entailed giving up her hard-won professional identity. She wonders whether "women who really did a lot of reading when they were kids go through more inner turmoil when they make decisions" because they "experience [life] more intensely." In this situation, she's set herself the challenge of reading all forty-seven of Anthony Trollope's novels, which she admires because in them he constructs "very complicated women" characters who have to make "consistently difficult" decisions such as whether to marry. These characters, who often appear in more than one book, "are all dealing with fundamental issues," she notes, "and I just find it very comforting to see characters over a life span and see them reappear and have an impact on others' lives." Reading over her interview transcripts, Nancy commented, "Reading has really organized my life, and I just thought of it as something that I did. I never saw it as a driving force."

Reconstructing "the Woman Reader"

According to Nina Baym, women have "always needed print more than men did for all sorts of basic information" (15). Until recently, women needed print because they had less access than men to formal education and relied on self-education through reading.[8] Women could not learn from experimenting and making mistakes as men often did, because for women, Baym points out, "the consequences of error were so often irremediable" (15). The stories Kim, Sylvia, and Nancy tell suggest that their reading experiences did indeed stand in for other avenues of experience, providing them with basic information, theoretical concepts, and models of behavior unavailable to them through other channels.

Novels could help girls, for instance, make sense of the confusing area of gender roles. Like Clarissa, those of us who grew up in the 1950s and 1960s confronted contradictory messages from social institutions, which touted gender equality while implicitly disparaging girls and women. Like Kim, many of us read and reread novels from the canon of "girls' literature" that, as Shirley Foster and Judy Simons point out, "engage directly with the conceptualization of girlhood and the development of a gendered identity" (xii). The classic girls' books, like most children's literature, present resistant, even radical, roles for young characters. Thus the heroine is often set apart from more ordinary girls.

Lucy Maud Montgomery's narrator makes this distinction clear in speaking of Gilbert Blythe's impressions of Anne Shirley in *Anne of Avonlea*:

> [Anne] held over [Gilbert] the unconscious influence that every girl, whose ideals are high and pure, wields over her friends; an influence which would endure as long as she was faithful to those ideals

and which she would as certainly lose if she were ever false to them. In Gilbert's eyes Anne's greatest charm was the fact that she never stooped to the petty practices of so many of the Avonlea girls—the small jealousies, the little deceits and rivalries, the palpable bids for favor. Anne held herself apart from all this, not consciously or out of design, but simply because anything of the sort was utterly foreign to her transparent, impulsive nature, crystal clear in its motives and aspirations. (366)

Anne is thus valuable partly because she is not like more girlish girls; the implication is that she is more like a boy than most girls are. Like the March girls in *Little Women*, she is set against more manipulative, boy-crazy girls who are materialistic, overly concerned with clothes, dishonest, or too self-involved to think of others.

While these portrayals of heroines as unlike ordinary girls could be interpreted as sending a message to girl readers that being a girl is unfortunate, Kim found in them a positive message. She took them as proof that having ambitions and values different from those of one's family and the surrounding social world was legitimate. She was clearly looking for evidence that one could live with integrity, and be integral, even when one is a girl. Kim's repeated readings of specific books also enabled her to envision and practice potential future roles. Rachel Brownstein argues that novels have traditionally provided the only place where girls and women could practice active lives, explore what it would mean to be understood, or even experience having their words and feelings attended to. Thus Brownstein asserts, "Girls, enjoined from thinking about becoming generals and emperors, tend to live more in novels than boys do, and to live longer in them" (xv). Kim's long-term and intense relationships with characters and authors support Brownstein's point.

But the women I interviewed read for information beyond gender concepts, although gender often figured in this larger quest as well. Sylvia, like many girls, cast a wide net for reading materials, selecting genres meant for boys as well as girls, for adults as well as

children, and reading popular literature along with literary classics. She depended on extensive haphazard reading in order to
happen on reading experiences that would turn out to be meaningful. As she says, she couldn't define her questions and thus
didn't know what she was looking for.

Sylvia also felt an urgent need to combine fragmented pieces of
information into some sort of holistic view of life. Established systems of knowledge were of little help here, since her goal was to
"find out whatever the message in the universe was for me." To
understand the whole of history, she supplemented history books,
from which women are largely absent, with novels, where they are
active participants. To understand other people, she opened herself to "permeability" by characters in novels, gaining experience
by "being in the book."

Nancy worked toward a holistic view as well. As she absorbed
novelistic experience, following female characters' lives "over the
life span," she tried to see how these lives fit together. How did
other women make decisions? How did they reconcile the private
self with the public contributor to the community, women's traditional roles with professional ambition, the past with the present
and future? What could be the consequences of various choices
characters—and Nancy herself—might make? Nancy never felt
obligated to settle on particular answers to these questions.
Instead, she left them open-ended, dependent on the myriad special circumstances that might turn up in an individual woman's
life. It's no wonder that, having seen in novels so many options for
women and the possible consequences of various decisions, Nancy
came to feel that passionate readers agonize more over decisions
than nonreaders do.

To achieve the personal results they expected from reading,
these women treated novels not as self-contained texts or as historical artifacts but as extensions of their own lives. Therefore academic literary practices, such as those advocated by Mills, worked
against their purposes. Nancy, in fact, describes being unable to
resume her independent reading agenda after college until she

shook off the compulsion to analyze and could "feel like I was reading for fun again, that it was recreational, using another side of my brain, whichever side it is that responds intuitively rather than rationally." Offered a choice of reading rationally, Nancy opted instead to tap into what Foster and Simons call a "collective cultural inheritance" passed down through generations, often by mothers who handed down to daughters the books they read as girls (ix). Women readers who embrace this inheritance rely on a parallel tradition of reading practices that persist even though the conditions from which they derived seem to have changed. Kathryn Shevelow illustrates, for instance, how seventeenth- and eighteenth-century advice manuals and articles in the *Tatler* that were aimed toward women readers conditioned those women to read as part of a social situation involving an author who was a father, mother, or trusted friend. I would suggest that this actively engaged, dialogic social approach to reading has been passed on by mothers to daughters and by authors to readers, so that the concepts of author speaking intimately to reader and author participating in a conversation are included in the assemblage of reading practices that I am calling "reading like a woman." Through similar practices, women in the past have, as Barbara Sicherman has suggested, "found in reading a way of apprehending the world that enabled them to overcome some of the confines of gender" and experience a "freedom of imagination . . . in books [that] encouraged new self-definitions" (202).

We who read like women have been "naughty" and "sensitive" and "impressionable" and allowed ourselves to be "nouseled" by books because choosing that tradition of reading provided the practical and emotional experience we needed to compose lives and relationships we could imagine only through reading. In favoring "unsettled" reading methods over more academic, structured ones, we have absorbed knowledge that wasn't available through established knowledge systems. Certainly other women, in previous eras, enveloped in similar historical and cultural situations, have done the same.

NOTES

1. I majored in English at a small Virginia women's college in the early 1960s, where the professor in my one course on the novel explained what each novel meant in its historical context and how it achieved unity. Although in my notebooks I reproduced her diagrams of how themes and plots worked, I did not, as far as I know, change any of my reading practices, perhaps because I despaired of ever knowing as much as my professor did.

2. For further comparisons of academic and nonacademic reading, see Radway (*Feeling*) and Pearce. Radway distinguishes between "dry" academic reading and the kind of engaged reading the Book-of-the-Month Club reviewers believed their "general readers" enjoyed. These reviewers spoke of "inhaling" novels, being "captured," "mugged," "swept away," (116–17). Pearce distinguishes between her academic or "hermeneutic" reading and what she calls "implicated" reading, which happens when her feminism is "off-duty" and she opens herself to "the chaos and the confusion" of reading, engaging in "dialogic text-reader interactions" with the attendant possibility of "emotional disturbance" and vulnerability, in an experience she argues is analogous to romance (2–3).

3. My sources, which discuss English and American women readers, almost always refer to privileged white women. For some examples of African American and working-class women's reading, see Gere (esp. ch. 6) and Tinsley and Kaestle.

4. Radway herself has had second thoughts about her interpretations of the Smithton women's reading. She suggests in *A Feeling for Books* that the Smithton readers "structured and controlled our interviews . . . and, I suspect, resisted my questions in creative ways. In fact, it occurs to me now that because I was less familiar with their linguistic patterns and habitual ways of talking, I was probably less able to pick up on the nature of their resistance and their manner of polite acquiescence to my volunteered interpretations. In fact, I suspect now that they were often humoring me" (363n13).

5. As Radway notes in her 1991 introduction to *Reading the Romance*, this argument reflects particular personal circumstances and academic theories current in 1984, when the book was originally published. If she had begun the research in 1991, she would have written much more self-reflexively, included some transcripts, and separated more clearly her respondents' assertions from her own.

6. In examining their fiction-reading practices, Bleich found that women "*enter* the world of the novel, take it as something 'there' for that purpose, [while] men *see* the novel as a result of someone's action and construe its meaning or logic in those terms" (239). Bleich explained these differences

psychoanalytically, as resulting from girls' different gender positioning relative to their mothers and fathers. He argued that because narrators speak in the "mother's tongue" (264), women readers identify with that voice and are able to enter the world it creates without feeling othered.

7. Some of these women were acquaintances I knew through a book club, and some I met for the first time at arranged meetings. In the interviews, I asked thirty-five questions, beginning with, What are your earliest memories of reading or being read to?, and ending with, What books have you loved recently, and why? Usually, however, I did not follow the questions rigidly, since I was reluctant to interrupt an enthusiastic flow of stories and thoughts. For follow-up interviews, I gave respondents transcripts of earlier interviews to add to or clarify. All these women were white, all but one were married at the time of the interviews, all but one had children, and all had grown up with stay-at-home mothers, although one mother managed a bakery in the home.

8. As Elizabeth Bennet remarks in *Pride and Prejudice*, "such of us as wished to learn, never wanted the means. We were always encouraged to read. . . . Those who chose to be idle, certainly might" (110; ch. 6). For some idea of the extensive education of middle-class English girls in household economy in the eighteenth century, see Vickery. For insight into the education of American girls at the end of the nineteenth century, see Sicherman.

Works Cited

Austen, Jane. *Pride and Prejudice*. 1813. Ed Donald Grey. 3rd ed. Norton Critical Editions. New York: Norton, 2001.

Barritt, Loren, and Ton Beekman et al. *Researching Educational Practice*. Grand Forks: U of North Dakota Monograph Ser., 1985.

Baym, Nina. *American Women Writers and the Work of History, 1790–1860*. New Brunswick: Rutgers UP, 1995.

Bleich, David. "Gender Interests in Reading and Language." Flynn and Schweickart 234–66.

Brownstein, Rachel M. *Becoming a Heroine: Reading about Women in Novels*. New York: Columbia UP, 1994.

Flint, Kate. *The Woman Reader: 1837–1914*. Oxford: Clarendon, 1993.

Flynn, Elizabeth A., and Patrocinio P. Schweickart. *Gender and Reading: Essays on Readers, Texts, and Contexts*. Baltimore: Johns Hopkins UP, 1986.

Foster, Shirley, and Judy Simons. *What Katy Read: Feminist Re-readings of "Classic" Stories for Girls*. Iowa City: U of Iowa P, 1995.

Gere, Anne Ruggles. *Intimate Practices: Literacy and Cultural Work in U.S. Women's Clubs, 1880–1920*. Urbana: U of Illinois P, 1997.

Lucas, Caroline. *Writing for Women: The Example of Woman as Reader in Elizabethan Romance*. Philadelphia: Open UP, 1989.

Millett, Kate. *Sexual Politics*. London: Virago, 1977.

Mills, Sara. "Authentic Realism." Mills, Pearce, Spaull, and Millard 51–82.

Mills, Sara, Lynne Pearce, Sue Spaull, and Elaine Millard. *Feminist Readings / Feminists Reading*. Charlottesville: UP of Virginia, 1989.

Montgomery, Lucy Maud. *Anne of Avonlea*. 1909. New York: Avenel, 1985.

Pearce, Lynne. *Feminism and the Politics of Reading*. London: Arnold, 1997.

Radway, Janice. *A Feeling for Books: The Book-of-the-Month Club, Literary Taste, and Middle-Class Desire*. Chapel Hill: U of North Carolina P, 1997.

———. *Reading the Romance: Women, Patriarchy, and Popular Literature*. 1984. Chapel Hill: U of North Carolina P, 1991.

Schibanoff, Susan. "The Art of Reading as a Woman." Flynn and Schweickart 83–106.

Shevelow, Kathryn. "Fathers and Daughters: Women as Readers of the *Tatler*." Flynn and Schweickart 234–66.

Showalter, Elaine. "Feminist Criticism in the Wilderness." *Critical Inquiry* 8.2 (1981): 179–205.

Sicherman, Barbara. "Sense and Sensibility: A Case Study of Women's Reading in Late-Victorian America." *Reading in America: Literature and Social History*. Ed. Cathy N. Davidson. Baltimore: Johns Hopkins UP, 1989. 201–25.

Tinsley, Katherine, and Carl F. Kaestle. "Autobiographies and the History of Reading: The Meaning of Literacy in Individual Lives." *Literacy in the United States: Readers and Reading since 1880*. By Kaestle, Helen Damion-Moore, Lawrence C. Stedman, Tinsley, and William Vance Trollinger, Jr. New Haven: Yale UP, 1991. 225–44.

Vickery, Amanda. *The Gentleman's Daughter*. New Haven: Yale UP, 1998.

Watt, Ian. *The Rise of the Novel: Studies in Defoe, Richardson, and Fielding*. Berkeley: U of California P, 1967.

"Both a Woman and a Complete Professional": Women Readers and Women's Hard-Boiled Detective Fiction

Erin A. Smith

> *But down these mean streets a man must go who is not himself mean, who is neither tarnished nor afraid. The detective in this kind of story must be such a man. He is the hero; he is everything. He must be a complete man and a common man and yet an unusual man. He must be, to use a rather weathered phrase, a man of honor. . . . He must be the best man in his world and a good enough man for any world.*
>
> —RAYMOND CHANDLER 1944

> *The mystery field has become so overrun with women private eyes one can only marvel at the ingenuity of the authors and the tolerance of readers that keep them all gainfully employed.*
>
> —DICK LOCHTE 1992

In the early 1980s, something dramatic happened to the field of mystery publishing—second-wave feminism. The number of women writing novels about female (and sometimes feminist) detectives increased dramatically. By 1992, 40% of the new mystery books published were written by women. Significantly, the initial onslaught involved a small set of professional ("hard-boiled") detectives who appeared in the late 1970s and early 1980s. Marcia Muller's 1977 *Edwin of the Iron Shoes* was the first such novel, but little attention was paid to this invasion of the field by women until the first of Sara Paretsky's V. I. Warshawski novels, *Indemnity Only*, and the first of Sue Grafton's Kinsey Millhone series, *"A" Is for Alibi*, appeared in 1982. By 1985, the phenomenon was important enough to warrant an article in the *New York Times Book Review*. With recognition by one of the nation's most important literary gate-keepers came a firestorm of debate about gender, reading, and the politics of this popular genre.[1]

Although publishers usually do not make public demographically based market surveys, the common wisdom is that the audience for women's hard-boiled detective fiction is mostly women—significantly more than half, according to accounts from booksellers, authors, agents, and editors (Walton and Jones 43, 278). Although mysteries, unlike westerns and romances, are read by large numbers of men and women (64% of American women and 60% of American men reported having read a mystery novel in a 1986 survey—see Maron; Wood), there are important differences between men's and women's reading preferences. Hard-boiled mysteries were preferred by 47% of male readers but only 14% of female readers; "romantic" mysteries appealed to 49% of female readers but only 13% of male readers (Wood 18). Anecdotal evidence confirms the gender divide. For example, the 1977 fan compendium *Murder Ink* includes "A Slight Debate: A Hard-Boiled Fan and a Country-House Fan Discuss the Genre." This is a fictional disagreement over the breakfast table between a husband who likes hard-boiled novels and a wife who prefers that her murders take place in English country houses. The argument ends with the husband shooting his wife with a .38 automatic only to drop dead himself several moments later because she had slipped a fast-acting poison in his breakfast (Stasio and Hummler). Women's hard-boiled detective novels straddle this gendered divide. They belong to an established men's genre, but they are written by and about women.[2]

These texts are written, published, and read by historical actors in social and institutional situations that, according to Elizabeth Long, form the "social infrastructure" and "social framing" of reading practices. Social infrastructure is the specific social relations under which reading is taught and carried out—families, schools, a social milieu in which books are in the air in a way that inspires people to read. Social framing means that "collective and institutional processes shape reading practices by authoritatively defining what is worth reading and how to read it" ("Textual Interpretation" 196). Social framing thus dictates what gets published, reviewed, circulated in libraries, and taught in schools, as well as which ways of reading get privileged in which contexts. My concern here is to reconstruct the complex and sometimes politically contradictory ways writers, publishers, and fan-readers have taken up women's hard-boiled detective stories to address their psychological, social, and economic needs. I read reviews, advertisements, and book catalogs that encourage specific ways of reading; analyze the sales patterns at a single mystery bookstore; and interview members of a women's-mystery fan organization about the ways this fiction functions in their lives. Why did a significant number of well-educated white women take up this historically misogynist genre in the early 1980s? How does casting a woman as the hero of a "men's genre" transform it? How does a publisher market this hybrid fiction and to whom? Which readers would be engaged by this fiction and in what ways? What can these collective fantasies tell us about the relations among gender, work, and feminism at this historical moment?

Mysteries and Second-Wave Feminism

What is most striking about the 1985 *New York Times Book Review* article on women's hard-boiled detective fiction is the overtly political motivation of many of its writers. For them, this fiction was a feminist intervention into a particularly antifeminist area of culture, an attempt to enter and transform yet another bastion of male dominance. Paretsky explains:

> When I started writing, I wanted to do something very different about the way women are depicted in detective fiction. . . . As a reader of mysteries, I always had trouble with the way women are treated as either tramps or helpless victims who stand around weeping. I wanted to read about a woman who could solve her own problems. . . . I was determined to write a hard-boiled sleuth who was both a woman and a complete professional, someone who could operate successfully in a tough milieu and not lose her femininity (Stasio 39).[3]

Marilyn Stasio suggests that these new women detectives are not only the embodiment of women's demands for equal access but also the beginning of a transformation of the mystery genre: women writers do not just make the detective-hero a woman, they "redefin[e] the mystery genre by applying different sensibilities and values to it" (39). Whether feminist writers transform the genre or get co-opted by the masculinist literary tradition remains a contentious question.

Politics aside, Stasio acknowledges that the publishing industry was more than a little ambivalent about trying to sell these stories about women sleuths claiming the mean streets. She explains, "Those in the industry hold that most readers of hard-boiled fiction are men, and the trade does not see them racing to buy books written by and featuring women. They are not so sure that women want to read them either" (39). The publishing professionals Stasio quotes to prove her point are noteworthy both for their essentialist notions about gender and mystery reading and for the heat of their rhetoric. Joan Kahn, an editor at St. Martin's Press with over thirty years of experience with mysteries, insists that "the behavior in these books [hard-boiled fiction] is too crude and simplistic for most women. 'I punched him, I shot him, I killed him, I dragged his body away.' I am sure that women could write that kind of bloodthirsty prose if they really wanted to. I'm just not convinced that they like to read it" (Stasio 39). As a consequence, many women writers had trouble finding editors willing to buy their manuscripts about female private investigators in the early 1980s, and the books that did appear were not widely promoted or reviewed. The authors themselves tell stories about stumbling across the works of Marcia Muller accidentally, having been completely unaware that others were also writing about female private investigators (Walton and Jones 19).

Male writers in the field were not very encouraging either. "Women don't fit well into a trench coat and a slouch hat," argues Lawrence Block, the author of books about the hard-boiled New York detective Matthew Scudder.

> The hard-boiled private eye is a special figure in American mythol-
> ogy. . . . It's a staple of the myth that he should be a cynical loner,
> a man at odds with society and its values. That is not something
> women normally relate to. Women aren't cynical loners—that's not
> how they like to work. It seems to me that if they want to go into the
> profession seriously, women writers will have to change the myth
> itself, instead of trying to fit themselves into it. (Stasio 39)

Block wants these women out of his locker room. He is not trying to bar them from writing detective fiction of their own, but they
should do so behind a door clearly marked "Ladies."

Block's argument ought to sound familiar to historians of American literature. As Nina Baym points out, the founding critics of
American literature of the 1940s and 1950s claimed literary excellence was constituted by a quality called "Americanness" (65). The
emblematic American in this critical tradition was inevitably a man,
a rugged individual who struggles to maintain his autonomy in the
face of a society that threatens to entrap him and a wilderness that
needs to be conquered, both cast in unmistakably feminine terms.
The valorization of this particular narrative left women writers in a
"double bind" (76). If they wrote stories about traditionally feminine concerns, women writers were dismissed as trivial, but if they
wrote stories about rugged individual women, their tales were read
not as great American literature but as stories about the frustration of female nature (74). Block places women authors like Grafton
and Paretsky in a similar catch-22. If they write domestic murder
stories, they are not situating themselves within the great American tradition of hard-boiled writing, but if they write about female
investigators—however cynical, solitary, and hard-drinking—Block
will acknowledge them not as mythical American heroines but as
women with some issues about their gender identity.[4]

Block's argument is nothing new. The founding writers of hard-
boiled detective fiction, a circle of men paid by the word for prose
they churned out for the cheap pulp magazine *Black Mask* and its
competitors in the 1920s and 1930s, made similar claims. *Black Mask*,

the most important publishing outlet for hard-boiled detective fiction between the two world wars, was subtitled *The He-Man's Magazine*. Its most prominent editor, Joseph Thompson Shaw, published an editorial in the April 1933 issue describing the ideal *Black Mask* reader:

> He is vigorous-minded; hard . . . responsive to the thrill of danger, the stirring exhilaration of clean, swift, hard action. . . . [He is] a man who knows the song of a bullet, the soft, slithering hiss of a swift-thrown knife, the feel of hard fists, the call of courage. (Shaw 7)

This rhetoric was typical. The phallic imagery with which this ideal reader is described not only genders him but also makes it clear that the reading experience was sexualized. The hypermasculinity of *Black Mask* editorial content was echoed by the advertisements published alongside the fiction for guns, motorcycles, and bodybuilding programs guaranteed to make a reader a "real, honest-to-jasper he-man."[5]

There are both historical and literary-historical reasons for the hypermasculine packaging of hard-boiled detective fiction, whose pulp magazine origins suggest it initially targeted a working-class audience. First, as all-male work and leisure spaces eroded from working-class communities, imagined communities of working-class male readers emerged in part as psychic compensation.[6] Women became voters in 1920, transforming the once all-male world of partisan politics (Baker). Between 1880 and 1930, the female wage-labor force increased twice as fast as the adult female population. By 1930, half of all single women and one-quarter of all adult females were in the paid workforce. Moreover, these working women were increasingly working side by side with men. The number of ("invisible") women workers employed in domestic service in private homes declined while those employed in offices, stores, and other public places increased (see Meyerowitz, esp. xvii, 5).

Not only were all-male workplaces disappearing but working-class men and women increasingly spent their leisure time engaging in mixed-sex activities. Kathy Peiss argues that between 1880 and

1920 there was a transition in working-class life from the homosocial cultures of the previous Victorian era to the heterosocial cultures of the modern world. The center of working-class communities moved from the men-only saloon, where leisure, mutual aid, and male bonding were of a piece, to an increasingly mixed-sex world of commercial leisure—the movies, amusement parks, dance halls—where young men and women met and socialized in heterosexual couples. This loss of all-male work and leisure spaces required a variety of material and ideological compensations. Hard-boiled writing culture functioned as a homosocial imagined community that addressed some of the same needs once met on the shop floor, in the voting booth, and in the saloon. The male writers of the pulps saw themselves not as artists but as workmen who produced a lot of piecework prose sold to and read by a lot of people like themselves. Furthermore, the imagined worlds of hard-boiled fiction are filled with gendered spaces—the mean streets (where women, as in turn-of-the-century saloons, do not go unescorted), boxing matches, tobacco shops, bars.

Second, male writers of detective fiction were opposing the domination of the mystery field by more successful women writers. The best-selling British mystery authors of the 1920s and 1930s were overwhelmingly women—Agatha Christie, Dorothy Sayers, Ngaio Marsh, Josephine Tey, Margery Allingham. Although a significant number of the detective-fiction writers of the period were men, women were prominent enough to gender the occupation of mystery writing feminine, in the same way that teaching and nursing are "women's professions," although men have also practiced them. Tough, hard-boiled tales were a reaction against the effeminate stories of civilized murders in English country houses solved by the nosy spinster next door.

Raymond Chandler's 1944 essay "The Simple Art of Murder" is the best example of the way hard-boiled writers distinguished their brand of masculine, American, more (self-proclaimed) realistic detective fiction from the genteel, often female-authored British stories that dominated the market. Chandler has nothing but disdain for the grossly improbable plots and insufferably silly detectives that fill the pages of classic detective novels. According to Chandler, Dashiell Hammett rescued crime fiction from its decline into this "arid formula" (12) by relocating it from country estates to the mean streets of an inherently corrupt world. As Chandler puts it in the most quoted passage of the essay, "Hammett gave murder back to the kind of people that commit it for reasons, not just to provide a corpse; and with the means at hand, not hand-wrought dueling pistols, curare and tropical fish" (14). Moreover, as my first epigraph suggests, the detective hero in this new kind of fiction was, above all, a man, a point Chandler makes clear through sheer force of repetition.

What the hard-boiled writers of the 1920s and 1930s were doing, then, was attempting to wrest control of a specific section of the literary marketplace for men and their (embattled) concerns from the women who had dominated the field. What women like Paretsky, Grafton, and Muller are doing now is trying to introduce feminism to this particularly recalcitrant area of culture. Not surprisingly, they meet resistance.

In 1985, the *New York Times* reviewed eighty-eight mysteries. Although 40% of the crime fiction published that year was female authored, only 16% of the reviews in the *Times* were of books by women. In addition, some female writers found that male colleagues of comparable success were being given $5,000 to $10,000 more than they were in advances from publishers (Lange). This realization led to the founding in 1986 of Sisters in Crime, of which Sara Paretsky was the driving organizational force. As defined in its bylaws, the purpose of Sisters in Crime is "to combat discrimination against women in the mystery field, educate publishers and the general public as to inequalities in the treatment of female authors, and raise the level of awareness of their contribution to the field" (*Introduction*). Sisters in Crime is an international organization of over two thousand members, mostly in the United States, Canada, and Great Britain. Members include (male and female) writers, readers, editors, agents, booksellers, and librarians. Publications of Sisters in Crime include a how-to-get-published pamphlet called *Shameless Promotion for Brazen Hussies* and other guides intended to help women writers get the attention and material rewards they deserve but are not receiving.

Part of the social infrastructure that shapes ways of reading contemporary hard-boiled women's detective fiction, then, is the "hostile environment" from which it emerges. First, the hard-boiled detective genre was founded in the 1920s by men who defined themselves in opposition to all things genteel, feminine, and female-authored and who therefore filled their texts with misogynist scenes and language. Second, publishers and reviewers treated women writers of detective fiction in the 1970s and 1980s as second-class citizens of this particular republic of letters. As a consequence, writing, reading, and advocating for this fiction is, among other things, an act of resistance to the exclusion of women from the literary field and to the devaluation of their contributions to it.

Advertising and Ways of Reading

The publishing industry's initial ambivalence about women's hard-boiled detective fiction evaporated in a hurry. The impressive hardcover and paperback sales of books by Paretsky, Grafton, Muller, and others spawned a "mini-explosion of women detectives" by the late 1980s (Klein, *Woman Detective* 231). There was a significant resurgence in sales of detective fiction in general during this period. Mystery writers made it onto hardcover best-seller lists, publishers began to acquire more mystery fiction, the Book-of-the-Month Club chose a crime novel as its main selection, and membership in mystery book clubs increased dramatically. *Publishers Weekly* christened the 1980s a "new golden age of mysteries," and the growing market made the industry particularly hospitable to new writers, including those whose main characters were women (Anthony). Although both men and women read mysteries, the membership in the Mysterious Book Club (the Book-of-the-Month Club mystery wing) and in the Mystery Guild (an independent book club) is more than half female (Carter).

That women readers dominate the mystery audience might explain the marketability of female private-eye novels. However, a case study of sales at a single mystery bookstore in a medium-sized southeastern city suggests that the audience for women's hard-boiled fiction is more varied than those in the industry would suspect. According to the owner, the best-known writers of women's hard-boiled fiction—Paretsky and Grafton—sell to men and women in almost equal numbers, although the owner often has to "lean" on male readers to get them to read lesser-known female authors (personal communication, 20 Feb. 1993). How do we explain these purchasing patterns, given publishing experts' conviction that men who read hard-boiled fiction have no interest in women protagonists and that women who like to read about female heroes find the hard-boiled genre too violent and bloodthirsty for their tastes? Part of the answer is suggested by publishers' use of a marketing strategy that the media critic Todd Gitlin calls "recombination" (64). The idea is to create a genre that is a eugenic hybrid of sorts—a genre that combines two generic traditions with distinct audiences into a single text that can attract readers from both traditions. In an ideal world, women's hard-boiled detective fiction would attract both the men who are fans of tough-guy detectives from the 1930s to the present and the (usually women) readers who, inspired by second-wave feminism, demand strong, independent heroines in their fiction. The promotional blurbs on the covers of women's hard-boiled fiction are chosen to attract and combine just these audiences. They come in two clusters. The first prominently features words like *woman* and *female*. Specimens of this type include "the toughest female detective" and "best of the new breed of female detectives" (front pages of *Burn Marks* and *Blood Shot* by Paretsky). The other cluster prominently name-drops Raymond Chandler and Dashiell Hammett and uses words like "hard-boiled." Specimens of this type include "ranks among the very best of the many heirs of the Raymond Chandler / Ross Macdonald tradition" and "first-rate exponent of the hard-boiled school of detective writing" (front pages of *Where Echoes Live* by Muller and *Bitter Medicine* by Paretsky). Some of the blurbs do both at once: "a quirky blend: part Sam Spade

[Hammett's 1930s private eye], part contemporary woman" (front pages, Paretsky's *Indemnity Only*).

The idea is to attract male readers by placing these books into the gendered hard-boiled tradition while reassuring women readers that the story is about someone with whom they can identify. What women writers view as a feminist intervention into a particularly misogynist area of culture ends up being a profitable enterprise for the writers and the mainstream publishing houses that put them into print. Moreover, many of these writers are savvy businesswomen who attend to the marketing of their work. In an interview in *Armchair Detective*, Grafton describes herself as "in effect, in business with Henry Holt and Bantam [her publishers]. We're partners" (Grafton, "G" 10–11).

"Sexy" is another word that figures prominently on the covers of women's hard-boiled fiction and in promotional literature. Paretsky's V. I. Warshawski is "smart, tough, sexy," and Grafton's Millhone is "smart, sexual, likable" (*Deadlock*, front pages; *"B" is for Burglar*, back cover). Women's hard-boiled detective fiction seems to be an erotically charged genre. Titles of review articles in large, metropolitan newspapers include "Female Dick" and "When the Dick Is a Dame" (see Morgan; Lochte). The appeal of this fiction lies in part in the gender trouble it creates. Not only does the genre cast a woman in a historically masculine position, the wordplay repeatedly calls attention to the woman's sexualized appropriation of male privilege. For feminist readers, the representation of women in powerful, nontraditional positions might be appealing. In addition, the juxtaposition in phrases like "female dick" destabilizes the customary binaries of gender and sexuality. According to Priscilla Walton and Manina Jones, "This in-between locus can counter dominant constructions of gender and sexuality by placing in question the clear-cut and essentialized character of the norms established by previous practices of the hard-boiled mold" (105).[7] However, a fan of the masculinist hard-boiled tradition might find that the sexualizing of this uppity woman, in part, neutralizes her bold foray into a once all-male profession. She is not a detective, she is a female dick, which both sexualizes her and makes her sound as if she is a profoundly unnatural woman.

Advertisement for Bantam Dell Mysteries, from the 1992
catalog of Mystery Books–Dupont Circle. Used by permission
of Dell Publishing, a division of Random House, Inc.

The use of sex to sell this kind of fiction is much more salient in visual advertisements. For example, the ad above is really two ads. The language appeals to female or feminist readers; the image, to what feminist film critics call "the male gaze" (Mulvey). The language of the ad interpellates the same kinds of readers attracted by Paretsky's self-conscious feminism and the framing of these novels as specifically about women detectives. "The best man for the case is a woman!" invokes a specific brand of liberal feminism. Moreover, "We put the Ms. in Mystery" makes special appeal to women who welcomed the availability of a professional title that made a woman's marital status irrelevant. Not coincidentally, *Ms.* is also the name of an important feminist periodical that named Paretsky one of its 1986 Women of the Year for her activism on behalf of women detective-fiction writers. However, the visual part of the ad interpellates another kind of reader, the (usually) male reader of hard-boiled fiction, who might be a little anxious about this woman in Sam Spade's shoes. We do not see the woman's face, which would make her character and emotions apparent to us. Instead the shot includes only her legs and lower torso, costumed so as to foreground her sexuality. This represents the woman as both a sexual object and a fairly useless pursuer of criminals. It might be difficult to chase after thugs in spike heels and a short skirt. The phallic, snub-nosed pistol nestled against her leg suggests the male privilege she is appropriating, but the rest of her costuming qualifies its message. She may have a tough and independent streak, but she is still defined first and foremost by her sexuality.

Although it is easiest to read this sexualized image as a male anxiety-defusing mechanism, that is not the only available reading of the image in the ad. It could be taken as evidence that, following Paretsky, this detective is "both a woman and a complete professional, someone who could operate successfully in a tough milieu and not lose her femininity." To be an accomplished professional woman and look terrific in a revealing outfit suggests that competence and sexiness are not mutually exclusive. Such a reading of "sexy" makes sense as a reaction to previous fictional female detectives. In turn-of-the-century dime novels, there were two breeds of women detectives—the pretty (incompetent) ones who went into sleuthing only to clear the name of a lover in order to get married and retire, and the big, strapping (competent) ones with visible facial hair who did not wed (Klein, *Woman Detective* 31–53). In the light of such a tradition, looking good in one's spike heels and short skirt while being gainfully employed solving crimes seems like a remarkably liberating achievement.

The social framing of this fiction, then, tells us that women's hard-boiled detective stories are deeply enmeshed with contemporary debates about gender, work, power, and sexuality. These texts are simultaneously marketed to feminist readers seeking stories about independent, professional (often sexually liberated) women and to readers of a misogynist literary tradition who find that sexualizing a professional woman can effectively return her to her appropriate, subordinate place. Reading such fiction may offer reassurance that a woman's professional accomplishments in a male-dominated field do not reduce her sexual attractiveness or reassurance that even the most competent professional woman is still a sexual object. If male fans of traditional hard-boiled fiction are a significant part of the market, maintaining this uneasy tension may be critical to achieving the sales necessary to make women's detective fiction profitable.

The Politics of Women's Detective Fiction

Most of the existing scholarship on detective fiction comes out of a formalist or structuralist tradition that attends to texts as sign systems but not to the social and economic worlds out of which ways of reading these texts emerge. Literary critics have focused particularly on the denouement of detective novels, where the mystery is solved; the various clues woven together into a seamless and coherent narrative; and social order restored. Fredric Jameson argues that mystery readers "read for the ending," so that the rest of the novel is degraded to a means to that end (132). Such exclusive focus on the form of detective fiction has a number of troubling consequences. First, it tends to reify the genre, privileging formal continuities over differences in subgenre, setting, and protagonist that are of great importance to fan-readers. Second, it ascribes a monolithic, reactionary politics to detective fiction—that the fiction inevitably recommends an ideology of competitive individualism or that it affirms existing power structures by locating crime in evil individuals rather than corrupt social institutions (Palmer 66; Cawelti 35, 105).[8] Third, it ignores differences in the conditions of production and primary readership over time and in different media. For example, the 1920s and 1930s readers of Hammett in the cheap pulp magazine *Black Mask* are not the same readers (demographically speaking) who buy his novels in expensive Vintage Crime Classics paperbacks in 2000. Reading these texts as classics is not at all the same as reading them as trash. The different reading protocols these labels invite, in effect, rewrite the text. As the historian of the book Roger Chartier reminds us:

> Against a purely semantic definition of the text (which inhabits not only structuralist criticism in all its variants but also the literary theories most attuned to a reconstruction of the reception of works), one must state that forms produce meaning and that a text, stable in its letter, is invested with a new meaning and status when the mechanisms that make it available to interpretation change. (*Order* 3)

In this essay, I am rethinking what constitutes literature. Instead of studying texts as linguistic artifacts, I am concerned with texts as social processes—economic, political, and psychic transactions among writers, editors, publishers, and the readers who encounter texts either individually or as part of reading communities.[9] The politics of this fiction, then, depend not only on the language of the text but also on the ways of reading specific to given interpretive communities and to the contours of the institutions readers, writers, and publishers inhabit.

There is a great deal more disagreement about the specific politics of women's hard-boiled detective fiction in the scholarly literature. Maureen T. Reddy's *Sisters in Crime: Feminism and the Crime Novel* and Kathleen Gregory Klein's *The Woman Detective: Gender and Genre* are surveys, tracing women detectives and women's crime fiction back to the nineteenth century, but they have substantial chapters on contemporary hard-boiled heroines as well. Reddy argues that women "have created female heroes who challenge received wisdom about women's role and novels that subvert genre conventions" (149). However, Klein insists in a chapter suitably entitled "An Unsuitable Job for a Feminist?" that women protagonists do not transform the genre but are co-opted by its masculinist conventions into complicity with an oppressive patriarchal system. Sally Munt's *Murder by the Book? Feminism and the Crime Novel* is an overview of the wave of feminist detective fiction that appeared in Britain and the United States in the 1980s.

Munt focuses on more marginal works—lesbian novels, socialist-feminist work, and other texts lacking mass-market publication. Although she sees these texts as Gramscian sites of struggle over meaning, texts that lack an inherent politics, she is uniformly critical of the work of Paretsky, Grafton, and others. Munt describes their work as "liberal feminist crime fiction" and maintains their "progressive surface text" (feminism) gets undermined by the "conservative depth text" (the liberal humanism) on which it is based (31). Munt claims that progressive rewritings of the genre are carried out almost exclusively by lesbian writers and writers of color, many of whom are not published by mainstream houses. In contrast, in *Detective Agency: Women Rewriting the Hard-Boiled Tradition*, Walton and Jones argue that

> feminist agency is possible not just within the confines of or despite the conventions of the genre, but *through* those very conventions. The feminist appropriation of the hard-boiled mode can redefine textual and cultural boundaries precisely because it comes into intimate contact with them. In other words, such practices make it possible to renegotiate the "generic contract" between industry, authors, audiences, and texts. (87)

Although textual analysis is a useful tool, it is nonetheless impossible to predict the political effects of reading these texts on the basis of their language and structures alone. Texts can only do work in the world once they are appropriated by individual readers and reading groups, whose social and institutional positions determine, in part, what these texts mean. The historian of the book Robert Darnton argues that reading is "doubly determined" and maintains that its study necessarily involves both books and the general codes a reader has internalized from his or her culture as acceptable ways of reading (187).

In contrast to the critical commonplaces about detective fiction as a thoroughly commodified form whose politics encourage uncritical acceptance of the status quo, the reports of people who are fans of the genre reveal a variety of ways of reading, only some of which have anything at all to do with the structural imperative to restore narrative coherence and social order at the close. Fan-readers emerge in my analysis as what Michel de Certeau calls "poachers," readers who actively appropriate mass-produced fictions to meet their psychological and social needs. These readers become active makers of meaning rather than passive consumers of stories they may or may not find satisfactory. Such idiosyncratic reading practices—identification with minor characters, attention to details of locale or a character's hobbies, ignoring what happens at the end of texts to privilege other moments—were a constant in the reading practices of mystery fans. Such multiple and highly personal ways of reading resonate with Chartier's redefinition of "popular" to refer not to texts themselves but to "a kind of relation, a way of using cultural products" ("Culture" 233).[10] This "popular" way of reading or appropriating cultural artifacts is like de Certeau's "poaching" in that cultural consumption becomes an active production of meaning that is useful given one's situation, goals, and personal history. Readers do not, or do not only, find in their mysteries reassurance that the status quo is perfectly satisfactory. They also find in the best mystery texts what Kenneth Burke calls "equipment for living"—structures, characters, scenes, and an idiom through which to make sense of their own experience.

These multiple and more complex ways of reading detective fiction have consequences for its politics. Jameson argues that mass culture is not "empty distraction or 'mere' false consciousness, but rather . . . transformational work on social and political anxieties and fantasies which must then have some effective presence in the mass cultural text in order subsequently to be 'managed' or repressed" (141). The management comes in evoking (or acknowledging) utopian longings, which are then symbolically reintegrated into the current social order. Jameson fails to carry the implications of his argument to their logical conclusion, however. There is no guarantee that such transcendent elements will be effectively managed or their effects circumscribed within the boundaries of the text. As Alison Light remarks in her study of women's popular fictions, "reading is never simply a linear con-job but a process of interaction . . . a process which helps to query as well as endorse social meanings and one which therefore remains dynamic and open to change" ("Returning" 8). The utopian or transcendent aspects of hard-boiled detective fiction have been overlooked largely because so little work has been done on how audiences appropriate this fiction to address their concerns and preoccupations.[11] Indeed, the conservative nature of detectives (they, by definition, catch those who have violated the social order) can be read as providing a safe space for certain other kinds of transgressive fantasies (violating gender scripts, murdering members of one's idealized nuclear family).[12]

The Uses of Mystery: The Case of Sisters in Crime

Having examined the specific ways writers and publishers frame women's hard-boiled detective fiction and having offered a theoretical framework for understanding the variety of popular reading practices, I now examine what readers have to say about this fiction. I worked with a chapter of Sisters in Crime that was forming in 1993. I attended four monthly meetings; collected twenty fifty-three-question surveys on detective fiction and how it fits in with other forms of leisure and work in the lives of readers; and conducted six interviews, one to two hours long, each with chapter members who volunteered to talk to me after the first meeting. Interviews were open-ended, focusing on readers' histories as mystery readers and on their favorite books and authors. One interview involved two readers who were coworkers; the others were one-on-one. The readers who volunteered to be interviewed were all well-educated, middle-class, and professional white women between thirty-five and fifty-five years old, readers whose decisions about work and family were profoundly influenced by second-wave feminism. Those completing surveys (everyone who attended the meeting that month) were also a demographically homogeneous group. All had some college education and over two-thirds had done some graduate work. Sixty percent were between thirty-five and fifty-five years old, the rest were over fifty-five. They were teachers, professors, researchers, or administrators at colleges and universities; they were writers, librarians, lawyers, journalists, technical writers, editors, advertising professionals, accountants, and business owners. Half were married; half were single, widowed, or divorced. Only sixty percent had children, most of whom were grown and living away from home. Roughly ten percent of those attending chapter meetings were men, and two of my twenty respondents were male. The critical consensus is that mystery readers in general are disproportionately well-educated, middle- and upper-middle-class professionals, but most studies suggest that the genre attracts only slightly more women than men (Winn 441; Cawelti 105; Klein, *Woman Detective* 8; and Maron 13). Although socioeconomically representative, my sample appears particularly heavy on readers who work in academic settings (an artifact of location), on older readers, and on writers (who were using the group as a networking and resource group). The vast preponderance of women readers is no doubt a result of the organization's mission of advocacy for women's mysteries. In addition, these readers may have been different from most fans of the genre in that their careers and family situations allowed them the leisure to read mysteries for an average of eleven to fifteen hours a week and to attend monthly meetings, a time commitment more difficult for those in the initial stages of building careers and families. Although this small, overwhelmingly female sample makes it difficult to generalize with regard to gender and reading, the complexity and variety of readers' interactions with texts is particularly striking given the similarity of their backgrounds.

The most important analytic category for these fan-readers is character. Readers discuss characters not as if they were the deliberate creations of a designing author but as if they were real people. The first meeting of the chapter, in March 1993, opened with the statement that the organizers started the group because they wanted to find people with whom they could "talk about characters as if they were people we knew." One reader describes her books as "a companion," taking them on long plane trips "for company" (personal communication, 30 Mar. 1993).[13] This equation of main characters with friends is particularly noteworthy given the tendency of these readers to prefer protagonists like themselves—well-educated, professional women who often have similar occupations.

Writers speak about this fiction similarly. Marcia Muller describes what it was like to be writing private-eye novels in the early 1980s: "we wanted to write about people like us, like the women around us. The time was ripe" (Brainard). Margaret Maron, a mystery author, argues that reading a series detective is "like having several sets of old friends. You can hang out with them for a few hours, catch up on their lives and then go on with your own without any of the demands required of real-life friendships" (13).

In my interviews, a query about a particular book—"I don't know that one. Tell me about it"—is generally interpreted as a question about the protagonist. Responses invariably start with "Well, she's a . . ." and give the details of the character's past—her marriage, her job, where she lives, and so forth. Elements of the story seldom make it into descriptions. At the close of a response, I have no idea what happens in the book at all. If I press for details of plot, I get accounts that are sketchy at best. Readers, particularly with series detectives, do not remember what happens in specific books, often cannot tell one book in a series from another, and usually have problems re-creating titles.[14] Typically, several moments of inarticulate description are cut off with an apology and an excuse—"They all run together." The text is bounded for these readers by the personality or subjectivity of the protagonist, not by the plot structure that figures so importantly for scholarly readers. For fan-readers, the plots of individual books are artificial divisions, divisions seldom recalled with ease or accuracy. The writer Maxine O'Callaghan confirms this: "The comments I get from fans are about what's happening to Delilah [her fictional PI] personally, not often about plot" (qtd. in Walton and Jones 153).

Elizabeth Long found the same pattern of discussing characters as real people in her work with Houston book discussion groups.[15] She argues that this way of discussing books offers a basis for challenging cultural authority. While readers might accept the evaluations of teachers, reviewers, and other cultural authorities on the literary merits of a work, they feel free to judge individual characters because their experiences interacting with people every day make them experts of human behavior ("Women" 606–08; "Reading" 317, 319). I suspect the pattern for mystery readers is more complex, however. Readers overwhelmingly prefer protagonists who are like themselves. This preference suggests that there is an element of rehearsal in these readings. It is easy to think about one's own professional and personal situation through the life of a fictional character whose background or occupation resembles one's own. Identification with a character gives readers the opportunity to imagine having physical courage or the boldness necessary to talk back, to try on such ways of being in the world. Paretsky claims her mail is full of just such testimony: "A lot of women write and tell me that V. I. helped them get through some difficulty in their own lives by making them feel they could resolve their own problems. I think that women are getting the message of empowerment" ("What").

Such pleasurable identifications are not limited to the protagonist, however. Both Light and Cora Kaplan have found that women readers and viewers are able to take up a variety of different subject positions in a text, finding pleasure in identification with minor characters and details of setting as well as with the protagonist. Light argues that "the identifications which all literary texts offer are multiple and conflictual, even irreconcilable" ("Young Bess" 69). It follows that a mystery novel could offer all kinds of potentially pleasurable identifications. One might enjoy vicariously murdering particularly bothersome family members or coworkers. Pleasure might come from identification with the detective, who sees everything but is seen by no one.

Multiple identifications do in fact come up in interviews with mystery readers. One reader who is a gourmet cook loves any mystery with food in it. Another reader finds the voice in hard-boiled detective novels—regardless of the sex or race of the protagonist—irresistible, discovering in the cynicism and wisecracks the same dry sense of humor she enjoyed in her friends and colleagues. An artist married to a police officer believes that Ngaio Marsh's novels, featuring a police detective and artist couple, get the interplay of temperaments just right.

Settings were also important. One of the first projects suggested for this chapter of Sisters in Crime was the compiling of an atlas giving titles of mysteries set in each city. One reader read a string of New Orleans mysteries before visiting the city for a conference. Another spent the three months before her trip to Italy reading about murders set in the Italian cities she would visit. One reader goes to the mystery bookstores in every city she visits and buys the works of all the local mystery writers to read while she is there (personal communications, Mar.–Apr. 1993).

As with protagonists, the more realistic the place descriptions are the better.[16] The publisher's blurbs on Marcia Muller's San Francisco mysteries are telling: "Muller's observations of the Bay Area remain as fresh as they were when the series began . . . every locale rings true, even to a native" and "Muller excels at creating a sense of place. Should a major earthquake ever destroy San Francisco again, you could use her books as a guide to reconstructing the city" (front pages of *Where Echoes Live* and *Trophies and Dead Things*).

Romance readers are similarly preoccupied with the realism of settings and historical periods in their favorite books. The readers Janice Radway interviewed believed (accurately) that most writers, particularly established writers, researched historical settings and strived for geographical accuracy. In this way, readers accumulated knowledge (facts) that justified their pleasurable leisure reading to disapproving spouses and observers. In addition, Radway suggests that romance novels function, in part, as a substitute for the travel these mostly working-class, stay-at-home moms were unable to do (109–12). Mystery readers' preoccupation with place functions in several different ways. Mysteries are used to build up anticipation about visiting an unfamiliar city, much as glossy brochures from the travel agent are. The focus on realism indicates that some kind of rehearsal may be occurring as well. Reading about places one will visit offers a way to imagine being or living in such a place, to prepare emotionally and mentally for what it might be like. In addition, like photographs, these mysteries may operate as invitations to remember one's own experiences in the same places.

Although I have no way of knowing how male readers talk about the mysteries they read in similar contexts, the way these women read their lives into these texts and these texts into their lives does bear some resemblance to gendered ways of reading that emerge from research on readers in university classrooms. Both David Bleich and Elizabeth Flynn have found this mode of reading to be more characteristic of women's readings of narrative than of men's. Whereas men tend to focus on the plot and the "facts" of the narrative as presented by the author, women tend to freely enter the world of the text, speculating on the relations between characters and interpreting on the basis of insights gained from their personal experience (Bleich 239, 256). Although this research was based on students' in-class written responses (in other words, readers may have been concerned with giving the right answer in ways not relevant to situations of reading for pleasure), it is nonetheless suggestive. Long found the boundaries between texts and readers' lives were remarkably fluid for readers of both sexes in Houston book clubs, but particularly for women readers ("Women" 603; "Reading" 317). The passionate women readers in Anne Berggren's essay in this volume, "Reading like a Woman," similarly experienced life and fiction as intimately enmeshed.

These patterns of interacting with texts resonate with the work of the feminist psychoanalyst Nancy Chodorow. Chodorow maintains that because women in our society are the primary caretakers of small children, boys and girls develop fundamentally different ways of being in the world. Girls define themselves as being like their primary caretaker, so their primary sense of self is connected to others, is a self-in-relationship. Boys define themselves as being different from their mothers, so their primary sense of self is separate or autonomous. Men and women in all these studies interact with texts in these gendered ways. The boundaries between women's lives and texts are much more fluid than those between men's lives and their texts, as this brand of psychoanalytic theory would predict.

This discussion of what readers find important—characters like themselves and their friends, vividly drawn places, a familiar voice or intriguing hobby or minor character—departs dramatically from scholarly preoccupation with plots and structure. However, plots are important in a paradoxical way. Readers consistently rank plot elements—pace, red herrings, well-hidden motives, surprises, narrative twists and turns—as very important in surveys. Yet these same readers, as previously discussed, have little or no recollection of plots and will not talk about them unless prodded—and even then, not well. The plot structures are probably a necessary, but not sufficient, condition for pleasurable reading of mysteries. What would make a reader a fan of mysteries is the play of plot elements, but what constitutes a good mystery depends on the identifications a reader is able to make because of his or her personal history.

The process of detection—the restoration of narrative coherence and social order at the close—may meet some specifically modern and postmodern needs. Theorists of postmodernity like David Harvey have characterized industrialized, capitalist countries in the twentieth century as so complex and swiftly changing that they resist being narrated in a simple, linear way, resulting in the construction of fractured histories and incoherent subjectivities. Slavoj Žižek points out that the detective novel is fundamentally preoccupied with the same formal problem—"the impossibility of telling a story in a linear, consistent way" (48–49). The detective novel tells the story of how one individual (the detective) pieces together clues to make a coherent narrative of how the crime occurred. This linear narrative is presented to the reader at the denouement. Detective fictions may operate, then, as a symbolic resolution of problems posed to human consciousness by the conditions of modernity. For a reader faced with fragmentation and unnarratable complexity, a story of how an individual detective achieves a coherent narrative of events from these fragments may be a comforting sort of wish fulfillment. Identifications too can figure here. The achievement of order from the chaos of a life that resembles mine may be far more satisfying than the ordering of someone else's life.

Musing on why she writes mysteries and speculating about why women read them, Maron says, "Women seem to enjoy reading these books because they speak directly to them in the middle of a life that is busier, more demanding, more fragmented. Mysteries can give a brief sense of order, the illusion that someone's dealing with the chaos and getting a handle on it" (13). Maron acknowledges that modern women's lives are characterized by both a dizzyingly fast pace and a good deal of difficulty making the different roles women play coalesce—a specifically feminine version of the postmodern condition. Thus the denouement where a coherent narrative is told and social order restored ultimately has importance for fans. This return to form, however, is still indelibly marked by the detour taken through the words and life situations of the fan-readers of this fiction. If formal aspects of detective novels are important, the satisfaction they can provide readers is constrained and complicated by the locale, voice, preoccupations, and personalities that inhabit these structures and enmeshed with the reader's own personal history.[17]

For some writers, women's hard-boiled detective fiction is a feminist intervention into a particularly antifeminist area of culture, an attempt to enter and transform yet another bastion of male dominance. For publishers, the genre produces incredibly profitable books that attract a sizable audience of women and men. White, middle-class female readers have found in these books a type of fiction into which they can more easily read themselves and their lives. Ways of reading women's hard-boiled fiction are clearly a good deal more complex, contradictory, and deeply involved with the personal and institutional histories of writers, publishers, and readers than the textual analysis of individual books could predict.

After thoroughly reviewing the scholarly literature on detective fiction, I entered the ethnographic phase of this research prepared to talk at length about plots, plot structures, and the comfort offered by the sense of order and coherence detective stories provide. I was astonished that not only did fan-readers have little interest in these topics, they were largely unable to recall even their favorite books in these terms. In many ways, these detective stories were not experienced as detective stories at all—they were books about gutsy, independent women, local color stories, witty dialogues, or sources for culinary tips and relationship advice. The gulf between scholarly readings and fan readings of these texts ought to give scholars pause. Since texts can only do work in the world once they are appropriated by individual readers and reading groups (who are in turn re-created by the texts with which they come in contact), good cultural studies must engage how texts function in this living context. Cultural studies of this nature are hard to come by.[18]

John G. Cawelti closed his 1976 book *Adventure, Mystery, and Romance* with the acknowledgement that "there is a lack of solid data about audiences" (298). Ten years later, Long could assert with equal validity, "Ignoring the audience and its reception of cultural products is, in fact, a problem common to most cultural studies, whatever their disciplinary origin or subject matter" ("Women" 593). The kind of interdisciplinary or cross-disciplinary collabora-tive work necessary to study living texts is hindered by a variety of institutional barriers—departments, tenure committees, intellec-tual traditions that make it difficult for the humanities scholars who read cultural artifacts to work with the social scientists who study mass publics. The reading practices of female fan-readers of hard-boiled fiction challenge not only critical commonplaces about the politics of this fiction but also the way cultural studies is done and the disciplinary structures we inhabit while we undertake that work.

Notes

1. For a brief history of the emergence of hard-boiled women detectives in the 1980s, see Klein (*The Woman Detective*, 230–42). Also see Irons; Walton and Jones.

2. There is some ambiguity about whether a mystery featuring a female pri-vate investigator should be called hard-boiled at all. Two readers I inter-viewed spent a long time discussing whether Paretsky was a hard-boiled writer or not. Rather than fit her into the industry's typology of "hard-boiled," "cozy," "police procedural," or "spy thrillers," they created their own category for "women detectives" to describe her work. The 1992

Mystery Books catalog includes a section called "Mean Streets" for hard-boiled detective stories (all men's) and another section called "Crime on Her Mind," which features women detectives, professional and amateur.

3. Paretsky's comments echo those of Carolyn Heilbrun, who writes academic mysteries under the name Amanda Cross. Heilbrun insists she began to write mysteries because she could no longer find any she wanted to read—"detective stories which combined conversation with literary mysteries and which treated women as people in their own right, rather than decorative appendages" (qtd. in Binyon 55).

4. The misogyny of hard-boiled detective fiction is a critical commonplace. Leslie Fiedler commented on the genre's "native birthright of antifeminism" long before most critics took this literature seriously (498).

5. The phrase is Phil Cody's, an editor of *Black Mask*. The best publishing history of *Black Mask* is Nolan's "History of a Pulp." See also Smith, *Hard-Boiled*, ch. 1. For an analysis of pulp magazine advertising, see Smith, "How the Other Half Read."

6. See Anderson on "imagined communities" created by print capitalism and their role in fostering nationalism and other forms of community not characterized by face-to-face interactions.

7. The plasticity of these categories is particularly salient in lesbian detective fiction. Walton and Jones report forty-two series novels featuring a lesbian professional investigator beween 1991 and 1995, tripling the number in the previous five-year period (42). Also see Munt, ch. 5; and Klein, "Habeas Corpus."

8. For a sampling of theorists arguing for the conservative politics of the form, see Žižek, ch. 3; Hamilton, ch. 1; Holquist; Knight, ch. 5; and Mandel 71–73. For further discussion of the complicity of detective fiction and other realist texts with the bourgeois order, see Belsey, ch. 3; and Seltzer.

9. Davidson similarly redefines "literature" as "not simply words upon a page but a complex social, political, and material process of cultural production" (viii). McGann argues that a text's meaning is "a set of concrete and always changing conditions: because the meaning is in the use and textuality is a social condition of various times, places and persons" (21).

10. Chartier's redefinition of "popular" as a way of using artifacts resonates with Bourdieu's work on the differences between "the aesthetic disposition" (28), which privileges form over function and recommends aesthetic distance as a worldview, and the "popular aesthetic" (32), which asks what cultural artifacts are good for.

11. Walton and Jones report the findings from a survey posted to the e-mail discussion list DorothyL, which is dedicated to discussion of women's mystery fiction. Also see Kelly, ch. 7.

12. Kaplan argues that the "reactionary political and social setting" of some

women's popular narratives "secures, in some fashion, a privileged space where the most disruptive female fantasy can be 'safely' indulged" (143). Thompson notes that whereas progressive positions on class issues are undermined by conservatism on issues of gender in hard-boiled fiction, British mystery fiction of the period between the two world wars undermines its progressive gender politics with reactionary stances on issues of class (143–44).

13. Reviews of detective fiction similarly speak of protagonists as though they were real people. For examples, see Patrick ("Old Drunk" and "Life Styles"); Weiner.

14. This tendency to forget details of plot contrasts sharply with Radway's findings about romance readers. Romance readers remember the events of specific books with ease and can recall favorite titles and authors with amazing detail. There is some evidence that writers and publishers are aware of the difficulties mystery readers have remembering titles. A number of detective series feature devices to aid memory in the titles. Karen Kijewski, who writes mysteries about a California detective, Kat Colorado, always features the protagonist's name in her titles—e.g., *Katapult, Katwalk, Kat's Cradle*. Joan Hess, who writes mysteries set in the small town of Maggody, also uses alliteration— *Malice in Maggody, Mischief in Maggody, Madness in Magoddy*. Grafton's alphabetic mystery series functions similarly.

15. Kelly (170–73) reports a similar finding among subscribers to DorothyL, an e-mail discussion list for fans of women's detective stories.

16. According to Kelly, subscribers to DorothyL are similarly taken by the "realism" of the settings in the novels they enjoyed (173).

17. There is some surface similarity between these ways of reading and an older formulation from reader-response criticism, Holland's "identity theme." Holland argues that a reader has an invariant "identity theme," a customary mode of psychological defenses, adaptations, fantasy projections and transformations that constitute a style of interacting with and adapting to the world. A text read with pleasure, Holland argues, is one through which a reader can reenact, reinscribe, and elaborate his or her identity theme. Similarities between the psychological structures of a reader and the available structures in a text, then, would dictate whether identification takes place and pleasurable reading follows. Just as poaching involves producing a useful appropriation based on one's situation, concerns, and personal history, Holland's reader produces readings based on his or her psychic needs and structures that may or may not correspond to those intended by the writer. Although I would argue that how one poaches has everything to do with one's nationality, gender, class, race, region, religion, age, sexuality, and other factors of personal history, Holland is adamant that his "identity theme" has nothing to do with such things (205).

18. The exception is work done by media studies scholars. Some of the most widely cited include Ang; Allen; and Jenkins. Notably, none are focused on print culture. For a recent interdisciplinary overview of work on reception, see Press.

Works Cited

Allen, Robert C. *Speaking of Soap Operas*. Chapel Hill: U of North Carolina P, 1985.

Anderson, Benedict. *Imagined Communities*. 2nd ed. New York: Verso, 1991.

Ang, Ien. *Watching* Dallas: *Soap Opera and the Melodramatic Imagination*. New York: Methuen, 1985.

Anthony, Carolyn. "Mystery Books: Crime Marches On." *Publishers Weekly* 13 Apr. 1990: 24.

Baker, Paula. "The Domestication of Politics: Women and American Political Society, 1780–1920." *Unequal Sisters: A Multi-cultural Reader in U.S. Women's History*. Ed. Vicki L. Ruiz and Ellen Carol DuBois. 2nd ed. New York: Routledge, 1994. 85–110.

Baym, Nina. "Melodramas of Beset Manhood: How Theories of American Literature Exclude Women Authors." *The New Feminist Criticism*. Ed. Elaine Showalter. New York: Pantheon, 1985. 63–80.

Belsey, Catherine. *Critical Practice*. New York: Routledge, 1980.

Binyon, T. J. *"Murder Will Out": The Detective in Fiction*. New York: Oxford UP, 1989.

Bleich, David. "Gender Interests in Reading and Language." Flynn and Schweickart 234–66.

Bourdieu, Pierre. *Distinction: A Social Critique of the Judgment of Taste*. Trans. Richard Nice. Cambridge: Harvard UP, 1984.

Brainard, Dulcy. "Marcia Muller: 'The Time Was Ripe.'" *Publishers Weekly* 8 Aug. 1994: 362.

Burke, Kenneth. "Literature as Equipment for Living." *The Philosophy of Literary Form*. 3rd ed. Berkeley: U of California P, 1973. 293–304.

Carter, Robert A. "Scene of the Crime." *Publishers Weekly* 29 Mar. 1991: 21.

Cawelti, John G. *Adventure, Mystery, and Romance: Formula Stories as Art and Popular Culture*. Chicago: U of Chicago P, 1976.

Certeau, Michel de. *The Practice of Everyday Life*. Trans. Steven R. Rendell. Berkeley: U of California P, 1984.

Chandler, Raymond. "The Simple Art of Murder." 1944. Rpt. in *The Simple Art of Murder*. New York: Vintage, 1988. 1–18.

Chartier, Roger. "Culture as Appropriation: Popular Cultural Uses in Early Modern France." *Understanding Popular Culture: Europe from the Middle*

Ages to the Nineteenth Century. Ed. Steven L. Kaplan. New York: Mouton, 1984. 229–54.

————. *The Order of Books: Readers, Authors, and Libraries in Europe between the Fourteenth and Eighteenth Centuries.* Stanford: Stanford UP, 1994.

Chodorow, Nancy. *The Reproduction of Mothering.* Berkeley: U of California P, 1978.

Cody, Phil. Editorial. *Black Mask* 8.11 (1926): n. pag.

Darnton, Robert. *The Forbidden Bestsellers of Pre-revolutionary France.* New York: Norton, 1995.

Davidson, Cathy N. *Revolution and the Word: The Rise of the Novel in America.* New York: Oxford UP, 1986.

Fiedler, Leslie. *Love and Death in the American Novel.* 1966. New York: Anchor, 1992.

Flynn, Elizabeth A. "Gender and Reading." Flynn and Schweickart 267–88.

Flynn, Elizabeth A., and Patrocinio P. Schweickart, eds. *Gender and Reading: Essays on Readers, Texts, and Contexts.* Baltimore: Johns Hopkins UP, 1986.

Gitlin, Todd. *Inside Prime Time.* New York: Pantheon, 1983.

Grafton, Sue. *"B" Is for Burglar.* New York: Bantam, 1986.

————. "G Is for (Sue) Grafton: An Interview with the Creator of Kinsey Millhone Private Eye Series Who Delights Mystery Fans as She Writes Her Way through the Alphabet." Interview by Bruce Taylor. *Armchair Detective* 22 (1989): 14–13.

Hamilton, Cynthia S. *Western and Hard-Boiled Detective Fiction in America.* Iowa City: U of Iowa P, 1987.

Harvey, David. *The Condition of Postmodernity.* Cambridge: Blackwell, 1990.

Holland, Norman. *Five Readers Reading.* New Haven: Yale UP, 1975.

Holquist, Michael. "Whodunit and Other Questions: Metaphysical Detective Stories in Postwar Fiction." *The Poetics of Murder: Detective Fiction and Literary Theory.* Ed. Glenn Most and William Stowe. New York: Harcourt, 1983. 149–74.

An Introduction to Sisters in Crime. Pamphlet.

Irons, Glenwood, ed. *Feminism in Women's Detective Fiction.* Toronto: U of Toronto P, 1995.

Jameson, Fredric. "Reification and Utopia in Mass Culture." *Social Text* 1 (1979): 130–48.

Jenkins, Henry. *Textual Poachers: Television Fans and Participatory Culture.* New York: Routledge, 1992.

Kaplan, Cora. "*The Thorn Birds*: Fiction, Fantasy, Femininity." *Sea Changes: Essays on Culture and Feminism.* London: Verso, 1986. 117–46.

Kelly, R. Gordon. *Mystery Fiction and Modern Life.* Jackson: UP of Mississippi, 1998.

Klein, Kathleen Gregory. "*Habeas Corpus*: Feminism and Detective Fiction." Irons 171–90.

———. *The Woman Detective: Gender and Genre*. 2nd ed. Urbana: U of Illinois P, 1995.

Knight, Stephen. *Form and Ideology in Crime Fiction*. Bloomington: Indiana UP, 1980.

Lange, Karen. "Mysteries by Women Writers Will Be Topic." *Durham Herald-Sun* 9 Mar. 1993: C3.

Light, Alison. "'Returning to Manderley'—Romance Fiction, Female Sexuality, and Class." *Feminist Review* 16 (1984): 7–25.

———. "'Young Bess': Historical Novels and Growing Up." *Feminist Review* 33 (1989): 57–71.

Lochte, Dick. "When the Dick Is a Dame." Rev. of *"I" Is for Innocent*, by Sue Grafton. *Los Angeles Times* 10 May 1992: 2.

Long, Elizabeth. "Reading Groups and the Postmodern Crisis of Cultural Authority." *Cultural Studies* 1 (1987): 306–27.

———. "Textual Interpretation as Collective Action." *Ethnography of Reading*. Ed. Jonathan Boyarin. Berkeley: U of California P, 1993. 180–211.

———. "Women, Reading, and Cultural Authority: Some Implications of the Audience Perspective in Cultural Studies." *American Quarterly* 38 (1986): 591–612.

Mandel, Ernest. *Delightful Murder: A Social History of the Crime Story*. Minneapolis: U of Minnesota P, 1984.

Maron, Margaret. "Women of Mystery." *Independent Weekly* 14 July 1993: 13.

McGann, Jerome. *The Textual Condition*. Princeton: Princeton UP, 1991.

Meyerowitz, Joanne. *Women Adrift: Independent Wage Earners in Chicago, 1880–1930*. Chicago: U of Chicago P, 1988.

Morgan, Susan. "Female Dick." *Interview* May 1990: 2.

Muller, Marcia. *Trophies and Dead Things*. New York: Mysterious, 1991.

———. *Where Echoes Live*. New York: Mysterious, 1992.

Mulvey, Laura. "Visual Pleasure and Narrative Cinema." *Screen* 16.3 (1975): 6–18.

Munt, Sally R. *Murder by the Book? Feminism and the Crime Novel*. New York: Routledge, 1994.

Mystery Books. Catalog. Washington: Mystery Books, 1992.

Nolan, William. "History of a Pulp: The Life and Times of *Black Mask*." *The Black Mask Boys*. Ed. Nolan. New York: Morrow, 1985. 19–34.

Palmer, Jerry. *Thrillers: Genesis and Structure of a Popular Genre*. New York: St. Martin's, 1979.

Paretsky, Sara. *Bitter Medicine*. New York: Ballantine, 1988.

———. *Blood Shot*. New York: Dell, 1989.

———. *Burn Marks*. New York: Dell, 1991.

———. *Deadlock*. New York: Ballantine, 1989.

———. *Indemnity Only*. New York: Dell, 1991.

———. "What Do Women Really Want? An Interview with V. I.'s Creator." *Professional Communicator* 10.3 (1990): 13.

Patrick, Vincent. "In Search of an Old Drunk." Rev. of *Guardian Angel*, by Sara Paretsky. *New York Times Book Review* 31 May 1992: 45.

———. "Life Styles of the Rich and Quirky." Rev. of *"E" Is for Evidence*, by Sue Grafton. *New York Times Book Review* 1 May 1988: 1.

Peiss, Kathy. *Cheap Amusements: Leisure in Turn-of-the-Century New York*. Philadelphia: Temple UP, 1986.

Press, Andrea L. "The Sociology of Cultural Reception: Notes toward an Emerging Paradigm." *The Sociology of Culture: Emerging Theoretical Perspectives*. Ed. Diana Crane. Cambridge: Blackwell, 1994. 221–45.

Radway, Janice. *Reading the Romance: Women, Patriarchy, and Popular Culture*. Chapel Hill: U of North Carolina P, 1991.

Reddy, Maureen T. *Sisters in Crime: Feminism in the Crime Novel*. New York: Continuum, 1988.

Seltzer, Mark. "The *Princess Casamassima*: Realism and the Fantasy of Surveillance." *American Realism: New Essays*. Ed. Eric J. Sundquist. Baltimore: Johns Hopkins UP, 1982. 95–118.

Shaw, Joseph Thompson. Editorial. *Black Mask* 16:2 (1933): 7.

Smith, Erin A. *Hard-Boiled: Working-Class Readers and Pulp Magazines*. Philadelphia: Temple UP, 2000.

———. "How the Other Half Read: Advertising, Working-Class Readers, and Pulp Magazines." *Book History* 3 (2000): 204–30.

Stasio, Marilyn. "Lady Gumshoes: Boiled Less Hard." *New York Times Book Review* 18 Apr. 1985: 3+.

Stasio, Marilyn, and Richard Hummler. "A Slight Debate: A Hard-Boiled Fan and a Country-House Fan Discuss the Genre." Winn 14–16.

Thompson, Jon. *Fiction, Crime, and Empire*. Urbana: U of Illinois P, 1993.

Walton, Priscilla, and Manina Jones. *Detective Agency: Women Rewriting the Hard-Boiled Tradition*. Berkeley: U of California P, 1999.

Weiner, Ed. "Who Killed the Town Lolita?" Rev. of *"F" Is for Fugitive*, by Sue Grafton. *New York Times Book Review* 21 May 1989: 17.

Winn, Dilys, ed. *Murder Ink*. 1977. Rev. ed. New York: Workman, 1984.

Wood, Leonard A. "The Gallup Survey: American Readers Love a Mystery." *Publishers Weekly* 21 Nov. 1986: 17–18.

Žižek, Slavoj. *Looking Awry: An Introduction to Jacques Lacan through Popular Culture*. Cambridge: MIT P, 1991.

"That, My Dear, Is Called Reading": Oprah's Book Club and the Construction of a Readership

Rona Kaufman

Reading inside and outside the Academy

Oprah's Book Club began the same month I returned to graduate school. Before that, I worked in a bookstore for two years—long enough to see the impact Oprah could have on the sale of books. Customers often came into the store with half-heard titles and approximated authors' names: piecing together their word clues, my coworkers and I would try to puzzle out the right book. On some days, so many people came in looking for the same book that the game shifted from Which title? to Why that title? We could often trace the answer to Oprah. Oprah would feature (or even simply mention) a favorite book of hers—a book, say, like Sarah Ban Breathnach's *Simple Abundance*—and viewers would rush to buy it; her references set off little earthquakes in the daily operations of the bookstore. When I heard that Oprah was starting her own on-air book club, I was excited to see how Oprah's organized call to books—her announcements that were designed precisely to send people out to bookstores and libraries in search of books—would affect the rhythm of the bookstore. And, as a member of one reading group and a sometimes eavesdropper on other reading groups, I was interested in seeing how Oprah's readers would talk about books. Oprah's decision to start a book club just as I was

221

leaving the bookstore made me feel as if I was being cheated out of the opportunity to witness a huge cultural event.

So I paid attention to the event from my new environment. I looked in bookstores (now as a customer rather than a worker) for evidence of the success of Oprah's Book Club. I saw signs—sometimes literally—everywhere. I saw displays—piles and piles of books heaped near registers and on tables throughout the store. I saw the *New York Times* best-seller list, where Oprah's Book Club selections often occupied the number-one space in fiction. In my new cramped living room that could barely fit both my computer and my television, I watched women testify on Oprah's show about the power of reading and their return to the book. But I saw few signs of this large-scale literacy project in the university. Most people around me hadn't heard of Oprah's Book Club, hadn't noticed the displays in the bookstores, hadn't thought about why some eight-year-old books were achieving newfound popularity. Some graduate students looked at me when I talked about Oprah's Book Club as though I was brave or stupid—or, I imagine, possibly both.

Scholars who I thought could help me think about how my worlds overlapped sometimes failed me. Most notably, that semester (fall 1996) I read Kurt Spellmeyer's "After Theory: From Textuality to Attunement with the World," which makes its own call to literacy. In the article, Spellmeyer laments the academy's inability to move beyond theory. He argues that even while critics believe that we are now in an era of "post-theory," we still cling to textuality, using theory as a way both to support posttheory arguments and to distance readers from the page and consequently from the world. We are "trapped," he says (893). The danger of being trapped in theory, of being trapped in the text, is that "we soon lose the capacity to differentiate between actions that can lead to meaningful change and those symbolic practices that substitute for action all too easily" (894). Spellmeyer calls for the (real) end of theory and a return to the arts, which are grounded in our experience of the world. He envisions a "pursuit of wholeness," which contains the "basic grammars of emotional life" (910, 911). He wants less mediation between the reader and the page and more "open space" in which readers can navigate their own experiences with language and meaning. He argues that we "need to become ethnographers of *experience* . . . who find out how people actually *feel*" (911).

Spellmeyer's article is problematic for many reasons, including his across-the-board dismissal of theory and his reluctance to acknowledge that his own championing of experiential reading requires theorizing. Yet it should nonetheless be an exciting one, especially for a returning graduate student like me interested in reading practices both inside a composition classroom and outside the academy, since Spellmeyer is interested in how the professionalization of reading affects nonprofessionals. But the article is remarkably shortsighted. Spellmeyer's principal framework is the academy; his addressees are scholar-teachers and their students. He is most concerned with the teacher-student hierarchy—tying the persistence of theory to the decline of teaching. Theory, he says, "is symptomatic of a widening gap between the concerns of elites who produce what counts as knowledge . . . and the needs of those to whom this knowledge gets strategically parceled out" (904). Still, Spellmeyer also refers to a "lay clientèle" (897), "the ordinary reader" (898), and "nonspecialists" (903). Out of the corner of his eye he sees a larger vision for the future; he hopes the impact of his redirected pedagogy of experience will be felt in waves and will perhaps lead to "a future beyond the university" (911). And right there I see a missed opportunity. If Spellmeyer were to look beyond his framework now—look outside the university now—he could see, in the abundance of reading publics, models of experiential reading already in existence. And he might find both comfort and instruction in seeing through that different lens.

In the same December that Spellmeyer's plea was published in *College English*, members of Oprah's Book Club were taking a break from their monthly reading, "so [they] don't have to rush through the holidays" ("Oprah's Book Club" 18 Nov. 1996). The book club began meeting in October 1996, after Oprah announced that she "wanted to get the country reading again" (18 Oct. 1996). Therefore, she would select a book—a book that she had read and been moved by. She would announce the title on the air and give her viewers one month to read it. She also gave publishers and booksellers advance notice so that they could print more copies and increase stock to meet buyers' demands. She invited viewers to write letters about their experiences with or feelings about the books, and from those thousands of viewers who wrote letters, four or so would be selected to go to Chicago (or, sometimes, to another location that was significant to the author or the book) for the in-person book club, which would include Oprah and the author. The aired presentation changed as the book club aged, but it typically included a videotaped biography of the author, highlights of the book-club dinner meeting, and an interview of the author by Oprah.

It is difficult to know how many of her viewers actually read, but in terms of sales and ratings, Oprah's Book Club was a wild success. All the selected books—including Jacquelyn Mitchard's *Deep End of the Ocean*, Toni Morrison's *Song of Solomon* and *Paradise*, Jane Hamilton's *The Book of Ruth*, Wally Lamb's *She's Come Undone*, Ursula Hegi's *Stones from the River*, Maya Angelou's *Heart of a Woman*, Mary McGarry Morris's *Songs in Ordinary Time*, and Bill Cosby's *Little Bill Books for Beginning Readers*—wound up on the *New York Times* best-seller list. Ratings of the aired book-club meetings, despite initial fears that people would not tune into television to watch people talk about books, especially books they have not read, were strong enough to merit longer excerpts telecast on the Lifetime television network. And many, many women (and some men) wrote to Oprah or testified on her show about how they were affected by the books. Oprah's excerpts underscored reading as a transformative—and by all means relevant—act. The tone of these shows was unfailingly upbeat. Even when a woman confessed to a painful past experience, such as the death of a child, Oprah applauded the connection she made between the book and her life and saw the reading process as one that facilitates healing. "That's why I love books," Oprah said. "Because you read about somebody else's life but it makes you think about your own" (18 Oct. 1996).

Still, reading that elevated people's experience had to take into account busy holiday schedules, hence the December break.

In juxtaposing Oprah's Book Club and Spellmeyer, I am aware that they represent two distinctly different sites of reading that, ironically, show no awareness of each other. Oprah's Book Club, with the exception of the *Paradise* meeting, made no reference to school, and because the purpose of the club was to reunite literature (or literary fiction and nonfiction) with those who can read it but have chosen not to, that lack of reference points to the failure of a kind of academic reading for these club members.[1] In proposing a kind of experiential reading that gives agency to the reader, Spellmeyer leaves (makes, perhaps) room for practice that takes place outside the university. But when he writes that we need to be "scholar/teachers who find out how people actually feel," he implies, as I read him, that people need us to find out how they feel before they can participate in an act of reading that allows them to feel. His movement goes from the academic to the nonacademic, from the professional to the amateur; the influence is unidirectional, always going out.[2]

Reading outside the academy has, of course, a rich and extensive tradition. I could situate Oprah's Book Club in a history of literacies and discourses—a history that stretches into other centuries, into communities that are gendered, raced, and classed. We know, for example, that reading groups have been around for hundreds of years; we know that particular ways of reading have received institutional validation since the formation of English departments;[3] we know that race and gender affect what and how one reads.[4] These would all be fruitful paths of inquiry to take. But what I do in this essay is think about how Oprah's Book Club produced meaning through literacy and how it offered an alternative literacy to the academy's dominant literacy; to do so, I make use of cultural studies. Precisely because cultural studies does not see the making of culture—the making of meaning—as solely a top-down process, it offers an important lens through which to view Oprah's Book Club.[5]

As John Fiske notes, cultural studies is interested not in aesthetics but rather in the "generation and circulation of meanings in industrial societies" (284). Seeing culture as an open and contested space, the bearer of tensions along all lines of difference, cultural studies asks, Who gets to say what culture is or should be? Answering that question requires examining relations between knowledge and power to determine what people can make or say and what kind of capital (economic and cultural) those productions and meanings carry with them. Cultural studies makes room for resistance and sees agency, rather than passivity, in the people who shape and are shaped by culture. While cultural studies acknowledges a grand narrative of dominance, a narrative embedded in media texts as what Stuart Hall would call the "preferred reading," it at the same time allows room for resistance by identifying contradictions both in a text and in a reader's own subjectivity. "What matters," Hall argues, "is *not* the intrinsic or historically fixed objects of a culture, but the state of play in cultural relations: to put it bluntly and in an oversimplified form—what counts is the class struggle in and over culture" (235).[6]

The media serves as an important site in cultural studies because of its appeal to mass audiences and its technological ability to reach them. Douglas Kellner claims that "media culture *is* the dominant culture today . . . replac[ing] the forms of high culture as the center of cultural attention and impact for large numbers of people" (17). He continues, "Moreover, media culture has become a dominant force of socialization, with media images and celebrities replacing families, schools, and churches as arbiters of taste, value, and thought, producing new models of identification and resonant images of style, fashion, and behaviour" (17). Herman Gray notes that media texts "provide materials (and cultural spaces) that people can appropriate, circulate, and recombine for their own meanings and uses beyond just those intended by the industrial commercial system" but that "are not inherently resistant or automatically progressive" (5). Media texts, then, are not depositories of static, rigidly embedded meaning: they require reading, interpretative acts, to shore up the dominant culture, to resist it, or both.

Oprah's Book Club served as a site where literary and cultural studies married. A reading group that took place largely but not exclusively on television, the book club united a variety of locations (the television studio, the book-club meeting place, the location of the individual reader and viewer) and a multitude of relationships (between reader and text, between reader and writer, between Oprah and everyone). The club also did much to illuminate the existence of the competition between the dominant reading practice of the academy and the alternative reading practice of the book club. I've based my arguments on the first year of the club's life (the club read eight novels from September 1996 to August 1997) as well as a second appearance by one of Toni Morrison's novels in the club's second year.

Before I begin to lay out my understanding of the cultural work done by and through the club, let me offer a few caveats. First, Oprah's Book Club was a living organism, not only because it was made up of living, breathing people but also because it continued to develop—every month (just about) it offered a new selection. Certainly the club's reading changed as the club aged; this evolution was evident in the club's first year alone. Second, as I argue that Oprah's Book Club was about literacy (about the definition, practice, and promotion of a particular kind of reading), I admit that I'm defining *literacy* in a pretty narrow way—to mean the reading of literary fiction and nonfiction. My definition goes beyond a functional literacy of reading street signs, cereal boxes, newspapers, or even nondiscursive signs of the world—all important forms of literacy, I know—because the reading that united the book-club members shared one location: the literary text. Similarly, I use the word *aliteracy* to refer to having the skills to read literary texts but opting not to. The move that was most celebrated early in the club's history was the move from aliteracy to literacy, from people's having rejected the book to their embracing the book. The club was never about *illiteracy*: the club assumed people could read. The club members once inhabited the curricular space of school, which was always invisibly present in their extracurricular book-club space. Finally, because the meetings, even with the cameras rolling, happened behind closed doors and because what was aired was edited, there are limits to what we can know about the club. We need to make a distinction, then, between the book club and the aired book club. Still, by paying attention to what the camera shows, we can know what the fifteen to twenty million people who watched Oprah's show knew.

Making an Unlikely Marriage

In a *Time* article, Walter Kirn looks at what he sees as the reemergence of reading: "At the least, it appears, reading books (or listening to them in the Jeep) is to the 1990s what gymgoing was to the '80s: something we plan to do, something we *want* to do and, by all appearances, something everyone else is doing, even Oprah viewers. Perhaps *primarily* Oprah viewers" (102). Caryn James, in the *New York Times*, characterizes Oprah as a "cheerleader for reading" (C15). People can try to belittle or dismiss the success of (or interest in) Oprah's Book Club as only a trivial experience of talk-show women, but the numbers were too vast.[7] And people can look at the money that flew from the consumer to the book industry and discount or condemn the reading group as the commodification of literature. But to do so would be to trivialize (again) acts of literacy that took place in and because of the book club. What's important to notice is that Oprah's Book Club reenergized literacy, providing a forum for reading that is encouraging and that relies on a spirit of trust. The book club worked from the beginning to construct a particular readership—to value and enact a particular way of reading. By highlighting certain reading testimonies, celebrating and literally applauding them, by using Oprah as the model of the success and usefulness of this form of literacy, the book club created its own culture of reading.

In Oprah's Book Club, a successful text was one that sent a reader back into his or her own life, a text that made a reader rethink his or her life and that led to some type of change on the reader's part. In the first aired book club, for Mitchard's *Deep End of the Ocean*, the first thing that we heard was that the book club has received impressive attention (from *Time*, *Newsweek*, and the *Washington Post*) and overwhelming response (from viewers turned letter writers—"Girl, did you break our mailman's back"). Women, one after another, read excerpts from their letters that revealed how the book affected them and effected change: "I find myself hugging my six-year-old daughter so much"; "I kissed my daughter twice every night while reading it"; "It made me question whether or not I really want to be a parent right now" (18 Oct. 1996). We also heard about how the novel changed the dailiness of its readers' lives: "The sink is full of dirty dishes, laundry piled up"; "I took the book with me everywhere"; I "[s]natch[ed] a few minutes of reading time in the carpool lane and even waiting for red lights." We heard from a woman who said, "[I] actually never liked to read before. And this has—this has really gotten me interested in reading." Oprah spoke to the "power of books," which causes you not only to "share someone else's life, use your own imagination in creating the images for yourself that the author allows you to by his or her words" but also to "think more deeply about yourself" (18 Oct. 1996).

We learned, from the beginning, that the book creates a community of readers that is intellectual and amiable. One of the four readers selected to meet Mitchard for the in-person book club reported back to the much larger television readership that "it was incredible how we all sat together—we bonded so well. It was like we've known each other for our whole lives. . . . We all have different opinions. And it was great to hear the other opinions that represented, I'm sure, millions of people." That they all had different points of view was "really quite neat" (18 Oct. 1996). Oprah said—as she said many times that first year—that the club members became her good friends. This sense of community was important because it helped elide differences in race and gender and because Oprah needed to ask people to believe in her vision for the club to work. She announced the next book-club selection, Morrison's

Song of Solomon, by acknowledging the difficulty of the project and by asking readers for patience and faith: "I just encourage you to stay with Ms. Morrison, stay with the author. Put your trust in her because she knows what she's doing. A lot of people feel that she's mystical. And as I said, I think that she's magical and . . . you'll find that you need to sometimes reread a page. You want to like spoon-feed the words to yourself. Stay with the author, trust her. She knows what she's doing" (18 Oct. 1996). And, of course, though she didn't say it, Oprah recognized that readers had to trust her first: she counted on the large-scale success of her show and the individual success of this first book-club meeting to convert even the most resistant readers. Oprah asked, near the end of this first show, "See what conversation we've stimulated?" and indeed it was impossible not to notice the enthusiasm for reading generated in and through that conversation and how that conversation established the terms of many future conversations.

Oprah's Book Club was a dynamic conversation made up of participants who surprised many people. Certainly it united books and television in ways that some people found disconcerting—people who read serious fiction or who read fiction seriously are not supposed to watch talk shows. It also brought together people who would most likely not have met—for example, Toni Morrison and Celeste, "the rich white woman from Dallas," who initially was annoyed with Oprah for choosing a "black" novel that could have nothing to do with her (3 Dec. 1996); Jane Hamilton and Julian, the club's "first man" who said that with a good book, "you can relate to the character" regardless of gender (22 Jan. 1997); Wally Lamb, who can effectively write a woman character, and women readers, who are moved by that character. And it also connected testimony, or at least a talk-show version of testimony, to literacy or aliteracy. One of the most noteworthy things about Oprah's Book Club was its appeal to women who once had rejected the book. The testimonies of their return to literacy were included in almost every broadcast. One woman announced that she was forty-six years old and had read only five books in her lifetime—*Deep End of the Ocean* is her sixth (18 Oct. 1996). Another woman said that *The Book of Ruth* was the first book she "actually read all the way through" in twenty years (22 Jan. 1997). When Oprah asked her, "How have you lived?" she explained, "I've just been busy, you know, doing what people do and not taking the time to be introspective of myself. And when Oprah said, 'You know, let's get reading,' I said, 'Yes, ma'am.'" The power that Oprah wielded was breathtaking— frightening, even—but we can see in the testimonies the creation of a community of people who want to claim or reclaim literacy.

Oprah herself pointed to the unlikely marriage between television and books. She asked, "Doesn't [reading] take you in in a way that watching t.v. cannot?" (22 Jan. 1997). She placed herself—and her show—in the space between experience and empathy. In introducing *Deep End of the Ocean*, a novel about a child who disappears, Oprah said, "I think I'm just like everybody else. And I have read over the years. I love books. But I have over the years interviewed lots of people who have experienced the loss of a child. We've done many, many shows about it. But this was the first time I felt like I was in the inside of a family" (18 Oct. 1996). Nevertheless, she held the television experience of her book club closer to reading than to viewing—it existed somewhere between the page and the screen—opening the "Behind the Scenes at Oprah's Dinner Party" show with Toni Morrison with the claim that it was "a dinner that transformed our lives. It was an evening that we will always remember. And even if you haven't read the book, it could help change yours" (3 Dec. 1996).

Perhaps this acknowledgment of the difference between, yet coexistence of, readers and viewers is why the edited book club focused so much on personal experience and so little on the content of the text. Plot, theme, and character development were rarely discussed. Much of the time was spent showing how the readers are frustrated or inspired by the characters ("I have grown and Ruth did not" [22 Jan. 1997]) and on readers' personal revelations. Perhaps that is how the marriage had to play out: keep the testimony format of the talk show but have it prompted by books.

And perhaps that is why Oprah never feared that she would have—to take liberties with Habermas's concept—a legitimation crisis, in which her show would be so successful in restoring literacy (and therefore for Oprah, agency) to its viewers that they no longer needed the show.[8] Oprah mentioned often that the Toni Morrison dinner lasted for four hours, but the first broadcast allotted only thirty minutes to the experience as a whole, which included Morrison's biography (focusing on her life struggles), an interview with her, and the audience's reaction. Oprah later did an hour-long behind-the-scenes look at the dinner party, which highlighted Morrison reading *Song of Solomon* but also spent a significant amount of time talking about how the table was set and what kinds of food were served. Oprah said at the beginning of that show, "Even if you haven't read the book, *Song of Solomon*, you haven't heard of Toni Morrison, there's still so much wisdom that you can get out of this dinner, as I did . . . But if you're more into party planning than life lessons, you can get some great tips on planning a dinner party, too" (3 Dec. 1996). All this is to say that we got very little of the club, but what was presented to viewers not lucky enough—or not driven enough—to have been included in the intimate space was the reading of a text that represented us and our lives.

Elizabeth Long notes that people tend to get involved with a reading group as a method of self-definition. It serves as

> an occasion for people to define who they are culturally and socially and to seek solidarity with like-minded peers. For many, joining a reading group represents in itself a form of critical reflection on society—or one's place within it—because it demands taking a stance toward a felt lacuna in everyday life and moving toward addressing that gap. (197–98)

But I wonder what happens when one joins a group whose membership is by and large anonymous? There were layers to Oprah's Book Club—people who read and took part in the dinner, people who read and watched from the audience or from their televisions, and people who did not read but watched the show.[9] These anonymous viewers may have had a sense of who the typical Oprah viewer was, but they could not give particulars outside their circle of acquaintances. The club's placement outside the academy allowed for freedom and flexibility of participation. Simply put, it wasn't school. Membership was optional. There was no penalty for dropping out. Members could decide not to read and not to watch the book-club episodes with no penalty—other than a sense of being left out of a growing cultural conversation. The identification seemed to lie more with the "felt lacuna" than with the anonymous makeup of the group.

But Oprah was not anonymous. She was a celebrity—and that set this book club apart from the tradition of reading groups. Her celebrity became authority in almost every aspect of the book club. She was not an authority in an academic sense—she was not a literary critic—but she was an authority on self-help, on transformative experience. She was her own poster child for the type of reading that she advocated: she was a poor, black, abused child who is now one of the wealthiest and most well-recognized women in the world, and she credited reading with helping her in her journey. Books were "my way out," she said. "That's why I love them so much" (18 Oct. 1996). She clearly wanted readers to follow her "out." The word *follow* is important: there was a hierarchy at work here, and Oprah was almost always at the top of it. She selected the novels; she chose which letter writers would be invited to dinner; she decided whether to drink lemonade or wine. And she also did most of the talking. The hierarchy played out discursively from the first meeting. At the end of the dinner, Jacquelyn Mitchard toasted first to Oprah, second to books (18 Oct. 1996). And as the only stable component in the intimate book club, Oprah was in the position to shape it. When we think about how edited the presentation of this book club was, we know that Oprah—certainly with a staff but with the final word left to her—pulled together all components of this literacy occasion. She sanctioned the stories. Foucault asks what fills the space that is left by the death of the author. In this case, it was Oprah.[10]

Readers were aware that Oprah was the stabilizing force in the club's history, and we heard them make comparisons of and pronouncements about the books that were read. Toni Morrison got more air time than the other authors and books: an hour-long behind-the-scenes look at the *Song of Solomon* meeting and a second book-club selection. But even in the initial half-hour *Song of Solomon* segment, time was spent acknowledging the difficulty of the text as well as the larger payoff. One club member told Oprah that she was brave for choosing *Song of Solomon*, and Oprah responded by saying, "I do think it was a little daring to do it as the second book for the book club. Because I didn't have enough people who were followers who could trust me. That's why when I did it, I said trust her, even if you don't trust me" (18 Nov. 1996). And Oprah and another female club member, who had marked and color-coded almost every page of the novel, had this exchange:

MELINDA: Like *Deep End of the Ocean*—I appreciated the book, but there were not . . .

OPRAH: Moments—you don't have moments; you don't have moments.

MELINDA: Right. You know, that's all the way through.

OPRAH: I had to get you in. I had to get you to wade in with me.

MELINDA: Right. I mean, it was the—you lured me in. I appreciate it.

Later, after the book club struggled through Toni Morrison's *Paradise*, Oprah promised them a next book that would be "much easier" and a romance "almost every woman can relate to" (24 Feb. 1998). Oprah's Book Club was always situated both textually (some texts are more difficult, more engaging, more rewarding) and temporally: the book club had a living life, one with ebbs and flows, and each meeting responded in some way to the one that had come before it.

I admitted early on that I am working with a narrow view of the term *literacy*. I want to turn, though, to Wai Chee Dimock's broader definition of literacy to think more about how club members are situated as readers. Dimock includes in her understanding of reading "a wide range of activities that have to do with the interpretation of signs, the adjudication of meanings, and the construction of reality" (86). Reading is an act of survival. We are all readers because of life gaps, "between immediate experience and apprehended meaning, between what we see and what we think it signifies" (87). We become professional readers, she argues, when we move to the literary form. But Oprah's readers, even as they turned to the literary form, still came to their own understanding of what reading is. Oprah told her viewers that after she read *Song of Solomon* but before the club met, she called Morrison and asked, "Do people tell you they have to keep going over the words sometimes?" Morrison answered, "That, my dear, is called reading" (18 Oct. 1996). Consequently, a large amount of time was spent showing the difficulty of the experience of reading *Song of Solomon* and how Oprah acted as a bridge between the club women and Morrison. In the *Paradise* meeting, the meeting that was explicitly set up to mirror a classroom, club members continued to reflect on (and, according to Morrison, enact) the nature of reading. Oprah asked Morrison if she was surprised that readers needed to set up a study group to read *Paradise*. Morrison responded, "Novels are for talking about, and quarreling about, and engaging in some powerful way—however that happens: in a reading group, a study group, a classroom, or just some friends getting together." She continued: "Reading is solitary, but that's not its only life. It should have a talking life, a discourse that follows it" (24 Feb. 1998). And Oprah led that discussion: she positioned herself as a link between the club members and Morrison. Oprah was the club's leader because she was one of them (not an academic, not a career schoolgirl) who was ahead. She spoke the same language, but she was more experienced. Her authority was demonstrated in these instances not so much as teacher but as spiritual mentor, championing the return to the self. But the club members' lack of professionalism played out importantly in the experience of reading, in this reading of experience. Their status as nonacademics and nonauthorities with most of their texts allowed them to reconstruct the author into friend and the text into point of introspection and potential catalyst of transformation.

But to say that the club members read in a nonacademic way is grossly inaccurate. Oprah's Book Club honored some of the positions observed by academics as well—most notably, Roland Barthes's position on authorial intention. Barthes announces in *Image, Music, Text* that the author is dead; with the author dies authorial intention. Only a momentary transmediator of words, the author creates no fixed meaning in a text. Indeed, intention is essentially meaningless in the process of meaning making. What matters—what is knowable—is what is on the page, not what was in the writer's mind. The reader, instead, is left to fill in gaps (to borrow Wolfgang Iser's term). Intention is surrendered to semiotics. Barthes writes, "[T]he birth of the reader must be at the cost of the death of the Author" (148). He later claims, "It is not that the Author may not 'come back' in the Text, in his text, but he then does so as a 'guest'" (161).

I like to think of this image of the author as guest, especially in terms of Oprah's Book Club. The authors were indeed guests. They were invited to dinner; they were invited to the show. Jane Hamilton was invited to bowl.[11] The writers became participants in the book club, and that participation, complicated though it was, distinguished Oprah's Book Club once again from other reading groups. Certainly in most groups the author has a presence that emanates from the page, not from the other side of the table. With Oprah in some ways, the author occupied a position of privilege: the author and his or her book were magically selected, the author did not have to submit a letter and wait, and he or she was enriched literally and most likely figuratively by the experience.[12] But while the videotaped biography of the author did much to enhance the author as a person, as a real live functioning human being, it did little to reify the author's authority. Certainly authors are used to losing their authority once their books fall into the hands of critics and reviewers, even into the hands of academics and the general reading public. But it seems to me that the key difference with Oprah's Book Club was that the author was bodily present in a roomful of people talking about his or her novel and constructing meaning from it. Furthermore, the meetings—indeed, the entire reading experience—promised a spirit of trust and congeniality between the writer and the readers.

What happens to this author who is both on the page and in the room? Gender aside, Barthes once again plays out well here: "If he is a novelist, he is inscribed in the novel like one of his characters, figured in the carpet; no longer privileged, paternal, aletheological, his inscription is ludic. He becomes, as it were, a paper-author: his life is no longer the origin of his fictions but a fiction contributing to his work" (161). Thus the fiction of the biography speaks to the fiction of the book. We heard that *Deep End of the Ocean* came to Mitchard in a dream, months before the sudden death of her husband. We saw Jane Hamilton at work on her midwestern farm, where *The Book of Ruth* takes place. At the beginning of the *Song of Solomon* show we were even offered glimpses into Toni Morrison's life—we learned that her house burned down after she won the Nobel Prize and that Morrison is a divorced mother of two whose sons used to spit up on her manuscripts as she wrote. These personal narratives add to the textual narratives and highlight the personal connection of reading.

This is not to say that the writer gets the last word. After bowling, Hamilton, Oprah, and the four book-club members (three women and one man, the first man) sat down to talk about the novel. Oprah, who first read the book in 1988, admitted that she grew frustrated with Ruth during the second reading: "Well, after seven more years of doing 'The Oprah Winfrey Show,' I was not as empathetic with Ruth this time. . . . I have grown and Ruth did not" (22 Jan. 1997). As Oprah explained her frustration, Hamilton jumped in to offer "one last defense" of Ruth: "you have to admit that she's got a great attitude and that she finds love in her heart for things that people don't ordinarily have love . . . I just wanted to make that point." Oprah, however, dismissed her with a quick "Okay," and then made a toast to books. Hamilton was present to make the last defense, but she clearly was not in charge of the conversation or, ultimately, of the treatment of Ruth. She nourished this character, to use Barthes's term, and leaves her to the reader. Hamilton in no way assumed an authoritarian posture: she responded as any reader might. What's more: she was granted by the readers who surrounded her, who bowled with her and ate french fries with her, no more authority over meaning or evaluation than they claimed for themselves.

And it is also not to say that all writers were treated equally. Toni Morrison and Maya Angelou were clearly placed on a higher plane than the others. Oprah announced that Morrison was her "all-time favorite author, living or non-living" (18 Nov. 1996) and that Angelou was like a mother to her. She ranked the evening with Morrison and a time when Angelou read to her as two of the top three experiences of her life (the third: making the movie version of Alice Walker's *The Color Purple*). Morrison's and Angelou's positions as favorites allowed them more speaking time: they got to be teachers offering lessons not about dinner parties but about life. "Life is big," Morrison said. "We make life small. We make life tiny and think it's only our income. Life is big. And we have it now. I mean this is it. So let's do it" (18 Nov. 1996). Angelou offered life lessons as well, although hers sat more easily with me since her book, *Heart of a Woman*, is nonfiction and offers explicit life lessons. But Angelou was quick to deflect any type of superior status. *Heart of a Woman* was the weepiest club meeting: club members took turns reading excerpts from their letters around the dinner table in Angelou's house, acknowledging that they had been raped or abused, and thanking Angelou and her books for saving their lives. Angelou, for her part, declined to be sole teacher and told one woman, who was a teacher herself:

> The truth is, you know me to be an inspiration, and look at you. You're a teacher. We have no idea the range of your influence. Now I had someone who went before me. I didn't make it up. Someone went before me. And it is my blessing to have Oprah as my own chosen daughter, friend. And who she influences . . . and who you influence . . . Who knows? . . . Somebody's watching you. You have no idea who you'll influence. (18 June 1997)

One question that Oprah asked most writers is what they want their readers to "feel, know" after reading their books. Jane Hamilton demurred: "Well, Oprah, I don't know that's why a writer writes a book, for somebody to actually learn something" (22 Jan. 1997). But Morrison claimed her authority as author of *Song of Solomon*; she said, "Some of the messages I want to convey are, you know, pastel strokes, not the heavy, thunderous ones. But the willingness to take risks with one's own life. The willingness to live an enchanted life, a life where these things mean something, a willingness to see the other side of things. It's like turning up the volume of your life" (18 Nov. 1996). She talked, too, about the craft of writing and authorial intention: "I really wanted to be a good read. I want people to want to turn the pages. At the same time, I want there to be enough there after you turn those pages, not just about the plot. It really is about something going on with the characters and something under that and something under that and something under that" (3 Dec. 1996). She then explained the significance of an image—the watermark on a table—in the text. In the *Paradise* meeting, Morrison said that she's been asked many times in the past by a variety of groups to come and teach her own work. She always declined, in part because she "knows too much" but also in part because she "didn't want to 'impose' on students who had asked [her] these questions about the fundamental and final reading—as though [she] had it" (24 Feb. 1998). Still, she came to this meeting. She sat in the front of the room (a library, it looks like) with all of the club members facing her, some literally at her feet. She taught. Morrison never disappeared, she never simply visited her fiction, and she was never just a guest. And, in the end, the two Morrison visits shed a great amount of light on the complicated cultural space that housed this book club.

Understanding Middlebrow

James notes that what separates Morrison from the other writers is that she is "high art," they are "middlebrow" (C15).[13] Reading groups seem to exist in this middlebrow cultural space. Long argues that most reading groups believe in a hierarchy of books in which classics and serious contemporary works are placed at the top and genre fiction is placed at the bottom. She notes, "Groups do establish differing relationships to this hierarchy, but all recognize it" (203) and draws on Pierre Bourdieu's work with class factions and cultural capital to explain that "many of the readers have a strong sense of cultural entitlement that derives from their own position of educational and social privilege, so they can eschew with ease the pronouncements of the academy, which is to them just another fraction of the sociocultural elite" (203).

Long argues that the category middlebrow only partially explains how reading groups determine literary merit and that it is likewise difficult to pin down exactly what is meant by middlebrow. She writes that "the category is drawn from the domain of aesthetics or taste" (203). But what domain of aesthetics or taste? In a satiric letter to the editor published shortly after her death, Virginia Woolf sketches out portraits of highbrow and lowbrow (as people rather than as cultural space) in an attempt to define middlebrow. She acknowledges that she does not succeed. The highbrow "is the man or woman of thoroughbred intelligence who rides his mind at a gallop across country in pursuit of an idea" (43); the lowbrow is "a man or a woman of thoroughbred vitality who rides his body in pursuit of a living at a gallop across life" (44). But the middlebrow is "betwixt and between. . . . The middlebrow is the man, or the woman, of middlebred intelligence who ambles and saunters on this side of the hedge, now on that, in pursuit of no single object, neither art itself nor life itself, but both mixed indistinguishably, and rather nastily, with money, fame, power, or prestige" (45). The middlebrow is the one Woolf cannot admire. Richard Brodhead makes clear connections between middlebrow and middle class in his discussion of Louisa May Alcott, although Janice Radway, in her recent talk on the Book-of-the-Month Club, criticizes his use of the term as anachronistic. Radway, in turn, contends that the term *middlebrow* was first used derogatorily by critics but then was later claimed by the "general reader"—educated and professional but in need of reading advice—who took it as a "culture of preference." Radway argues that proponents of the middlebrow use the term *academic* "to dismiss books they did not like in much the same way my academic colleagues and I had used the word 'middlebrow' to dispense with texts we judged inadequate" (9).

Radway uses the Book-of-the-Month Club as a model of middle-brow reading, and in a lot of ways that model parallels the kind of reading that is done in Oprah's Book Club: the reading is affective, the reading is transformative. Of course, the comparison doesn't hold up completely, nót just because Radway wants to situate the Book-of-the-Month Club at a particular moment in time—at the intersection of particular social, material, and cultural changes—but also because, although there's some overlap, the two clubs deal with different populations of readers. Book-of-the-Month Club draws its readers from the professional and managerial class; an early Book-of-the-Month Club editor envisioned his ideal reader as one who "had passed through the usual formal education in literature, who reads books as well as magazines, who, without calling himself a lit-terateur, would be willing to assert that he was fairly well read and reasonably fond of good reading" (Radway 296). The editor saw this reader as the general reader, but Oprah clearly saw the general reader as one who has, for all intents and purposes, stopped reading. This reader eventually needs help with choices and options, but he or she first needs someone to champion the book, to demonstrate its appeal, to help the reader open the cover.

Once that cover is opened and the world of the book is entered, both the practiced and the hesitant reader, as club members, may participate in a similar kind of reading. Book-of-the-Month Club people saw literary writing as writing

> conducted in a highly personal language and according to an idio-syncratic sense of truth. When used successfully, they believed, this personal idiom could illuminate the world in unusual ways and endow the reader with new eyes as well as tools for making sense of it. When done badly, however, the result was mere gibberish, in their opinion, self-referential nonsense that resisted translation and there-fore comprehension. (67)

Some texts are readable and some are unreadable—but readability has more to do with pleasure than with ability, a question of why rather than how. Radway insists on the centrality of pleasure—not so much "the cognitive pleasure of solving a difficult puzzle or following the trail of a difficult argument" as a pleasure that seems "more emotional and absorbing; it seemed to have something to do with the affective delights of transport, travel, and vicarious social interaction" (19). Consequently, story, plot, and characters are the most important markers of a good book. Book-of-the-Month Club editors place themselves between two kinds of readers: "an unthinking body—readers unwilling to perform intellectual work as they read—and those who indulged in rationality and contemplation to such an extent that they denied the sentimental claims of the heart and the sensual demands of the corporeal" (113–14). The middlebrow, Radway argues, values use over aesthetic.

The insistence on use makes a lot of sense in reading groups in general and Oprah's Book Club in particular, because reading is meant to illuminate aspects of the reader's life. If the act of reading only involves the world of the text, not the world of the reader, then the book has failed. And Oprah set up the definition of use to mean books that sent the reader back into his or her own life. With this definition in mind, viewing Toni Morrison as high art rather than middlebrow only partially explains her different treatment. Morrison was acknowledged to be the most difficult of the writers, highlighting the complexity of her aesthetic, but she was also the most affective. One club woman explained her desire to be part of the *Song of Solomon* dinner: "It just blew me away. I mean, I lived on a doctor's street. I lived in Danville. I lived in Shalimar. I mean, I was there. And I just closed that book and I said, 'I have got to see the person who wrote that. I've just got to see her'" (3 Dec. 1996). But it was Celeste, the wealthy white Texan, who got more air time than any other club member in club history, probably because the gap that Morrison filled for her was the largest. Early in the hour-long episode, Celeste shared part of the letter that got her to Chicago: "I've never been black; I've never been poor; I've never been abused. So what could I have in common with this odd group of characters? Too much, way too much" (3 Dec. 1996). Later in the show, Celeste explained why she "connected" to the character Ruth, who breast-fed her son for five years, which made Celeste recall how she felt "connected to all of mankind" when she herself breast-fed, which made her think about the child she lost, which made her cry for the first time in sixteen years. She said that the lesson was that "by not feeling the pain, I wasn't feeling the joy." My point here is that call-ing Morrison highbrow and the others middlebrow insufficiently explains her distinguished status. The same insistence was placed on use and affect with *Song of Solomon* as with *She's Come Undone*. Yes, we heard about the difficulty of the text, but, at the same time, we heard Celeste's story because the novel has prompted a transformation.

But the second Toni Morrison novel, *Paradise*, told another story. Oprah remarked that this was the first time "our book club became a class" (24 Feb. 1998). It was the first time for a lot of things. Certainly, this was the first book-club meeting where Oprah consciously took on the language of school. *Paradise* "was yet another dream come true being taught by Toni Morrison." The book-club meeting took place at Princeton University, its "natural setting, not only because it's a place of higher learning—woo, girl, do we need that—but also because it's where author Toni Morrison teaches." And the twenty-two people who were selected for the in-person club became "*Paradise* pupils for a day" (24 Feb. 1998). As with the *Song of Solomon* discussion, much of the club time was dedicated to talking about the difficulty of reading the novel. This time, however, the focus was more on the ability—or the inability—of the readers to overcome that difficulty. This was the first time we heard about competition among readers—Oprah asked at the beginning, "We all tried to come prepared, but who could compete with these scholars?" and the next voice we heard was that of a club member saying, "We all go along in a contemporary religion that's dogmatic." This was the first time we heard about club mem-bers going outside their selves to make sense of a text ("Aren't you the one who went back to the Latin dictionary in Genesis to figure this out?" Oprah asked); the first time there were factions within the group ("Over our heads!" Oprah said, bellowing each word and lifting one woman's hand into the air in response to another woman's comment, and then she asked Morrison, "Whose version is correct?"); and the first time we heard readers question their own competence (Gayle, Oprah's best friend, asks, "Ms. Morrison, are we supposed to get it on the first read?" adding plaintively, "I went to college—I'm really kind of smart—but there were times when I read a page three or four times").

This is also the first time we saw a reader explicitly not trust Oprah—the first time a reader became a nonreader. Before Oprah showed the tapes of the Morrison interview and the book-club meeting, she talked to a woman in the studio audience who did not finish the novel. This woman said she was so lost that she gave up: "I really wanted to read the book and love it and learn some life lessons and when I got into it it was so confusing. *I question the value of a book that is that hard to understand*—and I quit reading it" (24 Feb. 1998; my emphasis). Oprah gave her some reading advice—points Morrison made in the interview that was shown later—and, for all intents and purposes, dismissed the woman's complaint, but the complaint was out there. It made it into the show—into the edited, aired show. At that moment, this book club bore little resemblance to the one, more than a year earlier, in which one woman said, "Oprah said get reading and I said, 'Yes Ma'am.'" This woman read because of Oprah. The woman who questioned Oprah's book choice did not. And though this woman eventually accepted Oprah's advice, accepted that the text, with guidance, was readable, she articulated a position no one else did: "I question the value of a book that is that hard to understand." I see this as a key moment in the book-club's history in part because the woman asked this question, but in even greater part because the aired book club gave no explicit answer.

What the woman in the studio audience expected—what anyone who watched other book-club meetings came to expect—is to "read the book and love it and learn some life lessons." That is what Oprah's viewers did not get. Ultimately, what made the *Paradise* meeting different from the *Song of Solomon* meeting was not that one text was necessarily more difficult than the other but that the personal never took center stage. We never had a Celeste—someone whose journey through a difficult text did not stop with the last page but continued into the difficulties of her life. With *Paradise*, we had one quick global life lesson: battered women who stay with their batterers need to see themselves through the eyes of their children. It's a fast point, one that's made and dropped, and it's a point about others, not about these readers.

The Toni Morrison novels show that, heretofore with Oprah's Book Club, it hadn't been the books that were middlebrow, it had been the reading. But in the *Paradise* meeting, the club members did not do middlebrow reading. Although the readers' relation to *Song of Solomon* was complicated (more complicated than it was with *The Book of Ruth* or with *She's Come Undone*), their struggles successfully yielded middlebrow readings—readings that were affective, transformative, personal. The *Paradise* meeting, however, broadened the club's cultural space. It moved the readers into an academic realm—literally, since the meeting took place at Princeton, and figuratively, since the discussion used the language of school and emphasized the cognitive over the emotive. The meeting ended on a note of consensus and seeming victory: after a club member made a point about the nature of paradise, drawing on her knowledge of the Bible, Oprah said, "And that is paradise." She looked around the room. "That is paradise," she repeated. The meeting was over: something had been decided. But it was a very different ending point: something had been decided about the text (maybe: it's difficult to gauge, by the looks on members' faces, that they know that "that" really is paradise) rather than about how to connect that decision, that lesson, to the daily living of life. This is uncharted territory for the club.

And it is complicated territory to read. I can see the *Paradise* meeting as a calculated risk on Oprah's part—she purposely chose both a difficult novel and a different method of talking about the novel as a way to insist on growth in the book club. We know that

Oprah strategized about book choices—selecting *Deep End of the Ocean* before *Song of Solomon* to lure readers in, choosing a longer book as the season's last book so that readers had plenty of time (and plenty of text) to read during the taping hiatus. And certainly Oprah could opt to change the terms of the conversation as a way to illustrate that different texts make different demands on readers, that readers can experience a different (more cognitive, more intellectual, more analytic) kind of reading pleasure. Oprah tried to help readers develop their repertoire of reading practices and showed them that there is more than one worthwhile way to read. It's possible too that while the meeting did not end with the same kind of certainty we've seen before, perhaps we simply did not see enough—and that it may take longer for the readers to come to terms with *Paradise*, certainly the most difficult novel in the book club's history. Oprah admitted after the meeting that she's headed back to read *Paradise* again, even though, she said, "I thought I knew something." And I like to see the decision to hold the meeting at Princeton as Oprah invading the Ivy League, claiming it as a legitimate space for nonelite readers. Along those same lines, her insistence on using the language of school, oversimplified though it was, may have been a kind of reclaiming of a credible studentship for adults.

At the same time, I also want to point out that as Oprah pursued the difficult, she also to some extent reinstated some of the restrictions that have kept some readers from reading. The physical space was quite different in the *Paradise* meeting than it had been in the past: set up less as a conversation and more as a lecture—Morrison faced all the club members, some, again, literally sitting at her feet. Readers were therefore literally not positioned to claim the text as their own. And while Oprah appropriated a kind of language of school (she used words like *pupil, assignment, class, study* no fewer than a dozen times to introduce the club meeting), she never articulated and elucidated how and why to read academically, though she was able to demonstrate how and why to read personally. She radically changed, at once and without explanation, the terms of the conversation. If Oprah wanted club members to reach a different reading destination, she did not provide enough tools to help them get there (though I must admit, as I write this sentence, I hear echoes of a conversation with a respected professor who told me, "I have no idea how I would teach *Paradise*!" And I'm not sure how I would either).

Finally, the different treatment of both Morrison and her book, *Paradise*, is never completely divorced from the personal. Even though we know that Morrison is an academically canonized author, we know at the same time that she is the most elevated member of Oprah's personal canon. In a fascinating study of gender and discourse in talk shows, Gloria-Jean Masciarotte looks at the role of stories and shifting subjectivity in the format of the shows. The "storied life" is always privileged over the expert guest: "No matter who is featured up on stage—Ph.D. from Harvard, presidential candidate, head of the Nuclear Control Commission, or incest survivor—the real expert on the issue at hand, the 'true' voice, is the storied voice of the audience and the caller" (86). The purpose of a talk show is not to resolve the issue but to "display the space for stories" (88). What separates Oprah from other hosts, Masciarotte argues, is that she is a storied person too. Oprah's "host function is consumed by the story function. She too performs as talker, as a storied subject among a host of storied subjects. . . . [S]he was always already one of her own guests" (94). Morrison could retain her authority over her work—can remain an author rather than become a guest, to recall Barthes's language—because her doing so suited Oprah's story. Again, Oprah repeatedly contextualized the Morrison visit as one of the three most important events in her life. Significantly, the other life-changing events involved black women's texts—making the film version of *The Color Purple* and "having Maya [Angelou] read to me in her own house" (18 Nov. 1996). Race and gender matter.[14] By announcing the impact these women writers had on her life, Oprah claimed a position in a living black female literary culture.

It was easy to see Oprah as ultimate reader—and with regard to Morrison and Angelou, as ultimate student. But we should not overlook Oprah's position as author. If we think about the ways in which Oprah constructed the meetings, the ways in which she authorized particular readings and comments, including her own, we can see her as the author of a canon—for herself and the millions of viewers who follow her. Her canon reversed usual hierarchies: black women are at the top, white men at the bottom. (She announced Wally Lamb's *She's Come Undone* with qualification and explanation: "Our next book in the reading club is by a male author. Yes. But you'd never know it by the way he writes about women. He really gets women . . . I just couldn't believe when I was reading it that a man wrote this book until I saw the picture in his book. That's not a sexist statement" [22 Jan. 1997].) But Oprah clearly placed herself in a particular narrative of literacy and the literary. Her role was just as important as Morrison's and Angelou's: she established the terms of the conversation.

In the end, we have layer upon layer of story: the author's story, the character's story, the reader's story, Oprah's story. Everything is personal. Personal stories circulate and prompt more personal stories—enacting conversations that can lead to more personal insight and revelation. Books that do not speak, that do not give way to another voice, are not useful and therefore fail. The stories are cumulative, always expansive. But Oprah's is the master narrative. She constructed and enforced the model. Success, on both an author's and a reader's part, is determined by how that individual story fits into Oprah's larger one.

Reinvigorating Reading

Two groups have come into play in this essay—one more prominently than the other. Both Oprah's Book Club and the academy claim culture: both involve the production and circulation of meaning. The problem, it seems to me, is that each group saw the other as marginal to its endeavors; each community of readers recognized itself as dynamic, as always shifting, but saw the other as rigid, lifeless. With the *Paradise* meeting, Oprah's Book Club made the move to honor—or at least try out—an academic approach to reading (even if members struggled to adapt those practices for their own purposes). The academy too would have benefited from recognizing Oprah's Book Club as a significant and complicated site of reading, one that could have helped to concretize the idea that we read differently in different locations and that those acts of reading allow us to locate ourselves in a social world. Long notes that scholars often fail to acknowledge approaches that are not their own: "Academics tend to repress consideration of variety in reading practices due to our assumptions that everyone reads (or ought to) as we do professionally, privileging the cognitive, ideational, and analytic mode" (192). Yet if we believe that reading is laudable, if we want to encourage people, specialist and nonspecialist alike, to read books, we have to acknowledge that Oprah affects people (millions of people) in a way that the academy does not. The call for reading as a transformative practice was heard and obeyed. General readers believe in the personal. Books continue to be valued, and the voice initially sanctioning that value came from outside the university.

Understanding the workings and appeal of Oprah's Book Club has pedagogical implications as well. We need to think of our students as having many cultures and different ways of knowing that can enrich a classroom. Anne Ruggles Gere writes, "Our students would benefit if we learned to see them as individuals who seek to write, not to be written about, who seek to publish, not be published about, who seek to theorize, not to be theorized about" ("Kitchen Tables" 89). In a response to Gere, Susan Miller writes, "We might . . . think of our teaching as a way to facilitate practices already underway, not as a vocation that must inevitably separate students from their culture, by virtue of its superior entree to vaguely 'better' worlds" (106). We should think too about our students who don't read or who don't like to read—how we might use our understanding of the reading practices in Oprah's Book Club as a way to help to lay a foundation of engagement for our students. If our job is to teach students to be critical readers, that foundation of interest must be there.

I am most pointedly not calling for the academy to appropriate Oprah's Book Club as the model for all reading. One of the reasons that Oprah's Book Club was so successful was because it offered an alternative reading practice. And even as I saw Oprah reinvigorate reading for millions of readers, the book club did not present an uncomplicated, unproblematic performance of literacy.[15] What's more: the academy enacts a valuable way of reading: critical reading skills allow for agency in negotiating and crafting one's experience in the world and, perhaps ironically, can yield wonderfully personal results. The danger, though, is believing that culture can be produced only in one way and move in one direction; the danger is refusing to see beyond one particular location and having only one narrative. We should expand—explode, perhaps—our notions of how and why one reads.

Notes

1. For an argument about how and why literature has come not to matter in schools, see Bleich's "What Literature Is 'Ours'?" included in this volume. Like Bleich, I see Oprah's Book Club members make affective, largely individualistic responses to their readings. But unlike Bleich, I see club members working to change their social and material lives as a result of those responses. Club members insist that reading matters.

2. Certainly not all academics fail to look beyond the walls of the academy. Both Gere ("Kitchen Tables") and Long, among others, caution against views of the relation between the academy and the public that do not take into account cross-influence. Gere uses the term *extracurriculum* to name and therefore make visible the space for learning that occurs outside the academy. To neglect composition in other contexts is to "run the risk of talking past those on the other side, of constructing walls as divisions rather than means of communicating. A more productive alternative involves considering our own roles as agents within the culture that encompasses the communities on both sides of the classroom wall" ("Kitchen Tables" 90). And Long insists that we should see reading as a social act, worthy of attention even as it takes place outside sanctioned academic instruction, in order to tear down the "pervasive assumptions in social science that there exists a strict and exclusive dichotomy between public and private life, and that significant social development and change occur only within the public realm" (185–87).

3. In her work with turn-of-the-century women's clubs, Gere argues that the difference in approaches to literacy development has its roots in the formation of English departments in the nineteenth century. Academic views of literacy development focused on formalistic approaches: "learning to extract a specific meaning (the one suggested by the instructor) from a text and to analyze specific features of that text . . . [which] left students little opportunity to explore what the text might mean to them" ("Literacy" 254). Literacy development for clubwomen, however, involved collaboration and play, "discovering multiple meanings in a single text and considering the affective as well as intellectual dimensions of that process of discovery" (254).

4. Many critics (including Flint; Schweickart; Flynn; Kennard; Bleich; and Pearce) reject reading theory, namely Fish's and Iser's, based on a reader— the reader—who is objective, solitary, undistinguished socially by race, class, or gender. Miner, relying on Baym's work, marks the mid-nineteenth century as the beginning of a split between what men and women read: "That male and female readers should have parted company when electing texts comes as no surprise; after all, they inhabited 'separate spheres,' and these spheres defined possibilities not only of experience, but also of imagination" (188). And black women in particular have engaged in a tradition of writing and reading that has at its foundation humanism and didacticism. Tate argues that many critics of Afro-American literature have insisted that literature should both delight and instruct, serve "as a vehicle for promoting social protest and reform" (111). These same critics have resisted structuralist and poststructuralist methodologies, she argues, "which place, or seem to place, more emphasis on form rather than content," because reading then loses its usefulness (111). Tate celebrates reading that speaks to experiences and involves a call to action.

5. For Spellmeyer, cultural studies, as well as other critical methods that have replaced theory, could be a worthy successor to theory because of its "commitment to descending from textuality into the particulars of everyday life" (893)—if it truly could move away from the theory it pronounced dead.

6. Class plays a central role in (British) cultural studies; the intellectual inheritance of the working-class founders of the field comes largely from the Frankfurt school. Class plays out semantically—in the battle between the use of "popular culture" or "mass culture" (see Hall; Ohmann; Kellner; among others). I'm interested in class too, but I want to think about other locations of difference—in this case, the nonprofessional status of readers seen through the eyes of professionals.

7. Masciarotte argues that much of the criticism directed at talk shows centers on who is talking and what they are talking about: "the critical comments are usually off-the-cuff condemnatory remarks aimed at the obvious site of woman talking, woman taking pleasure in talking, even when it is about

painful subjects. Sad women? Silly women? Manipulated women? Victims further victimized by the evil empire of television and mass culture? Hmmmm . . . perhaps it is more than just the clichéd objection to prattling women. Perhaps it is the fact that the women are talking, taking pleasure in talking, and talking about painful experiences, ongoing and ill-defined struggles?" (82).

8. In 2002 Oprah ended the book-club segment of her show, not because viewers and readers were no longer watching it but because, she said, it had become difficult to find books she wanted to share with her audience. And, in 2003, she resurrected her book club with a new focus on classic works of literature.

9. There is also, perhaps, as my former colleague at the University of Michigan, Jeremy Wells, pointed out to me, a fourth layer of people who did not know they were participants: people who do not know about the existence of Oprah's Book Club but read the selections because of friends' recommendations, the *New York Times* best-seller list, and bookstore displays. But this unaware fourth layer was perhaps less likely in the second half of the book club's existence, since "Oprah's Book Club" was then printed on the covers of the selected books.

10. Oprah's name was always linked with the book club. The name of the group clearly showed possession: it was Oprah's Book Club, not My Book Group or Bookpeople or University of Texas Group, like the reading groups that Long studies. Even with a change in medium, Oprah's name was omnipresent. America Online had a chat room set up for book-club discussion. The keyword? Oprah.

11. Feldman notes that Oprah is able to control the use of her name and her words by insisting on a guest relationship with the writers. Because they are "guests of the Oprah Winfrey show," Harpo Productions makes the arrangements and pays for the accommodations, whereas in most other situations the publisher plans and pays because the appearance is seen as promotional.

12. Oprah constantly pointed out that she in no way benefited financially from the book sales. She said, "I want you all to know—I don't own any interest in any of these books. I got some letters from people saying, 'Are you taking a profit from the books?' No. I'm hoping that the authors can. But I get nothing from the book, just the pleasure of you reading it. And I'll be reading it again along with you" (18 Nov. 1996).

13. Kirn uses different terminology to describe the same difference. He sees two categories: "solidly challenging fare [such] as Toni Morrison's *Song of Solomon*" and "worthy popular entertainments [such] as Wally Lamb's *She's Come Undone*" (104).

14. So much more could be said, I recognize, about race in Oprah's Book Club. To address it adequately would require another paper in itself. You

don't have to look hard to notice that race mattered in whose texts were selected (Oprah honors an African American canon) and who is invited to read (the in-person book club is never all white). But race, though mentioned sometimes, and never with white writers, was rarely a sustained topic of conversation (Morrison talked briefly about the opening line of *Paradise*—"They shoot the white girl first"—and gave a history of black American towns).

15. Oprah determined too much of the agenda for the group to be truly democratic, and the group's conversation was too much about the individual, not enough about the social. Members' discussions carried in them the implicit assumption that the individual is largely responsible for the path of his or her life, that systemic forces are not working against him or her. The discussions told the Horatio Alger story again and again. Or they told the Oprah Winfrey story from the beginning. Perhaps this focus on the individual is what happens when the person with one of the most celebrated rags-to-riches stories in American history is in charge.

Works Cited

Angelou, Maya. *Heart of a Woman*. New York: Random, 1981.

Barthes, Roland. *Image, Music, Text*. Trans. Stephen Heath. New York: Hill, 1977.

Breathnach, Sarah Ban. *Simple Abundance: A Daybook of Comfort and Joy*. New York: Warner, 1995.

Brodhead, Richard. *Cultures of Letters: Scenes of Reading and Writing in Nineteenth-Century America*. Chicago: U of Chicago P, 1993.

Cosby, Bill. *Little Bill Books for Beginning Readers*. New York: Scholastic, 1997.

Dimock, Wai Chee. "Feminism, New Historicism, and the Reader." *Readers in History: Nineteenth-Century American Literature and the Contexts of Response*. Ed. James L. Machor. Baltimore: Johns Hopkins UP, 1993. 85–108.

Feldman, Gayle. "Making Book on Oprah." *New York Times Book Review* 2 Feb. 1997: 31.

Fish, Stanley. *Is There a Text in This Class? The Authority of Interpretative Communities*. Cambridge: Harvard UP, 1980.

Fiske, John. "British Cultural Studies and Television." *Channels of Discourse, Reassembled: Television and Contemporary Criticism*. Ed. Robert C. Allen. Chapel Hill: U of North Carolina P, 1992. 284–326.

Flint, Kate. *The Woman Reader, 1837–1914*. Oxford: Oxford UP, 1993.

Flynn, Elizabeth A. "Composing as a Woman." *College Composition and Communication* 39 (1988): 423–35.

Flynn, Elizabeth A., and Patrocinio P. Schweickart, eds. *Gender and Reading: Essays on Readers, Texts, and Contexts.* Baltimore: Johns Hopkins UP, 1986.

Foucault, Michel. "What Is an Author?" *Textual Strategies: Perspectives in Post-structuralist Criticisms.* Ed. Josue Harari. Ithaca: Cornell UP, 1979. 141–60.

Gere, Anne Ruggles. "Kitchen Tables and Rented Rooms: The Extracurriculum of Composition." *College Composition and Communications* 45.1 (1994): 75–92.

———. "Literacy and Difference in Nineteenth-Century Women's Clubs." *Literacy: Interdisciplinary Conversations.* Ed. Deborah Keller-Cohen. Cresskill: Hampton, 1994. 249–65.

Gray, Herman. *Watching Race: Television and the Struggle for "Blackness."* Minneapolis: U of Minnesota P, 1995.

Hall, Stuart. "Notes on Deconstructing 'The Popular.'" *People's History and Socialist Theory.* Ed. Raphael Samuel. New York: Routledge, 1981. 227–39.

Hamilton, Jane. *The Book of Ruth.* New York: Anchor, 1988.

Hegi, Ursula. *Stones from the River.* New York: Simon, 1995.

Iser, Wolfgang. *The Act of Reading: A Theory of Aesthetic Response.* Baltimore: Johns Hopkins UP, 1978.

James, Caryn. "Harnessing TV's Power to the Power of the Page." *New York Times* 21 Nov. 1996, late ed.: C15+.

Kellner, Douglas. *Media Culture: Cultural Studies, Identity, and Politics between the Modern and the Postmodern.* New York: Routledge, 1995.

Kennard, Jean. "'Ourself behind Ourself': A Theory for Lesbian Readers." Flynn and Schweickart 63–80.

Kirn, Walter. "Rediscovering the Joy of the Text." *Time* 21 Apr. 1997: 102–06.

Lamb, Wally. *She's Come Undone.* New York: Pocket, 1992.

Long, Elizabeth. "Textual Interpretation as Collective Action." *The Ethnography of Reading.* Ed. Jonathan Boyarin. Berkeley: U of California P, 1993. 180–207.

Masciarotte, Gloria-Jean. "C'Mon Girl: Oprah Winfrey and the Discourse of Feminine Talk." *Genders* 11 (1991): 81–110.

Miller, Susan. "Things Inanimate May Move: A Different History of Writing and Class." *College Composition and Communication* 45.1 (1994): 102–07.

Miner, Madonne M. "Guaranteed to Please: Twentieth-Century American Women's Bestsellers." Flynn and Schweickart 187–214.

Mitchard, Jacquelyn. *Deep End of the Ocean.* New York: Viking, 1996.

Morris, Mary McGarry. *Songs in Ordinary Time.* New York: Viking, 1995.

Morrison, Toni. *Paradise.* New York: Knopf, 1997.

———. *Song of Solomon.* New York: Knopf, 1977.

Ohmann, Richard. *Selling Culture: Magazines, Markets, and Class at the Turn of the Century.* London: Verso, 1996.

"Oprah's Book Club." Transcripts.*The Oprah Winfrey Show.* Harpo Productions.

Pearce, Lynne. *Feminism and the Politics of Reading.* London: Arnold, 1997.

Radway, Janice. *A Feeling for Books: The Book-of-the-Month Club, Literary Taste, and Middle-Class Desire.* Chapel Hill: U of North Carolina P, 1997.

Schweickart, Patrocinio P. "Reading Ourselves: Toward a Feminist Theory of Reading." Flynn and Schweickart 31–62.

Spellmeyer, Kurt. "After Theory: From Textuality to Attunement with the World." *College English* 58 (1996): 893–913.

Tate, Claudia. "On Black Literary Women and the Evolution of Critical Discourse." *Tulsa Studies in Women's Literature* 5 (1986): 111–23.

Wells, Jeremy. Personal communication. 7 Apr. 1997.

Woolf, Virginia. "Middlebrow: A Letter Written but Not Sent." *Atlantic Monthly* Sept. 1942: 43–47.

Rhetorizing the Contact Zone: Multicultural Texts in Writing Classrooms

Laurie Grobman

In the last decade, compositionists and literary specialists have produced a great deal of critical and pedagogical work on multiculturalism, much of it in response to Mary Louise Pratt's conception of the classroom as a contact zone, a social space "where cultures meet, clash, and grapple with each other, often in contexts of highly asymmetrical relations of power" (34).[1] Although Pratt describes an exhilarating experience in the contact zone of an interdisciplinary course, many instructors have more difficulty creating a composition contact zone in which students engage the issues of cultural diversity.[2] Despite our best intentions, we as multiculturalists find ourselves facing numerous challenges: identity politics; issues of authority; appropriation by other fields; the discomfort of new pedagogical terrain; and, most significant, students' apathy, resistance, and hostility.

Pratt theorizes a classroom that enacts conflict and contact rather than community so that conflicting belief systems are made visible for extended scrutiny and so that the diverse perspectives students and instructor bring to class are aired and exposed rather than ignored, marginalized, or silenced. What kind of classroom would be required to transcend resistance and fear to make the contact zone come to life in positive and productive ways? Phyllis van Slyck astutely observes that we as instructors must realize the profundity of what we are asking students to do when we invite them to reconsider and question cherished beliefs (151). Such challenges led me to rethink the notion of the contact zone as I planned my spring 1999 semester's composition course. I sought to create a classroom that would embrace the diversity implicit in Pratt's original conception but that would promote simultaneously a space in which students might engage the issues of multiculturalism without the fear, resistance, and defensiveness that too often hinder learning. I found my answer through what I call "rhetorizing the contact zone" of multicultural texts.

I use the term *multicultural text* to refer to literature by nonwhite ethnic minority American populations, those historically oppressed, marginalized, and silenced in literary and cultural discourse. No doubt, words like *multicultural, color, minority,* and *ethnic* are awkward and linguistically dissatisfying on a number of levels.[3] Obviously, white people have ethnicity and most have multicultural backgrounds, when culture is defined to include gender, ethnicity, class, sexual orientation, religion, and so forth. Moreover, scholars have recently begun to interrogate the notion of whiteness as racialized and ethnic. However, the terms multicultural and multiculturalism in English studies are associated with specific politics, viewpoints, and literary texts. Multiculturalism carries with it a recognition of white privilege, an acknowledgment of the power relations and advantages that nonwhites in America lack, and thus refers to the demand by traditionally marginalized cultures to be heard and represented in the literary, cultural, and social history of America.[4] The multicultural movement in English studies initially referred to the literature of nonwhite racial and ethnic minorities— those texts previously excluded from the traditional canon of American literature. Multiculturalism has since been expanded to include class and sexual orientation, but my focus here sustains its initial emphasis on ethnicity and race.[5]

Thus, although terms like multicultural are unsatisfactory, they must suffice, at least for now. Otherwise, the groundbreaking work of scholars to construct a more inclusive canon, which is ongoing, would be ill-served. Perhaps one day the phrase *American literature* (and by implication the canon of American literature) will come to be all-inclusive and diverse—based on race, ethnicity, gender, class, and sexual orientation. But, as Betsy Erkkila observes, we are not there yet: "White studies, with a few ethnic or gendered satellites, remains the dominant model of American literary and cultural studies. Ethnic and women writers are added on to traditional models of American literature and culture; they do not force a reconceptualization of the theory and practice of American literature and studies" (587).

This article argues that multicultural texts can be read as contact zones where competing discourses intersect as reader and writer make meaning of converging and diverging value systems, ideologies, and cultural structures. Mikhail Bakhtin's concept of heteroglossia—the stratification of languages within a language—helps us understand that a text consists of diverse cultural elements. As Bakhtin has argued, fiction is saturated with multiple discourses that compete with and animate one another. Discourse participants construct meaning not in isolation but through exchange and interaction. Wayne Booth, moreover, has helped us appreciate that all literary texts are rhetorical—they use persuasion and make arguments (*Rhetoric*). Together, these theories support the notion that multicultural texts are sites of rhetorical struggle, not simply expressions of personal or cultural struggle. Unlike canonical, white American texts, which associate whiteness with universality, multicultural texts engage the clash of cultural codes and expose the whiteness of the canonical texts they speak to and through. When we rhetorize the multicultural text, its embedded cultural systems become recognizable as conflicting and competing discursive and rhetorical systems.

This approach situates multicultural texts in writing classrooms in ways that distinguish the pedagogical objectives of composition from literature classrooms, an important distinction often glossed over.[6] The objectives of using multicultural texts in composition must take into account not only the (perhaps over simplistic) notion that multicultural literature has a particular power to promote multicultural understanding but also the concern of compositionists to develop an understanding of the complex relation between language and meaning, literacy and power. Subsequently, the debate over academic discourse—whether in teaching such discourse we are encouraging students to resist or adapt exclusionary language practices—intertwines with multicultural literature in ways that remain largely unexplored.[7] Many of us who address multiculturalism in our classes recognize students' pragmatic reasons for learning to write, and we hope we can give them the critical edge they need to make informed decisions about how they will use academic discourse. In multicultural writing classrooms, therefore, we must pay careful attention to issues of writing and rhetoric. While we hope for attitudinal change, multicultural composition must pay at least equal attention to students as writers—as producers of future texts that will be complicit in creating a more just society. Writing is not simply a matter of mastering a set of skills, but the political focus of a multicultural classroom must not be severed from the processes and strategies of writing and writing instruction.

In this essay, I describe a semester-long experiment on the use of a multicultural text, *The House on Mango Street*, by Sandra Cisneros, as a contact zone in a composition classroom. The metaphor of a contact zone has been productively extended and re-formed from Pratt's original reference to apply to diverse theoretical and pedagogical situations of difference, politics, and conflict. Patricia Bizzell uses the notion of a contact zone as a way to rethink the basic structure of English studies (see "'Contact Zones'"; "Negotiating Difference"). Kristine Blair uses the term *electronic contact zone* to refer to the democratizing potential of the composition computer classroom (see also Selfe and Selfe). In my earlier work, I extend the notion of the contact zone to the professional writing classroom, suggesting that professional writing's emphasis on internationalization ignores the critical complexities of multiculturalism and, consequently, language's inextricable connections with ideology, privilege, and subordination (see "Beyond Internalization"). Clearly, then, compositionists see in the idea of the contact zone useful ways of conceiving the political and pedagogical work of the discipline beyond the earliest uses of Pratt's term to apply to the composition classroom itself.

By viewing the multicultural text as a contact zone of competing, conflicting, and interconnected discourses, I hope to expose the clash of rhetorics in these texts and to show students the ways in which the cultural commonplaces of fear, prejudice, and hate are themselves rhetorics with their own "internalized systems, self-sustaining logics, and justifications" (Miller 408). In so doing, I encourage students to learn to "negotiate and to place [themselves] in dialogue with different ways of knowing" (Miller 407) as they enter, accept, and resist the diverse rhetorics embedded in the multicultural text. Reading multicultural texts as rhetorical contact zones enables students to consider the range of positions and voices from and against which the author speaks and writes. As Richard Miller has pointed out, "the most important work that can be begun in a composition course" extends beyond the multicultural content to students' understanding of rhetorical choice (404).

A product of multiple cultural and literary influences, *Mango Street* traverses various discursive and cultural systems to both reinforce and challenge the various ideologies they represent. By so doing, *Mango Street* rhetorically engages issues of import. As I turn to the experiences of my students' rhetorizing the contact zone of *Mango Street*, I show that this approach to multicultural texts in composition has three primary advantages: it fosters serious and invested critical thinking as it foregrounds rhetorical issues and writing instruction; it encourages students to engage the issues of multiculturalism they might normally reject and thus plants the seeds for students' emerging social consciousnesses; and it introduces students to the rhetorics of academic discourse. Although I present each arena separately, I want to stress that in practice they are inextricably connected.

Rhetorizing The House on Mango Street: Composition, Multiculturalism, and the Contact Zone

Although it is a short, accessible text, *Mango Street* embodies a complex web of intersecting and competing discursive systems that may be explored through rhetorical analysis. In my composition classes, we examined four of these discourses throughout the semester. Our goal was to understand how Cisneros situates herself in relation to these discourses and how she offers counterrhetorics. First, *Mango Street* engages the American dream that bombards young Chicanos and Chicanas with glorious images but denies them its possibilities. Second, Cisneros examines the American notion of individualism and its relation to Chicano and Chicana cultural values. Third, she engages rhetorically with American and Chicano male bildungsroman traditions. Finally, in its promotion of a Chicana feminist position, *Mango Street* comes into rhetorical contact with the gendered fairy tales that have shaped white students' lives, specifically "Cinderella" and "Rapunzel."

As the course began, I explained that we would be examining *Mango Street* as a contact zone: we would not be approaching it from the literary perspective students most likely learned in high school. Rather than examine formal characteristics such as plot, character development, symbolism, and so on, we would scrutinize Cisneros's rhetorical engagement with a variety of discursive systems that each reflect specific ideologies and beliefs. We began the course by reading the novel, supplemented by excerpts from Edward Stewart and Milton Bennett's *American Cultural Patterns*, to examine the discourses of individualism and the American dream. Next, we turned to the rhetorics of American and Chicano male bildungsroman traditions by reading William Faulkner's "Barn Burning" and Tomás Rivera's . . . *Y no se lo tragó la tierra / . . . And the Earth Did Not Devour Him*. I assigned two scholarly articles for our next unit on fairy-tale rhetoric and feminist critique, Madonna Kolbenschlag's "A Feminist's View of 'Cinderella'" and Ella Westland's

"Cinderella in the Classroom: Children's Responses to Gender Roles in Fairy-Tales." My students thus read *Mango Street* in the context of a wide variety of other readings relevant to the issues Cisneros raises. Through their own written work, students began to find their voices and positions in the discourses that compose her novel—and our world.

For each of these units, class discussions and writing assignments centered on how Cisneros converses with these diverse rhetorics. Through an asynchronous electronic conference board, students were able to work through their earlier ideas in the context of the responses and comments of other students.[8] I also required multiple drafts of essays addressing the discourses in the primary text. To encourage alternative ways of seeing and to emphasize the larger significance of the cultural debates in *Mango Street*, I devised assignments that allowed students to go beyond the text itself to the larger issues it raised. For example, in our unit on bildungsroman traditions, students could write about any of the three required readings, singly or in combination, and some of the questions and topics encouraged them to circle back to the first unit's readings from *American Cultural Patterns* (Stewart and Bennett). In the unit on fairy tales, students could write about the extent to which Cisneros assimilated or subverted traditional fairy tales, or they could write about feminist perspectives on fairy tales or popular culture more generally. One of the questions provided the opportunity for students to address the issue of male stereotypes in fairy tales or other forms of popular culture. In each assignment, students were required to draw from the academic articles they had read. For the fifth and final essay, for which research was required, students revisited various issues raised by the rhetorical contact zone of the novel.

By presenting *Mango Street* as a site of rhetorical struggle, I could emphasize our shared understanding that writing evolves from the social, that writing is "as much a product of the community as of the individual writer" (Winterowd 49). The discursive practices in the text reveal the communities in which Cisneros resides and, equally significant, from which she is excluded. If students could understand rhetoric's role in the production and reproduction of cultural claims and belief systems, they could begin to realize their own role as speakers and writers in these cultural processes. By engaging the rhetorics implicit in Cisneros's novel, students situated themselves as part of discursive communities in which they also reside, thus creating spaces from which they could read, speak, and write and from which they could begin to enter the discourses of communities from which they are otherwise excluded.

Writing Instruction in the Contact Zone

The contact zone of *Mango Street* provides rich opportunities for promoting critical thinking, reading, and writing. In its scathing critique of the discourses of the American dream, *Mango Street* traces the emotional, intellectual, moral, and artistic development of Esperanza Cordero, the protagonist, as she struggles with the realities of being poor, Mexican American, and female. Esperanza's changing conception of the American dream is a crucial aspect of her developing consciousness. To engage students in the problem solving of Esperanza's transformation, I asked them to analyze the extent to which Esperanza embraces—in the beginning and end of the book—the American dream promoted by American pop culture. Because the assignment required students to apply different sets of ideas to one another (the American dream, pop culture, and *Mango Street*), it promoted the kind of higher-level critical thinking educators are justly calling for (see Anson) and to which writing assignments in composition classes should strive.[9]

Many students' first drafts were mired in vague abstractions, such as "The American dream is whatever an individual wants it to be." Other students were willing to identify a particular component of the American dream (nice house, good job, etc.) but could not conceive of culture's complicity in the dream's construction (the dream is itself an absolute, an unquestioned assumption, a tenet by which we should all live). Some students could even see how

Esperanza's desire for a house is an expression of the American dream, but they could not appreciate the ways in which the forces around her shaped her aspirations. Most significant, very few students could understand the relations among these various concepts, much less articulate them in writing. Many also failed to see how Esperanza's transformed American dream was actually unlike the one promoted in pop culure.

However, students' work from one draft to the next demonstrates how *Mango Street* can promote critical thinking in the classroom. One student, Katherine,[10] began her first draft with the following thesis: "When Esperanza is a young girl the American Dream is important to her, but by the end of the book when she is a young adult she wants [to] escape from her life and culture on Mango Street." In this draft, Katherine demonstrates little understanding of the mental tasks required by the assignment, and her reading of the novel is distorted (Esperanza does not simply seek to escape Mango Street but vows to return to help her community). Katherine understands that Esperanza initially desires the American dream, but she does not connect that desire to external, cultural forces acting on Esperanza: "There is no set definition for the American Dream, it is what the person wants for themselves to make them happy. Usually it is material, especially in the American materialistic society."

Like most students in the class, Katherine gravitates toward familiar ground in this draft, adhering to the kind of assignment that asks students to define a concept without the broader contexts from which the definition would arise. To enable her and the other students to move beyond their familiar ways of seeing the world, I had them read and reread *Mango Street* to reconsider its rhetorical claims. With each reading, students had to pay careful attention to the text's subtleties. We compositionists seem to share the opinion that reading is important for writing students, even if we do not necessarily agree on what students should be reading (see Otte). Multicultural readers have become widely used in composition, but increasingly scholars have pointed out the problems in them, specifically their tendencies to essentialize race and ethnicity as well as reinforce dominant-marginal binaries (see Sadarangani; Stockton).

An in-depth, semester-long examination of a multicultural text can alleviate some of these problems and foster more nuanced, critical reading abilities. As a rhetorical space, the text becomes more than a story of growing up, oppression, political protest, or whatever else its plot may reveal. Instead, the text becomes what Barbara Johnson calls "warring forces of signification" (qtd. in Blum 94); as such, the text invites students into the conversations in it, to question and interrogate rather than absorb and regurgitate. By supplementing *Mango Street* with other literary and academic texts, I reinforced the importance of careful, critical reading and provided a sense of how texts and writers speak to one another, thus charting a path for students to follow.

The writing assignments that grew out of reading and teaching Cisneros's novel in this manner offered students a wide range of possibilities for experimenting with critical thinking. As they revisited both their own writing and the contact zone of *Mango Street*, students could reimagine and reshape the interpretations in their own texts. Katherine's revised thesis demonstrated the intimate connection between writing and thinking and her intellectual growth as she responded to the demands of the assignment: "When Esperanza is a young girl she gets her perception of the American dream from popular culture, but she does not hold the same dream by the end of the book." In this draft, Katherine adeptly implicated popular culture—from Bill Gates to *Beverly Hills 90210* and the models on magazine covers—in the materialism she saw in Esperanza's childhood American dream. She went on to explain the transformation in Esperanza's desires:

> Her dream also changes because of everything and everyone she has been controlled by her whole life on Mango Street. Throughout the book Esperanza realizes that her dream is to escape from all of the things that are keeping her down. She talks about a house all her own where she can have her privacy and independence.

Although arguably Katherine implied that forces within Chicano and Chicana culture (gender oppression, attachment to family and community), rather than those of the dominant culture, are the controls from which Esperanza seeks to escape, she nevertheless showed an ability to engage critically with the discourse of the American dream as it is addressed in the novel. Because Cisneros addresses so many discourses simultaneously, writing assignments were varied and interesting and promoted in students the kind of intellectual growth we experience as writers struggling with ideas. As critical thinkers, students became active learners engaged in intellectual issues of cultural diversity rather than passive recipients of the multicultural mission.

Individualism, Social Responsibility, and Bildungsroman Traditions

The advantages of rhetorizing multicultural texts in composition extend beyond encouraging students' participation in higher intellectual thinking and writing to engaging them in the specific content associated with multiculturalism and diversity. As van Slyck argues, the literary text is a site "where an important kind of cultural debate and dialogue can take place" and where "contradictory positions create a contact zone within the same text" (167). Much of the work on multiculturalism and composition implicitly or explicitly takes into account the changes on college campuses as minority presence continues to rise nationwide.[11] But the student population at the college at which I teach, located in an affluent suburban Pennsylvania community ten minutes from Reading and sixty minutes from Philadelphia, remains largely homogeneous.[12] Incorporating multicultural content into such a class is enormously difficult; students vehemently resist exploring issues of power, particularly when related to race or ethnicity. Moreover, in the absence of minority voices, the dialogue often seems inadequate. In the discussion that follows, I present two examples of how reading the contact zone of *Mango Street* offered my students the opportunity to participate in meaningful, multicultural dialogue.

To move students toward a genuine engagement with some of the threatening issues raised by *Mango Street*, I had the class explore the rhetorics of individualism and self-reliance, which are particularly American concepts. Using ideas from Stewart and Bennett as points of departure, students began to unravel Cisneros's complexly layered philosophies of individualism and self-reliance, what Margot Kelley calls "the negotiations of characters and a culture 'caught in the transition' between the collective and the individual orientation" (65). But students had a difficult time going beyond their majoritarian-based values. Stuck, like Candace Spigelman's students, "in the abyss of individual culpability" (53), they were at first unable or unwilling to suspend their belief that anyone who works hard enough can achieve success in this country and, perhaps even more significant, felt that Cisneros agreed with them on this point. Many students who acknowledged Esperanza's commitment to return to the Mango Street community resisted going beyond the idea that Esperanza is "strong enough" or "has the drive to make it." If the other community members remain trapped in barrio life, students argued, it was their own doing.

Cisneros's intertextual critique of the white male bildungsroman literary tradition helped students situate *Mango Street* in a literary-rhetorical community with specific conventions and practices representing shared and conflicting value systems and representing various coming-of-age narratives.[13] Students in their early drafts dealt mainly with surface similarities and differences, failing to see how themes and content were part of larger rhetorical claims. Many students resisted the notion that Cisneros, Rivera, and especially Faulkner (who occupied status as a white male writer on the collective list of authors most students had either read in high school or heard of as a literary master) wrote in response to a certain set of values and ideological positions.

We closely examined the final words in the short story "Barn Burning," "He did not look back" (1565), which suggested to many of my students (as well as scholars who have read and studied this Faulkner classic) that this story is a white, American male version of individualism and of the bildungsroman tradition. I asked students to question the story's implicit commentaries on American individualism. It may appear that Sarty Snopes "lights out" in the manner of that self-made man Huck Finn. However, by informing DeSpain of his father's, Abner Snopes's, plans to burn DeSpain's barn, Sarty's break from his father and family may be a gesture to the larger human community. We then turned our analysis back to *Mango Street*, since the conflicting impulses of individualism and social responsibility are at its core. Esperanza seeks to balance her need for a space of her own with her desire to give back to her community. We talked about how Esperanza's story differs from and intersects with Sarty's. While I hoped students would realize that the issues are rarely black and white, that even Faulkner critiques his own society, students' initial readings of the passage in which Sarty gazes with awe at DeSpain's mansion reinforced in their minds the rightness of the American dream. Few were willing to concede any justification for Abner Snopes's violence, unable to imagine the shameful conditions in which his family was forced to live and the systematic exploitation they faced. Indeed, most students blamed the family's abysmal conditions on the father's shortcomings. It is difficult for students to imagine the exploitation of white sharecroppers, especially at the hands of other whites. However, through sustained inquiry and careful rereading, students began to negotiate the claims of these texts. One student, Christine, addressed Abner Snopes's violent behavior in her research paper, in the light of what she had learned about the life of sharecroppers after the Civil War:

> Migrant farm workers, also known as sharecroppers, worked for a farm owner. In exchange, they received a place to live and some money. Most migrant farm working families lived on the property of the owner. . . . Most times these people could not afford land of their own. This was hard work for little or no benefits. . . . I feel that Faulkner understood what Abner felt and the troubled life he led.

Like most students in the class, Christine was initially unforgiving of Abner Snopes, blaming him for the hardships his family endures and the violence he commits. However, her research led her to a more careful reading of the text and its comments on issues of power, class, and poverty. While she did not forgive Abner Snopes, she gained some compassion for his circumstances. Through continued, invested dialogue with bildungsroman traditions, students were able to break out of their resistance and consider what it must be like for white families, such as the Snopes, and Chicano families, such as the Corderos, to have the American dream so far out of reach. Rivera's . . . *Y no se lo tragó la tierra* / . . . *And the Earth Did Not Devour Him*, the most canonized Chicano story of growing up, gives a Chicano spin on the coming-of-age narrative represented by "Barn Burning." Numerous critics recognize the intertextual relations between Rivera's text and *Mango Street*, written fifteen years later by a Chicana. Moreover, scholars tend to interpret both texts within the larger American bildungsroman and female bildungsroman traditions. In my class, I provided a bit of literary history to give students a framework for considering the extent to which Cisneros challenges or conforms to the traditions that precede her writing.

Students' writing discussed the ways in which Rivera's text questions the philosophy of the American white male tradition: perhaps the stories of pulling oneself up by one's bootstraps do not apply in Rivera's world, where children are exploited as laborers and families are denied basic human needs such as a place to sleep. Students' initial response was to try to fit Rivera's story into familiar bildungsroman themes (e.g., the protagonist's egocentric questioning of God). They saw in the young protagonist their own rebellion against their parents' religion, something they felt was common to teenagers everywhere. However, on closer examination, students began to see that the narrator's questioning revolved around the suffering of his family and community. The competing rhetorics in these texts compelled students to reconsider notions of individualism and the American dream. Through careful and close study of Chicano and Chicana history and cultural contexts, students entered into dialogue with Rivera and Cisneros. In so doing, they discovered—in ways that were completely new to most of them—how the history of Chicano and Chicana oppression affects the freedom and possibilities in the American bildungsroman tradition and the cultural values it assumes and espouses.

Haley, for example, began her first draft on Rivera's novel by pointing to the protagonist's Mexican American background and his struggles against poverty and prejudice. She then wrote: "The book, in it being a story of development and growing up, is in most respects an example of a bildungsroman. However, in its cyclical structure and lack of an actual physical adventure, . . . [it] does not completely conform to a white male bildungsroman, it also challenges some of the characteristics as well." In this draft, Haley astutely observed those points of divergence and convergence between Rivera's text and the white male tradition. However, despite the foregrounding of the boy's Mexican American heritage and the poverty and prejudice that confront his growing up, her draft remained largely free of cultural contexts. In our conference on her paper, I encouraged Haley to consider the why of her assertions—to consider how the Chicano cultural contexts she raised in her introductory paragraph might influence Rivera's dialogue with Faulkner. How could she enter their conversation? What would she say?

Because writing assignments often circled back to earlier issues and texts, students were able to see and enact the revision process in their writing by producing multiple drafts of each essay and by drawing on earlier essays as they created new ones. This sequencing of assignments not only fostered deeper analysis in general but also promoted the kind of dialogue about specific issues related to cultural diversity that students in these classes often resist. In her revision, Haley wrote:

> In its challenging of the typical patterns of the white male bildungsro-
> man, . . . *And the Earth Does Not Devour Him* is an excellent exam-

ple of a typical bildungsroman integrated to include a distinct sense of identity and values, in a society that does not provide this to those of an ethnic background.

Notwithstanding the errors and awkwardness of the sentence, Haley's revision displayed a deeper understanding of how Rivera's text involves clashing rhetorics—the claims Rivera makes about the bildungsroman's ideological positions and their relation to Chicanos' lives. Subsequently, Haley entered the cultural debate played out in Rivera's and Faulkner's stories. In her supporting points, Haley tried to integrate the cultural contexts into her analysis, with varying degrees of success. For example, Haley wrote about the hero's break with authority in Rivera's story:

> In this chapter, the boy's father, then brother, become ill with sunstroke. In showing his complete disgust with the whole situation in which he is in, the boy goes against his family's and his own beliefs and curses God himself. After this incident he feels as though he has freed himself: "for the first time he felt capable of doing and undoing anything that he pleased" (Rivera 112).

This attitude of achieving one's goals is typical in the bildungsroman. Haley made the connection between the exploitative and destructive situation of Chicano migrant farm workers and the boy's crisis of faith. She picked up on Rivera's discursive strategy as the boy curses his God.

Students also compared and contrasted *Earth* and *Mango Street*, particularly in terms of the values Rivera's text espouses and the extent to which Cisneros critiques them. It was important for students to come to terms with the unique ways these writers use language to uproot and shatter accepted views. Revisiting the issues raised by *Mango Street*, students began to understand that the commonplace "we can achieve if we try hard and work hard" might not apply to those who confront socioeconomic and political forces beyond their control.

However, although most students were able to acknowledge the extent to which both writers comment on racial and class oppression, they were less willing to accept the gendered codes in Rivera's text. Thus we returned to *Mango Street* to consider how Cisneros writes against prescribed gender roles, and we thus entered the cultural conversations of feminist discourse. Cisneros subverts the circular journeys of the female bildungsroman tradition when Esperanza circles back to her community, not out of a sense of futility but from a commitment to a community ethic. As Esperanza envisions her departure from Mango Street, the stories "inside [her] head" become communal: "They will not know I have gone away to come back. For the ones I left behind. For the ones who cannot out" (110). In her essay, Betsy effectively tied together the intersecting claims of *Mango Street*. She blended the discourse of political and social oppression with the Chicana feminist critique of gender as she analyzed how Cisneros's text differs from Rivera's:

> Chicano culture also dictates to Esperanza that she will be submissive to men and will be the weaker race. She breaks against both gender and ethnic oppression, brave to stand for what she wants. Again, this is what makes Esperanza's bildungsroman different. She tells how she grows up and at the same time tells the concerns of the oppressed culture she lives in every day. A characteristic of Chicano literature is that it is a response to domination and oppression. Certainly Esperanza shows such a response through her actions to ignore the given ways and fight for what she wants.

Fairy Tales and Feminist Rhetorics

The gendered fairy tales that typically surround white American girls as they grow up—for example, tales presented by Disney in movies, cartoons, and toys—are girls' versions of rags-to-riches stories, the female protagonist rescued by a wealthy and handsome prince. Cisneros directly engages these fairy tales, and Esperanza knows that neither these stories nor the lives of the women around her represent the destiny she wants for herself. Breaking cultural codes about women's roles, Esperanza refuses to accept gender limitations, as her recurring use of fairy tales like "Cinderella" and "Rapunzel" suggests. The class read two scholarly articles: Kolbenschlag's critique of "Cinderella" and Westland's social-science study of the effects of fairy tales on girls' and boys' gender identity. At first, most students, particularly the males, vehemently resisted the notion that fairy-tale messages impart any harm, even though they admitted its prevalence in our culture. Some appeared angry, as indicated by the following comments on the class's asynchronous conference board:

> First of all Kolbenschlag must have been bored out of her mind and needed something to get headlines. She felt that if she would criticize the story of Cinderella she would make a name for herself. . . . She is very good at her feminist viewpoints but the extent at which she goes is just unbelievable. I really detest this woman.

> I believe in women's rights. If an equal job is being done by a man, or a woman the benefits and consequences should be equal. The only thing I have a problem with is putting the blame on stupid fairy tales. It is probably the most bull I have heard this year. . . . Also men by nature are dominant!!

These students' hostile, emotional rhetoric, however, did not preclude more productive dialogue in our class discussions and students' writing, primarily because Cisneros's engagement with fairy-tale rhetorics opened the door for students to converse with Cisneros. Barry's early draft centered on how Cisneros uses fairy tales to "emphasize how much women are oppressed in the Chicano culture." Through group work, the class examined Cisneros's specific use of fairy tales in relation to Esperanza and the other women in *Mango Street*. To what extent did Esperanza see herself as a Cinderella or Rapunzel? What kind of claims was she making? Did her use of fairy tales bring her into a more transformative realm?

In his next draft, Barry's thesis became more complex, accounting for Esperanza's social consciousness: "Cisneros places some of these fairy tales in her book . . . to emphasize how much women are oppressed in the Chicano culture, but at the same time Esperanza is rebelling against these fairy tales so she can stay out of the oppression cycle." In entering Cisneros's rhetoric, Barry gained a broader understanding of Cisneros's efforts to situate herself within and against a number of discursive practices in order to effect change. Perhaps even more important, he entered the critique with her. As Joseph Harris and Jay Rosen suggest, our classrooms are "not only zones of contact but spaces of possibility" (67); thus our task as teachers is to provide opportunities for students to "see certain texts or events in a different or unusual light" (66) so they can "begin to resist the power of discourses, to transform their rules, to become critics" (66–67).

Students' initial resistance to Cisneros's apparent rejection of men was also tempered by the extent to which Cisneros dispels stereotypes of poor Chicanos by portraying their humanity. Chicana feminists' affinities with both the white feminist movement and the Chicano movement, sharing analyses of gender and sexuality with the former and analyses of race, culture, and class with the latter (see Rebolledo), add another layer to the rhetorical battles in her text. The Chicana feminist's dilemma—she is "caught between two perspectives which appeal strongly to different aspects of her experience" (Yarbro-Bejarano 140)—induces a doubleness that students recognized in *Mango Street*: Cisneros critiques white oppression and Chicano sexism without reinforcing stereotypes of Chicano men. Esperanza thinks about "those who don't know any better" and who inadvertently end up in her neighborhood "scared" of the men they do not know (28). Kenny wrote:

> We see they [outsiders] judge the people in the neighborhood by how their houses look. They think that just because there are crumbling brick buildings and old houses that this is a bad neighborhood. They are afraid of violence and bad people. Esperanza learns from this that people that judge things by their looks are not always right. She knows that her neighborhood is old and wretched, but she also knows there are a lot of good people in her neighborhood too.

Cisneros's use of counterrhetorics to dispel stereotypes of Chicanos and Chicanas influenced Kenny, whose enlightenment about how individuals and cultures unfairly judge (and are judged by) others extended to how he understands Esperanza's developing consciousness:

> Esperanza is learning throughout the book how unfairly the society treats people. . . . she does not want to be like those people when she grows up. She makes her own dream of being happy and does not care what others think of her. She wants to be a good person and still respect others. . . . By the end of the book, Esperanza has her own dream, her own American Dream. . . . she will still not forget the others that she has left, and will always go back to them in their time of need. She will never totally leave those who cannot escape the wrath of society.

From Academic Discourse to Broadened Perspectives

The academic discourse paradigm currently dominating composition studies holds that first-year students become authorized in the academic community by their ability to appropriate academic discourse, to operate inside it.[14] Academic discourse encourages students to move from feeling to thinking, from adhering to perspectives for their familiarity to judging their logic or humanity. Academic discourse encourages students to use writing to make meaning and empowers them to participate in the construction of knowledge. By rhetorically investigating *Mango Street*, my students used academic discourse to expand their understanding of this text to larger, related issues: the feminist movement and women's issues, cultural diversity issues, literary value, the influence of mass media on children and teenagers, moral relativism, individualism and social responsibility, and the American dream's potentialities and pitfalls.

How does appropriation of academic discourse and larger meaning making occur? If sequenced appropriately, each assignment builds on the others so that writing assignments, as Ann Berthoff suggests, "encourage conscientization, the discovery of the mind in action." Students "learn . . . how meanings make future meanings possible, how form finds further form" (755). While academic discourse itself is highly contested (see Bartholomae; Elbow; Kraemer), at the risk of oversimplification, I like to think of it broadly as the knowledge-making process specific to the academy. Though variations in this process as well as in what constitutes knowledge exist both between and within disciplines, we cannot ignore the common thread: knowledge builds on prior knowledge as the inquirer-writer engages with other points of view.

Sharon's research essay demonstrated how academic discourse strategies—the broadening of views through increased knowledge and the building of perspectives through engaged inquiry—can lead to broader understanding of issues of social justice. Researching Chicano cultural and historical contexts, Sharon explored the extent to which Cisneros's text accurately reflects Chicano and Chicana culture. She began by using a sociological study to counteract stereotypes of barrio life:

> The Chicano people were not welcomed by the Americans. Because of this Chicanos created a Mexican-American world in something called barrios. . . . Ronald Takaki, the author of *A Different Mirror*, explained that "though their neighborhood was a slum, a concentration of shacks and dilapidated houses, the barrio was home to its residents" (334). The Chicanos felt safe among people of the same heritage. Even though it wasn't a nice place to live, it was home to them.

Although Sharon initially could not imagine how Esperanza or any of her friends could feel safe in their neighborhood, the knowledge she gained through research broadened her understanding:

> Sandra Cisneros' story *The House on Mango Street* is about a girl named Esperanza who grows up living in the barrios. She writes, "All brown all around, we are safe. But watch us drive into a neighborhood of another color and our knees go shakity-shake and our car windows get rolled up tight and our eyes look straight" (28).

Cisneros explains exactly how history portrays the situation. In the barrios they felt safe, but as soon as they left the community, they were frightened of the people who were a different color than them.

Next, Sharon moved from Esperanza's apparently secure feelings about life in the barrio to Cisneros's larger claim about social responsibility:

Robin Ganz explains that "Sandra Cisneros derived inspiration from her cultural specificity and found her voice in the dingy rooms of her house on Mango Street, on the cruel but comfortable streets of the barrio, and in the smooth and dangerous curves of borderland arroyos" (19). She shows that Cisneros was inspired by the barrios and wanted to write so the reader would know what it would be like to live there.

Sharon attempted, quite skillfully, I think, to find a rational basis for Cisneros's claims that readers should understand rather than judge the lives of the barrio residents. Moreover, she began to comprehend how Esperanza felt obligated to her neighbors, despite her own ability to break free from many of her community's constraints. Sharon thus used academic discourse to broaden her understanding of Cisneros's rhetorical claims. Like any academic writer, she executed a blend of research and her own analysis to construct a truly dialogic argument. As Min-Zhan Lu argues, allowing students to negotiate multiple discourses gives them the ability to choose to resist or adapt academic discourse "in the context of the history, culture, and society in which they live" (458).

Betsy left *Mango Street* and used the research essay to explore the achievements and needs of the feminist movement in the United States. After three paragraphs explaining the accomplishments of women over the last fifty years, Betsy concludes that "the movement has lost what it originally intended to do." She returned to Cisneros's arguments about popular culture's influences on gender identity, pointing to television shows like *Ally McBeal*, which, she claimed, "moves the feminist movement backward by portraying the stereotypical woman." Betsy cited her experiences in college classrooms and dorm rooms as further evidence for her claims:

> Time and time again, I have seen girls who will rather spend time fix-
> ing their hair in time for a party than completing a paper, intimidated
> to speak in class or take action on their campus. The boys on campus
> also seem to encourage this. They refute a girl's opinion without an
> open mind or they talk over her when she is trying to speak.

Not surprisingly, Betsy pointed to the gendered relations in our classroom and to the resistance to and dismissal of feminist criti-cism by some of the male students in the class. In addition to the conference-board postings about feminist critiques of fairy tales, Betsy believed she heard some students muttering sexist comments under their breath and was dismayed by some of the male students' uncritical dismissal of rap music's misogynist tendencies. But Betsy was able to transcend these circumstances, examining *Mango Street*'s feminist rhetoric in its larger contexts. She used the obstacles faced by Esperanza as a starting point from which to examine her own world and the barriers women still face, even those like her who seem to have limitless opportunity:

> The feminist movement is dwindling. Men continue to act in demean-
> ing ways towards women and see them as less than themselves. The
> movement needs to survive in order to review with men that women
> are equally as capable and deserve respect. These same ideas need
> to be also presented to women. Women have forgotten that there is
> something that they need to fight for.

The increasingly dominant multicultural perspective in compo-sition studies goes to the heart of our mission as rhetoricians and teachers of writing. Rhetorizing the contact zone through multi-cultural texts allows nonwhite voices to be heard in homogeneous composition classrooms.[15] However, I am wary of Jody Swilky's use of the term "ideological transformation" (21), not only because of the extent to which students can conform their writing to what instructors want to see (Miller; see also Knoblauch), but also because I think that in one semester (or even two) of English composition it is more likely we will see glimmers of emerging social consciousness rather than full-fledged ideological transformations.

In the contact zone of my first-year composition course, students explored connections as well as difference, what Steven Athanases refers to as "fostering empathy" (26) and "find[ing] common ground" (27), and they were subsequently more comfortable with the difficult material I asked them to confront. The contact zone, according to Miller, should neither "establish a community where a simple pluralism rules and hate speech is just one of its many voices" (395–96) nor become an "environment that is relentlessly threatening, where not feeling safe comes to mean the same thing as feeling terrified" (396). van Slyck also says we should avoid dividing the class into hostile camps when discussing differences but instead bring about a "reflective, dialogic approach to any given text and the cultural issues it raises" (153). When we rhetorize the multicultural text, the dialogue springs from it, and students can enter easily and nonthreateningly. Without a safer contact zone, we undermine the student-centered, collaborative pedagogy so important to the way we understand the composing process and to the improvement of student writing, for collaboration works best in a community of trust (see Brooke, Mirtz, and Evans; Bishop). In the contact zone of my classroom, as in Pratt's, "no one was excluded" (39), but most felt safe.[16] From the relaxed classroom atmosphere to the level of participation by most students in a variety of classroom activities, students indicated that, for the most part, they felt comfortable to engage with the text, the issues, Cisneros, one another, and me. Jerry's introduction to his final essay described his experience in the composition contact zone:

> Since I have been in college I have been doing more thinking on certain topics than I have ever done before. Instead of jumping to a conclusion of what is right or wrong all of a sudden I have learned to be more open to arguments, instead of being set in my own opinion. To my surprise I have found that I tend to agree with many things that I never thought I would.

If my classroom experience with *Mango Street* was successful, it was not because I produced any immediate converts but because I saw in students' texts the kind of rhetorical battles they saw in Cisneros's text. Their drafts became contact zones of their own. Cy Knoblauch asserts that his white, middle-class students do not "recognize a dialectical relationship between states of belief and acts of reading, where two sets of meaning interact to produce altered understanding" (18). His students could only reclothe their initial middle-class readings of Toni Cade Bambara's "The Lesson" in a liberal package. Significantly, though, he remarks that it might have been different, "given sufficient time and trust, given more courage on both sides" (18). I believe that rhetorizing *Mango Street* fulfilled much of Knoblauch's wish list in ways that a piecemeal gathering of texts from a multicultural reader simply does not allow. By immersing students in the discourses of *Mango Street*, the classroom became a contact zone where students participated in clashing rhetorics and cultural debate, appropriated academic discourse, and, finally, used language to generate meaning and value.

Notes

1. The recognition that all language intersects with ideology and has both political and ethical implications has led compositionists increasingly to incorporate issues of gender, race, ethnicity, and class into instruction, seeking to "promote ideological transformation" as students gain critical understanding of dominant and subordinate ideologies and structures (Swilky 21). Indeed, as Silva, Leki, and Carson write, "there is no disputing that in recent years mainstream composition studies has been at great pains to articulate and promote a multicultural perspective that honors diversity" (398). Multicultural literature—most often in the form of nonfiction and fiction in multicultural readers—has become a staple of these classes because, we seem to agree, it has a particular power to influence attitudes and promote multicultural understanding.

2. In some instances, students do not feel free and comfortable to voice their beliefs, fearful of what may happen when the claims of their cultures come into contact—and conflict—with the claims of others' cultures. Miller observes that the classroom as contact zone rarely occurs because students are skilled at what he calls "hyperconformity": avoiding "conflicts about or

contact between fundamental beliefs and prejudices" (396, 399). Furthermore, scholar-teachers who write about homogeneous classes frequently note the level of resistance and anger multicultural literature evokes in white students (see Swilky; Ruzich). Knoblauch points out the irony of teaching critical pedagogy to those who are not marginalized and implores us to think clearly about the objectives of such a pedagogy (15–16). Spigelman notes "that almost palpable silence in a classroom" that "signal[s] profound discomfort" (48) with issues of power.

3. For more on the debate over terminology, see Alberti; Gates; Franco.

4. The term is commonly used in this fashion, as is evident in the work of Alberti; Bizzell; Bjork; Goebel and Hall; Peterson; Primeau; Trimmer; and many others.

5. Other terms that are used somewhat interchangeably are *multiethnic literature, ethnic literature, nontraditional literature,* and *noncanonical literature.*

6. Booth's "The Ethics of Teaching Literature" is a good example. Though Booth's article focuses on the reading of literature, giving little if any attention to students' writing, Booth premises his discussion on Leonard's article in *College Composition and Communication.* Leonard's poignant question, "if I'm changing students, how do I change them in the ways that I feel are most useful to them?" is specifically directed to students in writing classrooms (222).

7. Literary multiculturalists have also paid a great deal of critical attention to multicultural pedagogy, but in ways different from those I am suggesting here. Elsewhere I have identified the three most pressing conflicts in multicultural studies today: the debate over interpreting and evaluating multicultural texts according to Western paradigms and criteria; racial conflicts; and whether to teach multicultural literature according to ethnic-specific or general multicultural paradigms ("Toward a Multicultural Pedagogy").

8. I used *CourseTalk*, Penn State University's Web-based, asynchronous electronic conferencing software. This program enables students to post and respond to other students' comments online. Rather than write their homework assignments for my eyes only, students can write for one another as well. Because *CourseTalk* does not occur in real time and students can comment at their convenience outside class, it extends our class discussions beyond the class period and closely simulates a back-and-forth conversation.

9. The assignment was worded as follows: Arguably, the young Esperanza gets her ideas about the American dream from American culture. How is the American dream portrayed in popular culture today? Does it match her ideas of the American dream as portrayed in *Mango Street*? Be specific.

10. I am using pseudonyms for my students. Excerpts from student essays are unedited, except for obvious typos.

11. Many studies specifically use student writing as multicultural texts (see, e.g., Lu; Bartholomae). However, these approaches presume a multicultural student population.

12. In my two composition sections in the semester discussed here, totaling forty-five students, I have one Hispanic student, no African American students, and no Asian American students.

13. The richness and complexities of bildungsroman traditions defy simple summary, but I believe it is necessary to give students such a framework while informing them of its limitations.

14. I recognize that not all compositionists subscribe to the academic discourse paradigm; however, I do believe it dominates the current thinking in the field, and it is the one to which I subscribe.

15. Clearly, colleges like mine need to make other voices and perspectives real, not just textual, and my college has begun to think about ways to tap into the minority population ten minutes away. In the meantime, however, we cannot bury minority voices simply because they are absent from the classroom.

16. Pratt distinguishes the multicultural classroom contact zone from "safe houses" such as ethnic or women's studies, "places for healing and mutual recognition, safe houses in which to construct shared understandings, knowledges, claims on the world that they can bring into the contact zone" (40). However, "safe houses," it seems, are reserved for individuals and cultures "where there are legacies of subordination" (40). I suggest, instead, that all students, regardless of their legacies of subordination or domination, deserve to feel safe in our classrooms, especially if we want them to grow morally and intellectually.

Works Cited

Alberti, John. "Teaching the Rhetoric of Race: A Rhetorical Approach to Multicultural Pedagogy." Brannon and Greene 203–15.

Anson, Chris. "Response Styles and Ways of Knowing." *Writing and Response: Theory, Practice, and Research.* Ed. Anson. Urbana: NCTE, 1989. 332–66.

Athanases, Steven Z. "Fostering Empathy and Finding Common Ground in Multiethnic Classes." *English Journal* 84.3 (1995): 26–34.

Bakhtin, Mikhail. *The Dialogic Imagination.* Trans. Caryl Emerson and Michael Holquist. Ed. Holquist. Austin: U of Texas P, 1981.

Bartholomae, David. "Writing with Teachers: A Conversation with Peter Elbow." *College Composition and Communication* 46 (1995): 62–71.

Berthoff, Ann. "Is Teaching Still Possible?" *College English* 46 (1984): 743–55.

Bishop, Wendy. "Helping Peer Writing Groups Succeed." *Teaching English in the Two-Year College* 15 (1988): 120–25.

Bizzell, Patricia. "'Contact Zones' and English Studies." *College English* 56 (1994): 163–69.

———. "Negotiating Difference: Teaching Multicultural Literature." *Rethinking American Literature*. Brannon and Greene 163–74.

Bjork, Patrick Bryce. "Teaching toward a Multicultural Perspective in the Land That Time Forgot." Goebel and Hall 81–95.

Blair, Kristine. "Literacy, Dialogue, and Difference in the 'Electronic Contact Zone.'" *Computers and Composition* 15 (1998): 317–29.

Blum, Jack. "Poststructural Theories and the Postmodern Attitude." Winterowd with Blum 92–111.

Booth, Wayne C. "The Ethics of Teaching Literature." *College English* 61 (1998): 41–55.

———. *The Rhetoric of Fiction*. 2nd ed. Chicago: U of Chicago P, 1983.

Brannon, Lil, and Brenda Greene, eds. *Rethinking American Literature*. Urbana: NCTE, 1997.

Brooke, Robert, Ruth Mirtz, and Rick Evans. "Our Students' Experiences with Groups." *Small Groups in Writing Workshops*. Ed. Brooke, Mirtz, and Evans. Urbana: NCTE, 1994. 31–51.

Cisneros, Sandra. *The House on Mango Street*. 1984. New York: Vintage, 1991.

Elbow, Peter. "Reflections on Academic Discourse: How It Relates to Freshmen and Colleagues." *College English* 53 (1991): 135–55.

Erkkila, Betsy. "Ethnicity, Literary Theory, and the Grounds of Resistance." *American Quarterly* 47 (1995): 563–94.

Faulkner, William. "Barn Burning." *The Heath Anthology of American Literature*. Ed. Paul Lauter. 2nd ed. Lexington: Heath, 1997. 1553–65.

Franco, Dean. "Ethnic Writing / Writing Ethnicity: The Critical Conceptualization of Chicano Identity." *Post-Identity* 2.1 (1999): 104–22.

Ganz, Robin. "Sandra Cisneros: Border Crossings and Beyond." *MELUS* 19 (1994): 19–29.

Gates, Henry Louis, Jr. " 'Ethnic and Minority' Studies." *Introduction to Scholarship in Modern Languages and Literatures*. 2nd ed. Ed. Joseph Gibaldi. New York: MLA, 1992. 288–302.

Goebel, Bruce A., and James C. Hall, eds. Introduction. *Teaching a "New Canon"? Students, Teachers, and Texts in the College Literature Classroom*. Urbana: NCTE, 1995. xi–xv.

Grobman, Laurie. "Beyond Internationalization: Multicultural Education in the Professional Writing Contact Zone." *Journal of Business and Technical Communication* 13.4 (1999): 427–48.

———. "Toward a Multicultural Pedagogy: Literary and Non-literary Traditions." *MELUS: The Journal of the Society for the Study of the Multi-Ethnic*

Literatures of the United States 26.1 (2001): 221–40.

Harris, Joseph, and Jay Rosen. "Teaching Writing as Cultural Criticism." Hurlbert and Blitz 58–67.

Hurlbert, Mark, and Michael Blitz, eds. *Composition and Resistance.* Portsmouth: Boynton/Cook, 1991.

Kelley, Margot. "A Minor Revolution: Chicano/a Composite Novels and the Limits of Genre." *Ethnicity and the American Short Story.* Ed. Julie Brown. New York: Garland, 1997. 63–84.

Knoblauch, Cy. "Critical Teaching and Dominant Culture." Hurlbert and Blitz 12–21.

Kolbenschlag, Madonna. "A Feminist's View of 'Cinderella.'" *Writing and Reading across the Curriculum.* 6th ed. Ed. Laurence Behrens and Leonard J. Rosen. New York: Longman, 1997. 533–39.

Kraemer, Don. "Abstracting the Bodies of/in Academic Discourse." *Rhetoric Review* 10 (1991): 52–69.

Leonard, Elizabeth Anne. "Assignment #9—A Text Which Engages the Socially Constructed Identity of Its Writer." *College Composition and Communication* 48 (1997): 215–30.

Lu, Min-Zhan. "Professing Multiculturalism: The Politics of Style in the Contact Zone." *College Composition and Communication* 45 (1994): 442–58.

Miller, Richard E. "Fault Lines in the Contact Zone." *College English* 56 (1994): 389–408.

Otte, George. "Why Read What? The Politics of Composition Anthologies." *JAC: Journal of Advanced Composition* 12 (1992): 137–49.

Peterson, Nancy J. "Redefining America: Literature, Multiculturalism, Pedagogy." *Teaching What You're Not: Identity Politics in Higher Education.* Ed. Katherine J. Mayberry. New York: New York UP, 1996. 23–46.

Pratt, Mary Louise. "Arts of the Contact Zone." *Profession 91.* New York: MLA, 1991. 33–40.

Primeau, Ronald. "Writing Portfolios in the Multicultural Literature Class." Goebel and Hall 180–95.

Rebolledo, Tey Diana. "The Politics of Poetics, or, What Am I, a Critic, Doing in This Text Anyhow?" *Chicana Creativity and Criticism.* Ed. Rebolledo and Eliana S. Rivero. Tucson: U of Arizona P, 1988. 129–38.

Rivera, Tomás. *. . . y no se lo tragó la tierra / . . . And the Earth Did Not Devour Him.* 1971. Trans. Evangelina Vigil-Piñón. Houston: Arte Público, 1992.

Ruzich, Constance M. "White Students' Resistance to Multicultural Literature: Breaking the Sullen Silence." *Teaching English in the Two-Year College* 26 (1999): 299–304.

Sadarangani, Umeeta. "Teaching Multicultural Issues in the Composition Classroom: A Review of Recent Practice." *Journal of Teaching Writing* 13

(1994): 33–54.

Selfe, Cynthia L., and Richard J. Selfe, Jr. "The Politics of the Interface: Power and Its Exercise in Electronic Contact Zones." *College Composition and Communication* 45 (1994): 480–504.

Silva, Tony, Ilona Leki, and Joan Carson. "Broadening the Perspective of Mainstream Composition Studies: Some Thoughts from the Disciplinary Margins." *Written Communication* 14 (1997): 398–428.

Spigelman, Candace. "Taboo Topics and the Rhetoric of Silence: Discussing *Lives on the Boundary* in Basic Writing." *Journal of Basic Writing* 17.1 (1998): 42–55.

Stewart, Edward, and Milton Bennett. *American Cultural Patterns.* Rev. ed. Yarmouth: Intercultural, 1991.

Stockton, Sharon. "'Blacks vs. Browns': Questioning the White Ground." *College English* 57 (1995): 166–81.

Swilky, Jody. "Resisting Difference: Student Response to Multicultural Texts." *Writing Instructor* 13.1 (1993): 21–33.

Takaki, Ronald. *A Different Mirror: A History of Multicultural America.* Boston: Little, 1993.

Trimmer, Joseph F. "Teaching Others: A Cautionary Tale." Brannon and Greene 249–56.

van Slyck, Phyllis. "Repositioning Ourselves in the Contact Zone." *College English* 59 (1997): 149–70.

Westland, Ella. "Cinderella in the Classroom: Children's Responses to Gender Roles in Fairy-Tales." *Gender and Education* 5 (1993): 237–49.

Winterowd, W. Ross, with Jack Blum, eds. *Composition in the Rhetorical Tradition.* Urbana: NCTE, 1994.

Yarbro-Bejarano, Yvonne. "Chicana Literature from a Chicana Feminist Perspective." *Chicana Creativity and Criticism: Charting New Frontiers in American Literature.* Ed. Maria Herrera-Sobek and Helena Marma Viramontes. Houston: Arte Público, 1988. 139–45.

What Literature Is "Ours"?

David Bleich

This essay is not an argument. It is a series of questions combined with several reports of classroom experience. For better or worse, this essay reflects the experiences of one person and his experiences of others, their readings, their bearings, their opinions. I hope readers wish to continue discussing the issues this essay is putting on the table.

Is Any Literature Not "Ours"?

The opening of the traditional reading lists to the voices of the traditionally unheard reminded me of how I overlooked what now matters a lot: for example, the bigotry of the figure whose work was the subject of my bachelor's thesis, T. S. Eliot. I became aware that I was a member of several constituencies in society and that it was part of my professional responsibility to take and give accounts of those memberships. I began to wonder how I, the son of immigrants from eastern Europe, could "profess" to others about Shakespeare, Henry James, and Eliot. Sure, it is the American dream, but after a while it seemed to be the time to wake up.

One result of waking up is the title question of this essay: How do I know when I can adopt the literature I am assigned in school and feel that it is my own? How does anyone know? And because people like Judith Fetterley needed to "resist" Hemingway and Faulkner, "culture wars" broke out in academia about "whose" literature will appear in the reading lists of courses that introduce people to literature in college. To understand these disputes a little better, I came up with a course titled, What Literature Is Ours? that studied the extent to which class members affiliated themselves with specific works of literature. The literary response processes that have been part of my pedagogy for thirty-five years have provided a disciplined basis to inquire into the collective responses, memberships, and values that have emerged in the political climate of the academy. We wanted to think about the processes of how individuals internalize literature and how groups of individuals, including the national society, come to decide how single works and genres are ours.

For about five years, my course—a first-year undergraduate seminar—discussed and reflected on the extent to which readers from one culture or one constituency can overtake literature seemingly meant for other groups. Is Kafka for male critics, European philosophers? Is Shakespeare for kings and aesthetes, or, perhaps, for bigots? Is Morrison for African American women? Is Melville for white male sailors? Sometimes women, African Americans, or Jews showed a decisive sympathy with characters from their group. However, in general, each reader and each group of readers had partial and mixed identifications and possessions, none of which were predictable from affiliations provided readers by current identity politics. The interest of this course was, in fact, in the anticipation of the surprises of identification that turned up as new people read the materials, as I, the "same" teacher, reread them, but in a new context, in new times.

Of course, many readers and critics have known for a long time that any reader can respond fruitfully to any work. Despite changes in the political climate, many teachers have understood from experience that there are no limits to literary response easily related to one's membership in society. If permitted, the careful reading and study of literature, through almost any pedagogy, will teach readers that their capacities for response are greater than previously assumed and that they are finally available to unlimited new experiences marked by the otherness that any literature has become for any reader. Yet as the course progressed, this issue of the otherness of literature revealed itself in an unexpected way: the thought arrived that written literature does not matter very much in American society or even perhaps in all Western society. The paths through which literature once mattered no longer exist: for most of the history of the West, to read or perform written texts transmitted vital information, values, and perspectives of the kind now promulgated by the many media we use. In my seminars (for the privileged and already well educated), few students felt affiliated with literary works as a result of their study or analyses of these works; few students expected works from their culture to be anything but "other" to begin with. The category "our literature" was not to be found.

My reading of and thinking about the students' work suggested that literature no longer matters in today's privileged Western society and that what literature is ours seems to matter even less. I am not alone in having these thoughts. In 2000, St. Martin's Press advertised a textbook by John Schilb and John Clifford entitled *Making Literature Matter*. Shortly before that, in 1992, Dana Gioia came out with *Can Poetry Matter?* The concern is not a new one: Plato thought literature should be censored because in his society it mattered more than it does in ours. Perhaps these recent titles are just eye-catchers, but would they catch any eyes if people today are not already thinking about the question?

This essay discusses the connections between literature not mattering and the processes of individual and collective assimilation of literature. It suggests that literature doesn't matter because writing has been separated from speaking. It further suggests that language in general is thought of only as a transparent instrument of conveyance. If language were presumed to be material, literature would not be just an amusement and most literature would be ours.

The concept of the materiality of language is the premise of this essay. The questions of mattering come from materiality. Because language is matter, it does matter (see my "The Materiality of Rhetoric" and "The Materiality of Language"). I further discuss this idea briefly as the announcement of the premises for a more realistic writing pedagogy than we now practice (*Know and Tell* xv–xviii). In the great majority of language uses in the West, the materiality of language is unrecognized. Students, participating in this nonrecognition, do not "see" the languages of literature but, instead, see through it to its "substance." As the discussion and examples that follow suggest, literature does not matter because its substance is considered interchangeable with similar substances available from a variety of media.

Does Literature Matter?

What does it mean for literature to matter to begin with? Plato thought it mattered and he advocated censorship to control its effects. The Roman Catholic Church thought it mattered and they created an Index of censored works. Stalin and Hitler thought it mattered and they burned books. Americans thought film mattered so that a code of the filmable had to be established. If literature can matter only under conditions of censorship, what does this say about how our societies work? To say that literature matters must mean, at least, that if people read and go to literary performances, the effects of reading and public involvement must be plain for all to see. If literature is censored, it must mean that the censors think that letting people read will harm, at least, the censors. This is an effect of literature.

In America today, one can barely earn a living as a poet, playwright, or novelist. A writer can only either starve or become a millionaire. A serious, nonpopular writer today is in a separate social class whose audience, with few exceptions, is marginal, usually academic. Most "creative writers" in universities have very small audiences; few are national figures. Towns, communities, regions do not have poets and writers who live there, write for local audiences, and play a role in the local culture. Young people can't aspire to such a role. If there were such people seeking to contribute to the cultural life of the community, no one would pay them. If such figures become faculty members, they then teach others writing—as a hobby.

Film and television matter more. Those who learn to write for the media often do become professional writers and language users. But such work is hard to get on a national level and is not respected on a local level. Local television stations don't have their own arts and entertainment shows; they just have news, weather, and sometimes sports. The film industry also needs writers, but it is still so competitive that one's only reasonable aspiration can be to make it big. Merely to be employed is to remain a hack. In these senses, literature in the form of written novels, lyrics, and plays matters only as part of "a liberal humanities education" but not as a force in our society, much less in societies struggling for food and medical sustenance.

Literature did not suddenly stop mattering, and to some people, such as children, it continues to matter. Children's literature is usually part of a social relationship between parents and children and among children. It is often very popular and au courant among large numbers of children. The current Harry Potter series is today's instance of Anne of Green Gables, the Oz books, Nancy Drew, the Bobbsey twins, and so on. In illiterate societies of the past, such as classical Greece and Elizabethan England, literature was performed and thus "lived" in senses similar to how children's literature lives today: it was part of many people's social relations with one another. Children's literature in its common uses remains both oral and written and has still not been touched by academic tropes and schemata, except that it is a required course for most students preparing to teach primary grades. It is as if adult literature has become a subject separate from language. In the performances of the Greek epics, the Greek dramas, the medieval mystery plays, Elizabethan drama, the literature mattered because people heard it in collective scenes. It was easily folded into the language of everyday life: because it was heard by many, it could be repeated by anyone, and in the process of memory and repetition, it could teach through language while never forgetting the linguistic transmission of the experiences.

Shakespeare's work mattered because the dramatist filled theaters with people who actually communicated vocally with the performances. The material in the plays was understood to describe the politics of the time. Plays about kings and other tragic figures communicated something about how England was being ruled. The theatergoers did not need to be literate, but to go to a play also meant to learn about how business was being conducted by government figures and about how people in high places spoke. Because the audience was illiterate and because they heard rather than read the plays, they could pick up the language much more easily than if they had only read the plays, as in the case of contemporary students. People who do not read continue the processes of language acquisition in the infantile modes, namely, through hearing others speak and selectively internalizing the language, sometimes and in various degrees repeating it in new contexts. In this way, audiences take possession of the literature through the language, a process sharply curtailed by reading. To acquire literary language through reading, it must be studied and discussed, an activity done only to a small degree in postsecondary education.

What we now call literature requires its audience to be members of a comfortable class of educated people, but in this social class, the literature itself is amusement; at best, it is aesthetic pleasure. The enacted, living language that illiterate Elizabethan people learned in the theater we learn through genres that are more obviously ours: TV news, docudrama, and fictionalized history. For the audiences in preliterate societies, literature was thus inherently pedagogical. It functioned, perhaps, the way Oliver Stone films do now: as uncertain hints of what "really" happens in places to which most people can have no access, thus teaching people how things might really be arranged. Less consciously, but just as influentially, preliterate audiences "acquired" the literary language they heard as they identified (or failed to identify) with characters and stories. The preeminence of writing as the path to the cultivation of language in postsecondary education has actually limited the scope of our ability to let our language grow and become a true ingredient of social health. Literature does not matter to literate adults because its existence in texts has been separated by those of us in the academy from its life in the spoken language. In 1999, a student with 1300 SAT scores wrote the following:

> It always takes me quite a long time to read any Shakespeare, I struggle through the text . . . always having to . . . refer to the footnotes for almost every line. . . . Yet, when I see the plays performed, whether it be on film or on stage, I can follow it with such ease that it seems . . . ridiculous that I couldn't get so much out of the text. For some reason, it just comes to me when I see it acted out. All of the "weird" language seems to go away and I can follow the plot along so easily.

Similarly today, the lyric teaches those who hear lyrics—in songs on radio and television. Few people learn the lyrics written by reading what academics call lyric poets.

In class, the question, What literature is ours? means, variously, do we feel a kinship with the works, with their situations, with their characters or their culture? Students report to all of us some of the history of the books they have read and films they have seen, perhaps, that they remember from any time before the present moment. Many have good answers and discuss the questions thoughtfully. Some write about peer-group literature, like Nancy Drew and *Lord of the Flies*; others about social films like *Mississippi Burning* or cultural films like *The Red Violin*. Every student writes (almost entirely) about literature read and films viewed in school. The students I meet already know that literature from a variety of other cultures is accessible to them in one way or another, but they do not know that making the literature their own also means recognizing the other already in themselves. It is still "them" and "us". This sense of the otherness of all literature is closely connected with the assumed transparency of the language. Because the students rarely internalize the language of the literature, they perceive the works as packaged in an other zone of existence altogether. Literary response means to students response to the references of the works and not to the formal articulations that produce the sense of reference. The degree of students' relating to the references varies with the materials, with the stories and characters, but not with the language; most of the time language is not considered part of a work's materials. To a small extent, literature matters to students temporarily as stories or references—more commonly, if films are viewed, as images—but it does not matter as language, as a moment during which their own language is growing or becoming more adept and agile.

My students overlook the language they read and speak, and they respond to issues they see that do not require the awareness of language. Almost always, literature is a narrative or a sequence of images and issues to be discussed. How these issues are verbally formulated by the works of literature students read is irrelevant to most of them. They rarely speak or know other languages, and while they try hard, they are almost completely unfamiliar with what happens in any culture except American popular culture. They know little about French, German, African American, Asian, Jewish, or farm culture; and they are definitely not familiar with Mexican or Chinese cultures, even though they respond well to the films from these cultures. The literature can be made their own on an affective or purely individualist basis, but there is no cultural kinship with it, no immersion in it, no sense of love of the literature and the whole world of it. The students do not think that literature says things in a way that they too can say things and have no sense that new voices in texts can speak at once for them and for the other group represented by the voices' literary identities. Rather, they are caught up in the hermeneutic conundrums posed by the academic standards that come from long ago through universities that trained their teachers in conventional academic tropes. The students are excellent, thoughtful, witty, and they have a desire to understand more. But this understanding is not to come through language, and it is not to come through a process of widening collective cultural identities. Their understanding comes through the moral weight of the literature as applied to their individual lives, which they experience as now slightly enhanced by the growing political awareness that people in the rest of the world are really different from Americans in their ways and values. In the following discussion, I try to show the modes of response, the intelligence of the students, their embeddedness in traditional academic mores, and the great difficulty they have in recognizing the determining roles of language in the literature and in their readings.

Getting the Language: Toni Morrison's Sula

In our course, three of the American novels were *Sula*, by Toni Morrison; *Benito Cereno*, by Herman Melville; and *A Thousand Acres*, by Jane Smiley; the film of Smiley's novel was on reserve. Most of the students in this class, now and in the past, have been women. I cite this fact because, as a rule, female students are both more interested in and more adept at understanding the questions of social affiliation that are the subjects of my course. Yet these students are guided by the values in our society: female students, while less dogmatic than male students are about individualist values, know no other basis for literary response, though in some instances identification with women as a class poses itself as a new basis for literary response. Here are samples of response to Toni Morrison's *Sula*:

> Ms. A: I didn't have to force myself to read this novel, but found myself wondering what would happen next. . . . Sula was . . . a truly independent woman whose belief in herself got her through hardships she faced. . . . The friendship between Nel and Sula is so strong that each girl knew what the other was thinking. . . . but, things change. Nel expects Sula to understand that Jude is her husband and that he is the one man that Sula shouldn't go after. Yet, Sula expects that Nel should be happy to share Jude because they have always shared everything. . . . Sula was able to get through this change, while without Sula, Nel loses herself.

> Ms. D: [*Sula*] was one of the few books that kept my attention because I actually read it word for word. I found *Sula* to be a very fascinating look at friendships and female relationship during a

period of racial disharmony. . . . I appreciated Morrison's openness on the issue of female sexuality. The other aspects I related to was the friendship of Sula and Nel. . . . I found myself reading the book and forgetting that it even dealt with race relations. Most of the time it felt like I was reading a book about women of any racial background. . . . *Sula* is definitely part of my literature because anyone can feel comfortable reading it.

Ms. K: The ending of this novel stays with me. . . . The last scene is so touching. I know what it's like to wish for childhood days, when life was much simpler, when promise and hope stretch out in front of you as far as the eye could see. Like Nel, I've thought of an old friendship gone wrong and just cried at the sheer unfairness of it all. . . . [Sula and Nel] were taught . . . that sex is no more than a game, that children are loved but not liked, that life is to be lived but not enjoyed. It's really no wonder, then that both ended up the ways they did. . . . Yes, when slicing off the end of her finger she hurt herself worse than those boys ever would, but she was the one controlling it. She took their power away and made it her own. . . . More than anything I really feel sorry for Sula and Nel. Neither was able to break the cycle of destructiveness although each tried to in different ways.

These three students were taken with this novel. They were absorbed in it, and in class they spoke about it with detailed knowledge of the text. Consider their perceptions and interpretations of it. Ms. A focused on how to treat rivalry for a husband, Ms. D on female sexuality, and Ms. K on how Sula takes the boys' power away. Each of these issues is important today: the ethics and politics of domestic loyalty and affiliation, the recognition of how female sexuality is different from male sexuality, and the accession to social power by women. This looks good, doesn't it? It looks as if the students, even in their first responses to the novel, have put material on the table that will raise the questions of social affiliation asked by the course's title question. I, the teacher, took up these issues and we discussed them; the students participated with interest and excitement. In the end, I could tell myself that I had reached these students. I could tell because they came to class religiously and worked as hard as they could. Why am I complaining?

I suppose because I read all of what the students wrote. Because I see the issues I want to discuss embedded in a set of values that, if I think about it a bit longer, overwhelms the topics of the course, which will have practically no effect on these students, except for the fact that it was a pleasant experience (this counts as literature not mattering). Consider other things in Ms. A's response—Sula was a "truly independent woman whose belief in herself got her through hardships she faced." Holy cow! This sounds more like Horatio Alger than Toni Morrison. Nel loves Sula regardless of what Sula does. Why does the friendship supersede the "borrowing" of Nel's husband? Does Nel really "lose herself"? In fact, are we justified in separating Nel and Sula from the fate of Bottom? from the fate of Ohio? from the fate of America? Is there any inclination on the part of Ms. A to overtake the passions of Nel and Sula, much less their words, which were not cited by any of these three readers?

Ms. D says that this work takes place "during a period of racial disharmony." Again: Holy cow! Has America ever emerged from "racial disharmony"? This student implies that bigotry is a thing of the past or that we are no longer affected by the two hundred years of slavery or by the national refusal to cope with the aftereffects. Can I the teacher depart from the issues of the course and stop on formulations like this? How many class sessions will it take to disabuse this student, and most other students at my university, of this view? The context in which Ms. D's "good" reading takes place is imaginary! My approach was to use the occasion where new ideas of female sexuality are brought up. But does even the term "female sexuality" refer to what black women experience in the same way that it refers to what white women experience? As there were no black members of this class, what does it mean to speak about it at all? And if there were one or two black women in this course, what would they say, seeing that there is a white male teacher giving out the grades?

Ms. K notes the dramatic scene in which Sula, at age twelve and menaced by "four white boys in their early teens" (53), cuts off the end of her finger and says to the boys in a "quiet" voice, "If I can do that to myself, what you suppose I'll do to you?" (55). She interprets this scene responsibly from a literal and political standpoint as Sula's taking the boys' power and "making it her own." Ms. K also makes reference to the "cycle of destructiveness," which refers, at the least, to what she just noted: self-injury to preempt injury at the hands of the white boys. However, Ms. K does not cite the text and, in particular, does not cite the fear, anger, and desperation on the part of both Nel and Sula. Rather, Ms. K notes the "wish for childhood days, when life was much simpler." Once again: Holy cow! Much simpler? Ms. K forgets that in those "much simpler" days Sula killed Chicken Little by throwing him into the river, that Eva killed Plum by pouring kerosene on him and setting him on fire, that Sula stood by while her mother burned to death. In relating herself to the scene she cites, Ms. K writes that "I know what it's like to wish for childhood days" and notes the "unfairness" of a "friendship gone wrong." Neither Sula nor Nel had "childhood days" they might wish to recover, and their friendship did not "go wrong"; but Ms. K, perhaps through none of her own fault the American dreamer, does wish for those days.

Because this is a classroom, it is not surprising to find that one student cited the text in the service of her response, seeming to overtake the language and to document the material brought up by the other students. Ms. J observes that the "immense amount of pain suffered by these characters struck me most." What was the bond between Sula and Nel? Ms. J says, "From the beginning Sula and Nel discovered 'they were neither white nor male, and that all freedom and triumph was forbidden to them'" (52). Was Sula a "truly independent woman"? Ms. J says, "Sula lived against the grain in any way possible but it was in this rebellion that she found her strength. Sula found no qualms whatsoever in trying out men and 'discarding them without any excuse the men could swallow'" (115). Is this the betrayal of Nel that Ms. A referred to? I don't think so. Ms. J was affected by the language, and, for reasons she did not reveal, she was able to discern the departures, social and linguistic,

taken by this novel from what has been received by students like
her. Finally, just what sort of "female sexuality" did Ms. J find? Is
the following description, cited by Ms. J, a sign of Morrison's "openness"? Sula almost enjoyed "the utmost irony and outrage in lying
under someone, in a position of surrender, feeling her own abiding
strength and limitless power" (123). Of course, it is not erroneous
to see such a sentence as describing female sexuality. Yet the
"utmost irony and outrage" belongs to a figure in this, Morrison's
society, in the world Morrison has been evoking repeatedly in her
novels, where the moments of what is ordinary intimate pleasure
to some people are extraordinary and stolen moments of enfran-
chisement to Sula and to others like her. Ms. J observes, "It is this
ability to survive that is so inspirational about the encounters of
this novel because these are hardships I have not personally experienced but [should I meet them] I would hope to discover the
courage that these characters demonstrated."

Like the other respondents I cite, Ms. J is white. In general she is a
less conventional student and probably a bit more "inner-directed,"
to use David Riesman's term of the 1950s. In addition, she is a poetry-
writing minor, who has won the recognition of the faculty. From the
standpoint of "outcomes assessment" I have no idea which student
got how much from this novel. But Ms. J's response suggests that
the acquisition of literary language accompanies the acquisition of
the otherness. To teach the culture alone is bordering on proselytiz-
ing, and, besides, there are so many of one culture teaching works of
other cultures that it is not possible to establish any procedures. Yet
Ms. J's response suggests that a fixed procedure is not needed but
for the following consideration: the literary language must be
understood as the key to cultural and interpersonal otherness.
Imagine: which of us could actually be in position to say, "If I can do
that to myself, what you suppose I'll do to you?" Understanding that
we are not in that position comes from using that phrase among ourselves. To make the language our own, we arrive at where we actually are, relative to Sula, to Bottom, to Ohio, to, perhaps, "National
Suicide Day" when the tunnel comes crashing down on the black

workers. Once we recognize our distance from Bottom, using Sula's language establishes our kinship with her, however much we affirm our difference.

Getting the Genre: *Herman Melville's* Benito Cereno

As a critic, Toni Morrison has tried to outline new conditions for letting literary language show us more porous boundaries between selves and cultures. As I discuss elsewhere, she proposes the "writerly perspective" as a way to understand the social reach of any literary work (*Know* 56–59). This perspective views literary language as necessarily referring to the total society that produced the work. Her example of idealized whiteness in *Moby-Dick*—the chapter entitled "Whiteness of the Whale"—may be understood in reference to whiteness in American society. In Melville's novel, whiteness refers to the color of the hunted whale, and it is part of why Ahab is obsessed with this whale. Because from the standpoint of the writer this term must have carried its social reference, albeit "unconscious" to the novel (that is, not explicitly marked as including reference to white people), it carries the same social reference for readers taking a writerly perspective: the perspective of the one actively using language, of the one remembering the words and their usages in society and actively recording them in different permanent forms. Assuming the writerly perspective in reading makes the actual words matter, which in turn makes the literature matter as language in addition to story and character. Given Morrison's idea, it seems plausible to attribute the writerly perspective to Ms. J's reading above: one whose business it is to pick the right words to render society for and to others. This is one basis on which poets and creative writers could work and function in communities: to provide renditions, on a regular basis, of community events and history—without the exaggerated fanfare and praise that now accompanies national recognition. If all readers took a writerly perspective, if literature were taught by teaching readers to use a writerly perspective, the language of literature would come to seem material and not transparent. New types of social relations would emerge from such styles of reading.

Here is an example of a response to *Benito Cereno* that begins to think through a writerly perspective:

> Ms. B: I can't entirely appreciate [the blacks'] hardships. However, [Delano's] statements weren't considered "racist" at the time. My mindset continued through the book. . . . I was looking at it through the eyes of the narrator, presumably a white seaman . . . because that's who I seemed to relate to the most, or that's whose mind the reader was meant to follow. . . . I followed along the lines of "Why can't Delano see the uprising here?" instead of "Can't he see that slavery is bad?"

To start, the writerly perspective picks out the issue of Delano's perception as the point of this narrative, rather than whether racism or even slavery is bad. So far, however, Ms. B's identifying with the narrator or writer leads to a reflection that, in general, does not happen enough in literature classes to make literature matter:

> Ms. B: This whole concept [of Delano's perception] made my mind twirl a bit more. It wasn't so much about relating to the time period as it was to the way things were written. Why is it that we seem to think such things shouldn't be written, or read, or said: I can say nigger in some contexts (when referring to works such as [Ann Petry's] "Like a Winding Sheet" or other works). I can write the word nigger. Neither of these, I'll admit, I can do entirely comfortably (it is still an awful word in my mind). But I think (most importantly for this case) I can read the word nigger without feeling disgust or contempt towards the author or asking why he or she couldn't have used another word. In fact, I think it is imperative that such words as these (which might include other stereotypical comments . . .) are used in literature. Literature should be unrestricted.

One salient feature of this response is that assuming a writerly perspective leads Ms. B directly to the feeling of social censorship. Consider: she writes that it is "imperative"—not merely desirable or interesting—that literature record the use of *nigger*. She is reacting in part to events in our class, in which most students claimed that they would not want to say the word *nigger*. She honors this spontaneous self-censorship and records her partial participation in it. Yet that some feel disgust or contempt for the word should lead not to its censorship but to the search for all its uses. Regardless of what we feel about it, this term matters, and we readers are in a position to learn about why without participating in its harmful functions.

Ms. B identifies with the narrator she presumes to be white ("non-negro"). The sense in which the literature is hers is marked by this identification and by the issues to which it leads. Ms. B relates Delano's failures of perception in Melville's novel to the different uses of the term *nigger* by the two black figures in Petry's story. There, the husband, Johnson, having been demeaned by white women who called him "nigger" at work, beats his loving wife uncontrollably when she calls him "nigger" in a sympathetic way. Ms. B's focus on the necessary recording of the word facilitates comprehension of why both stories and their special language matter in society; in fact, it is only the reflection on the necessity of the verbal record that leads Ms. B to the issue immanent in both stories: the American subjugation of black people during and after slavery. Literature had been censored (in part by students in this class) to suppress the violence of the stories of slavery. To say the words in the story is to remove the censorship and tell the story.

A failure to overtake the writerly perspective in this novel works at the level of genre as well as language. One student writes the following:

> Ms. L: I enjoyed the generous and charitable attitude of Captain Delano, but then I start questioning. What is the point in all the hemming and hawing and suspicion and drawn out and convoluted conversations if the whole mess could be cleared up in a deposition at the end of the book (the true story not confirming any of Captain Delano's suspicions)?

Ms. L had not situated author and work historically as a few others had. The result was that the story of Delano's error became only that: an error of perception rather than a story of how the acceptance of the normality of slavery prevents accurate perception permanently. Delano, at the end, still could not understand why Benito Cereno was destroyed by "the negro" even though the slave takeover was defeated. However, Ms. L's error was in assuming the veracity of the deposition: if all the details are there, why are we wasting time reading why Delano does not see the truth? In other words, Ms. L is deceived, in part, by the status of a legal deposition and its air of authenticity: a sworn statement. Another respondent was not thus deceived on first reading:

> Ms. J: Although Captain Delano had certainly been entertaining, it is the more courageous and "generous" portrayal of his character at the end that leaves me with a more serious picture of him, and indeed the "white" race. He had been transformed into the "hero" in the investigation report [the deposition]; meanwhile I had just read [in the main narrative] something of the complete contrary. The "negro Babo" is depicted as this evil man, leading the large crowd of Negroes, and described [in the depositions] as "restless and mutinous." They were slaves, who fought to regain the human right of freedom! The report, of course, did not take much notice of that very important fact, and that disturbed me greatly.

The deposition had the effect of distracting readers from consideration of the underlying social (in)justice of the scene of the novel—the normality of slavery. Readers like Ms. L concentrated on "what really happened" rather than on how Delano understood what happened. The role of the deposition in this novel is similar to the role of the legal considerations of Captain Vere in Melville's *Billy Budd*. They both obfuscate the actual issues of justice, which in each case is established by the total social context of American society and not just of the novel.

Ms. L, a gifted student, was embarrassed by her misplacement of emphasis. But, in fact, the error happened not because of any failure of intelligence on her part but, on the contrary, because she has been throughout her time in school such a good student, completely trained to separate the work of literature from everything else and to analyze it on its internal terms alone. On hearing other people's response, Ms. L quickly grasped what happened and offered the following reflection in an extended essay soon after having responded to Melville.

> Ms. L: I can conclude that I bring defensiveness to the reading. I honestly do feel a little guilty for being part of the privileged majority, not because I have specifically done anything to harm a minority group, but perhaps because slave owning has impacted me as slavery has impacted black people. I associate myself with fairly well-to-do white men with power. I am not saying that I identify with men in general or with men with political power, but my father, uncles, brother, cousin, and friends all enjoy being "white, free, and twenty-one" . . . and they are a part of my life.

Ms. L's reflection is an important step in starting to learn through a writerly perspective. She could see the deposition genre in different terms—as having a relatively narrow role in society. In the novel considered in isolation, the deposition does seem to have that "oh that's what really happened" function. But the deposition genre is just as written as the words, just as fictional as the story—and just as consequential as the other social and historical realities to which the story is referring. The legal genre, accurately portrayed in the novel, plays a role in concealing the total outrage of slavery, a fact well-detected by Ms. L. However, because in America most good students have been educated just as Ms. L was, young people—and thus future citizens—learn that literature does not matter because it is "only words," only stories or other genres, which themselves are institutionally, conventionally separated from the issues that led to their having been created to begin with.

Saying the Words: Jane Smiley's A Thousand Acres

Students' responses to Jane Smiley's *A Thousand Acres* suggest that, potentially at least, the language and reference of this novel can more easily enter their repertoire. However, in this case, the writerly perspective has possibly collaborated with society and readers to censor, partially, the issue of fathers' sexual abuse of daughters. The novel is about an Iowa farm family whose patriarch, Larry Cook, has had sexual relations with and beaten his two oldest daughters, Ginny and Rose. Ginny is the childless narrator who takes over caring for Rose's children after Rose dies prematurely of cancer. Rose had always admitted to herself what had happened. Ginny admitted it only belatedly. Two responses to *A Thousand Acres*:

> Ms. B: Two things about this novel that I didn't like were Ginny's initial denial of the events that took place between her and her father and also between her father and Rose. Ginny had the attitude that if you ignore it, it will no longer be there to haunt you, but yet it does come back to her. When it does, it changes her life. The second thing about the novel that I did not like was the fact that Larry never had to admit to his daughters, to himself, or the people of the town what he had done. Because of this it seems like it is unfinished business for everyone, Ginny, Rose, and us, the readers.

> Ms. J: I was taken aback at Ginny's transformation throughout the novel. She begins as a sweet, gentle, submissive creature who gradually transforms into a violent figure full of anger and pain. Ginny's physical, emotional, and mental submission to her father was an entrapment of which I truly cannot imagine. . . . Ginny and Rose did not have a chance. Similar to the situation in Bottom in *Sula*, the characters inflict violence upon themselves. Even Rose and Ginny end up turning on each other once they realize they cannot conquer their enemy. Their father held so much power over them. He literally owned them. Everything these girls did throughout their lives was somehow affected by the presence of their father. . . .

These responses are similar to those collected by Brenda Daly when she taught the novel. In *Authoring a Life*, Daly writes, "It seems that students, like Rose's children, don't have much faith in Ginny either. Even though I pointed out that Ginny is the novel's narrator, student writers consistently overlooked Ginny's narrative role, even when it was relevant to their arguments" (174). Daly is referring to the fact that the story is told by the figure who seems to avoid facing the underlying perversion of the family structure and business. Ms. B might have come to a different judgment had she recognized that the denial in the narration is the result of the trauma and that the articulation of this history is itself supposed to be the path toward reducing its damage. Similarly, Ms. B has an implied criticism of the novel when she notes how the father never does account for himself. Ms. B, like Daly's students, is holding something back from this tale. Yet she seems to acknowledge her implication in its experience.

Ms. J, as she did in her response to *Sula*, notices violence, anger, and pain in this narrative but is dismayed by Ginny's transformation. She, too, it seems, does not assimilate Ginny's narrative role, as that narration is the machinery that should counteract the pain and violence. Because Ginny is narrating, something is not said. Some articulation expected by the students is not there—undoubtedly an account of the incestuous events as well as some acknowledgment by the perpetrator. Ms. J seems less affected by these omissions than Ms. B, but as Daly describes, the reading of Ginny's story as having omitted these two things was common in her class and amounts to an issue that implicates the author, readers, and society.

Daly's student and collaborator, R, wrote:

> In *A Thousand Acres*, we have both ends of the spectrum: one daughter who is presumably too angry to speak, the other too emotionally disembodied to speak with authority. This may accurately reflect the effect of sexual abuse on victims; however, readers are not likely to understand—without a few clues from Smiley—why Ginny speaks almost as if she were a reporter, rather than a participant in the tragic events. (175)

R is expecting something important from Smiley—a more active role as a combatant of the crime she narrates. R implies, and I agree with this judgment, that the presentation of such a narrative is not strong enough to teach the actual meaning of what is narrated, although people like R and Daly, themselves incest survivors who spent years reconceiving, articulating, and understanding the traumatic events, can have immediate access to Ginny's narrative.

As if to confirm this point, one of my students, whose response to this novel is not included here, claimed that "the people of this novel are my people as well" without mentioning the underlying situation of the incestuous, predatory father. Ginny projects, from the first sentence, an overwhelming attachment to the land-rooted farming process, so that it is possible from this narrative to think that Larry's actions with his daughters are a kind of "bad thing" that invades the lives of families as drunkenness or gambling does in other families.

Daly's skeptical judgment rests to a great extent on Ginny's often mild presentation of the history. R also mentions with some impatience that Ginny permits herself only one sentence—there is more than one sentence, but not many—that alludes to the memory of the father's sexual action with her. After she narrates that sentence, she screams for a while, and then there is no further effect, except the transformation of her life into something different: she leaves her husband. Ginny is also too angry and emotionally disembodied to speak. Daly objects to Rose's statement to Ginny: "He didn't rape me, Ginny. He seduced me" (168; Smiley 190). Daly keeps to this objection even though, later in the novel, Rose, imploring Ginny to "say the words," says:

> But he did fuck us and he did beat us. He beat us more than he fucked us. He beat us routinely. And the thing is, he's respected. Others of them like him and look up to him. He fits right in. However many of them have fucked their daughters or their stepdaughters or their nieces or not, the fact is that they all accept beating as a way of life. We have two choices when we think about that. Either they don't know the real him and we do, or else they do know the real him and the fact the he beat us and fucked us doesn't matter. Either they themselves are evil, or they're stupid. That's the thing that kills me. This person who beats and fucks his own daughter can go out into the community and get respect and power, and take it for granted that he deserves it. (302)

In this speech "the words" are said repeatedly. Rose can say them, but Ginny cannot. In addition to the words, Rose describes the state of normalcy in which Larry Cook's behavior exists. All the men in the county belong, potentially, in the same category as Larry Cook because, even if they are not abusers, it "doesn't matter" to them that it takes place to begin with. Despite this clear announcement of the systemic evil in the men of Zebulon County, Brenda Daly is troubled by the term "seduced."

This critique focuses on a fundamental matter of language use. Daly understands that many incest survivors think just this way and that this may well be an acceptable verisimilitude. But Daly observes that Smiley, speaking of Larry Cook in an interview, said, "He pursues a kind of seduction of Rose that he would be ashamed of if he could look at it with any perspective" (168). Daly's student, R (also an incest survivor), says, "In my view, Smiley's word seduction is an excuse for the father's action, a way of condoning rape" (168). Daly and her student are claiming on the evidence of the interview that Smiley herself is still backing away from the truth of her own story. This truth is, Daly writes:

> What else is the sexual act committed upon a child, if not rape? Does lack of resistance constitute consent? Rose's denial of the raping of her body by her father is another continuation of the tradition of violence against women in literary works. Smiley is not deconstructing this myth; she is supporting and promulgating it throughout her novel.

In raising this point, seemingly only about diction, Daly is showing why Plato thought literature should be censored. At first, her point could seem harsh; after all, it must have taken some courage to print this novel in the first place, seeing as how rarely such stories are told in public forums. Yet the vocabulary does fix certain not-quite-conscious features of the story. When the story says that the daughters were seduced, that is what we hear; we then say that is horrible, but we hear "seduced" and not "raped." The difference between the two terms is that rape is a crime and seduction is not. Rose does say "he beat us and fucked us"; she says father and his friends are "evil." But neither Rose nor Smiley says that Larry Cook and those who accept his behavior are criminals who deserve prosecution and incarceration. Daly says that because Larry Cook's behavior is not identified as a crime, the criminal behavior is tolerated. Does Daly not have a point? If Rose and Ginny both said, in addition to "he beat us and fucked us," "he raped us," would there not be a different light on Larry Cook, on the men of Zebulon County who looked away, on our society, which deplores but does not prosecute the crime of rape of daughters by fathers?

The Necessary Conversations

How can it be that Daly is complaining about a novel on this account? Aren't novelists supposed to be good at choosing the right word for the story and for the society? My reading is that Daly is assuming a right few of us claim: to consider that the literature matters. This means that the words themselves matter. To some, she may seem to come close to censorship. But she is not censoring; she is commenting, criticizing, and, above all, taking a stance that says, "Jane Smiley: what you say about this really matters, especially to those of us who know this subject. I am taking my place as your critic by telling you, an artist, what language may be better than the language you use." Better for what? Well, certainly better for students who, like my own, are naive about the subject of this novel. But we see they are less naive about this issue than about those encountered by Sula. Somehow, students responded, important things were not said. The students felt unspoken words coming; they felt them to be a part of the scenes of the novel, the whole logic of this family, the enormity of the crime that transforms an industrious, idealistic agricultural operation that helps and feeds thousands into a plantation. As Ms. J wrote, "He [the father] literally owned them [his daughters]."

Daly's complaint is comparable to the complaint made to Patricia Williams by her sister, who urges Williams to make public an injustice in law school: unless you say it, the sister said, others will say "it didn't happen" (91). The reason for this demand for candor and "saying it" is that those who wish to deny that "it" happened are far more numerous than those willing to acknowledge that it happened. In America, literature has assumed the position of not mattering; one can be indirect. One can be elliptical—after all, literature is an aesthetic undertaking, not a social one. This aesthetic condition of literature renders it something that does not matter. We are removed from aesthetic literature—just a thing of beauty. We are also removed from moral literature—just a message on how to conduct our lives in a general way. Most students in our classes move toward those two views of literature. No teacher, certainly no student, is ready to do what Brenda Daly did: object to an author's chosen words and then tell her what the right words would be!

Yet for literature to matter, this is what has to be done. Sure, all authors can answer, can disagree, can speak. But this is a conversation, a discussion that we do not see because writers have no formal place in living communities. Brenda Daly's response to Smiley took place in part in a university community, where both were faculty members in a department. Suppose, however, that that kind of conversation were conventional. Suppose it were common for people to discuss with authors how to say local thoughts, how to choose the right words for each situation. Suppose that the convention of the sacred text were no longer the rule and that reading involved public participation in how stories were written. Then the study and role of literature in society would matter. Yet this is not a strange proposition. It is how television works. There are focus groups and tryouts for each new program. Producers actively seek out public interests and create shows that might speak to those interests. The public is viewed as having different segments that have different preferences.

In this volume, Rona Kaufman brings to our attention the work of scholars like Anne Gere and Elizabeth Long, who have studied women's reading and writing groups. These groups reflect what can happen in a more general sense in our communities, but they differ in one significant way: they are responses to exclusions from formal education and other reading sites populated by men. Groups like these do reduce the sacred-text syndrome, but they have remained marginal: have the groups studied in such detail by Anne Gere been recognized in any curriculum? Do they even play a role in the history of education courses? If it were not for Gere's work, would students know that such groups existed?

Oprah Winfrey's reading initiative, discussed in detail by Kaufman, is a contemporary extension of the reading groups studied by Gere. Winfrey tried to use the popular reach of television to promulgate a kind of reading experience that changed the nature and status of reading. Her attempt was original and came out of both the obscure (but widespread) reading-group tradition and the enterprising (now mainstream but once marginal) Hollywood tradition, which made use of existing popular outlets (such as the nickelodeons) to lead an existing audience into new popular genres. Indeed the popular art form of film and television is now fully ensconced worldwide. Will similar moves work with reading and literature? Of course, we don't know. Yet, as with Hollywood, "minority" initiative is, first, intrinsically interesting to everyone, and then the "everyone" changes as more minority or marginal groups enter the public discussion. There is evidence that the genres of many "others" are percolating to make new genres of "reading matter" and to change the status of reading as well as its place in society. However, this club has stopped functioning, then restarted, and we are at this time uncertain of the effects it can have.

At the same time, consider this. Toward what kind of lives is the majority in the wealthy industrialized West motivated? Are writers not identified with the technological tidal waves likely to "find a voice" in this "perfect storm" of software and online idolatry? In the current atmosphere, is there room for collective achievement and egalitarian education? It is one thing for writers to become temporarily known and read as a result of television coverage; it is another for the society to function under circumstances where writers and readers speak to one another on an everyday, ordinary, community level. The everyday exchange between writers and readers is the ideal toward which my remarks are oriented. Relative to this ideal, literature does not now matter to the general public.

Similarly, if even university discussions of literature took on some of the shape of the conversation between Daly and Smiley, some of the energy and purpose of Winfrey, creative writers would no longer be either impecunious or millionaires but more ordinary citizens with more familiar roles to play, and their participation in social debates would start to matter. Now, however, few authors are in a position to explore with students and readers what the right words may be for this or that story. They cannot share the stories; and what author will ask an audience what to write? Those authors employed by universities can function in this mode, but, as a rule, they dare not and most do not wish to.

Unfortunately, the answer to my title question is that very little literature is really ours—not because we are removed from it culturally but because we play no role in its creation. We may read some of it, and others like us who are professional readers and critics will overtake the language and enrich our lives, our minds, our language. Yet see how even intelligent, highly motivated, good-natured students struggle, how distant they feel from the language of the American literature they read. See how rarely they identify a literary idea with what actually exists in society. And these are American students reading American writers, writing about issues that implicate all American people. There is no culture gap. There is, however, the presupposition that literature and language do not matter: there is only the most distant sense that overtaking the language of literature and making it our own changes how we are as social figures.

For teachers of literature and language, there is so much to do that there is no sense in even accounting for it. Sharon Crowley in *Composition in the University* and Robert Connors[1] in *Composition-Rhetoric* recently called for the end of required first-year writing. I realize how much trouble this view has caused in many colleges and universities, but perhaps we can amend Sharon's and Bob's calls: substitute a year of studying how language is used for the writing courses that now do not respect the intelligence of our students. This substitute approach is not acknowledged by the academic mores that consider literacy a priority over oral language and over language in general. In a sense, the vitality of acquiring language in childhood has been repressed by the almost obsessive emphasis on reading and writing in schools. This repression is closely related to the repression of feelings and of the language of feelings that some zones of literary response criticism have tried to counteract. To become responsive again to the living language, that is, the language that we learned from having heard and internalized it, is to provide a clearer path toward the full range of how we overtake literature and, if we are lucky, make it our own. We English teachers need to teach, day in and day out, how much language matters in literature, in other writing, on television, in the living room. By orienting ourselves toward the spoken, living forms of literary language, we are also deindividualizing subjectivity, calling attention to the particular forms of sharing that our shared languages and genres make visible. At the same time, we are recognizing the inevitability of subjectivity and the identical inevitability of ever wider intersubjective connections borne by each individual. We teach literature and writing because language has always mattered to us, and we would be serving many to say these words, to show that they matter. To begin to recognize and teach literature as though its language matters is to recognize the human in the humanities.

NOTE

1. Let me take this moment to mourn the premature loss of this important young scholar.

WORKS CITED

Bleich, David. "The Materiality of Rhetoric, the Subject of Language Use." *Realms of Rhetoric: The Prospects for Rhetoric Education.* Ed. Joseph Petragalia and Deepika Bahri. Albany: State U of New York P, 2003. 39–60.

―――. *Know and Tell: A Writing Pedagogy of Disclosure, Genre, and Membership*. Portsmouth: Heinemann, 1998.

―――. "The Materiality of Language and the Pedagogy of Exchange." *Pedagogy* 1.1 (2001): 117–42.

Connors, Robert. *Composition-Rhetoric: Backgrounds, Theory, and Pedagogy*. Pittsburgh: U of Pittsburgh P, 1997.

Crowley, Sharon. *Composition in the University: Historical and Polemical Essays*. Pittsburgh: U of Pittsburgh P, 1998.

Daly, Brenda. *Authoring a Life: A Woman's Survival in and through Literary Studies*. Albany: State U of New York P, 1998.

Fetterley, Judith. *The Resisting Reader*. Bloomington: Indiana UP, 1978.

Gioia, Dana. *Can Poetry Matter? Esssays on Poetry and American Culture*. Saint Paul: Graywolf, 1992.

Melville, Herman. Benito Cereno: *A Cultural Edition*. Ed. Jay Fliegelman. New York: Bedford, 2003.

Morrison, Toni. *Sula*. New York: Plume, 1982.

Schilb, John, and John Clifford. *Making Literature Matter: An Anthology for Readers and Writers*. Boston: Bedford–St. Martin's, 2000.

Smiley, Jane. *A Thousand Acres*. New York: Knopf, 1991.

Reading "Whiteness," Unreading "Race": (De)Racialized Reading Tactics in the Classroom

AnaLouise Keating

Having demolished and condemned as racist the idea that observed group differences have any objective, biological foundation, the liberal intellectual community has revived the "race" concept as an essential category of human experience with as much ontological validity as the discarded racist notion of biologically distinct groups.
ORLANDO PATTERSON

Race is a text (an array of discursive practices), not an essence. It must be read with painstaking care and suspicion, not imbibed.
HENRY LOUIS GATES, JR.

Reading "Whiteness"

It is by now almost a commonplace to argue that United States readers (of all colors) have been trained to regard "whiteness" as the unmarked, nonracialized norm.[1] Generally, the argument goes something like this: in the United States, "whiteness" has functioned as a pseudouniversal category that hides its specific values, epistemology, and other attributes under the guise of a nonracialized, supposedly colorless human nature. Its presence erased, "whiteness" operates as the unacknowledged standard against which all so-called minorities are measured and marked. Applied to theories of reading, this unmarked "white" norm has become the framework, subtly compelling us to read ourselves, our texts, and our worlds from within a hidden "whiteness." As Rebecca Aenerud asserts, "Unless told otherwise, the reader, positioned as white, assumes the

314

characters are white" (37).[2] By thus positioning readers of all colors as "white," conventional reading and writing practices acculturate us into "whiteness," and reinforce the unjust status quo. How can educators interrupt this "white" acculturation and assist student readers in recognizing the hidden "white" framework they unconsciously employ when they read? As anthologies like *Displacing Whiteness: Essays in Social and Cultural Criticism* (Frankenberg), *Off White: Readings on Race, Power, and Society* (Fine, Weis, Powell, and Wong), *Whiteness: A Critical Reader* (Hill), *White Trash: Race and Class in America* (Wray and Newitz), and *White Reign: Deploying Whiteness in America* (Kincheloe, Steinberg, Rodriguez, and Chennault) indicate, this question and related issues have become increasingly urgent.[3]

Throughout the 1990s a growing number of scholars, writers, and activists called for (and began enacting) analyses of "white" as a racialized category. Toni Morrison, for example, challenges scholars to reread canonical United States literature and recognize how "literary whiteness" has shaped our understanding of what it means to be "American" (*Playing* 9). Arguing that "[a] criticism that needs to insist that literature is not only 'universal' but also 'race-free' risks lobotomizing that literature, and diminishes both the art and the artist" (12), she urges literary scholars to adopt new reading practices that expose the hidden racial discourse in United States literature. Similarly, some educators have begun emphasizing the importance of developing critical pedagogies that examine how "whiteness" has (mis)shaped knowledge production in United States culture. Thus in the introduction to *White Reign* Joe Kincheloe and Shirley Steinberg underscore the need for "a critical pedagogy of whiteness" (14). Because they believe that "[w]hite ways of being can no longer be universalized, white communication practices can no longer be viewed unproblematically as the standard, and issues of race can no longer be relegated to the domain of those who are not White," they stress the importance of "denormalizing whiteness" by exploring its racialized, nonuniversal characteristics (18).[4]

While I agree with these scholars and others who call for an examination of the ways "whiteness" has been socially constructed, I am troubled by their lack of attention to the implications reading "whiteness" holds for classroom dynamics. Because "whiteness" has functioned as an oppressive, mythical norm that negates persons (whatever their skin color) who do not conform to its standard, we need to understand and expose it. However, I worry that this analysis—if not carried out with great care—simply revives the "'race' concept" Orlando Patterson alludes to in my first epigraph and reifies students' already existing hegemonic conceptions of "race." Moreover, as Michael Apple, Charles Gallagher, and others suggest, all too often this interrogation of "whiteness" turns into a "crisis" for "white"-identified students, leading to what Apple describes as "the production of retrogressive white identities" (ix) or what Gallagher calls "whiteness . . . as an identity that evokes victimization and racist, reactionary thinking" ("Redefining" 33). When students who identify as "white" begin reading "whiteness" in previously unmarked texts, they are compelled to recognize the insidious roles "whiteness" plays in United States culture. Because they associate "whiteness" with "white" people, this recognition triggers a variety of unwelcome reactions—ranging from guilt, withdrawal, and despair to anger and the construction of an extremely celebratory racialized "whiteness." In short, they enact a "white" backlash that encompasses a sense of heightened alienation from people identified as "nonwhite" and the belief that "white" people are an oppressed group.[5]

It is not enough simply to begin reading "whiteness" into previously unmarked texts, for to do so inadvertently contributes to this "white" backlash and reinforces the belief in permanent, separate racial categories. Nor should we encourage "white"-identified students to develop "a positive, proud, attractive, antiracist white identity" (Kincheloe and Steinberg 12), for even the most progressive forms of "white" pride inadvertently reaffirm "white" superiority. As Ian F. Haney López argues:

> The dominant racial discourse already fashions Whites as the superior opposite to non-Whites; an uncritical celebration of positive White attributes might well reinforce these established stereotypes. At the same time, because races are constructed diacritically, celebrating Whiteness arguably *requires* the denigration of Blackness. Celebrat-

ing Whiteness, even with the best of antiracist intentions, seems likely only to entrench the status quo of racial beliefs. (172)

In this essay, I suggest that educators can challenge the hidden "white" framework and the racial identities it holds in place by employing what I call (de)racialized reading tactics. I bracket the prefix to underscore the paradoxical, seemingly contradictory dimensions of this enterprise: on the one hand, we must encourage students to adopt new reading practices that enable them to recognize and explore how all characters and texts are racialized—marked by name, language, location, and color. But on the other hand (and simultaneously), we must describe and enact these racialized readings very carefully, in unexpected, temporarily non-racialized ways that destabilize conventional understandings of "race" by underscoring the potentially fluid, relational nature of all racialized identities. Because the contemporary science fiction writer Octavia Butler's novels have played a pivotal role in my thinking on this topic, I begin with a discussion of her work and then move on to apply her (de)racializing tactics to the classroom, and I propose four pedagogical strategies designed to reveal the hidden "whiteness" of conventional reading practices and thus to alter student thinking and perceptions.[6] These tactics invite students to enact a twofold (de)racialized reading process that exposes "whiteness" and explores the artificial, unstable nature of "white," "black," and all other racialized identities, without ignoring their concrete material effects. Drawing on my own classroom experiences, I then demonstrate how (de)racialized readings allow educators to invite students of all colors to read "race" in new ways and to begin divesting themselves of their own "whiteness." More specifically, these tactics enable educators to enact reading practices that investigate "whiteness" without reinforcing the retrogressive "white" identities described above.

Reading Butler's (De)Racialized Writing

Like the (de)racialized reading tactics referred to in the previous section, Butler's use of "race" to describe key characters and communities indicates a paradoxical, seemingly contradictory act: on the one hand, her characters are almost always racialized— marked by name, language, location, and color (generally in this order).[7] But on the other hand, this racialization occurs so subtly— in context-specific instances fully integrated into the narratives— that Butler seems to deracialize them. At times, Butler avoids racial categories almost entirely. In *Dawn*—which takes place after nuclear war has almost entirely destroyed the earth and depicts the interactions among Lilith, other human survivors, and their rescuers, the Oankali (an ancient, extremely alien-looking species of genetic engineers)—there are only four references to Lilith's color and none to her "race" per se. The first description occurs at the end of the first chapter; as Lilith reflects on her previous "Awakenings" she recalls when the Oankali "put a child in with her—a small boy with long, straight black hair and smoky-brown skin, paler than her own" (8). This description is context-specific and relational, triggered by her interaction with another human being.[8] Lilith's physical appearance is described but not labeled. Those readers who do not simply skim over this description cannot use it to ascertain Lilith's "race" in any definitive sense: she could be of African, Asian, or indigenous ancestry—or perhaps some intermixture of these with European.[9] The second reference occurs four chapters later, as Lilith leaves the only environment she has known during the past 250 years: "There had been little color in her world since her capture. Her own skin, her blood— within the pale walls of her prison, that was all. Everything else was the same shade of white or gray. . . . Now, here was color" (30). Like the earlier passage, this description is relational but does not allow readers to fix Lilith's "race." The third reference occurs when Lilith meets Paul Titus, the first adult human she has encountered in over 200 years: "She stared at him. A human being—tall, stocky, *as dark as she was*, clean shaved" (89; my emphasis). Once again, Lilith's physical appearance is described but not labeled, and again the description is relational. The final reference occurs almost one hundred pages later, when Lilith's "ooloi" mate, Nikanj, commenting on Lilith's alliance with Joseph Shing, states that although other Oankali believed she "would choose one of the big dark ones because they're like you," Nikanj knew she would choose Joseph "because he's like you. . . . During his testing, his responses were closer to yours than anyone else I'm aware of. *He doesn't look like you, but he's like you*" (171; my emphasis). As in the previous examples, the characters are described but not labeled or grouped according to "race." In this passage, and in Butler's work as a whole, affinity is based on ways of thinking and acting, not on appearance or "blood."

Even when Butler does label characters' "race" more overtly, the labels often appear unexpectedly. In *Parable of the Sower*, which depicts Lauren Olamina as she attempts to survive and create a new community in a radically altered United States, Butler does not immediately inform us of her characters' racialized affiliations.[10] The novel begins in the year 2024, but it is not until the following year, after readers have become acquainted with Lauren and her neighbors, that we read the following passage:

> We ran into a pack of feral dogs today. We went to the hills today for target practice—me, my father, Joanne Garfield, her cousin and boyfriend Harold—Harry—Balter, my boyfriend Curtis Talcott, his brother Michael, Aura Moss and her brother Peter. Our other adult Guardian was Joanne's father Jay. He's a good guy and a good shot. Dad likes to work with him, although sometimes there are problems. The Garfields and Balters are white, and the rest of us are black. That can be dangerous these days. On the street, people are expected to fear and hate everyone but their own kind. Our neighborhood is too small for us to play those kinds of games. (31)

Even within this paragraph—which occurs in the third chapter—Butler subtly and slowly racializes her characters, and once again this racialization is context-specific.[11] Significantly, the focus is not on "race" itself but rather on the implications "race" makes for the characters' survival. And as in *Dawn*, alliances are not based on simplistic racial designations but instead have their source in characters' thoughts, actions, and beliefs.

Kindred provides an even more remarkable example of this delayed racialization. Set simultaneously in 1976 California and pre–Civil War Maryland, this novel follows Dana Franklin and her husband, Kevin, as Dana is pulled back through time whenever the life of her ancestor, Rufus, is threatened. The "white" son of a slave owner, Rufus represents a shocking, previously hidden element of Dana's family heritage that she must learn to understand and accept. Significantly, it is not until the third chapter, and Dana's second trip into the past, that Butler identifies her as "black." Only thirty pages later does she label Kevin "white."[12] As in Butler's other novels, the descriptions are context-specific and relational. We learn that Dana is "black" only when Rufus refers to her in derogatory terms, and we learn that Kevin is "white" only when, employing a recursive narrative style, Butler describes Dana's first encounter with this man she would later marry.[13]

What are we to make of these (de)racializing tactics? Do they simply encourage some (perhaps "white"-identified) readers to ignore the important role "race" plays in Butler's texts? Do readers caught up in Butler's fast-paced narratives (unconsciously) assume that, because the characters are not overtly racialized, they have no "race"—in other words, that they are "white"? After all, as I explained above, United States readers (of all colors) have generally been trained to view "whiteness" as the unmarked, nonracialized norm. As Toni Morrison asserts, "To identify someone as a South African is to say very little; we need the adjective 'white' or 'black' or 'colored' to make our meaning clear. In this country it is quite the reverse. American means white, and Africanist people struggled to make the term applicable to themselves with ethnicity and hyphen after hyphen after hyphen after hyphen" (*Playing* 47).

I would suggest, however, that Butler adopts a different strategy. She forgoes the hyphens—and often even the word *American* itself—and depicts her characters first as people, marked by language, location, and color, but not by racial labels. Only later, when readers have already accepted the characters and entered into their lives, does Butler indicate the characters' color, and she does so contextually. By so doing, she compels readers to recognize both the relational, contingent nature of "race" and its profound social effects.

These (de)racializing tactics challenge us to read "race" in new ways. They offer an important alternative to the racial scripts circulating in contemporary United States culture,[14] which conflate color with "race" and divide people into distinct groups based on apparent (physical) differences. As David Shipler explains in his study of United States "black"-"white" interethnic relations, in today's highly racialized culture "there is no more potent attribute than the color of the skin" (232). We have been trained to classify and evaluate ourselves and those we encounter according to racialized appearances: "Color is the first contact between blacks and whites. It comes as the initial introduction, before a handshake or a word, before a name, an accent, an idea, a place in the hierarchy of class, or a glimpse of personality. . . . From across a room or across a street, from a magazine page or a television screen, it is this most superficial attribute that suggests the most profound qualities" (231).[15] Put differently, we have internalized a "white" reading practice that encourages us to read the bodies we encounter according to "race," defined simplistically by obvious physical differences. Marking color unobtrusively, Butler interrupts this color-based mode of reading and the racial scripts it simultaneously relies on and reinforces. Her (de)racializing tactics have a transformational impact on readers. Without clearly defined racial differences, her characters cannot be labeled and categorized by "race." As the boundaries break down, inviting readers to reexamine our preconceptions concerning racialized identities, we begin recognizing that affinity—and, by extension, alliances among people—cannot be reduced to "race" but instead depends on the choices we make.

Take, for example, the transformations in perception that occur while reading *Kindred*. Generally the pattern goes something like this: at the outset, we do not even think about Dana's ethnicity or, if we do, we assume she is "white."[16] When we discover that Rufus is the "white" progenitor of Dana's "black" family tree, we experience several shifts in perception. To begin with, we must confront our implicit assumption that because until this point Dana had been unmarked, she was "white." This confrontation exposes the limitations in the myth of a color-blind society—a myth that many United States readers hold dear—and the insidious ways "whiteness" provides the unspoken racialized framework.[17] Our own reading practice has demonstrated that contemporary United States culture is not as color-blind as we believe. We have not read the unmarked Dana as an unraced individual but instead have read her as "white," vividly illustrating how "whiteness" functions as the invisible, supposedly raceless norm. This hidden "whiteness" informs contemporary beliefs about the supposedly color-blind laws, thus reinforcing existing injustices. Second, and like Dana herself, we as readers are startled by the implications of her newly discovered "white" relative. The fact that Dana was unaware of her own "white" ancestor reveals the flawed nature of the racial scripts circulating in United States culture—scripts that rely on facile concepts of racial purity. People we identify as "black" cannot be so neatly categorized into a single "race." Indeed, as Naomi Zack suggests, "It has been estimated that between 70 and 80 percent of all designated black Americans have some degree of white ancestry" (*Race and Mixed Race* 75). And the fact that Rufus has two mixed-"race" children, one of whom looks "white," indicates that many people whom we read as "white" also have unknown mixed ancestry. A third, closely related transformation occurs when, having then assumed that Kevin must also be "black"—simply because he is Dana's husband, readers learn thirty pages later that he is not. Again, we must reexamine our racialized preconceptions and the racial scripts we have internalized and act out as we read, for alliances cannot be ascertained by focusing solely on "race."

Reading transforms us. As Françoise Lionnet asserts, "one does not enter into a fictional world without risk, the risk of being influenced by a specific point of view. Reading is a two-way street and by implicating myself in my reading, I am in turn transformed by that activity" (28). When we enter the fictional worlds of Butler's novels, our usual highly racialized ways of viewing the world are challenged. We risk being changed by the (de)racialized characters we encounter. Butler's textual revelations and the self-reflection they provoke compel readers to acknowledge and explore both their own assumptions concerning racial purity and the ways they label, categorize, and stereotype people according to "race." Despite commonly held assumptions that "we" have moved beyond "race" and judge people simply as individuals, readers' shock at discovering Kevin's and Dana's racialized identities demonstrates that in fact color and "race" shape our perceptions in unacknowledged, sometimes dangerous ways. We do not read the bodies we encounter simply as unmarked human beings; they are "raced"—even when that "race" is an unmarked "whiteness." Although it seems paradoxical, Butler's (de)racializing tactics challenge readers to recognize that those bodies that *seem* unmarked are actually marked "white." We learn that appearances can be deceptive and, quite possibly, that not one of us is unmixed. Indeed, the implicit belief in distinct races implies a false sense of racial purity, since we could all be described as multiracial. Furthermore, the suggestion that we can automatically identify ourselves and others according to "race" is inaccurate and misleading.[18]

(De)Racialized Reading Tactics in the Classroom

I was so struck by Butler's (de)racializing tactics that I determined to apply them to my own teaching and developed four tactics that I now employ in various ways when teaching about "whiteness" and "race." Without seeming to focus on "whiteness" or, more generally, on "race," these tactics—which encompass text selection, delayed racialization, denaturalized racialization, and the deconstruction of "whiteness"—enable educators to expose "whiteness" while de-essentializing all racialized identities. After outlining these pedagogical tactics, I explain how I applied them in an introductory literature course I taught last semester.

First, select texts carefully and think through what you want students to learn as they read. Like the larger United States culture in which they live, many students assume that "race" is an unchanging biological (and divine) fact, based on natural (God-given) divisions among people; each individual is born into a single "race," defined monolithically, which can be read simply by looking at physical appearance. When teaching about "whiteness" and "race," it is vital to challenge this naturalized taxonomy of "race" and help students realize that the belief in discrete, biologically separate "races" relies on nineteenth-century pseudoscientific theories that have been disproved.[19] Popular beliefs to the contrary, there are no genetically distinct "races" of people. "Race" is, rather, an economically and politically motivated classification system with highly destructive effects; and racialized identities are unstable, artificial, and relational. Perhaps not surprisingly, most students' beliefs about "whiteness"—if they have even thought about it—are equally misguided. As I explained earlier, because "whiteness" has functioned as the unmarked norm, students rarely have considered "whiteness" to be a racial category. When teaching about "whiteness" educators need to assist students in recognizing its pervasive yet invisible nature, as well as the power dynamics that underlie and reinforce "whiteness" and all other racialized identities. However, to prevent students from inserting "whiteness" into their already existing racial scripts and thus viewing it as just one more homogeneous "race," educators must emphasize that there is no monolithic definition of "whiteness" or of "white" people, just as there is no monolithic definition of "blackness" and "black" people, "Asianness" and "Asian American" people, or any other racialized group. To assume otherwise simply reinforces stereotypes and prevents us from recognizing potential commonalities.

Second, delay racialization. Do not focus on "race"; start with other issues and give students specific suggestions, topics to reflect on as they read. Significantly, these topics should not foreground "race," for to do so would simply make students defensive and inadvertently trigger already existing racial scripts. Plan classroom discussion carefully and lead students through questions designed to assist them in becoming aware of how they have unconsciously operated within a "white" reading framework. I find it effective to begin with seemingly universal topics (like quest motifs) and with theories of reading, rather than with "race."

Third, denaturalize "race." When you (finally) do introduce "race" in the classroom, present it in ways that historicize and pluralize racial categories. Offering students an overview of some of the ways racialized identities have functioned and changed in United States culture allows educators to demonstrate the artificiality in the racial scripts we have all been trained to read. For instance, throughout the nineteenth century many United States state and federal agencies recognized only three "races"—"White," "Negro," and "Indian." Given the extremely diverse mixture of people living in the United States, this three-part classification was, to say the least, confusing. How were United States Americans of Mexican or Chinese ancestry to be described: as "white," "negro," or "Indian"? The state of California handled this predicament in a curious way: rather than expand the number of "races," the government retained the existing categories and classified Mexican Americans as a "white" population and Chinese Americans as "Indian." This decision had little to do with outward appearance; it was motivated by socioeconomic and political concerns, since it allowed the state to deny Chinese Americans the rights accorded to people classified as "white" (Omi and Winant 82). Since then, both groups have been redefined numerous times. United States Americans of Chinese descent have been classified as "Orientals," "Asians," "Asian Americans," "Pan-Asians," and "Asian Pacific Americans." Yet these terms are inadequate and erroneously imply a homogeneity unwarranted by the many nationalities, geographical origins, languages, dialects, and cultural traditions supposedly contained within these politically motivated categories (Webster). Similar comments can be made about other United States ethnicities as well. The goal here is to reveal the limitations in the racial scripts students employ when they read—racial scripts that present "race" as permanent, monolithic components of each person's identity—and pluralize "race" by emphasizing that all racialized identities take diverse forms.

Fourth, after exposing the insidious nature of "whiteness," invite students to deconstruct it by divesting themselves of the "white" frames of reference that shape their reading habits. This final step entails an emphasis on the potential agency self-reflective reading practices offer. As students learn to read "whiteness" in previously unmarked bodies and texts, they can recognize the political implications of "race" and begin deconstructing the racial scripts they have been trained to read.

These (de)racialized reading tactics encompass a subtle movement designed to explore "whiteness" yet make "race" more unstable. After intentionally deracializing student reading practices and the classroom, we reracialize them through close textual readings of specific passages and class discussions that reveal that "race" is an artificial, unstable, relational meaning system that can (and must) change. By thus emphasizing the constructed, historically changing nature of "race" while exposing "whiteness," (de)racialized reading tactics give students agency and challenge them to unread "race" by reading it in new ways. To illustrate one form these (de)racialized reading tactics can take in the classroom, I describe a unit on "whiteness" and "white" studies I recently designed and taught in an introduction to literature course. It focuses first on text selection, then describes strategies for delaying racialization, denaturalizing race, and deconstructing whiteness.

TEXT SELECTION

I selected two texts for this unit—Don DeLillo's 1985 novel, *White Noise*, and Leslie Marmon Silko's 1977 novel, *Ceremony*. I selected DeLillo because on the surface it seems to have nothing to do with "race" yet (as I will explain later) contains highly racialized subtexts, including provocative references to "whiteness," and I selected Silko because it challenges and denaturalizes restrictive definitions of "whiteness." Like *White Noise*, *Ceremony* is filled with images of "whiteness" and "white" people. But unlike *White Noise*, *Ceremony* openly denormalizes "whiteness" by exposing it and putting it in dialogue with other racialized groups. Despite the many differences between them, the novels share a number of similarities. Both focus primarily on a single figure: in *White Noise* the protagonist is Jack Gladney—an upper-middle-class, highly educated man, creator of "Hitler studies" as an academic discipline and the chair of Hitler studies at College-on-the-Hill (a small liberal arts college somewhere in America), who, we later learn, is "white"; and in *Ceremony* the protagonist is Tayo, a light-skinned, mixed-blood World War II veteran suffering from posttraumatic shock, who feels personally responsible for the deaths of his uncle and cousin and the drought devastating New Mexico. Each protagonist experiences a crisis in identity. In *White Noise*, Jack is obsessed and paralyzed by his fear of death, a fear intensified by his perhaps deadly exposure to environmental waste during an "airborne toxic event"; and in *Ceremony* Tayo returns from the war alienated both from the larger dominant culture and from traditional Laguna Pueblo culture. As they attempt to make sense of their lives, each protagonist enacts a type of quest. Throughout much of *White Noise* Jack's quest is internal and self-reflective. During conversations and meals with family members and colleagues and excursions to the supermarket and shopping mall, Jack tries to master his fear of death; in the novel's final section Jack's quest takes a more outward form as he searches for Willie Monk, creator of Dylar, an experimental drug designed to cure people's fear of death. Tayo's quest is more visionary and externalized. Tayo attempts to understand his role in the cosmos through a series of ceremonies and rituals with Ku'oosh, the Pueblo medicine man; Betonie, the mixed-blood Navajo healer; and Ts'eh Montaño, the embodiment of a mythic mountain spirit. His quest culminates in a final conflict with his full-blood childhood friends, Emo, Harley, and Leroy, who have surrendered themselves to the witchery and the seductive "white" culture that Tayo must learn to resist.

DELAY RACIALIZATION

Before beginning this unit on "whiteness,"[20] I delayed racialization by telling students that we would focus on issues concerning character, identity formation, and quest motifs and suggested questions they should think about while reading the novels:

How would you describe Jack and Tayo? How do they view themselves? What similarities and differences do you find between them, and how do you account for these similarities and differences? How does each man attempt to construct his identity? What roles do other people and the larger dominant culture play in each protagonist's identity construction? How do Jack and Tayo change in the course of the novels? What specific crises do Jack and Tayo face? How do they respond to these crises, and how do you account for their responses? Do the texts use this crisis-and-response to comment on contemporary social issues and, if so, how?

On the surface, these questions seem to have nothing to do with "race." They simply focus on some of the most obvious textual issues that occur during a first reading of the novels.

I began with *White Noise* because it allowed me to introduce and (de)racialize the topic of "whiteness," a topic *Ceremony* picks up on in more obvious ways. During the first two days of this unit, we discussed the issues referred to above. Significantly, no one (including me) mentioned "race." This omission on my part was intentional and designed to mimic Butler's (de)racializing tactics, as well as the way my students had been trained to ignore "whiteness" while reading. By introducing "whiteness" and "race" in a larger context—that of each protagonist's identity crisis—I hoped to assist my students in recognizing the enormous roles "whiteness" and "race" play in United States culture without reinforcing their already existing racial scripts.

On the third day of this unit, I finally introduced the topics of "whiteness" and "race." Even at this point, I did not focus specifically on "whiteness" or "race" but instead discussed them in the larger framework of literary and cultural studies. In so doing, I hoped to challenge student skepticism about "whiteness" and prevent them from falling back on retrogressive essentialized "white" identities. I began class by announcing that "whiteness" studies was the topic of the day and explained why we would examine this topic, a topic that most of my students had never considered. Because "whiteness" studies is a growing field of cultural and literary studies, it is important that they be familiar with it. As I gave students background information on the development of this field, I repeatedly underscored its relevance to the study of literature. I explained that for at least the last two decades of the twentieth century scholars have looked at the racialized dimensions of literary works by authors identified as "African Americans," "Native Americans," "Chicanos and Chicanas," and so on, but not at the racialized dimensions of works by authors identified as "white." I offered concrete examples to reinforce my point: although we generally describe the Harlem Renaissance as a "black" literary movement (perhaps because those identified as Harlem Renaissance writers were people of African descent?), we do not describe Puritanism or transcendentalism as "white" movements, even though—to the best of my knowledge— the Puritans and transcendentalists were all people of European descent. We have studies of "Chicano" narrative, "Asian American" novels, "Native American" poetry, and so on. But, I asked students, imagine a course or a book devoted exclusively to white writers (as so many courses and books still are) that acknowledged this fact in its title: say, "Classics of the White Western World," "The White American Experience," or "White Regional Writers." In this schema, "minority" writings become deviations from the unmarked, unspoken "white" norm. By focusing on course titles and literary categories in this way, I (de)racialized them and invited students to think consciously about how we read and classify literature. That is, I racialized the categories in a manner that encouraged students to recognize their artificial, constructed nature. This approach allowed me to demonstrate the highly racialized nature of literary categories, the fact that as readers we are generally unaware of this racialization and the hidden "whiteness" of canonical United States texts.

Denaturalizing "Race"

We cannot talk about "whiteness" without also talking about "race." The trick, however, is to discuss these volatile issues without reinforcing essentialist concepts. To do so, I offered students a brief overview of the development of racialized identities in the United States, with special emphasis on the constructed, relational nature of "blackness" and "whiteness." I pointed out that although we generally view the terms "black" and "white" as permanent, ahistorical racial markers indicating distinct groups of people, they are not. Significantly, the Puritans and other early European colonizers did not consider themselves "white"; they identified as "Christian," "English," or "free," for at that time the word "white" did not represent a racial category. Racialization was economically and politically motivated: it was not until around 1680, with the racialization of slavery, that the term was used to describe a specific group of people, a group that excluded many people today considered "white."[21] I underscored the relational nature of racialized categories by explaining that the "white race" evolved in opposition to but simultaneously with the "black race." As peoples whose specific ethnic identities were Yoruban, Ashanti, Fon, Dahomean, and so forth were forcibly removed from their homes in Africa and taken to the North American colonies, the Europeans adopted the terms "white" and "black"—with their already existing implications of purity and evil—and developed the concept of a superior "white race" and an inferior "black race" to justify slavery.

I used the history of *passing* to destabilize this binary between "blackness" and "whiteness" even further. Drawing on my personal experience, I briefly informed students about my own family background—my grandmothers who tried to pass into "whiteness" and my family's attempts to deny the implications of our African ancestry. I emphasized that my family's experience is by no means unique. During the past three hundred years, many thousands of people passed from "blackness" into "whiteness."[22] By thus historicizing "race" and by exposing the fluidity and multiplicity in racial designations, I challenged students to reevaluate the racial scripts they have been trained to read.

Deconstructing "Whiteness"

After this extensive background discussion, I explained my rationale for examining "whiteness" in *White Noise*. The title's reference to an apparently nonracialized "whiteness" invites us to think further about what it means to be "white," and I led students through a close reading of specific passages that illustrate DeLillo's selective racialization, where only "nonwhite" or racially ambiguous people are marked and thus denormalized: the "woman who lived on our street with a teenage daughter and an *Asian* baby," "the *black* girl who's staying with the Stovers," the "*black* family of Jehovah's witnesses" Jack meets during the evacuation (39; 80; 132; my emphasis).[23] In these passages—as in the novel as a whole—Jack, his family, the Stovers, and other ("white") neighbors are not marked by color or "race." I used this textual evidence to demonstrate how an invisible "white" framework and the selective racialization it supports confer normalcy on the unmarked (and seemingly "nonraced") characters and single out "nonwhites" as different—deviations outside the ("white") norm. As I had suspected, my students had not noticed this selective racialization when reading *White Noise* because it paralleled their own reading habits. Consequently, as we examined this textual evidence, they were compelled to reflect on their own reading practices. They too have internalized this invisible "white" norm, a norm that makes it seem natural to read "race" selectively.

After discussing the hidden allusions to "whiteness" in *White Noise*, I reminded students that "whiteness" becomes more visible in the novel's final section, where we read that Jack himself is marked as "white." We read that he feels "white" (242) and that he walks on his "bare white feet" (244). During his encounter with Willie Mink, Mink refers to Jack several times as "white," first identifying him as "a heavyset white man" (308), later calling him "white man" and telling him that he is "very white" (310). Finally, the room where this confrontation occurs is itself a "white room" filled with a "white buzz" (312). This sudden proliferation of references to "whiteness"—which occurs when Jack's fear of death and, relatedly, his inability to control or make sense of his life grow even stronger—almost invites us to explore "whiteness" in *White Noise*.

At this point in class discussion, students were persuaded of the value in reading "whiteness" in *White Noise* and were willing to examine it in greater detail. I then discussed traits often associated with "whiteness"; distributed a handout, "Critics on Literary Representations of 'Whiteness'"; and invited students to apply these "white" traits to *White Noise*: in what ways does the novel substantiate, challenge, and revise scholars' descriptions of "whiteness"? How does incorporating an analysis of "whiteness" affect your interpretation of the novel? What do we make of the associations between Jack's consumerism, his fear of death, and his "whiteness"? We used this handout again one week later when we discussed Silko's representations of "whiteness" in *Ceremony*. In each instance, I presented this information as hypothetical and explained that, as we talked about "whiteness" in the assigned texts, we would not try to arrive at a definitive understanding of the concept. Instead, we would simply speculate on possible, temporary meanings of "whiteness" and the potential usefulness of examining "whiteness" in *White Noise* and *Ceremony*. By presenting "whiteness" in this fashion, I hoped to assist students in recognizing the fluidity of racial categories.

Class discussions of "whiteness" in *White Noise* and *Ceremony* were truly remarkable and allowed students to gain new insights about previously puzzling dimensions of each text, including Jack's fear of death and the ways his faith in science, technology, and consumption impede his development and interfere with self-understanding and Tayo's alienation, his sense of inferiority, and the dominant United States culture's multilayered, systemic oppression of native cultures. Perhaps not surprisingly, after examining "whiteness" in *White Noise* my students viewed "whiteness" and "white" people in highly critical ways and determined that "whiteness" is extremely destructive. "Whiteness" gave Jack an unspoken, unacknowledged sense of superiority and the unwarranted belief that he should be able to control his life. Students read Jack's fear of death and his role as creator of Hitler studies as an indictment of "whiteness" and an implicit equation of "whiteness" with death. In addition to concluding that Jack becomes paralyzed by his unacknowledged "whiteness," they associated his feelings of emptiness, his fear of death, his attraction to the supermarket and shopping mall, and his apparently meaningless life with his "whiteness." Several students decided that "white" spirituality is an enormous vacuum or void, promising fulfillment through a misguided (and perhaps deadly) faith in science, technology, and consumption.

I am aware that these depictions of "whiteness" border on demonization. As an educator, I want students of all colors to recognize the racialized nature of "white" identities. However, I do not want my "white"-identified students to assume that, because they are "white," these characteristics must automatically, inevitably apply to them. (What good would this awareness serve?) Nor do I want them to be filled with paralyzing guilt if they see in Jack's unspoken "white" superiority and privilege reflections of their own. Such personalized guilt is ineffective and prevents "white"-identified students from acting. And, although self-identified students of color might find it satisfying to see the "white" gaze that has marked them as inferior and other turned back on itself, such reversals are equally ineffective, for they inadvertently support already existing stereotypes of "race" and replicate the existing racial hierarchies. Instead, I want to assist students of all colors in developing an ethics of accountability that enables them more fully to comprehend how these oppressive racialized systems that began in the historical past continue misshaping contemporary conditions. Only then can they form new alliances that go beyond existing racial categories and empower them to work for social change.[24]

But to do so, students must recognize the constructed, contingent nature of "whiteness" and, more generally, of "race" as a whole. "Whiteness" is not synonymous with "white" people. That a person is born with "white" skin does not necessarily mean that she or he will think, act, and write in the "white" ways described above. Nor does the fact that a person has "brown" or "black" skin automatically guarantee that she or he will not think, act, and write in "white" ways. As Alison Bailey points out:

> The connection between "acting white" and "looking white" is contingent, so it is possible for persons who are not classified as white to perform in whitely ways and for persons who are white not to perform in whitely ways. Racial scripts are internalized at an early age to the point where they are embedded almost to invisibility in our language, bodily reactions, feelings, behaviors, and judgments. (34)

It is crucial for educators to assist students in recognizing the pivotal role "whiteness" plays in these racial scripts, for "whiteness" serves as the unacknowledged framework, a framework that has affected all of us. No matter how we identify—whether as "Hispanic," "Mexican," "Anglo," "American," "black, "white," or so forth—we all, to greater and lesser degrees, have learned to think, read, and act in "white" ways. We have internalized what Gloria Anzaldúa describes as a "white" "frame of reference." As she explains in a 1996 interview with Andrea Lunsford:

> In this country the frame of reference is white, Euro-American. . . . [W]e—the colonized, the Chicanos, the blacks, the Natives in this country—have been reared in this frame of reference, in this field. All of our education, all of our ideas come from this frame of reference. We're complicitous because we're in such close proximity and intimacy with the other. . . . I have a white man and woman in here, and they have me in their heads, even if it's just a guilty little nudge sometimes. (252–53)

Unlike Anzaldúa, however, many students are almost entirely unaware of this "white" framework until we assist them in recognizing its pervasiveness in their lives.

Although I mentioned this "white" framework and the racial scripts it holds in place during discussion of *White Noise*, it was not until students read *Ceremony* that they could recognize the contingent nature of "whiteness" and skin color: full-blood Native American characters such as Emo, Harley, and Rocky think and act in "white" ways, while the light-skinned, mixed-blood Tayo learns to recognize and resist "whiteness." Although Silko in many ways demonizes "whiteness"—in *Ceremony* the dominant "white" culture is associated with greed, restrictive boundaries, destruction, emptiness, absence, and death—she does not essentialize it. Instead, she offers an origin myth, told by Betonie. In response to Tayo's statement "I wonder what good Indian ceremonies can do against the sickness which comes from their ["white" people's] war, their bombs, their lies," Betonie asserts:

> That is the trickery of the witchcraft. . . . They want us to believe all evil resides with white people. Then we will look no further to see what is really happening. They want us to separate ourselves from white people, to be ignorant and helpless as we watch our own destruction. But white people are only tools that the witchery manipulates; and I tell you, we can deal with white people, with their machines and their beliefs. We can because we invented white people; it was Indian witchery that made white people in the first place. (132)

In this passage, and in *Ceremony* as a whole, "whiteness" is depicted as a highly destructive, immensely seductive worldview that—with great effort—can be resisted. It is not European ancestry that dooms white people to act in these evil ways but rather a system of values and a code of conduct potentially adopted by people of any color. Like James Baldwin (180), Silko in *Ceremony* represents "whiteness" as "a moral choice" rather than an essential, biologically based identity. As Betonie's creation story and Tayo's quest demonstrate, once we begin recognizing this previously invisible "whiteness," we can—if we so desire—resist it.

Through class discussion, I emphasized the role reading can play in challenging "whiteness." More specifically, I invited students to disidentify with the representations of "whiteness" they encounter in *White Noise* and *Ceremony*. As Anzaldúa explains in "To(o) Queer the Writer":

> Reading is one way of constructing identity. When one reads something that one is familiar with, one attaches to that familiarity, and the rest of the text, what remains hidden, is not perceived. Even if one notices things that are very different from oneself, that difference is used to form identity by negation—"I'm not that, I'm different from that character. This is me, that's you." (257)

(De)racialized readings trigger this identification-disidentification process. Before class discussion, students read "race" unthinkingly, thus reinforcing the "white" frame of reference that holds racialized identities in place. To borrow Anzaldúa's terms, they attached themselves to the hidden racial scripts they were trained to read. Be exposing these racial scripts—making students conscious of what they had unconsciously assumed—I opened space for disidentification to occur. Disidentifying themselves with the representations of "whiteness" they encountered in *White Noise* and *Ceremony*, they could begin defining themselves differently. This process of disidentification was especially important for "white"-identified students because it enabled them to recognize that they did not need to identify with Jack Gladney or the "white" people in *Ceremony*. Their "whiteness" does not doom them to act in "white" ways. As in Butler's novels, affinity is based on ways of thinking and acting, not (necessarily) on "race." They can disidentify themselves with the representations of "whiteness" in *White Noise* and *Ceremony* and begin developing new alliances based on ways of thinking and acting, not on "race."

Because reading "whiteness" into apparently nonracialized texts allows us to begin disrupting "whiteness" as the unspoken, unchallenged norm,[25] the (de)racialized reading tactics I employed in this unit on "whiteness" were extremely effective. Students (of all colors) could no longer ignore the insidious role "whiteness" plays in normalizing a hierarchical social system. Our readings and discussions vividly demonstrated that—popular rhetoric to the contrary—contemporary United States culture is not color-blind. We have all, to varying degrees, been socialized into an invisible, highly destructive "white" framework. This recognition made my students more accountable for the choices they make. Emphasizing the contingent nature of "whiteness" and the relational, historical dimensions of all racialized identities, I challenged them to begin questioning the unspoken "white" status quo and to decide whether they were willing to continue choosing to think and act in "white" ways. Perhaps most important, these (de)racialized reading tactics enabled me to expose the destructive components of "whiteness" without triggering the "retrogressive white identities" (Apple ix) and the "racist, reactionary thinking" (Gallagher, "Redefining" 33) that occur with growing frequency in the classroom.

Unreading "Race"

In this essay I argue that we cannot simply read "whiteness" into previously unmarked texts and bodies, for to do so recenters "whiteness," reinforces the false belief in separate "races," and leads to a "white" backlash and the development of retrogressive "white" identities. Instead, reading "whiteness" must be the first step in a larger process that enables us simultaneously to unread "race" by exposing the arbitrary, politicized nature of all racial identities. It is this twofold process that I describe as (de)racialized reading tactics.

Let me emphasize: I am not in any way suggesting that educators engage in a superficial color blindness that transcends "race" or ignores the impact of racism. I am, in fact, suggesting the reverse: (de)racialized readings are transformational and expose both the pseudo-universal assumptions we often make about "whiteness" and the highly destructive implications of racialized thinking and racism. Significantly, however, the reading tactics I propose do so without reifying "race," which is—as we all know but generally forget—a sociohistorical concept, not a biological fact. Racial divisions—and the concept of purity on which they rely—were developed to create a hierarchy that grants privilege and power to specific groups of people while simultaneously oppressing and excluding others. If, as Henry Louis Gates, Jr., implies in my second epigraph to this essay, "race" is a text that everyone in this country unthinkingly reads, we must begin reading—and rewriting—this text in new ways. (De)racialized reading tactics offer a variety of ways to do so.

Notes

Parts of this essay appear in my "Interrogating 'Whiteness,' (De)Constructing 'Race,'" *College English* 57 (1995): 901–18.© 1995 by the National Council of Teachers of English. Reprinted with permission.

Thanks to the Eastern New Mexico University students in my women's studies and introduction to literature courses, to Jesse Swan for our many conversations on "whiteness," and to Elizabeth Flynn for comments on earlier versions of this essay.

1. Throughout this essay I use the terms "white," "black," "whiteness," "blackness," and "race" in quotation marks to underscore their relational, artificial, and misleading nature.

2. Morrison makes a similar point: "Until very recently and regardless of the race of the author, the readers of virtually all American fiction have been positioned as white" (*Playing* xii).

3. For an extensive overview of recent investigations of "whiteness," see Fishkin.

4. According to Giroux and McLaren, the traditional Western view "of learning as a neutral or transparent process" is inaccurate and prevents us from recognizing the highly political, racialized nature of all pedagogical methodologies. They maintain that "[t]eachers need critical categories that probe the factual status of white, Western, androcentric epistemologies that will enable schools to be interrogated as sites engaged in producing and transmitting social practices that reproduce the linear, profit-motivated imperatives of the dominant culture, with its attendant institutional dehumanization" (160). McLaren makes a similar point when he says that "interrogating the culture of whiteness itself . . . is crucial because unless we do this—unless we give white students a sense of their own identity as an emergent ethnicity—we naturalize whiteness as a cultural marker against which Otherness is defined" ("Multiculturalism" 214). As I explain in

this essay, I have deep reservations about this desire to nurture a sense of racialized "whiteness." For other theorists demanding an interrogation of "whiteness" in pedagogy, see Mohanty; hooks.

5. For useful analyses of this "white" crisis, see Gallagher ("White Reconstruction") and McLaren (*Revolutionary Multiculturalism*). According to McLaren, "Feeling that their status is now under siege, whites are now constructing their identities in reaction to what they feel to be the 'politically correct' challenge to white privilege" (262).

6. Author of ten novels and a collection of short stories, Butler has been writing science fiction for over twenty years. Butler was one of the first African American science fiction writers, and her work represents a significant breakthrough. Her novels contain strong "black" female protagonists whose wisdom and actions make them agents of change. She deals with complex issues, including the struggle for power and control; the ways these struggles are inflected by gender, ethnicity, and class; fear of and confrontation with differences; and the creation of new communities where peoples of many colors, and often different species, interact.

7. The only protagonist who is not racialized is Teray in *Patternmaster*.

8. Earlier in the narrative Butler informs us that Lilith's married name is "Iyapo" and that her husband was originally from Nigeria; however, these cues do not necessarily tell us anything about Lilith's own ethnicity.

9. For example, according to Haraway, "illustrating the workings of the unmarked category, 'white,' *Dawn*'s cover art has allowed several readers whom I know to read the book without noticing either the textual cues indicating that Lilith is black or the multi-racialism pervading Xenogenesis" (381).

10. The Afrocentric nature of Lauren's surname (Olamina) does provide an important clue to her ethnicity for readers aware of the history of African American identities.

11. It is significant that in this dystopic future, where violence and intense disrespect for human life reign, people self-segregate based on color.

12. Earlier, we learn that Kevin has "the kind of pale, almost colorless eyes that made him seem distant and angry whether he was or not" (13). But since some "black"-identified people have pale eyes, this brief description generally does not inform readers of Kevin's color. In my experience, it certainly does not prepare readers for the shock they experience when they discover that Kevin is not "black."

13. Morrison employs a very different strategy but with remarkably similar effects. *Paradise* opens with the sentence, "They shoot the white woman first"; however, even after reading the entire novel, readers do not know which woman is "white." This ambiguity is intentional. As she asserts in a 1998 interview, "My point was to *flag* race and then to erase it, and to have the reader believe, finally—after you know *everything* about these

women—their interior lives, their pasts, their behavior—that the one piece of information you don't know, which is the race, may not in fact matter. And when you *do* know it, what do you know?"

14. I borrow the term "racial scripts" from Bailey.

15. Unfortunately, Shipler focuses on only "white-black" interactions; however, his remarks can be extended to other United States racialized groups as well.

16. Unless, of course, readers have looked carefully at the most recent cover page and read the author's biography. I am repeatedly struck by how few of my students pay attention to either.

17. See Crenshaw's discussion of the racist, hidden "white" dimensions of contemporary color blindness.

18. My theory is only partially speculative. For the past ten years, I have taught *Kindred* both in upper-level and graduate literature courses and in introduction to women studies and I have seen my students' perceptions transformed through their reading and discussion of this text. No matter how they self-identify—whether as "Hispanic," "Indian," "black," "American," or "white"— students' reactions have followed the path outlined in this section.

19. For discussions of the roles nineteenth-century pseudoscience played in naturalizing racialized taxonomies, see Appiah; Zack (*Race and Mixed Race*).

20. Not surprisingly, I did not describe this unit to the students in my introduction to literature course as a unit on whiteness.

21. Southern Europeans, light-skinned Jews, Irish, and Catholics of European descent, for example, were most definitely not "white" in eighteenth- and nineteenth-century America. See Webster 132–33.

22. "It was estimated on the basis of intercensual and birth-death rate comparisons that 25,000 blacks 'passed into the general community' *each year* from 1900–10" (Goldberg 344n12; see also Alcoff; Smith; and Zack [*Race and Mixed Race*; *American Mixed Race*]).

23. There are too many examples of this selective racialization to list, but additional examples include the "black" Pentecostal (135), the "Asian" child (154), the "Indians" (or are they "Pakistanis"? Jack's family doesn't know for sure) at drugstores (179), and the "Iranian" who delivers the newspaper (184).

24. Shohat and Stam make a similar point, stating that they "would therefore distinguish between a personalistic, neurotic guilt on the one hand, and a sense of collective and reciprocal answerability on the other" (343–44).

25. Aanerud makes a similar point: "Reading whiteness into texts . . . that are not overtly about race is an essential step toward disrupting whiteness as the unchallenged racial norm" (43).

Works Cited

Aanerud, Rebecca. "Fictions of Whiteness: Speaking the Names of Whiteness in U.S. Literature." Frankenberg 35–59.

Alcoff, Linda. "Mestizo Identity." Zack, *American Mixed Race* 257–78.

Anzaldúa, Gloria. Interview with Andrea Lunsford. "Toward a Mestiza Rhetoric: Gloria Anzaldúa on Composition and Postcoloniality (and the Spiritual)." 1996. *Interviews/Entrevistas.* Ed. AnaLouise Keating. New York: Routledge, 2000. 251–80.

———. "To(o) Queer the Writer—*Loca, escritora y chicana.*" *Inversions: Writing by Dykes, Queers, and Lesbians.* Ed. Betsy Warland. Vancouver: Press Gang, 1991. 249–64.

Appiah, Kwame Anthony. "The Uncompleted Argument: Du Bois and the Illusion of Race." Gates 21–37.

Apple, Michael W. Foreword. Kincheloe, Steinberg, Rodriguez, and Chennault ix–xiii.

Bailey, Alison. "Locating Traitorous Identities: Toward a View of Privilege-Cognizant White Character." *Hypatia* 13 (1998): 27–43.

Baldwin, James. "On Being 'White' and Other Lies." *Black on White: Black Writers on What It Means to Be White.* Ed. David Roediger. New York: Schocken, 1998. 177–80.

Butler, Octavia. *Dawn.* New York: Warner, 1987.

———. *Kindred.* 1979. Boston: Beacon, 1988.

———. *Parable of the Sower.* New York: Four Walls, 1993.

———. *Patternmaster.* 1976. New York: Warner, 1995.

Crenshaw, Kimberlé Williams. "Color-Blind Dreams and Racial Nightmares: Reconfiguring Racism in the Post–Civil Rights Era." *Birth of a Nation'Hood: Gaze, Script, and Spectacle in the O. J. Simpson Case.* Ed. Toni Morrison and Claudia Brodsky Lacour. New York: Pantheon, 1997. 97–168.

DeLillo, Don. *White Noise.* New York: Penguin, 1985.

Fine, Michelle, Lois Weis, Linda C. Powell, and L. Mun Wong, eds. *Off White: Readings on Race, Power, and Society.* New York: Routledge, 1997.

Fishkin, Shelley Fisher. "Interrogating 'Whiteness,' Complicating 'Blackness': Remapping American Culture." *Criticism and the Color Line: Desegregating American Literary Studies.* Ed. Henry Wonham. New Brunswick: Rutgers UP, 1996. 251–90.

Frankenberg, Ruth, ed. *Displacing Whiteness: Essays in Social and Cultural Criticism.* Durham: Duke UP, 1997.

Gallagher, Charles A. "Redefining Racial Privilege in the United States." *New Jersey Project Journal* 8 (1997): 28–39.

———. "White Reconstruction in the University." *Socialist Review* 94 (1995): 165–87.

Gates, Henry Louis, Jr., ed. *"Race," Writing, and Difference*. Chicago: U of Chicago P, 1985.

Giroux, Henry, and Peter McLaren. "Radical Pedagogy as Cultural Politics: Beyond the Discourse of Critique and Anti-utopianism." *Texts for Change: Theory/Pedagogy/Politics*. Ed. Donald Morton and Mas'ud Zavarzadeh. Urbana: U of Illinois P, 1991. 152–86.

Goldberg, David Theo. "Made in the USA: Racial Mixing 'n Matching." Zack, *American Mixed Race* 237–55.

Haraway, Donna. *Primate Visions: Gender, Race, and Nature in the World of Modern Science*. New York: Routledge, 1989.

Hill, Mike, ed. *Whiteness: A Critical Reader*. New York: New York UP, 1997.

hooks, bell. *Talking Back: Thinking Feminist, Thinking Black*. Boston: South End, 1989.

Kincheloe, Joe L., and Shirley R. Steinberg. "Addressing the Crisis of Whiteness." Kincheloe, Steinberg, Rodriguez, and Chennault 3–29.

Kincheloe, Joe L., Shirley R. Steinberg, Nelson M. Rodriguez, and Ronald E. Chennault, eds. *White Reign: Deploying Whiteness in America*. New York: St. Martin's, 1998.

Lionnet, Françoise. *Autobiographical Voices: Race, Gender, Self-Portraiture*. Ithaca: Cornell UP, 1989.

López, Ian F. Haney. *White by Law: The Legal Construction of Race*. New York: New York UP, 1996.

McLaren, Peter. "Multiculturalism and the Postmodern Critique: Toward a Pedagogy of Resistance and Transformation." *Between Borders: Pedagogy and the Politics of Cultural Studies*. Ed. Henry Giroux and McLaren. New York: Routledge, 1994. 192–222.

———. *Revolutionary Multiculturalism: Pedagogies of Dissent for the New Millennium*. Boulder: Westview, 1997.

Mohanty, Chandra Talpade. "On Race and Voice: Challenges for Liberal Education in the 1990s." *Beyond a Dream Deferred: Multicultural Education and the Politics of Excellence*. Ed. Becky W. Thompson and Sangeeta Tyagi. Minneapolis: U of Minnesota P, 1993. 41–65.

Morrison, Toni. Interview with Elizabeth Farnsworth. *News Hour with Jim Lehrer*. PBS. Mar. 1998.

———. *Paradise*. New York: Knopf, 1998.

———. *Playing in the Dark: Whiteness and the Literary Imagination*. Cambridge: Harvard UP, 1992.

Omi, Michael, and Howard Winant. *Racial Formation in the United States from the 1960s to the 1980s*. 2nd ed. New York: Routledge, 1994.

Patterson, Orlando. *The Ordeal of Integration: Progress and Resentment in America's "Racial" Crisis*. Washington: Civitas/Counterpoint, 1997.

Shipler, David K. *A Country of Strangers: Blacks and Whites in America*. New York: Knopf, 1997.

Shohat, Ella, and Robert Stam. *Unthinking Eurocentrism: Multiculturalism and the Media*. New York: Routledge, 1994.

Silko, Leslie Marmon. *Ceremony*. New York: Penguin, 1977.

Smith, David Lionel. "What Is Black Culture?" *The House That Race Built: Black Americans, U.S. Terrain*. Ed. Wahneema Lubiano. New York: Pantheon, 1997. 178–94.

Webster, Yehudi O. *The Racialization of America*. New York: St. Martin's, 1992.

Wray, Matt, and Annalee Newitz, eds. *White Trash: Race and Class in America*. New York: Routledge, 1997.

Zack, Naomi, ed. *American Mixed Race: The Culture of Microdiversity*. Lantham: Rowman, 1995.

———. *Race and Mixed Race*. Philadelphia: Temple UP, 1993.

Notes on Contributors

ANNE G. BERGGREN, a lecturer in the Sweetland Writing Center at the University of Michigan, has worked as a high school teacher, newspaper reporter, editorial assistant, and preschool teacher. She teaches writing and literature courses at the University of Michigan and is working on a book tentatively titled "The Passionate Reader: Women's Stories of Reading."

DAVID BLEICH teaches language, literature, writing, gender studies, film studies, science studies, and Jewish studies at the University of Rochester. His most recent book, edited and introduced with Deborah Holdstein, is *Personal Effects: The Social Character of Scholarly Writing* (2001). He also edited with Sally (Reagan) Ebest and Thomas A. Fox *Writing With: New Directions in Collaborative Teaching, Learning, and Research* (1994). He is the author of *Know and Tell: A Writing Pedagogy of Disclosure, Genre, and Membership* (1998), *The Double Perspective: Language, Literature, and Social Relations* (1988), *Utopia: The Psychology of a Cultural Fantasy* (1984), *Subjective Criticism* (1978), and *Readings and Feelings* (1975).

ELIZABETH A. FLYNN is professor in the department of humanities at Michigan Technological University, where she teaches courses in writing, reading, literature, and gender studies. She is author of *Feminism beyond Modernism* (2002), founding editor of the journal *Reader*, and coeditor, with Patrocinio P. Schweickart, of *Gender and Reading* (1986). She was president of the Women's Caucus for the Modern Languages and has chaired the Division on the Teaching of Writing and the Division on the Teaching of Literature of the Modern Language Association.

ANGELETTA KM GOURDINE is assistant professor of English at Louisiana State University. She teaches African, African American, and Caribbean literatures and courses in world literature by women. She is the author of *The Difference Place Makes: Gender, Sexuality and Diaspora Identity* (2003). Currently she is working on a book-length project about black women in beauty and fashion culture.

JANE GREER is associate professor of English and women's and gender studies at the University of Missouri, Kansas City, where she teaches courses on the history of literacy, literature, and gender as well as composition courses. She is the editor of *Girls and Literacy in America: Historical Perspectives to the Present* (2003), and she is currently completing a book-length study of the opportunities for literacy instruction available to working-class women in the United States from 1830 to 1940.

LAURIE GROBMAN is associate professor of English and co-coordinator of the professional writing degree program at Penn State University, Berks-Lehigh Valley College, where she teaches basic writing, first-year composition, rhetorical theory, multicultural literature, and women's literature. Her book *Teaching at the Crossroads: Cultures and Critical Perspectives in Literature by Women of Color* (2001) offers a transformative model for teaching literature by women of color. Her articles on basic writing, critical pedagogy, and multiculturalism in writing and literary studies have appeared in a range of composition and literary journals.

RONA KAUFMAN is assistant professor of English at Pacific Lutheran University, where she teaches courses in writing and literacy and directs the Writing Center. She completed her dissertation, "Reading Materials: Composing Literacy Practices in and out of School," in the Joint Program in English and Education at the University of Michigan. Her interests include composition theory, reading theory, pedagogy, cultural studies, and teacher education.

ANALOUISE KEATING is associate professor of women's studies at Texas Woman's University. She is the author of *Women Reading Women Writing: Self-Invention in Paula Gunn Allen, Gloria Anzaldúa, and Audre Lorde* (1996), editor of Anzaldúa's *Interviews/Entrevistas* (2000), and co-editor (with Anzaldúa) of *This Bridge We Call Home: Radical Visions for*

Transformation (2002). She has published articles on critical race theory, queer theory, United States women of color, and pedagogy. She is currently working on a multigenre anthology, "Entremundos: Creative and Critical Perspectives on Gloria E. Anzaldúa."

KELLY J. MAYS is assistant professor of English at the University of Nevada, Las Vegas. She has published articles on Chartist literature and nineteenth-century British reading and publishing practices and serves as an editor of the *Norton Introduction to Literature*. She is currently completing a study of representations of reading and literacy in nineteenth-century Britain.

JAMES PHELAN, professor of English at Ohio State University, is the editor of *Narrative* and the author of numerous books and essays on narrative theory, including *Worlds from Words* (1981), *Reading People, Reading Plots* (1989), and *Narrative as Rhetoric* (1996). He is also the author of essays on pedagogy and, with Gerald Graff, coeditor of two Bedford Case Studies in Critical Controversy, on *Huckleberry Finn* (1995), and on *The Tempest* (2000). The working title of his current project is "Living to Tell about It: A Rhetoric and Ethics of Character Narration."

PATROCINIO P. SCHWEICKART is professor of English and women's studies at Purdue University, where she teaches courses in feminist theory, theory and cultural studies, gender and literature, and gender and multiculturalism. She is coeditor, with Elizabeth A. Flynn, of *Gender and Reading: Essays on Readers, Texts, and Contexts.* Her current research focuses on theories of reading, theories of communicative action, and feminist theories of the ethic of care.

ERIN A. SMITH is associate professor of American studies, literature, and gender studies at the University of Texas, Dallas. Her first book, *Hard-Boiled: Working-Class Readers and Pulp Magazines* (2000), examines hard-boiled detective fiction of the 1920s, 1930s, and 1940s and the mostly working-class readers who encountered it in pulp magazines and cheap paperbacks. Her research focuses on gender and popular culture in the twentieth century.

LOUISE YELIN is professor of literature at Purchase College, State University of New York. She is the author of *From the Margins of Empire: Christina Stead, Doris Lessing, Nadine Gordimer* (1998) and of essays on Victorian literature, feminism, postcolonial studies, and globalization.

Index